한 권으로 끝내는

스파르타 토익 Vol.2

실전 1000제

LC & RC

English& 북스

한 권으로 끝내는
스파르타 토익
실전 1000제
LC&RC Vol. 2

1쇄 발행 2019년 11월 7일
5쇄 발행 2024년 8월 13일

저　자	김태훈, 김수현, 최영근
펴낸이	박성호
펴낸곳	잉글리쉬앤 (주)
편　집	박고우니, 장서원
영업마케팅	여주형, 김성윤, 방성출, 박훈효, 조민형, 이달님, 강정구, 이진희, 조병운
조예선, 이현정, 조광민, 노희동, 김정민, 최희성, 최인태, 윤종철, 엄주아
신현수, 오지현, 최유미, 최가연, 김정호, 안혜연, 조승채

주　소　서울 특별시 관악구 쑥고개로 67-1
대표전화　(02) 878-1945
출판등록　2002년 3월 3일 제 320-2002-00045호

ISBN 978-89-6715-136-2 13740

저작권자 2024 잉글리쉬앤(주)
이 책은 잉글리쉬앤(주)에 의해 출간되었으므로
저자와 출판사의 서면에 의한 허락 없이 글과 그림의 인용, 복제, 발췌를 금합니다.

* 가격은 뒤표지에 있습니다. 파본은 바꾸어 드립니다.
www.english.co.kr

Contents

- 토익 소개 ·· 4
- 파트별 유형 및 전략 ························ 6
- 학습 플랜 ·· 13

실전 모의고사

TEST 01 ·· 14
TEST 02 ·· 56
TEST 03 ·· 98
TEST 04 ·· 140
TEST 05 ·· 182

- 점수 환산표 ···································· 226

정답 및 스크립트

Answer Key ·· 228
1회 스크립트 및 해석 ······················ 231
2회 스크립트 및 해석 ······················ 247
3회 스크립트 및 해석 ······················ 264
4회 스크립트 및 해석 ······················ 280
5회 스크립트 및 해석 ······················ 298

- OMR 답안지 ···································· 315

온라인 모의고사 이용 방법

books.english.co.kr 접속 ▶ 상단 메뉴 '도서인증받기' 클릭
▶ 인증 내용 입력 ▶ 인증 완료 ▶ 테스트 응시

토익 소개

토익이란?

Test Of English for International Communication의 약자로, 영어가 모국어가 아닌 사람들의 일상생활이나 국제업무 등에 필요한 실용 영어 능력을 평가하는 국제 평가 시험

▶ 시험 구성

구성	Part	유형		문항 수	시간	배점
듣기(LC)	1	사진 묘사		6	45분	495점
	2	질의 응답		25		
	3	대화문		39	100	
	4	담화문		30		
읽기(RC)	5	단문 공란 채우기		30	75분	495점
	6	장문 공란 채우기		16		
	7	지문 독해	단일 지문	29	100	
			복수 지문	25		
TOTAL		7 Parts		200문항	120분	990점

▶ 시험 내용

Part	유형	유형 내용
1	사진 묘사	제시된 사진을 알맞게 설명하는 보기 고르기
2	질의 응답	질문을 듣고 알맞은 대답 고르기
3	대화문	대화를 듣고 질문에 알맞은 내용 고르기
4	담화문	담화를 듣고 질문에 알맞은 내용 고르기
5	단문 공란 채우기	빈칸에 맞는 내용을 골라 단문 완성하기
6	장문 공란 채우기	빈칸에 맞는 내용을 골라 장문 완성하기
7	지문 독해	단일 지문 또는 이중·삼중 지문을 읽고 문제에 맞는 내용 고르기

접수 방법은?

▶ 한국 토익 위원회 사이트 혹은 앱으로 접수 ➜ www.toeic.co.kr
▶ 인터넷 접수할 때 시험일, 고사장, 개인 정보 등을 입력 (증명사진 필요)
  ※ 접수 마감일 이후 추가 접수일에 접수 시 추가 비용 발생

응시 준비물은?

▶ 규정 신분증 (주민등록증, 운전면허증, 기간 만료 전의 여권, 중고등학생만 학생증 인정)
▶ 연필, 지우개 (볼펜이나 사인펜은 사용 금지)
▶ 아날로그 시계 (전자 시계 불가)

시험 진행은?

▶ **시험 시간이 오전일 경우** 오전 9:20까지 입실 (오전 9:50 이후 입실 불가)
▶ **시험 시간이 오후일 경우** 오후 2:20까지 입실 (오후 2:50 이후 입실 불가)

오전 시험	오후 시험	시험 진행
오전 9:30 ~ 9:45 (15분)	오후 2:30 ~ 2:45 (15분)	답안지 작성에 관한 오리엔테이션
오전 9:45 ~ 9:50 (5분)	오후 2:45 ~ 2:50 (5분)	수험자 휴식 시간
오전 9:50 ~ 10:05 (15분)	오후 2:50 ~ 3:05 (15분)	신분 확인
오전 10:05 ~ 10:10 (5분)	오후 3:05 ~ 3:10 (5분)	문제지 배부, 파본 확인
오전 10:10 ~ 10:55 (45분)	오후 3:10 ~ 3:55 (45분)	듣기 평가(LC)
오전 10:55 ~ 12:10 (75분)	오후 3:55 ~ 5:10 (75분)	읽기 평가(RC)

※ 읽기 평가(RC) 시간에 2차 신분 확인 실시

성적 확인은?

▶ 시험일로부터 약 2주 후에 토익 위원회 사이트(www.toeic.co.kr)에서 확인 가능
▶ 온라인 출력과 우편 수령은 1회 무료, 이후에는 유료 발급

파트별 유형 및 전략

PART 1 사진 묘사 **6문제**

파트 1은 4개의 보기 중에서 사진을 가장 잘 묘사하는 보기를 고르는 문제이다. 총 6문제가 출제되며, 인물 및 사물/풍경 사진 등 다양한 유형들이 등장한다.

| 핵심 전략 |

+ 사진 유형별로 자주 출제되는 어휘와 표현들을 익힌다.
+ 난이도가 높은 경우 주어가 사물인 보기가 자주 등장하므로 수동태, 현재완료 수동태, 수동태 진행형과 같은 문법을 완벽하게 숙지한다.
+ 오답 소거법을 통해 사진을 완벽하게 묘사한 보기가 아닌, 그 중 정답에 가장 가까운 Best Answer를 고르도록 훈련한다.
+ 유사 발음, 연상 어휘 등을 이용한 오답이나, 사람과 사물의 상태 및 동작을 잘못 묘사하는 오답들이 자주 등장한다.

| 문제 형태 |

1

Look at the picture marked number one in your test book.

(A) She is cleaning her desk.
(B) She is sharpening a pencil.
(C) She is filing some papers.
(D) She is holding a phone.

PART 2 질의 응답 ◀ 25문제

파트 2는 3개의 보기 중에서 질문에 적절한 응답을 고르는 파트이다. 문항 수는 총 25개로, 의문사 의문문, Yes/No 의문문이 출제된다.

| 핵심 전략 |

- 질문의 앞부분을 집중해서 듣고 질문 유형을 파악하는 연습을 한다.
- 의문사 의문문은 가장 자주 출제되는 유형으로, 답변 패턴이 정해져 있다. 의문사별로 정답 유형을 숙지해 두자.
- 평서문은 답변 패턴이 정해져 있지 않아서 어렵게 느껴질 수 있다. 오답 소거법을 이용하여 보기 중 가장 적절한 응답을 고르면 정답을 쉽게 찾을 수 있다.
- 유사 발음 어휘, 질문의 단어 반복 등을 이용한 보기가 오답으로 자주 등장하므로 이를 주의 하여 정답을 골라야 한다.

| 문제 형태 |

7 Mark your answer on your answer sheet.

How much longer do you need on this project?

(A) About ten pages long.
(B) Roughly half an hour.
(C) The project was successful.

PART 3

대화문 39문제

파트 3는 2~3명이 나누는 대화를 듣고 이와 관련된 3개의 문제를 푸는 파트이다. 총 39문제가 출제되며, 3인 대화가 1~2세트 출제된다. 화자 의도 파악 문제와 시각 자료 연계 문제가 각각 2~3세트 출제된다.

핵심 전략

- 대화를 듣기 전에 문제를 먼저 읽고, 키워드를 파악한 후 그 부분을 집중적으로 듣는 훈련을 하자.
- 첫 번째 문제는 주로 주제나 장소, 신분에 관한 문제로, 정답의 단서가 대화 초반에 나오므로 처음 부분을 놓치지 않고 들어야 한다.
- 의도 파악 문제는 먼저 제시된 표현을 확인하고, 음성을 들으면서 해당 표현이 나올 때까지 문맥을 정확히 파악해야 한다.
- 표나 송장, 지도 등의 다양한 시각 자료가 출제되며, 미리 시각 자료를 읽고 지문의 내용을 예측해 본다. 또한, 시각 자료와 음성을 연계하여 정보를 파악하는 능력을 길러야 한다.
- 3인 대화에서 화자는 국적에 따라 발음이 구분되므로, 미국, 영국, 호주 등의 다양한 발음에 익숙해지도록 연습한다.

문제 형태

32 What does the woman imply when she says, "I got one for my friend"?

(A) She is inviting the man to meet her friend.
(B) Her friend is the same size with his wife.
(C) She is willing to pay for the product.
(D) She is emphasizing it's a good product.

Questions 32 through 34 refer to the following conversation.

M: Hi, I'm looking for a birthday present for my wife. I think she'd like one of these sweaters, but do you have any in a smaller size?
W: I'm pretty sure everything we have is out here on the display table. But I can check the stockroom in the back if you'd like.
M: Thanks, that'll be great. You know they look perfect for early spring. Light, but warm. You can wear them indoors or outdoors.
W: That's right. <u>I got one for my friend</u> who wears it a lot, so I'm sure your wife would love one. And we're selling them for 30% off this week.
M: That's good to know. I hope you have one in my wife's size.

PART 4

담화문 30문제

파트 4는 담화를 듣고 이와 관련된 3개의 문제를 푸는 파트이다. 총 30문항이 출제되며, 녹음 메시지나 공지, 뉴스 등이 주로 출제된다. 파트 3와 마찬가지로, 화자 의도 파악 문제와 시각 자료 연계 문제가 등장한다.

핵심 전략

- 담화를 듣기 전에 문제를 먼저 읽고, 키워드를 파악한 후 그 부분을 집중적으로 듣는 훈련을 하자.
- 첫 번째 문제는 주로 주제나 장소, 신분에 관한 문제로, 정답의 단서가 담화 초반에 나오므로 처음 부분을 놓치지 않고 들어야 한다.
- 의도 파악 문제는 파트 3와 달리 한 사람의 담화이므로 문맥의 흐름을 더 쉽게 파악할 수 있다. 따라서 담화의 전반적인 문맥 흐름을 이해하고, 해당 문장의 앞뒤 상황을 정확히 파악하도록 하자.
- 표나 송장, 지도 등의 다양한 시각 자료가 출제되며, 미리 시각 자료를 읽고 지문의 내용을 예측해 본다. 또한, 시각 자료와 음성을 연계하여 정보를 파악하는 능력을 길러야 한다.

문제 형태

Tour Schedule	
Garden Tour	10:00 A.M.
Lunch	Noon
Museum Visit	1:30 P.M.
Theater Performance	4:00 P.M.

98 Look at the graphic. What time is this talk most likely being given?

(A) At 10:00 A.M.
(B) At noon
(C) At 1:30 P.M.
(D) At 4:00 P.M.

Questions 98 through 100 refer to the following talk and list.

Can I have everyone's attention at the front of the bus? I hope you enjoyed your lunch at Restaurant Baron. As I mentioned earlier, it first opened in 1880 and has been operating longer than any other restaurants in Charlestown. Now, if you look out the window on your right, you'll see the National Museum of History and according to our schedule, we're right on time. We'll be spending about 2 hours here. I'll pass out the brochures with the information about the permanent and temporary exhibits you'll be seeing today. We'll meet again at the main entrance at 3:30 for our next schedule. Enjoy yourselves.

PART 5

단문 공란 채우기 `30문제`

파트 5는 문장 안에 있는 빈칸에 적절한 단어나 어구를 채워 넣는 파트이다. 총 30문항이 출제되며, 문법 문제와 어휘 문제가 등장한다. 문제 유형에 따라 풀이 방식이 다르므로 이를 가장 먼저 파악하는 것이 중요하다.

| 핵심 전략 |

- 문제를 풀기 전, 보기를 통해 문제 유형을 파악하는 연습을 한다.
- 문법 문제는 문장 구조나 빈칸 주변의 문법을 통해 문제를 풀어야 한다. 문법 문제를 단시간에 풀기 위해서 명사, 동사, 형용사 등의 기본적인 문법을 확실히 익혀 두도록 하자.
- 어휘 문제는 해석을 통해 문맥에 가장 적절한 단어를 선택해야 한다. 가능한 한 많은 어휘를 암기하고, 예문을 통해 어휘가 어떻게 사용되는지를 이해하자.
- 자주 함께 쓰이는 단어 및 표현들을 숙지하여 빠른 시간 내에 문제를 풀어야 한다.

| 문제 형태 |

101 Sky Motors offers a variety of training programs to help enhance ------- in the workplace.

(A) productivity
(B) produce
(C) productive
(D) productively

102 The fundraising event recorded such high ------- that the proceeds will be higher than expected.

(A) representative
(B) consultation
(C) safety
(D) attendance

PART 6

장문 공란 채우기 — 16문제

파트 6는 지문 안에 있는 4개의 빈칸에 알맞은 보기를 선택하는 파트이다. 문법, 어휘, 문장을 넣는 문제가 등장하며, 총 16문항이 출제된다. 문맥에 맞는 문장을 고르는 문제는 각 지문마다 1개씩 출제된다.

핵심 전략

- 전체 문맥을 이해해야 풀 수 있는 문법 및 어휘 문제가 나오므로 지문의 흐름을 놓치지 않는 것이 중요하다.
- 빈칸에 알맞은 문장을 넣는 문제는 빈칸 앞뒤와 전체 맥락을 파악하여 정답을 골라야 하므로 전반적인 독해력을 늘려야 한다.
- 지문을 읽으면서 흐름상 다음에 나와야 할 내용을 예측하면 정답을 쉽게 찾을 수 있다.

문제 형태

Questions 135-138 refer to the following notice.

Important Notice about Hatter Industries

Please note that the contact information for Hatter Industries changed on March 21. Due to the closure of our Dabbley office and the ------- (135) of our operations in Buena, all correspondence concerning our products and services should now be sent to the following address: Hatter Industries, 642 Mandela Lane, Buena, CA.

Our employees' e-mail addresses, as well as our Web site's address, www.hatterindustries.com, remain ------- (136).

However, we are still waiting for our new telephone and fax numbers. ------- (137) will be updated on our Web site as soon as the new numbers are assigned as of March 25. ------- (138).

135
(A) decision
(B) relocation
(C) suspension
(D) result

136
(A) assigned
(B) even
(C) formal
(D) unchanged

137
(A) Yours
(B) Another
(C) These
(D) Theirs

138
(A) We apologize for any inconvenience and thank you for your understanding.
(B) Refer to the side of the packet for full details of instructions before applying.
(C) Her office location will also remain the same.
(D) For more information about the forthcoming event, visit www.lizard.org.br/events.

PART 7

지문 독해 54문제

파트 7은 지문을 읽고 지문과 관련된 문제 2~5개를 푸는 파트이다. 총 54문항이 출제되며, 지문은 편지, 문자 메시지, 광고, 공지문 등 다양한 유형으로 나온다. 단일 지문 10개, 이중 지문 2개, 삼중 지문 3개의 세트가 등장한다.

| 핵심 전략 |

+ 지문의 종류와 제목, 키워드를 파악하여 내용을 미리 예측하고 정답 단서를 찾는다.
+ 지문의 단서가 보기에는 다르게 패러프레이징될 수 있으므로, 단어를 암기할 때 동의표현을 함께 익힌다.
+ 복수 지문에서는 2개 이상의 지문을 연계하여 풀어야 하는 문제들이 출제되므로, 지문간의 관계를 파악하는 연습을 해야 한다.

| 문제 형태 |

Questions 162-164 refer to the following advertisement.

ACCOUNT SERVICE DIRECTOR WANTED

A leading financial service bank is looking for an account services director. —[1]—. He or she will be responsible for reclassifying income payment to ensure the accurate reporting of tax payments. —[2]—. Validating tax related information, determining reclassification amounts, processing reclassifications using various internal systems, and performing quality-control checks relevant to all tax-reporting processes will be some of the other responsibilities. —[3]—. In order to qualify, the candidate must have a college degree and previous tax or brokerage experience along with strong analytical skills. —[4]—.

If you are interested, please send your résumé to:

Rosabeth Moss Kanter / Lawrence Financial, Inc.
985, Andrew Park Avenue / Houston, TX 48954

---

162 What position is being advertised?

(A) Public official
(B) Real estate agent
(C) Accountant
(D) Financial consultant

163 Which of the following is required for the position?

(A) Communication skills
(B) A license approved by a related organization
(C) Background knowledge of Lawrence Financial, Inc.
(D) A college education

164 In which of the positions marked [1], [2], [3], and [4] does the following sentence best belong?

"They must also be able to work overtime and weekends when required."

(A) [1]
(B) [2]
(C) [3]
(D) [4]

학습 플랜

▶ 2주 완성

	Day 1	Day 2	Day 3	Day 4	Day 5
1 week	TEST 1 풀기	TEST 1 복습	TEST 2 풀기	TEST 2 복습	TEST 3 풀기
2 week	TEST 3 복습	TEST 4 풀기	TEST 4 복습	TEST 5 풀기	TEST 5 복습

▶ 4주 완성

	Day 1	Day 2	Day 3	Day 4	Day 5
1 week	TEST 1 풀기	TEST 1 LC 복습	TEST 1 RC 복습	TEST 1 RC 복습	TEST 2 풀기
2 week	TEST 2 LC 복습	TEST 2 RC 복습	TEST 2 RC 복습	TEST 3 풀기	TEST 3 LC 복습
3 week	TEST 3 RC 복습	TEST 3 RC 복습	TEST 4 풀기	TEST 4 LC 복습	TEST 4 RC 복습
4 week	TEST 4 RC 복습	TEST 5 풀기	TEST 5 LC 복습	TEST 5 RC 복습	TEST 5 RC 복습

MP3와 해설 파일은 온라인에서 제공됩니다.
▶ books.english.co.kr

TEST 01

test 01.mp3 | 정답 p.231

LISTENING TEST

In the Listening test, you will be asked to demonstrate how well you understand spoken English. The entire Listening test will last approximately 45 minutes. There are four parts, and directions are given for each part. You must mark your answers on the separate answer sheet.
Do not write your answers in your test book.

PART 1

Directions: For each question in this part, you will hear four statements about a picture in your test book. When you hear the statements, you must select the one statement that best describes what you see in the picture. Then find the number of the question on your answer sheet and mark your answer. The statements will not be printed in your test book and will be spoken only one time.

Statement (B), "They're shaking hands," is the best description of the picture, so you should select answer (B) and mark it on your answer sheet.

1.

2.

3.

4.

5.

6.

PART 2

Directions: You will hear a question or statement and three responses spoken in English. They will not be printed in your test book and will be spoken only one time. Select the best response to the question or statement and mark the letter (A), (B), or (C) on your answer sheet.

7. Mark your answer on your answer sheet.

8. Mark your answer on your answer sheet.

9. Mark your answer on your answer sheet.

10. Mark your answer on your answer sheet.

11. Mark your answer on your answer sheet.

12. Mark your answer on your answer sheet.

13. Mark your answer on your answer sheet.

14. Mark your answer on your answer sheet.

15. Mark your answer on your answer sheet.

16. Mark your answer on your answer sheet.

17. Mark your answer on your answer sheet.

18. Mark your answer on your answer sheet.

19. Mark your answer on your answer sheet.

20. Mark your answer on your answer sheet.

21. Mark your answer on your answer sheet.

22. Mark your answer on your answer sheet.

23. Mark your answer on your answer sheet.

24. Mark your answer on your answer sheet.

25. Mark your answer on your answer sheet.

26. Mark your answer on your answer sheet.

27. Mark your answer on your answer sheet.

28. Mark your answer on your answer sheet.

29. Mark your answer on your answer sheet.

30. Mark your answer on your answer sheet.

31. Mark your answer on your answer sheet.

PART 3

Directions: You will hear some conversations between two or more people. You will be asked to answer three questions about what the speakers say in each conversation. Select the best response to each question and mark the letter (A), (B), (C), or (D) on your answer sheet. The conversations will not be printed in your test book and will be spoken only one time.

32. Where is the conversation taking place?
    (A) At a library
    (B) At an electronics store
    (C) At an auto shop
    (D) At an Internet service company

33. What does the man want to check?
    (A) A receipt
    (B) A warranty period
    (C) A discounted price
    (D) A reservation time

34. What does the man ask the woman to do?
    (A) Complete a form
    (B) Visit again later
    (C) Pay for the repairs
    (D) Register the product

35. What is the woman's problem?
    (A) She left some documents in the office.
    (B) She forgot her password.
    (C) She cannot change her password.
    (D) She cannot access a room.

36. What does the man tell the woman to do?
    (A) Get a key from the security office
    (B) Install a new system
    (C) Contact a security officer
    (D) Change a secret code

37. How can the woman get into the office today?
    (A) By changing her password
    (B) By getting a different password
    (C) By getting help from the man
    (D) By signing up for a membership

38. What type of business is the woman calling?
    (A) A publishing company
    (B) An advertising office
    (C) A food manufacturer
    (D) A bistro

39. What problem are the speakers discussing?
    (A) A service cost was overcharged.
    (B) An order number was entered incorrectly.
    (C) Some details are incorrect.
    (D) The deadline for an advertisement was not met.

40. What does the man ask the woman to provide?
    (A) An order number
    (B) An order date
    (C) A shipping date
    (D) A menu

41. Where are the speakers?
    (A) At a bookstore
    (B) At a library
    (C) At a park
    (D) At a book fair

42. What does the man imply when he says, "Maybe you don't have to buy it"?
    (A) He will buy a new book.
    (B) He will lend a book to the woman.
    (C) He has two of the same books.
    (D) He can get a book for free.

43. What does the man suggest the woman do?
    (A) Recommend a book to read
    (B) Order a book on the Internet
    (C) Join a reading club
    (D) Update some information regularly

GO ON TO THE NEXT PAGE

44. Where most likely are the speakers?
   (A) At a dentist's office
   (B) At a travel agency
   (C) At a real estate agency
   (D) At a law firm

45. What does Laura request?
   (A) An afternoon appointment
   (B) A text message
   (C) A revised schedule
   (D) An informational booklet

46. When will the message be sent to Laura?
   (A) On May 20
   (B) On August 20
   (C) On August 21
   (D) On November 21

47. What are the speakers talking about?
   (A) Newly designed equipment
   (B) An extended deadline
   (C) Product manufacturing
   (D) A product advertisement

48. What does the man say about his company?
   (A) It specializes in design.
   (B) It has many branches abroad.
   (C) It offers items at reasonable prices.
   (D) It has been in business for a long time.

49. What will the man do tomorrow?
   (A) Bring some items
   (B) Order new materials
   (C) Think of some ideas
   (D) Conduct a survey

50. Where is the conversation taking place?
   (A) At a publishing company
   (B) At a newsstand
   (C) At a library
   (D) At a bookstore

51. What does the woman imply when she says, "I didn't see it"?
   (A) She lost some goods.
   (B) Some data are missing.
   (C) She couldn't find an item.
   (D) A place has changed.

52. What is suggested about *Independence Day*?
   (A) It is no longer available.
   (B) It is very popular.
   (C) It is an old product.
   (D) It can be purchased online.

53. Where does the woman work?
   (A) At a public utility
   (B) At a landscaping company
   (C) At a construction company
   (D) At an interior design firm

54. Why does the man want to make a change?
   (A) To enlarge a space
   (B) To make a place clean
   (C) To save money
   (D) To create a safer environment

55. What does the woman say she will do?
   (A) Contact another department
   (B) Write an e-mail
   (C) Print some material
   (D) Prepare some paperwork

56. What does the man want to order?
    (A) Furniture
    (B) Computer parts
    (C) A computer
    (D) A printer

57. Why does the woman apologize?
    (A) Some items are defective.
    (B) The wrong number of products was delivered.
    (C) Some items are no longer available.
    (D) The customer was overcharged.

58. What will the man most likely do next?
    (A) Inspect a system
    (B) Look at a Web site
    (C) Request a discount
    (D) Speak with a service engineer

59. Who most likely is the woman?
    (A) A culinary expert
    (B) A business consultant
    (C) A business reporter
    (D) A real estate agent

60. According to the man, what is the restaurant's biggest challenge?
    (A) Hiring reliable employees
    (B) Obtaining food materials
    (C) Managing franchises
    (D) Creating new menu items

61. What will the man do next year?
    (A) Add a new menu item
    (B) Make plans for an event
    (C) Produce his own ingredients
    (D) Expand his business

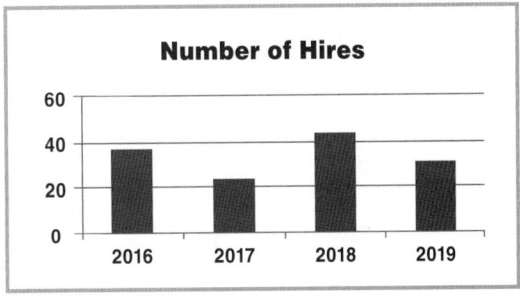

62. What is the conversation about?
    (A) A job interview
    (B) An annual sales report
    (C) A scheduling conflict
    (D) An orientation session

63. Look at the graphic. In which year was the man in charge of the orientation preparation work?
    (A) 2016
    (B) 2017
    (C) 2018
    (D) 2019

64. What task does the woman ask for help with?
    (A) Filing some documents
    (B) Booking a venue
    (C) Conducting a survey
    (D) Reserving equipment

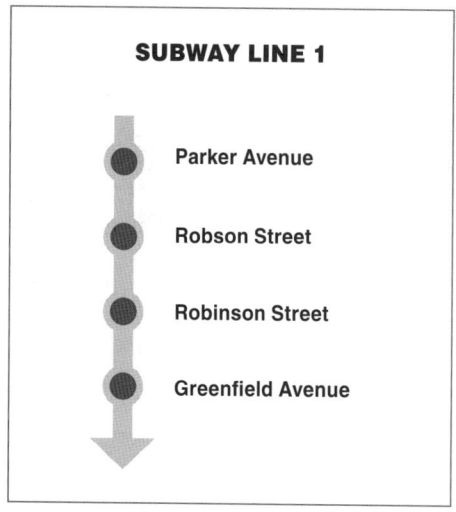

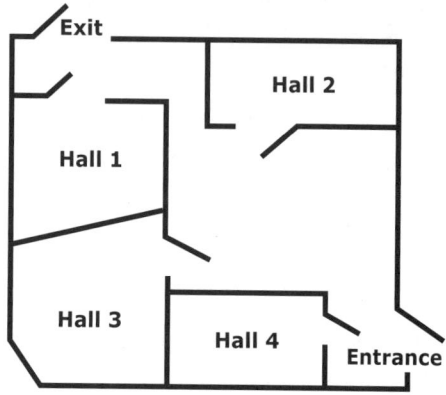

65. What event are the speakers going to?
    (A) A magic show
    (B) A live concert
    (C) A movie preview
    (D) An art exhibition

66. Look at the graphic. At which stop will the speakers get off the train?
    (A) Parker Avenue
    (B) Robson Street
    (C) Robinson Street
    (D) Greenfield Avenue

67. What does the man suggest doing?
    (A) Touring some facilities later today
    (B) Preparing an item to get an autograph
    (C) Taking a subway earlier than usual
    (D) Watching a performance on TV

68. What problem does the woman mention?
    (A) She is having difficulty finding a location.
    (B) She parked in the wrong parking lot.
    (C) She lost her admission ticket.
    (D) She was overcharged for parking.

69. Look at the graphic. Which hall will the woman go to?
    (A) Hall 1
    (B) Hall 2
    (C) Hall 3
    (D) Hall 4

70. Why does the man tell the woman not to rush?
    (A) There are still two hours left.
    (B) There are few cars in the parking lot.
    (C) She doesn't need to pay for parking.
    (D) A staff member will wait for her.

PART 4

Directions: You will hear some talks given by a single speaker. You will be asked to answer three questions about what the speaker says in each talk. Select the best response to each question and mark the letter (A), (B), (C), or (D) on your answer sheet. The talks will not be printed in your test book and will be spoken only one time.

71. What will be renovated?
- (A) A subway station
- (B) A shopping complex
- (C) Some amenities
- (D) A bus terminal

72. What problem does the speaker mention about the structure?
- (A) It is always crowded with people.
- (B) It is located on the outskirts of the city.
- (C) It is difficult to get there by public transportation.
- (D) It has some old facilities.

73. What will happen after the commercial break?
- (A) Some residents will ask questions.
- (B) The mayor will give details about a project.
- (C) There will be information on the use of some facilities.
- (D) A senior official will be interviewed.

74. What kind of service is being advertised?
- (A) Computer classes
- (B) Computer maintenance
- (C) Internet service
- (D) Online advertisements

75. According to the speaker, what do customers like about the service?
- (A) It provides a useful program for free.
- (B) It always takes care of problems quickly.
- (C) It often offers discounts.
- (D) It provides new products every year.

76. How can customers get a discount?
- (A) By applying for a service online
- (B) By purchasing new software
- (C) By making a contract for a certain period of time
- (D) By ordering multiple products

77. What is the talk mainly about?
- (A) How to run a blog successfully
- (B) Why blogs are so popular
- (C) Effective online marketing methods
- (D) Various topics of blogs

78. What does the speaker mention about power bloggers?
- (A) They don't need a lot of experience.
- (B) They should provide a variety of information.
- (C) They should write blog posts consistently.
- (D) They have to update only useful information.

79. What does the speaker recommend doing?
- (A) Looking at various blogs
- (B) Posting reliable content
- (C) Taking frequent trips
- (D) Collecting a lot of data

80. Where does the speaker work?
- (A) At a restaurant
- (B) At an amusement park
- (C) At a fitness center
- (D) At a travel agency

81. What does the speaker mean when she says, "I'm in charge of overall management"?
- (A) She wants more funding.
- (B) She can't do another job.
- (C) She can handle anything.
- (D) She can control labor costs.

82. What does the speaker want to discuss with the listener?
- (A) The value of an additional expenditure
- (B) The details of some expected costs
- (C) Current trends in tourism
- (D) Types of recreational programs

83. What type of art will the listeners see?
    (A) Photography
    (B) Sculptures
    (C) Craftworks
    (D) Paintings

84. What does the speaker imply when she says, "They'll probably have to come to the exhibition next time"?
    (A) There is no time to wait any longer.
    (B) The tickets are all sold out.
    (C) There are no additional vacancies.
    (D) Some people have changed their reservations.

85. What does the speaker ask the listeners to do?
    (A) Move quickly
    (B) Wait a little longer
    (C) Turn off the ringers on their phones
    (D) Speak quietly

86. Where do the listeners most likely work?
    (A) At an electronics shop
    (B) At a hospital
    (C) At a restaurant
    (D) At a factory

87. What type of policy has changed?
    (A) Vacation periods
    (B) Bonus payments
    (C) Working hours
    (D) Production goals

88. What does the speaker ask the listeners to do?
    (A) Work overtime
    (B) Submit sales reports
    (C) Make recommendations
    (D) Contact the winner

89. What will the listeners do next month?
    (A) Receive some training
    (B) Develop a Web site
    (C) Get an award
    (D) Purchase new software

90. According to the speaker, what field is Ms. Page an expert in?
    (A) Education
    (B) Politics
    (C) Web programming
    (D) Accounting

91. Why did Ms. Page win an award last year?
    (A) She taught quality classes.
    (B) She improved an educational environment.
    (C) She created an innovative Web site.
    (D) She developed some software.

92. What is the purpose of the workshop?
    (A) To strengthen the bond between employees
    (B) To come up with an efficient way to negotiate
    (C) To learn how to meet demand efficiently
    (D) To study how to make up for the shortcomings of a product

93. What kind of documents does the speaker ask the listeners to submit?
    (A) A training plan
    (B) A catalog of products
    (C) A product performance report
    (D) A team report

94. What will be given to the winning team?
    (A) Vacation time
    (B) A bonus
    (C) Gift certificates
    (D) New products

Special Movement Center	
Customer	Daniel Antonio
Address	86 North Hills Avenue
Arrival Time	8:00 A.M.
Payment	$1,640

95. What is the purpose of the message?
    (A) To ask for a payment
    (B) To change a moving date
    (C) To confirm the details of a contract
    (D) To inform the listener of the price of a service

96. Look at the graphic. What information has changed?
    (A) Daniel Antonio
    (B) 86 North Hills Avenue
    (C) 8:00 A.M.
    (D) $1,640

97. What does the speaker offer to do?
    (A) Finish the work quickly
    (B) Provide a free service
    (C) Send more staff members
    (D) Give a discount

North Edmonton Island

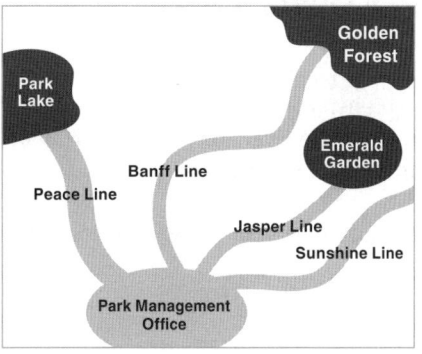

98. Look at the graphic. Which route will the listeners take?
    (A) Peace Line
    (B) Banff Line
    (C) Jasper Line
    (D) Sunshine Line

99. According to the speaker, why should the listeners refrain from taking pictures?
    (A) They don't have enough time.
    (B) It could cause an accident.
    (C) It's too dark there.
    (D) It may have a bad effect on wild animals.

100. What does the speaker suggest the listeners do?
    (A) Get enough rest
    (B) Buy some souvenirs
    (C) Get some animal food
    (D) Drink enough water

This is the end of the Listening test. Turn to Part 5 in your test book.

READING TEST

In the Reading test, you will read a variety of texts and answer several different types of reading comprehension questions. The entire Reading test will last 75 minutes. There are three parts, and directions are given for each part. You are encouraged to answer as many questions as possible within the time allowed.

You must mark your answers on the separate answer sheet. Do not write your answers in the test book.

PART 5

Directions: A word or phrase is missing in each of the sentences below. Four answer choices are given below each sentence. Select the best answer to complete the sentence. Then mark the letter (A), (B), (C), or (D) on your answer sheet.

101. Consumer surveys show that Golden Planet's newest mobile phone is too -------.

    (A) expense
    (B) expenses
    (C) expensive
    (D) expensively

102. You should carry your employee card at ------- times.

    (A) many
    (B) all
    (C) previous
    (D) one

103. Those who spend more than $300 will get a 20% -------.

    (A) refund
    (B) fund
    (C) discount
    (D) exchange

104. For further instructions, ------- go to our Web site and access the Customer link.

    (A) simply
    (B) greatly
    (C) highly
    (D) closely

105. Fresh Life's air cleaner comes with a warranty that is valid ------- three years.

    (A) during
    (B) for
    (C) on
    (D) about

106. Richard Business Consulting rewards employees for making ------- workplace suggestions.

    (A) upcoming
    (B) considerate
    (C) experienced
    (D) valuable

107. Access to public transportation was a ------- consideration when SJ Communications was looking for a new office for relocation.

    (A) large
    (B) largest
    (C) largely
    (D) largeness

108. Ms. Clinton advised that the shipments be placed ------- the security office.

    (A) out of
    (B) onto
    (C) inside
    (D) over

109. Dragons Motors ------- that it will no longer build sedans.
    (A) announcing
    (B) announced
    (C) have announced
    (D) to announce

110. The Washington-based Komerican Group ------- supports the continued innovation of its affiliates.
    (A) effect
    (B) effects
    (C) effective
    (D) effectively

111. Despite the meeting, delegates from the two companies ------- failed to reach an agreement on the terms and conditions of the contract.
    (A) seldom
    (B) still
    (C) even
    (D) already

112. Refunds from Ventors Broadband are made ------- two weeks of a service cancellation.
    (A) by
    (B) for
    (C) among
    (D) within

113. For the ------- of our customers, we are developing an application that allows users to view and order menus on their smartphones.
    (A) decision
    (B) convenience
    (C) security
    (D) permission

114. Mr. Kim was asked to ------- the report again, including last October's missing sales information.
    (A) approve
    (B) accept
    (C) submit
    (D) inform

115. Workshop organizers ------- planned to hold the event outdoors but failed to do so due to bad weather.
    (A) quickly
    (B) properly
    (C) usually
    (D) originally

116. At tomorrow's banquet, awards will be given to all ------- have contributed to achieving the company's record sales over the past year.
    (A) which
    (B) who
    (C) what
    (D) where

117. The team members going on a business trip to Chicago tomorrow must be at the airport two hours before the ------- departure time.
    (A) scheduled
    (B) arranging
    (C) delayed
    (D) expecting

118. The office supplies ordered three days ago were delivered just as the employees ------- for the day.
    (A) was leaving
    (B) were about to leave
    (C) will be left
    (D) have been leaving

119. Because the magazine didn't have enough time to interview the mayor, it had problems ------- this issue.
    (A) publish
    (B) published
    (C) to publish
    (D) publishing

120. Creativity and an outgoing personality are essential to become a sales ------- for World Travel Co.
    (A) associate
    (B) association
    (C) associating
    (D) associated

121. Current Economics reported that the unemployment rate rose to its ------- level ever in the second quarter of this year.
    (A) high
    (B) highly
    (C) higher
    (D) highest

122. At United Insurance Company, you ------- to go through a one-year probationary period to become a full-time employee.
    (A) required
    (B) are required
    (C) to be required
    (D) have required

123. To prevent accidents, all technicians should exercise ------- while inspecting the generator.
    (A) cautious
    (B) cautiously
    (C) cautioned
    (D) caution

124. Linda Sives enjoyed studying foreign languages very much when in school, but she ------- thought she would have a job teaching French.
    (A) most
    (B) otherwise
    (C) nevertheless
    (D) never

125. We will use the copier in the human resources office ------- the new one arrives.
    (A) after
    (B) once
    (C) now that
    (D) until

126. Mr. Kenzi was told to choose ------- that he thought would be his favorite.
    (A) other
    (B) anything
    (C) others
    (D) whichever

127. Please contact Mr. Pitt and Ms. Roberts and ask if ------- are available on April 6 for interviews.
    (A) they
    (B) their
    (C) theirs
    (D) themselves

128. ------- the underground parking lot is closed tomorrow morning, please park on the road opposite the office building.
    (A) In case
    (B) Unless
    (C) That
    (D) What

129. Mr. Hofmann was selected for ------- next month for his excellent management skills.
    (A) permits
    (B) credentials
    (C) promotion
    (D) transfer

130. We will be able to ------- up to 30% on costs by changing suppliers of raw materials.
    (A) prohibit
    (B) develop
    (C) produce
    (D) save

PART 6

Directions: Read the texts that follow. A word, phrase, or sentence is missing in parts of each text. Four answer choices for each question are given below the text. Select the best answer to complete the text. Then mark the letter (A), (B), (C), or (D) on your answer sheet.

Questions 131-134 refer to the following announcement.

Starting in the coming new year, some changes will be made to the vacation policy. You should let us know at least two weeks before the day you intend ------- on vacation. So far, you've filled out the forms
131.
and applied, but you'll have to apply on the company's Web site from next year. By doing so, the vacation application process will certainly be simple.

In addition, most importantly, we will allow up to three people in a team to be on vacation at the same time, except in August and December. -------. Of course, you can apply for ------- sick leave at any time
132. **133.**
like you used to. It will be ------- to a separate regulation that is different from the usual vacation policy.
134.
If you have any further questions or suggestions, please contact human resources.

131. (A) go
(B) going
(C) to go
(D) gone

132. (A) I hope many employees can enjoy the holidays together.
(B) It will keep our company running smoothly.
(C) You'd better choose a travel agency carefully.
(D) You can see a specific timetable on the bulletin board of the Web site.

133. (A) expected
(B) treated
(C) prepared
(D) sudden

134. (A) devoted
(B) allowed
(C) complied
(D) subject

Questions 135-138 refer to the following article.

CALGARY (February 18)—Star Grocery Factories, a U.S. food giant, today announced a ------- 135. to enter Calgary, Canada. The company is opening its first Canadian branch in Calgary. -------. 136. Moreover, the second and third stores will be opened one after another in Victoria and Edmonton this year. "We aim to provide all kinds of foodstuffs, ------- the best fruits and vegetables at a 137. reasonable price. These are available to ------- consumers throughout North America," said the 138. company's vice president Michael Jonadan.

135. (A) plan
(B) planner
(C) planning
(D) planned

136. (A) Many companies in the city have gone abroad.
(B) It will open on the 1st of next month.
(C) They have already gained a lot of fame.
(D) Star Grocery Factories is an international company.

137. (A) from
(B) concerning
(C) including
(D) between

138. (A) a little
(B) all
(C) every
(D) the other

Questions 139-142 refer to the following e-mail.

To: All customers
From: Asiana Electronics Service Center
Date: June 8
Subject: New office space

Dear Customers,

We are very pleased to announce that Asiana Electronics Service Center has ------- to a larger facility.
139.

Our new facilities in the Riverside Building offer a more spacious reception area and various convenient amenities. -------. In fact, we do not think there will be much confusion because we ------- moved to
140. **141.**
another floor of the same building. If you get off the elevator on the sixth floor, you will see our office on the right.

All contact information, except for our address, will remain unchanged. We are looking forward to

------- you in the better environment. Thank you.
142.

Sincerely,

Asiana Electronics Service Center

---

139. (A) relocated
(B) consolidated
(C) located
(D) confirmed

140. (A) We are considering canceling the contract because of the high rent.
(B) Budget issues forced us to choose a small space.
(C) These will enable our staff to serve you much more efficiently.
(D) Some deliveries have not arrived yet.

141. (A) regularly
(B) directly
(C) rarely
(D) just

142. (A) see
(B) seeing
(C) be seen
(D) being seen

Questions 143-146 refer to the following e-mail.

Date: November 17
To: All Management Team Members
From: Raymond Smith
Re: Grace White's departure

Dear colleagues,

Grace White, who has worked with us for a long time, is leaving the company. The ------- day she
143.
works will be Monday, December 30.

She has been in our company for the last eight years and has been recognized as a very versatile employee. ------- the past eight years, she's contributed to creating a strong working relationship
144.
among colleagues, and she's helped others gain business insight. -------. These will always be
145.
appreciated.

This Friday evening, we will hold a farewell party to wish her ------- success. I hope many of you
146.
will come and celebrate with us.

Regards,

Raymond Smith
Operations Manager
Management Team

143. (A) first
(B) next
(C) last
(D) latest

144. (A) To
(B) Over
(C) While
(D) About

145. (A) We will not forget her work ethic and humanity so far.
(B) She has always attended job seminars.
(C) Her replacement was already hired a month ago.
(D) You should no longer rely on her.

146. (A) continue
(B) continued
(C) be continued
(D) continues

PART 7

Directions: In this part you will read a selection of texts, such as magazine and newspaper articles, e-mails, and instant messages. Each text or set of texts is followed by several questions. Select the best answer for each question and mark the letter (A), (B), (C), or (D) on your answer sheet.

Questions 147-148 refer to the following coupon.

Next Saturday, July 6, Super Pizza, which specializes in handmade pizza, will finally open its second store. Take this coupon and visit our new place. During the day of the opening, you can enjoy more than 10 different kinds of pizza and beverages at a 50% discount.
Only one coupon can be used per person.

Super Pizza

Please refer to the directions on the back of the coupon for the location of the store.

---

147. What is suggested about Super Pizza?

(A) It has been in business for more than 10 years.
(B) It holds regular discount events.
(C) It will continue to open new stores.
(D) It offers a variety of pizza.

148. What is true about the coupon?

(A) It can be used in all branches.
(B) Customers can get a free beverage with it.
(C) It can be used on one day only.
(D) No expiration date has been set.

Questions 149-150 refer to the following advertisement.

Hawaii's Choice

Get a break from your busy life and go to paradise. Make some great memories at the new luxury mansion in Hawaii. You can feel the sun's energy while enjoying the picturesque scenery. Don't miss dinner with a variety of fresh seafood and a chance to enjoy Hawaii's best wine.

During the day, you can participate in various activities such as surfing and snorkeling. More detailed information can be found on our Web site at www.tourmanias.com.

Hawaiian Crystal Villa
1-689-555-0088

149. What is the purpose of the advertisement?
(A) To promote local specialties
(B) To publicize a resort area
(C) To encourage participation in sports activities
(D) To recommend a residence

150. What is NOT advertised as a feature?
(A) A fine view
(B) Quality food
(C) Pictures on display
(D) Various activities

Questions 151-152 refer to the following e-mail.

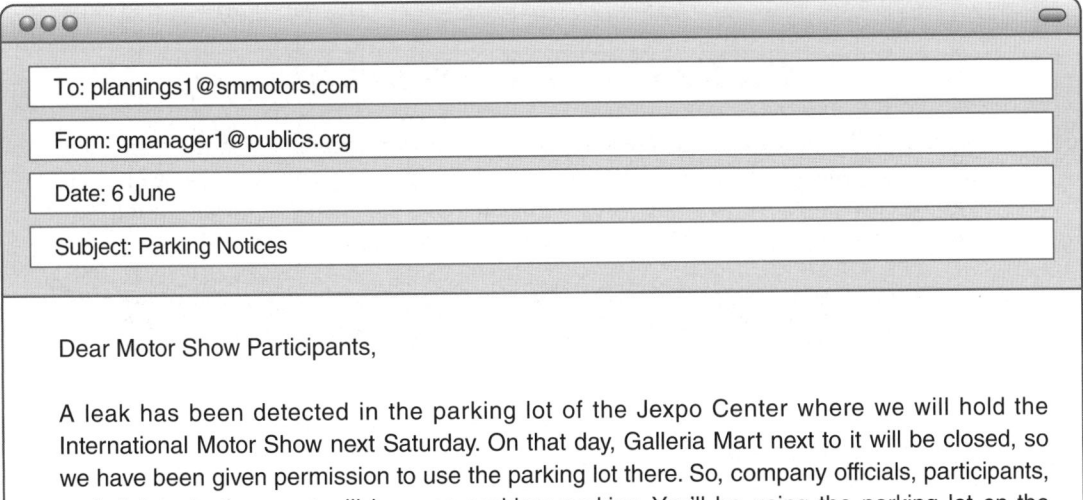

To: plannings1@smmotors.com
From: gmanager1@publics.org
Date: 6 June
Subject: Parking Notices

Dear Motor Show Participants,

A leak has been detected in the parking lot of the Jexpo Center where we will hold the International Motor Show next Saturday. On that day, Galleria Mart next to it will be closed, so we have been given permission to use the parking lot there. So, company officials, participants, and visitors to the event will have no problem parking. You'll be using the parking lot on the ground floor. Within three days, we'll send the authorization barcode to your mobile phone. Just scan it at the entrance to the parking lot and the barrier will open. If you have any questions, please contact me by e-mail.

Graham Wilson

151. Who most likely is Mr. Wilson?
(A) A technician
(B) A maintenance worker
(C) A security officer
(D) An event organizer

152. How can visitors get into the parking lot?
(A) By showing text messages to the security guard
(B) By registering the vehicle number
(C) By entering a password
(D) By scanning a specific image

Questions 153-154 refer to the following form.

Oasis Hotel Restaurant

We are glad that we were responsible for your precious mealtime. Please take a moment to complete the survey below. And when you pay for your meal, please give it to the cashier. Those who submit the form can have the chance to receive a free meal ticket through a drawing on the first day of each month.

	Completely Agree	Agree	Neutral	Disagree	Completely Disagree
The menu is very varied.		V			
The amount of food was sufficient.				V	
The quality of the food was good for the price.	V				
The service of the servers was satisfactory.			V		
The ordered food was served on time.	V				

Comments :

Serving staff were generally busy, but they were very kind and attentive. The quality of the food was very good, but the quantity was not enough for a meal.

Name : Olive Beck   E-mail : youngero1@kanmail.net

153. What is Ms. Beck most unsatisfied about?

(A) Diversity of options
(B) The amount of food
(C) Waiting time
(D) Attitudes of staff

154. What is indicated about Oasis Hotel Restaurant?

(A) Customers may receive a voucher once a month.
(B) The price is inexpensive.
(C) It is very famous in the area.
(D) It is always crowded with people.

Questions 155-157 refer to the following e-mail.

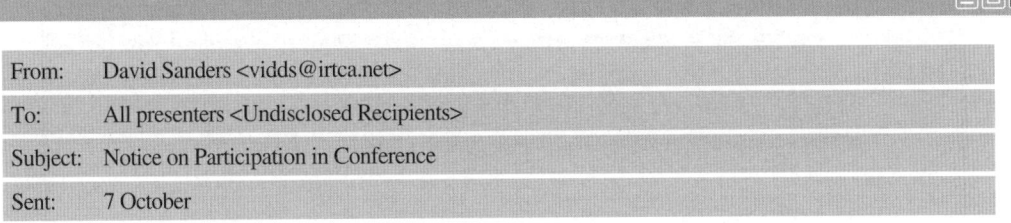

From:	David Sanders <vidds@irtca.net>
To:	All presenters <Undisclosed Recipients>
Subject:	Notice on Participation in Conference
Sent:	7 October

Welcome to the International Robot Technology Conference. When you arrive at the Future Technology Research Center, the venue, on 25 October, please be sure to register in the lobby on the first floor. After the registration process is over, you will receive some gifts and materials.

The presentation will be held at A-1 Hall on the second floor, and entries from each company will be displayed at A-3 Hall. The presentation equipment, including a projector, is fully equipped within A-1 Hall. You should save your presentation materials on a USB and bring them with you. Before the presentation, the security officer will check the USB with a separate laptop computer.

There are some companies that registered immediately after the list of participating companies was announced. If you need to adjust your participation status, please make sure to apply through our Web site by 15 October.

Sincerely,

David Sanders
Conference Organizer

---

155. Where should the event participants complete the registration process?

(A) In the first-floor lobby
(B) In A-1 Hall
(C) In A-3 Hall
(D) On the Web site

156. What should be done before the presentation?

(A) Preparing new equipment
(B) Reviewing some materials
(C) Checking a schedule
(D) Inspecting devices

157. What can participants do through the Web site?

(A) Cancel the attendance
(B) Ask for some equipment
(C) Register presentation materials
(D) Preview some entries

Questions 158-160 refer to the following online chat discussion.

[Pablo Antonio] Good morning, Ms. Brown and Mr. Roberts. I've finally confirmed an expert on the subject of next month's seminar.
09:16 A.M.

[Elle Brown] Great. Who is that? A famous person?
09:17 A.M.

[Pablo Antonio] It's Kenneth Jones, who is highly recognized in the field of social media marketing. Do you know about him? He's also good at Web design, so I think he's going to include some of that in the seminar.
09:18 A.M.

[Terry Roberts] That sounds good. I'm very interested in that field.
09:21 A.M.

[Elle Brown] I've heard of him. He probably wrote a best-selling book about social media and the Web.
09:22 A.M.

[Terry Roberts] I see. Then I'll send an e-mail to the department staff about the seminar today.
09:25 A.M.

[Pablo Antonio] Be sure to include in the e-mail that we are all having dinner with the presenter after the seminar.
09:29 A.M.

[Terry Roberts] Okay. I won't forget that.
09:30 A.M.

[Elle Brown] We'll each be given an opportunity to ask questions, right?
09:33 A.M.

[Pablo Antonio] Sure. Terry, add to the e-mail that all attendees should prepare questions in advance. I will call Mr. Jones at 2 P.M. to tell him how to get to the seminar's location.
09:36 A.M.

---

158. Why did Mr. Antonio send the message to his colleagues?

(A) To change the meeting schedule
(B) To introduce a new employee
(C) To get ideas about a seminar
(D) To inform them about the guest lecturer

159. At 09:21 A.M., what does Mr. Roberts most likely mean when he writes, "That sounds good"?

(A) He wanted to meet Mr. Jones.
(B) He already read a book written by Mr. Jones.
(C) He expects to enjoy the upcoming lecture.
(D) He thinks many employees are interested in the field of Web design.

160. What will Mr. Antonio do in the afternoon?

(A) Give a lecturer directions to the venue
(B) Send e-mails to employees
(C) Attend a meeting
(D) Ask for employees' opinions

Questions 161-163 refer to the following announcement.

City Hall Renovation Work

Glasgow is seeking a company for the renovation of City Hall. —[1]—. The company will be selected through an open bid, Mayor James Denver said. Once selected as a contractor, the company will be responsible for renovating or repairing much of City Hall over the course of two years. —[2]—.

Only companies that have worked in the construction industry for at least 10 years can apply for bids. —[3]—. The list of documents needed for the bidding can be found on the City Hall Web site's public notice board.

If the project is finished well, additional points can be awarded when bidding for construction or civil engineering works in the city. —[4]—.

161. What is the purpose of the announcement?

(A) To recruit staff at City Hall
(B) To award a prize to a superior company
(C) To announce a business to build a new building
(D) To find a business for a project

162. How can companies find out the details of the bidding?

(A) By contacting a public official
(B) By visiting City Hall
(C) By checking information on the Internet
(D) By presenting an estimate

163. In which of the positions marked [1], [2], [3], and [4] does the following sentence best belong?

"In addition, the necessary materials must be prepared in advance."

(A) [1]
(B) [2]
(C) [3]
(D) [4]

Questions 164-167 refer to the following article.

British Daily

GRIMSBY (6 July)—The Emerald Hotel Group, a global hotel chain, is entering the resort condominium business. —[1]—. Although based in London, England, the first condominium of the group will open in Namhae in South Korea. It will be the world's largest resort and will have state-of-the-art amenities, including an automatic parking guidance system.

Customers can buy memberships on a yearly basis, or purchase ownership of units if desired. —[2]—. In fact, it is said that famous real estate investors and entrepreneurs in Korea are already expressing a lot of interest.

Another noteworthy aspect is that the restaurant will be operated by Sejun Kim, one of Asia's top cooking experts. —[3]—. Travelers staying there will have the opportunity to enjoy a wide range of Asia's representative dishes.

With the creation of the great resort facility, the overall economy as well as employment rates in the region is expected to improve considerably. —[4]—. On the other hand, some experts are worried that real estate prices in the area may rise too much.

Locals are generally very positive about the changes that will take place in the region, which has not changed much for a long time.

- Anne Louis, Korean Correspondent

164. What is the purpose of the article?

(A) To explain a tourism trend in Asia
(B) To inform readers of the renovation of a hotel
(C) To announce the expansion of a business
(D) To attract investors for a project

165. What is suggested about the condominium?

(A) It is being built with the investment of Namhae citizens.
(B) A variety of advanced facilities will be included.
(C) Membership will be traded at an expensive price.
(D) A celebrity will own some facilities.

166. Where is the Emerald Hotel Group headquartered?

(A) In Hong Kong
(B) In Korea
(C) In England
(D) In Japan

167. In which of the positions marked [1], [2], [3], and [4] does the following sentence best belong?

"As it is an exceptionally excellent facility, it is expected to attract a lot of people to make a purchase."

(A) [1]
(B) [2]
(C) [3]
(D) [4]

Questions 168-171 refer to the following text-message chain.

Rebecca Taylor [2:11 P.M.]
Hello, Carol. It's Rebecca in the public relations department. Are you busy now?

Carol Thompson [2:14 P.M.]
No, what's going on?

Rebecca Taylor [2:15 P.M.]
I need to check some customer information, but I can't log in to the computer network.

Carol Thompson [2:18 P.M.]
Did you enter the wrong password?

Rebecca Taylor [2:19 P.M.]
That's not possible. Jim from your team already reset my password this morning.

Carol Thompson [2:20 P.M.]
I see. I'll have to check your computer. I'll go to your office now.

Rebecca Taylor [2:22 P.M.]
Okay, I'll be waiting.

168. What department does Ms. Thompson most likely work in?

(A) Marketing
(B) Human resources
(C) Information technology
(D) Management

169. What is suggested about Ms. Taylor?

(A) She often forgets her password.
(B) Her log-in information was changed.
(C) Her computer is not working properly.
(D) She is not used to handling computers.

170. At 2:19 P.M., what does Ms. Taylor mean when she writes, "That's not possible"?

(A) A computer is out of order.
(B) She knows the exact password.
(C) The network cannot be normalized.
(D) A project has not been completed.

171. What will Ms. Thompson do next?

(A) Go to Ms. Taylor's workspace
(B) Change the passwords
(C) Check some software
(D) Send a technician

Questions 172-175 refer to the following article.

Business News

EDINBURGH (1 November)—Roy Smith, who has led Kings Networks to grow into one of the top three companies in Britain, announced his retirement on 31 October.

He joined the Manchester branch of Kings Networks shortly after graduating from New York University in the United States. As a customer service representative, he became a highly reputable employee in a short period of time. Due to his superior ability, he was quickly promoted and landed the CFO position at the Edinburgh headquarters only four years after he joined the company.

By introducing a new management policy, he more than doubled the company's net profit within 10 years of being appointed CFO. Eventually, at the age of 43, he became the youngest CEO ever of Kings Networks.

As a result, Victoria Camden from the London branch has been chosen to temporarily replace Roy Smith, who has been a valuable asset for the company for the past 30 years, until his replacement is found. However, as there are no candidates that are as fit as her, most of the staff expect Ms. Camden to continue to serve as chief executive officer.

The company decided to give Mr. Smith the role of advisor, as he will continue to reside in the city where the head office is located even after retirement.

172. What is the purpose of the article?
 (A) To announce the closure of a business
 (B) To promote a company policy
 (C) To report on an executive's retirement
 (D) To explain the company's performance

173. The word "landed" in paragraph 2, line 8, is closest in meaning to
 (A) found
 (B) arrived
 (C) resigned
 (D) assumed

174. What is suggested about Ms. Camden?
 (A) She has been devoted to the company for nearly 30 years.
 (B) She is likely to continue to work as the leader of the company.
 (C) She has been promoted quickly.
 (D) She was an adviser to the company.

175. Where does Mr. Smith currently live?
 (A) In Edinburgh
 (B) In Manchester
 (C) In London
 (D) In New York

Questions 176-180 refer to the following flyer and e-mail.

The Grand Photo Festival

The 8th Grand Photo Fair will be held for three days from July 6 to 8 at the Stainley Art & Culture Center. In order to apply for this exhibition, you must first participate in the preliminaries. They run from June 8 to 12, and anyone can participate. Up to 500 people can submit their works on a first-come-first-served basis. Among them, 100 works will be chosen for the exhibition. We invited only photographers from the Rotterdam area last year, but this time, we abolished the regional restrictions. Each participant may submit up to two works.

To apply, please follow the steps below:

1. Download sign-up sheet from www.artfestival.org.ca. Then fill it out and access the 'Application' link on the Web site and upload it.

2. Mail the work to the Rotterdam Photography Association. The address can be found in the application form.

3. Finally, send the fee of $30 to the account number specified on the form. If submitting two works, you will have to pay $45.

The application deadline is June 1. In the preliminary round, the work will be selected by adding up the evaluation points by the judges and the Internet survey scores. Participants will be notified individually on July 1 regarding whether or not the work has been selected for the exhibition.

To:	nice_world@artfestival.org.ca
From:	ken11@sepmail.com
Date:	May 16
Subject:	Upcoming Photo Exhibition

I know that each participant can submit two works. I sent a single photograph and the registration fee last Friday. Then, can I send another one now? Of course, I will pay the additional $15 as well. Actually, I took a new picture, and I like it so much that I would like to submit it.

Please let me know if I can do that.

Thanks,

Rayleigh Bryk

176. According to the flyer, what is indicated about the Grand Photo Festival?

(A) It is held once a month.
(B) Only professional photographers are allowed to participate.
(C) Works will be displayed online.
(D) A requirement for participation has been changed.

177. In the flyer, the word "points" in paragraph 6, line 2, is closest in meaning to

(A) scores
(B) locations
(C) phases
(D) meanings

178. When will the participants know the results of the preliminary round?

(A) On May 16
(B) On June 12
(C) On July 1
(D) On July 8

179. How much did Mr. Bryk pay for the registration?

(A) $15
(B) $30
(C) $45
(D) $60

180. According to the e-mail, what does Mr. Bryk ask about?

(A) The payment amount
(B) The additional submission
(C) The cost refund
(D) The number of works

Questions 181-185 refer to the following press release and e-mail.

For Immediate Release
Contact: media_team@oceanworlds.com

Sydney, 16 February—One of the leading hotel companies, the Ocean Worlds Hotel Group, is hiring large numbers of new employees in the first half of this year. Applications will be accepted from 6 March to 6 April. In addition to our headquarters in Australia, we are looking for 300 people to work at our hotel branches in major European countries, including Switzerland, France, Germany, and the Netherlands. We are well-known for providing the most competitive salaries and generous benefits packages in our industry.

Open houses will be held at each branch in Europe. From branch managers, potential employees will not only be able to get information about our company but a great opportunity to look around the company's main facilities. They will be held every Friday in March. Those interested in attending a Friday open house should register online by 3 March at www.oceanworlds.com. Information about available positions can also be found there.

Ocean Worlds Hotel Group was founded in 1945 and now has 33 branches in 16 countries around the world. In addition, it is operating large, kid-friendly amusement parks in Australia, France, and England.

To: Leila Lütjens <lutjens_ace@naite.com>
From: Brigham Heyes <bh_ok@oceanworlds.com>
Re: Information
Date: 16 March

Dear Ms. Lütjens,

I was happy to have a conversation with you at our hotel last Friday. I'd like to offer you a job in the hotel's purchasing department. The purchasing manager and I, after reviewing your résumé, concluded that you would be a great fit for the department. Please come back to our hotel to discuss it further.

Are you available on Wednesday, 21 March, at 10 A.M.? Could you let me know if it is possible or when is convenient for you?

I look forward to seeing you again.

Sincerely,

Brigham Heyes

181. According to the press release, what will take place at Ocean Worlds Hotel Group?

(A) Opening a new branch
(B) Implementing a new policy
(C) Inviting customers to an event
(D) Recruiting new staff on a large scale

182. What is mentioned about Ocean Worlds Hotel Group?

(A) It is doing business for children.
(B) It is the largest company in the industry.
(C) It is hiring temporary workers.
(D) It is a newly established enterprise.

183. What is true about the open houses?

(A) A meal will be served to the participants.
(B) All job applicants must attend.
(C) They are held once a week in March.
(D) They can accommodate up to 300 people.

184. Why did Mr. Heyes send the e-mail?

(A) To provide a special gift
(B) To introduce a manager
(C) To offer a position
(D) To delay an appointment

185. What is suggested about Mr. Heyes?

(A) He is the president of a firm.
(B) He is a branch manager.
(C) He works in the personnel department.
(D) He is a new employee.

GO ON TO THE NEXT PAGE

Questions 186-190 refer to the following article, e-mail, and online review.

Karlstad Weekly

February 18—A new bicycle path is being built on the outskirts of Karlstad, reaching all the way to Green City Park. Work on the Riverside Trail began about two months ago. Harald Albinson, who works in the Karlstad office of the Swedish company Concord Industries, designed it. He is a veteran with more than 15 years of experience in civil engineering design.

Concord Industries has been involved in road work for cars and bicycles in many European countries, including Britain and France. As some of the surrounding roads also need to be renovated to suit the new bike paths, the project is the biggest ever. Therefore, if it is completed well, Mr. Albinson and all employees involved in the work will receive special bonuses and additional paid leave. The project is expected to be completed by October this year.

Many locals are very fond of the support to employment and tourism that the project brings. Concord Industries has hired hundreds of local residents to work on the path. Karlstad's tourism administration official expects the new bike route will increase activity in many service sectors, eventually boosting the local economy. Once the construction is over, a marathon will be held to commemorate completion in November.

To:	Harald Albinson <ha_smile@concordindustries.se>
From:	Hanna Vinter <hannavinter@concordindustries.se>
Date:	October 30
Subject:	Your achievement

Mr. Albinson,

I am writing to congratulate you on completing the Riverside Trail and the surrounding facilities well. This has made our company a stronger presence in Karlstad. In honor of your great achievement, Karlstad's mayor will give you a plaque of appreciation and a commemorative present this Thursday. We didn't even think about it, did we? In addition, you will enjoy a month off next month with your colleagues who worked with you.

Sincerely,

Hanna Vinter
Managerial Department, Concord Industries

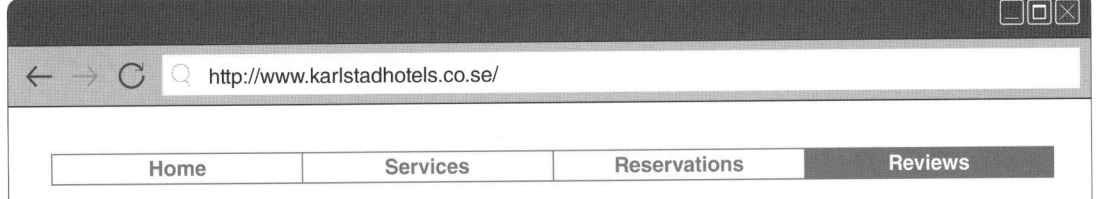

Berta Riverside Hotel

November 18 by Viola Strand

My name is Viola, and I live in Stockholm. A week ago, I participated in a marathon competition held in Karlstad with two friends. What a fantastic event! The event was very fun, of course, but the road we ran on was particularly impressive. The surrounding scenery was so nice that we stayed at the Berta Riverside Hotel for two nights. The hotel was also a wonderful place in harmony with the surrounding landscape. Every amenity was provided from comfortable rooms to free wireless Internet. The morning buffet was the best thing I've ever had. However, it was regrettable that we could not see part of the beautiful path from the hotel room.

186. What is the purpose of the article?

(A) To promote local events
(B) To explain the local traffic problem
(C) To encourage people to participate in a race
(D) To report on a construction project

187. What is suggested about Mr. Albinson?

(A) He will be given an added incentive.
(B) He won an award in a marathon.
(C) He is an expert in hotel management.
(D) He will be in charge of a larger project.

188. What is indicated in the e-mail?

(A) Mr. Albinson will be traveling to Karlstad.
(B) Mr. Albinson wants to go on vacation.
(C) Mr. Albinson is receiving some unexpected news.
(D) Concord Industries is headquartered in Karlstad.

189. What is true about Ms. Strand?

(A) She wants to work for Concord Industries.
(B) She was dissatisfied with the view at the hotel.
(C) She moved from Stockholm to Karlstad.
(D) She has friends in Karlstad.

190. What did Ms. Strand like best about the hotel?

(A) The breakfast
(B) The free Internet service
(C) The kindness of the staff
(D) The cleaning service

Questions 191-195 refer to the following advertisement and e-mails.

Top Smart Case

Top Smart Case has specialized in producing and supplying cell phone protection cases for the longest time in Korea. Our products are made of innovative materials that you've never seen. Before you choose a case, make sure to refer to the following attributes.

1. **Softness** – All the products produced by Top Smart Case do nothing to damage the cell phone they hold. It's easy to put the case on and take it off your phone.

2. **Impermeability** – The cases are impermeable to air and water. Products stored in our cases are well-protected and they are kept free of any dust.

3. **Harmlessness to the human body** – Our products are made of 100% high-quality silicon, so they have no adverse effect on the human body.

4. **Convenience** – Just wash with clean water and the cases will always look new.

5. **Style** – You can find various product designs on our Web site at www.topsmart.com. We also make custom-made designs for our customers.

To:	Paul Staunton
From:	Nancy Harris
Date:	June 1
Subject:	Promotional items

Dear Mr. Staunton,

Thank you for your kind explanation about the design of the case for use as our promotional items. As you said, our company logo on the back of the case should not be too big.

And, after discussing it with our team members, I think it's better to have the logo engraved rather than printed on the case. It's easy to keep your product clean, so customers will use it for a long time. Then, I think the printed logo will be erased over time. I wonder how long it will take and how much it will cost if you engrave the logo. Also, I'd appreciate it if you could let me know any other better ways or ideas.

Best regards,

Nancy Harris
Tanny Life Insurance

To: Nancy Harris
From: Paul Staunton
Date: June 5
Subject: Logo task

Dear Ms. Harris,

I reviewed your e-mail carefully. Well, most people don't throw away their cell phone cases in just a few days. As you mentioned, the printed logos will not last that long. If we use laser techniques to draw a logo on the surface of the case, it can last for quite a long time, but it's more expensive. If we make the engraved product as you said, it will probably take about five days longer than originally scheduled, but I don't think there will be any additional charges. Please let me know when the final decision has been made. We'll do our best to provide you with high-quality goods.

Best regards,

Paul Staunton
Top Smart Case

191. What is indicated about Top Smart Case?

(A) It is a new company.
(B) It produces packing boxes.
(C) It can make customized products.
(D) Its products are sold only in Korea.

192. Why did Ms. Harris send the e-mail?

(A) To ask for advice
(B) To request a discount
(C) To report some problems
(D) To recommend a manufacturer

193. Why does Ms. Harris want the engraved cell phone case?

(A) It is inexpensive.
(B) It is a rare item.
(C) People can use it for a long time.
(D) Advanced materials are used.

194. According to the first e-mail, what feature in Top Smart Case will affect customers?

(A) Softness
(B) Impermeability
(C) Harmlessness to the human body
(D) Convenience

195. What does Mr. Staunton acknowledge in his e-mail?

(A) Printing technology has developed very much.
(B) The printed matter does not have a long life.
(C) Making a logo requires a lot of money.
(D) The laser technique is most efficient.

Questions 196-200 refer to the following article, schedule, and e-mail.

Free courses held by local companies

By Jenny Houston

(February 16)—Several companies in Boston have been offering various education programs for local residents. They are benefiting local residents and maximizing publicity at the same time.

All free courses take place during regular business hours, and places are provided by local community centers. Representatives from each company guide prospective attendees to be assigned to courses that fit their interests.

Beneficial to both locals and businesses, the events feature courses that actually help get a job. Many job seekers who have completed the free curriculum have been successful in getting the jobs they want. In addition, many companies have become more interested in the program as they have hired more skilled employees. Martin Greaves, the human resources manager at Wells Bank, said, "Thanks to this training program, we're very satisfied that we don't have to educate our new employees separately."

Howard Community Center's
Weekly Education Program Schedule

Time Slot	Monday	Tuesday	Wednesday	Thursday	Friday
10 A.M. – 12 P.M.	Office Program Practice (Bill Anderson)	Basic Web Design (John Stevens)	Office Program Practice (Bill Anderson)	Basic Web Design (John Stevens)	Office Program Practice (Bill Anderson)
1 P.M. – 3 P.M.	Modern Landscape (Sam Stimson)	Undetermined	Modern Landscape (Sam Stimson)	Presentation Techniques (Sara Jeong)	Basic Web Design (John Stevens)
4 P.M. – 6 P.M.	Presentation Techniques (Sara Jeong)	Undetermined	Presentation Technique (Sara Jeong)	Undetermined	Modern Landscape (Sam Stimson)

※ All lectures are held three times a week.

TO:	Peter Mendes
FROM:	Jiyeon Lee
DATE:	March 16
SUBJECT:	Re: Education Program

Dear Mr. Mendes,

Thank you for contacting our community center about the education programs run by local companies. The curriculum has been in operation for four years, and many residents have learned useful expertise to get a job. People often question whether the lectures are really useful because they are free.

As the programs are sponsored by companies that represent our region, such as Planting Industries, all classes are taught by renowned instructors. Of course, as reported in last month's article, it could be very beneficial for your job search.

However, among the course schedules you are interested in, the 4 P.M. class on Friday will be changed to the same time on Thursday.

With best wishes,

Jiyeon Lee

196. What does the article mention about the free courses?

(A) They are becoming popular.
(B) Only job seekers can attend classes.
(C) They are related to employment.
(D) They help residents network in the community.

197. What is indicated in the schedule?

(A) All Web design classes are held in the morning.
(B) Some of the slots have not been set yet.
(C) The number of classes per subject varies.
(D) All students should attend every morning.

198. According to the e-mail, what is the advantage of all programs?

(A) Class hours are flexible.
(B) Free materials are provided by mail.
(C) Students can get a scholarship.
(D) Reliable lecturers are giving lectures.

199. According to the e-mail, what are residents concerned about the program?

(A) The quality of the lectures
(B) The preparations for lectures
(C) Scheduling conflicts
(D) The difficulty of the classes

200. What is implied about Mr. Mendes?

(A) He has attended the classes before.
(B) He is not available in the afternoon.
(C) He has to take a lecture on Friday afternoon.
(D) He may not require training after entering a company.

Stop! This is the end of the test. If you finish before time is called, you may go back to Parts 5, 6, and 7 and check your work.

MP3와 해설 파일은 온라인에서 제공됩니다.
▶ books.english.co.kr

TEST 02

test 02.mp3 | 정답 p.247

LISTENING TEST

In the Listening test, you will be asked to demonstrate how well you understand spoken English. The entire Listening test will last approximately 45 minutes. There are four parts, and directions are given for each part. You must mark your answers on the separate answer sheet.
Do not write your answers in your test book.

PART 1

Directions: For each question in this part, you will hear four statements about a picture in your test book. When you hear the statements, you must select the one statement that best describes what you see in the picture. Then find the number of the question on your answer sheet and mark your answer. The statements will not be printed in your test book and will be spoken only one time.

Statement (B), "They're shaking hands," is the best description of the picture, so you should select answer (B) and mark it on your answer sheet.

1.

2.

3.

4.

5.

6.

PART 2

Directions: You will hear a question or statement and three responses spoken in English. They will not be printed in your test book and will be spoken only one time. Select the best response to the question or statement and mark the letter (A), (B), or (C) on your answer sheet.

7. Mark your answer on your answer sheet.
8. Mark your answer on your answer sheet.
9. Mark your answer on your answer sheet.
10. Mark your answer on your answer sheet.
11. Mark your answer on your answer sheet.
12. Mark your answer on your answer sheet.
13. Mark your answer on your answer sheet.
14. Mark your answer on your answer sheet.
15. Mark your answer on your answer sheet.
16. Mark your answer on your answer sheet.
17. Mark your answer on your answer sheet.
18. Mark your answer on your answer sheet.
19. Mark your answer on your answer sheet.
20. Mark your answer on your answer sheet.
21. Mark your answer on your answer sheet.
22. Mark your answer on your answer sheet.
23. Mark your answer on your answer sheet.
24. Mark your answer on your answer sheet.
25. Mark your answer on your answer sheet.
26. Mark your answer on your answer sheet.
27. Mark your answer on your answer sheet.
28. Mark your answer on your answer sheet.
29. Mark your answer on your answer sheet.
30. Mark your answer on your answer sheet.
31. Mark your answer on your answer sheet.

PART 3

Directions: You will hear some conversations between two or more people. You will be asked to answer three questions about what the speakers say in each conversation. Select the best response to each question and mark the letter (A), (B), (C), or (D) on your answer sheet. The conversations will not be printed in your test book and will be spoken only one time.

32. What is the conversation about?
    (A) A new product
    (B) A sporting competition
    (C) A business-related event
    (D) Business travel

33. Where do the speakers most likely work?
    (A) At a travel agency
    (B) At a publishing company
    (C) At an advertising agency
    (D) At a home appliance company

34. What does the woman suggest the man do?
    (A) Check out what they need to do for an event
    (B) Present an idea to promote a product
    (C) Analyze European market trends
    (D) Register for an event in advance

35. What type of company do the speakers most likely work for?
    (A) A real estate agency
    (B) An architectural firm
    (C) An interior design company
    (D) A trading company

36. Why have the prices of solar panels gone up?
    (A) The cost of materials is high.
    (B) They take a long time to produce.
    (C) They do not consume much electricity.
    (D) They have become more popular.

37. What will the woman most likely do next?
    (A) Contact a colleague
    (B) Cancel a contract
    (C) Ask for funding
    (D) Send out an estimate

38. What kind of company does the woman work for?
    (A) A marketing firm
    (B) A construction company
    (C) A moving company
    (D) A cleaning service

39. How did the man know about the service provider?
    (A) He did a search on the Internet.
    (B) His acquaintance gave him some information.
    (C) He saw an ad near an apartment complex.
    (D) A moving company told him about it.

40. What information does the woman ask the man for?
    (A) The location of his residence
    (B) His preferred payment plan
    (C) His e-mail address
    (D) His appointment time

41. What event is the woman planning?
    (A) A departmental meeting
    (B) A retirement party
    (C) A charity event
    (D) A cooking seminar

42. What does the man ask about?
    (A) Preferred dishes
    (B) A reservation time
    (C) A mailing address
    (D) The number of attendees

43. What is suggested about the Topaz Room?
    (A) It is already booked.
    (B) It can accommodate more than 12 people.
    (C) It is a completely independent space.
    (D) It is equipped with amenities.

GO ON TO THE NEXT PAGE

44. Why is the woman calling?
   (A) To suggest a medical examination
   (B) To reschedule an appointment
   (C) To confirm a reservation
   (D) To report a system error

45. What time does Dr. Harris usually start working?
   (A) At 8:00 A.M.
   (B) At 9:00 A.M.
   (C) At 10:00 A.M.
   (D) At 11:00 A.M.

46. What does the man say he has to do next week?
   (A) Visit another hospital
   (B) Apply for sick leave
   (C) Enter some new information
   (D) Go on a business trip

47. What event are the women organizing?
   (A) A product demonstration
   (B) A trade fair
   (C) A sports competition
   (D) A grand opening

48. What do the women ask about?
   (A) Checking some equipment
   (B) Putting products on display
   (C) Promoting the details of an event
   (D) Using an elevator

49. What will the man do next?
   (A) Show the women to a place
   (B) Help the women carry some goods
   (C) Ask the women for a guidebook
   (D) Inspect a machine

50. What are the speakers mainly discussing?
   (A) Launching a new product
   (B) Correcting some wrong information
   (C) Preparing for an upcoming event
   (D) Recruiting new employees

51. What does the man imply when he says, "Will the meeting be held for only one hour tomorrow afternoon"?
   (A) The meeting should not take a long time.
   (B) The discussion will end earlier than scheduled.
   (C) The man doesn't have any time to spare.
   (D) The meeting should be extended.

52. What does the woman ask the man to do?
   (A) Call a manager
   (B) Make a document
   (C) Do volunteer work
   (D) Contact all employees

53. Where is the conversation taking place?
   (A) At an insurance company
   (B) At an Internet service provider
   (C) At an electronics company
   (D) At an advertising agency

54. What does the woman mean when she says, "there are so many ads on SNS"?
   (A) Everyone has a smartphone.
   (B) Many people do not use other forms of media.
   (C) Consumers will not be interested in advertisements.
   (D) SNS advertising is essential.

55. What is the woman concerned about?
   (A) Recruiting the right person
   (B) Expenses for advertising
   (C) A deadline for a report
   (D) Additional public expenditures

56. What are the speakers discussing?
    (A) A new album
    (B) A TV program
    (C) An Internet broadcast
    (D) A musical performance

57. According to the woman, what is new about the event?
    (A) The length of a performance
    (B) The prices of tickets
    (C) Livestreaming
    (D) The number of songs

58. What does the woman suggest doing?
    (A) Buying tickets as soon as possible
    (B) Arriving earlier than the starting time
    (C) Finding more information on the Internet
    (D) Paying attention to the weather

59. What problem does the man mention?
    (A) Some wrong information was announced.
    (B) A flight will not arrive on time.
    (C) Several passengers missed a connecting flight.
    (D) The staff did not remember the schedule properly.

60. Why will the woman contact Justin?
    (A) To change a plane reservation
    (B) To ask for transportation
    (C) To ask him to help carry baggage
    (D) To report an arrival time

61. What does the woman ask the man to do?
    (A) Call a coworker on the service support team
    (B) Announce a schedule again
    (C) Check some schedules
    (D) Reset the landing time

No Parking

Monday	7 A.M. – 12 P.M.
Wednesday	8 A.M. – 3 P.M.
Friday	2 P.M. – 8 P.M.
Saturday	11 A.M. – 5 P.M.

62. What problem are the speakers discussing?
    (A) They need to find an alternative parking space.
    (B) The man lost his parking ticket.
    (C) They are not allowed to enter the concert hall.
    (D) They arrived too late for the concert.

63. Look at the graphic. What day is it today?
    (A) Monday
    (B) Wednesday
    (C) Friday
    (D) Saturday

64. What does the man ask the woman to do?
    (A) Pay a bill
    (B) Book seats
    (C) Confirm a charge
    (D) Get tickets

GO ON TO THE NEXT PAGE

Subject	Schedule
Russian	Monday / Wednesday / Friday 7:00 P.M. – 8:20 P.M.
Spanish	Monday / Thursday / Friday 6:30 P.M. – 7:50 P.M.
German	Tuesday / Thursday / Friday 8:00 P.M. – 9:20 P.M.
French	Monday / Wednesday / Thursday 7:00 P.M. – 8:20 P.M.

Pine Apartment Directory	
1160	Roy Smith
1500	Robert Walker
1506	Kenneth Jones
1605	Frank Evans

65. What are the speakers mainly discussing?

   (A) Waiting lists for courses
   (B) Preparations for a business trip
   (C) A company-sponsored program
   (D) An orientation session

66. According to the man, why is the company policy good for employees?

   (A) They often go on business trips.
   (B) They can make good use of their spare time.
   (C) They can leave work earlier.
   (D) They do a lot of business with foreign companies.

67. Look at the graphic. Which class will the man most likely take?

   (A) Russian
   (B) Spanish
   (C) German
   (D) French

68. Where does the woman most likely work?

   (A) At a department store
   (B) At a car repair shop
   (C) At an electric company
   (D) At a customer service center

69. Why did the work take a long time?

   (A) There was an unexpected difficulty.
   (B) The demand for services has increased a lot.
   (C) There was a serious defect in the product.
   (D) Core parts were not supplied on time.

70. Look at the graphic. What is the man's name?

   (A) Roy Smith
   (B) Robert Walker
   (C) Kenneth Jones
   (D) Frank Evans

PART 4

Directions: You will hear some talks given by a single speaker. You will be asked to answer three questions about what the speaker says in each talk. Select the best response to each question and mark the letter (A), (B), (C), or (D) on your answer sheet. The talks will not be printed in your test book and will be spoken only one time.

71. According to the speaker, why will the event be delayed?
    (A) To meet the schedules of some participants
    (B) To avoid inclement weather
    (C) To prevent scheduling conflicts
    (D) To make further preparations

72. Why do organizers say the event will be special?
    (A) It will be broadcast on the radio.
    (B) People can listen to new songs.
    (C) It will run late into the evening.
    (D) Celebrities from abroad will be there.

73. Who is Tommy Holland?
    (A) An event organizer
    (B) An actor
    (C) A broadcaster
    (D) A musician

74. Where does the listener work?
    (A) At a hotel
    (B) At a restaurant
    (C) At a library
    (D) At a theater

75. Why is the speaker calling?
    (A) To check a reservation time
    (B) To get information about a menu
    (C) To request a change in a reservation
    (D) To cancel a reservation

76. What is the speaker apologizing for?
    (A) She gave the wrong information.
    (B) She didn't answer the phone.
    (C) She arrived behind schedule.
    (D) She should have called earlier.

77. What is being advertised?
    (A) A laptop computer
    (B) A hard drive
    (C) A camera
    (D) A mobile phone

78. What is suggested about the product?
    (A) It is inexpensive.
    (B) It is the lightest product.
    (C) Its memory is originally 8 gigabytes.
    (D) It is well packaged.

79. What should customers do to extend the warranty period?
    (A) Buy a memory chip
    (B) Register a product
    (C) Pay extra
    (D) Order an item within a week

80. Where does the talk most likely take place?
    (A) At a manufacturing plant
    (B) At a clothing company
    (C) At a construction company
    (D) At a hardware store

81. What does the speaker say the most important thing for the listeners to do is?
    (A) Wear working clothes
    (B) Follow safety regulations
    (C) Comply with working hours
    (D) Protect information security

82. What does the speaker mean when she says, "There is a drop box next to the exit in this conference room"?
    (A) Listeners should not throw away garbage.
    (B) The box should be moved to another room.
    (C) Papers should be dropped into the box.
    (D) Personal belongings should be kept in the box.

GO ON TO THE NEXT PAGE

83. Where is the speaker calling from?

    (A) An electronics store
    (B) A software company
    (C) A gift shop
    (D) A furniture store

84. What does the speaker imply when she says, "We need to make a manual"?

    (A) More detailed information should be provided to the supplier.
    (B) Many people find it difficult to install a program.
    (C) She wants to run a different operating system.
    (D) She needs a strategy to increase product sales.

85. What is the speaker going to do next?

    (A) Send some products
    (B) Revise a manual
    (C) Contact a supplier
    (D) Assist customers

86. What event is taking place?

    (A) A workshop
    (B) A company tour
    (C) A press conference
    (D) An anniversary celebration

87. What are the listeners advised to do?

    (A) Come up with ideas
    (B) Make presentations
    (C) Consult with a lecturer
    (D) Work overtime

88. What will happen in the afternoon?

    (A) Opinions will be exchanged.
    (B) A public hearing will be held.
    (C) Practical training will be implemented.
    (D) A publication will be introduced.

89. Where do the listeners most likely work?

    (A) At a telecom company
    (B) At an educational institution
    (C) At a Web design company
    (D) At an online shopping mall

90. According to the speaker, what is Mr. Jung an expert in?

    (A) Business management
    (B) Web site construction
    (C) International trade
    (D) Public relations

91. What does Mr. Jung say about teaching students?

    (A) It is not an easy task.
    (B) It requires thorough preparation.
    (C) It costs him a lot of money.
    (D) It makes him feel fulfilled.

92. What problem is being discussed?

    (A) Noise from vehicles
    (B) Some damaged roads
    (C) A reduction in public transportation
    (D) Traffic congestion

93. Why is the problem occurring?

    (A) Some roads were repaired poorly.
    (B) The number of buses has increased in a city.
    (C) There are too many cars on a road.
    (D) Public transportation is not available to residents.

94. What does Mr. Jones suggest?

    (A) Expanding existing roads
    (B) Restricting traffic to certain vehicles
    (C) Adjusting commuting times
    (D) Creating bus-only lanes

PRESENTATION SCHEDULE	
Dr. Baker	8:30 A.M.
Dr. Andy	10:00 A.M.
Dr. Lee	11:30 A.M.
Dr. Ruben	2:00 P.M.
Dr. Page	3:30 P.M.

Monthly Meeting Agenda	
March	Emerging Markets
April	Sales Analysis of the First Quarter
May	Online Shopping Mall
June	New Summer Products

95. What is the purpose of the message?

   (A) To send some materials
   (B) To apologize for an inconvenience
   (C) To confirm participation in an event
   (D) To inform the listener about the attendees

96. Look at the graphic. At what time is the listener's presentation?

   (A) 8:30 A.M.
   (B) 9:00 A.M.
   (C) 10:00 A.M.
   (D) 12:00 P.M.

97. What is implied about the event?

   (A) The survey is conducted every year.
   (B) The presenter must arrive half an hour early.
   (C) It is only for engineers.
   (D) Attendees must register in advance.

98. Look at the graphic. In which month is the staff meeting taking place?

   (A) March
   (B) April
   (C) May
   (D) June

99. What problem does the speaker mention?

   (A) A Web site connection is not smooth.
   (B) Some product pictures do not appear on screens.
   (C) There are problems locating products.
   (D) Deliveries are not being made on time.

100. What will the listeners most likely do after the meeting?

   (A) Inspect some machinery
   (B) Check a Web site
   (C) Call a specialist
   (D) Ship some orders

This is the end of the Listening test. Turn to Part 5 in your test book.

GO ON TO THE NEXT PAGE

READING TEST

In the Reading test, you will read a variety of texts and answer several different types of reading comprehension questions. The entire Reading test will last 75 minutes. There are three parts, and directions are given for each part. You are encouraged to answer as many questions as possible within the time allowed.

You must mark your answers on the separate answer sheet. Do not write your answers in the test book.

PART 5

Directions: A word or phrase is missing in each of the sentences below. Four answer choices are given below each sentence. Select the best answer to complete the sentence. Then mark the letter (A), (B), (C), or (D) on your answer sheet.

101. The Internet service company asked some customers to answer a survey about how often they use ------- computers each week.

    (A) their
    (B) they
    (C) them
    (D) themselves

102. Culture & Entertainment mainly creates ------- videos which are often used to promote corporate policies.

    (A) compelling
    (B) considerate
    (C) experienced
    (D) generous

103. Though the sales presentation was brief, the Prime Accounting Company decided to hire them ------- full-time accountants at once.

    (A) in
    (B) during
    (C) with
    (D) as

104. The marketing manager has an urgent need ------- a projector in order to deliver information more effectively.

    (A) use
    (B) using
    (C) used
    (D) to use

105. You can purchase tickets for the musical performance either online ------- by phone.

    (A) and
    (B) but
    (C) also
    (D) or

106. We just ------- a new printer and two color ink cartridges that Bryan Dylan ordered.

    (A) reported
    (B) regulated
    (C) suggested
    (D) received

107. The Payroll Department requested that all employees submit all business-related receipts ------- 5 P.M. tomorrow.

    (A) until
    (B) by
    (C) of
    (D) on

108. SH Technology Ltd. now reimburses the educational expenses of employees interested in the ------- of higher-education degrees.

    (A) planning
    (B) meaning
    (C) examination
    (D) completion

109. ------- day-shift employees prefer to eat lunch outdoors when the weather is nice.

    (A) Any
    (B) Much
    (C) Every
    (D) Many

110. Ella Bush ------- many books about various health-related topics, including how to get rid of stress, for the past 10 years.

    (A) writes
    (B) writing
    (C) wrote
    (D) has written

111. A supply order form was submitted yesterday afternoon, and the ordered items are ------- to arrive by 2 P.M. tomorrow.

    (A) committed
    (B) subject
    (C) expected
    (D) used

112. The new policy should prove ------- to new employees as well as to existing employees.

    (A) instructive
    (B) instructively
    (C) instructors
    (D) instructions

113. Mr. Graham requested that the contract ------- to him immediately because he has to revise some of the terms.

    (A) is sent
    (B) was sent
    (C) being sent
    (D) be sent

114. Ms. Swift doesn't know ------- sent her lost purse in the mail.

    (A) which
    (B) what
    (C) when
    (D) who

115. The sales manager asked that the product he ordered be placed ------- the copier.

    (A) into
    (B) next to
    (C) through
    (D) without

116. The president told me to ------- report on the progress of the construction of the shopping center.

    (A) fairly
    (B) evenly
    (C) timely
    (D) regularly

117. It is important for all employees in the Personnel Department to ------- tomorrow's seminar.

    (A) attend
    (B) recommend
    (C) arrive
    (D) participate

118. Kistar Construction submitted a very ------- offer but failed to win the contract.

    (A) competing
    (B) competitive
    (C) competitively
    (D) competition

119. ------- bicycling is so popular in Sydney, the city council approved plans to add a bicycle lane to every main road.

    (A) Whereas
    (B) Even if
    (C) Although
    (D) Because

120. The reclining seats on the latest express bus allow passengers to stretch out very -------.

    (A) quickly
    (B) upwardly
    (C) consistently
    (D) comfortably

GO ON TO THE NEXT PAGE

121. The amount ------- on the document is only an estimate and may vary depending on additional options.
    (A) shows
    (B) showed
    (C) shown
    (D) showing

122. Rich Mart, which supplies quality ingredients, will ------- customers with a 30-percent discount all next week.
    (A) give
    (B) provide
    (C) offer
    (D) inform

123. Violinist Sumi Lee's performances, widely advertised to the public, ------- a growing number of people.
    (A) attracts
    (B) may attract
    (C) are attracting
    (D) have been attracted

124. The London Museum of Art does not ------- visitors to take photographs of exhibits.
    (A) show
    (B) allow
    (C) enter
    (D) display

125. ------- moving Charles' desk, all his papers in the drawers got mixed up.
    (A) In the process of
    (B) In regard to
    (C) In addition to
    (D) On behalf of

126. Every restaurant owner is expected to comply with all applicable state ------- when disposing of food waste.
    (A) regulations
    (B) regulated
    (C) regulating
    (D) regulator

127. Personnel Department staff members will gather tomorrow ------- have a meeting with the new employees.
    (A) contrary to
    (B) even if
    (C) in order to
    (D) because of

128. Please send me a copy of the registration form ------- it is the most convenient for you.
    (A) whichever
    (B) whenever
    (C) wherever
    (D) whoever

129. We do not ------- customers' personal contact information to anyone without their consent.
    (A) find
    (B) handle
    (C) gather
    (D) disclose

130. Most people find the delay before the results of the awards ceremony are announced ------- to bear.
    (A) easily
    (B) enjoyable
    (C) hard
    (D) expected

PART 6

Directions: Read the texts that follow. A word, phrase, or sentence is missing in parts of each text. Four answer choices for each question are given below the text. Select the best answer to complete the text. Then mark the letter (A), (B), (C), or (D) on your answer sheet.

Questions 131-134 refer to the following press release.

The Case for Sensitive Items

Chief designer Frank Robinson of Mandelisa, a bag brand, announced that he has designed a case for fragile objects. It was developed ------- items vulnerable to impact when traveling. Mr. Robinson earned
131.
recognition for developing an innovative suitcase designed ------- for long journeys. -------. "Even if there
132.   133.
is plenty of space in a suitcase, travelers have to pay more attention to their belongings so that they fit well in their luggage. The surface of this case is very hard, ------- it is light and ideal for travel,"
134.
Mr. Robinson said.

131. (A) to protect
 (B) protection
 (C) protector
 (D) protect

132. (A) immediately
 (B) considerably
 (C) specifically
 (D) quickly

133. (A) However, it still had problems carrying sensitive goods.
 (B) They did not require additional equipment.
 (C) These days, travelers don't carry a lot of belongings.
 (D) A large suitcase is required for a long trip.

134. (A) provided that
 (B) since
 (C) or
 (D) but

Questions 135-138 refer to the following notice.

The Centum Premium Shopping Mall is happy to announce the inauguration of a shuttle service for shoppers. This service ------- to anyone visiting the mall. For those with disabilities, the bus
135.
is designed to carry passengers in wheelchairs. -------. The service is available from Tuesday
136.
through Sunday from 11 A.M. to 8 P.M.

In order to use the vehicle, you should make a reservation at least 30 minutes in advance -------
137.
we can plan accordingly. Although the shuttle service is free of charge, ------- donations are
138.
welcome. They will be of great help in maintaining quality service. Donations can be placed in the box next to the driver's seat.

135. (A) being offered
(B) was offered
(C) is being offered
(D) has been offered

136. (A) Rides are provided within a 3 km radius of the pickup location.
(B) The driver will be ready to depart in 10 minutes.
(C) Many shoppers will drive their cars.
(D) Buses are a cheap and practical means of transportation.

137. (A) as long as
(B) although
(C) except
(D) so that

138. (A) increasing
(B) contributing
(C) voluntary
(D) costly

Questions 139-142 refer to the following e-mail.

To: Cliff Clapton <cliff2@kitchensupplies.site>
From: Chris Stevens <stevenstar@skrestaurant.com>
Date: May 22
Subject: Contract Renewal

Dear Mr. Clapton,

For the past eight years, your company has been supplying us with dishes and containers.

-------. The contract ------- us is set to renew automatically every three years. I would like to make some
139.   **140.**

changes to the contract before the next renewal date.

These days, the government is urging self-employed people not to use disposable products. We have

decided to increase the percentage of ------- friendly products. Could you recommend some substitutes
                                        141.

for plastic utensils? I've seen recyclable products in your catalog before, so could you send me some

samples of them? You can also recommend products that are -------.
                                                          142.

Please send me some samples as soon as possible so that I can have enough time to consider the

products.

Best regards,

Chris

---

139. (A) Most customers prefer the lunch we provide.
(B) Repair work will be carried out in our store.
(C) I hope our relationship will continue in the future.
(D) We've had a lot of competitors lately.

140. (A) against
(B) inside
(C) between
(D) regardless of

141. (A) properly
(B) safely
(C) financially
(D) environmentally

142. (A) portable
(B) durable
(C) biodegradable
(D) thermal

Questions 143-146 refer to the following memo.

To: All Employees
From: William Jones
Date: September 26

Good afternoon,

It is with a mix of sadness and pride that I am announcing Richard Scott's decision to ------- Instar
                                                                                                143.
Electronics to pursue his own dream at top German automaker Vents. His last day with us will be

on Friday, November 28.

Since he started working here, he has played a key role in applying state-of-the-art features to all

of our products. In addition, Mr. Scott himself organized a more cost-effective and productive work

system. In the process, he made the bonds between employees more -------. -------.
                                                                    144.   145.

Please join us in ------- Richard the best of luck and continued success in his career.
                  146.
Regards,

William Jones
Assistant Manager
Research & Development Department

---

143. (A) leave
     (B) operate
     (C) establish
     (D) join

144. (A) free
     (B) hard
     (C) permanent
     (D) solid

145. (A) It is clear that he has contributed greatly to the improvement of the overall culture of our company.
     (B) He graduated from a college in New York with excellent grades.
     (C) He studied Asian markets for three months last year.
     (D) He will be working as a research and development manager starting tomorrow.

146. (A) wishing
     (B) wished
     (C) wishes
     (D) to wish

PART 7

Directions: In this part you will read a selection of texts, such as magazine and newspaper articles, e-mails, and instant messages. Each text or set of texts is followed by several questions. Select the best answer for each question and mark the letter (A), (B), (C), or (D) on your answer sheet.

Questions 147-148 refer to the following advertisement.

Perosque Symbolic Collection

For over 100 years, fashion lovers from around the world have appreciated Perosque's unique classic bags. We are pleased to introduce a new line of merchandise to add to our existing collections. Our traditional handbags and all kinds of bags are handmade by certified craftsmen, and all goods are made of the highest-quality natural leather. It is possible to order large quantities, but be aware that it may take longer than expected to complete because they are handmade goods. And we can supply our products to all of Europe and America. We would like you to take a look at the products on our Web site at www.perosque.com.

147. For whom is the advertisement intended?

(A) Tourists
(B) Clothing manufacturers
(C) Boutique owners
(D) Product designers

148. What is suggested about Perosque?

(A) It exports its products to various countries.
(B) It is looking for a leather crafts expert.
(C) It is planning to expand its business to the United States.
(D) It will continue to sell only the same products.

Questions 149-150 refer to the following information.

FRESH WORLD RESTAURANT

Monday – Saturday
Lunch: 11 A.M. – 3 P.M.
Dinner: 5:30 P.M. – 9 P.M.

Sunday
Breakfast: 8 A.M. – 3 P.M.
Dinner: 4 P.M. – 9 P.M.

In addition to our regular menu, we offer the following daily specials just for $12.00:

Monday: Lasagna
Tuesday: Ravioli
Wednesday: Risotto
Thursday: Bruschetta
Friday: Seafood Stew

We have live entertainment on Friday and Saturday evenings.
Making a reservation is suggested for Friday and Saturday evenings.

149. When does dinner start on Tuesdays?
(A) At 3:00 P.M.
(B) At 4:30 P.M.
(C) At 5:30 P.M.
(D) At 9:00 P.M.

150. What is mentioned about Friday?
(A) Having a reservation is required.
(B) Breakfast is available starting at 9 A.M.
(C) There is a live performance.
(D) Risotto is served as a special menu item.

Questions 151-152 refer to the following text-message chain.

John Breedlove 4:56 P.M.	Clara, are you still in the office?	
Clara Jones 4:58 P.M.	Yes, I was just about to leave. What's going on?	
John Breedlove 5:01 P.M.	I can't remember my new password for the remote computer system. It's hard to remember because the company asked me to set a long password.	
Clara Jones 5:02 P.M.	Is there any way I can help you?	
John Breedlove 5:06 P.M.	Yes, on my desk, I'm sure there's a piece of paper with my password on it.	
Clara Jones 5:08 P.M.	There are a lot of documents on your desk.	
John Breedlove 5:11 P.M.	Sorry! It's on a green piece of paper. I think it's in a book with a white cover.	
Clara Jones 5:12 P.M.	I see. I guess this is it. The code you need to know is aux1020855.	
John Breedlove 5:15 P.M.	Yes, thanks so much, Clara. See you tomorrow.	

151. What's Mr. Breedlove's problem?

(A) He can't open the door to his office.
(B) He lost an important document.
(C) He can't access a system.
(D) Some information on his computer has been deleted.

152. At 5:08 P.M., what does Ms. Jones imply when she writes, "There are a lot of documents on your desk"?

(A) She doesn't want Mr. Breedlove to postpone his work.
(B) She can't find what she is looking for.
(C) She has to work late this evening.
(D) She thinks cleaning is necessary.

Questions 153-154 refer to the following e-mail.

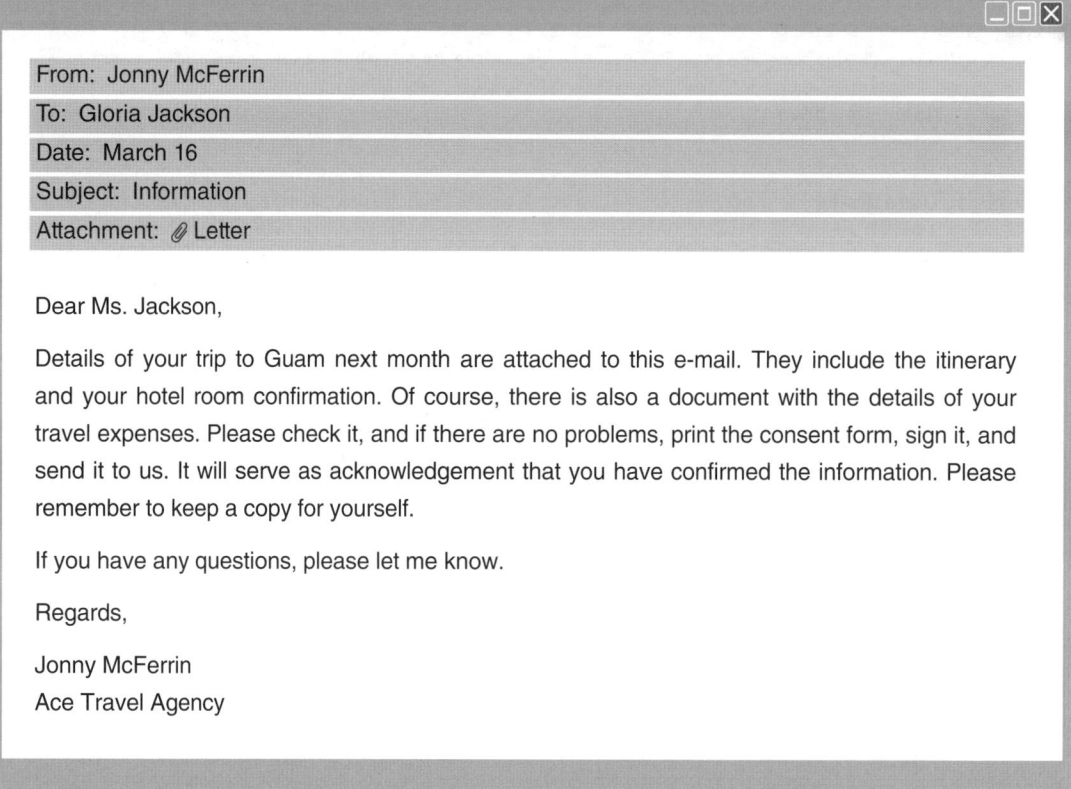

From: Jonny McFerrin
To: Gloria Jackson
Date: March 16
Subject: Information
Attachment: 📎 Letter

Dear Ms. Jackson,

Details of your trip to Guam next month are attached to this e-mail. They include the itinerary and your hotel room confirmation. Of course, there is also a document with the details of your travel expenses. Please check it, and if there are no problems, print the consent form, sign it, and send it to us. It will serve as acknowledgement that you have confirmed the information. Please remember to keep a copy for yourself.

If you have any questions, please let me know.

Regards,

Jonny McFerrin
Ace Travel Agency

153. What is the purpose of the e-mail?
 (A) To inform a person about some travel arrangements
 (B) To report the details of a sale
 (C) To ask for a copy of a document
 (D) To request approval for a budget

154. What is Ms. Jackson advised to do?
 (A) Fill in a form
 (B) Make a reservation beforehand
 (C) Keep a document
 (D) Provide additional information

Questions 155-158 refer to the following article.

Angelina Hale is a restaurant owner with an unusual history. She was a promising fund manager until a decade ago. —[1]—. She made a lot of money, but she led a busy life. As a result, she failed to eat regularly and had to eat a lot of unhealthy food such as fast food. Finally, she quit her job due to serious health problems. —[2]—. That's when she came up with the idea for her own restaurant, the Home Cook.

Starting as a small restaurant in her hometown, she cooked only with vegetables she grew herself as well as organic ingredients from reliable farmers. At first, the rather bland taste did not catch the public's attention.

—[3]—. However, gradually adding local flavor, she has consistently tried to develop recipes that both taste good and are nutritious. "It makes me happy to see my community becoming health-conscious," said Angelina Hale. —[4]—.

In fact, several local daycare center directors have recently decided to provide children with cuisine from the Home Cook.

155. Where did Ms. Hale originally work?

(A) At a food company
(B) At a doctor's office
(C) At a travel agency
(D) At a financial institute

156. What change has Ms. Hale observed in her community?

(A) A shortage of vegetables
(B) Increased interest in healthy eating habits
(C) A boom in the restaurant business
(D) A rise in the number of organic farms

157. What is true about the Home Cook?

(A) Its chefs provide their own ingredients.
(B) It serves only vegetarian dishes.
(C) It will increase its production of food.
(D) It will open a new branch soon.

158. In which of the positions marked [1], [2], [3], and [4] does the following sentence best belong?

"Now, her business is expected to grow even more."

(A) [1]
(B) [2]
(C) [3]
(D) [4]

Questions 159-161 refer to the following press release.

Busan Public Pools to Reopen in June

May 30 — The Busan Department of Health announced that renovations on two of the city's public swimming pools will be completed soon. Both pools are scheduled to reopen in June. Last year, after failing quarterly water quality tests, the pools remained closed for about 10 months. The Southern Pool will reopen in two days as only its water filtering equipment needed to be replaced. The pool will be available for use by the public as of June 1. However, it will take a little longer at Centum Swimming Pool because the floor of the pool has to be repaired. It is also the largest swimming pool in the country, and since it is used by so many people, all necessary safety precautions must be taken. As such, indoor swimming pools must be inspected periodically, and maintenance must be performed frequently.

159. What is the main topic of the press release?

(A) The maintenance of some city facilities
(B) The expansion of a swimming pool
(C) The revision of some health regulations
(D) The closure of an old swimming pool

160. What is the problem at the Southern Pool?

(A) There was a leak in the floor.
(B) The water was not properly filtered.
(C) It is not popular in the country.
(D) Safety accidents frequently occur there.

161. What is indicated about Centum Swimming Pool?

(A) It features a fitness center.
(B) Safety checks there are always done thoroughly.
(C) It is an indoor facility.
(D) It has grown in size this year.

Questions 162-164 refer to the following advertisement.

Contact: Bobby Petrov, bobbyp16@pacificcompany.com

The Pacific Development Company is pleased to announce the completion of its latest project, Ocean View Apartment. —[1]—. The complex has 160 townhouses still available. Most of the units were presold when the show house was open to the public.

Each unit features a well-equipped kitchen, three spacious bedrooms, and two bathrooms. Each room has a big window, so residents can enjoy the great view. —[2]—. Every unit also includes modern amenities, such as central air conditioning, an energy-efficient oven, a dishwasher, and a clothes washer/dryer. All home appliances can be operated with smartphones.

The Ocean View Apartment Complex is conveniently located near various government offices, shopping centers, and large discount stores. —[3]—. Additionally, all residents have access to the fitness center and the library on the property.

If you want to visit an available unit, please call 051-008-8949 in advance to schedule a visit. —[4]—.

---

162. What most likely is the Pacific Development Company?

(A) An interior design company
(B) A home rental operator
(C) A housing loan provider
(D) A homebuilder

163. What is indicated about the townhouses?

(A) They are all still available.
(B) They are fully furnished.
(C) They include some appliances.
(D) They each have three parking spaces.

164. In which of the positions marked [1], [2], [3], and [4] does the following sentence best belong?

"It is open for viewing from Monday through Saturday from 11 A.M. to 8 P.M."

(A) [1]
(B) [2]
(C) [3]
(D) [4]

Questions 165-167 refer to the following announcement.

Field Trip Coordinator Needed

Emerald Riverside Park is looking for a tour guide to lead our environmental education program. The job description includes preparing field trips, explaining the natural environment and ecosystem of the park to visitors, and scheduling field trip groups.

There are some restrictions on the qualifications. Qualified applicants must have previous experience managing and leading teams and should be familiar with the parks and environmental resources in the city. Biology or environmental studies majors are preferred. The ability to speak a foreign language such as Spanish or French is a plus.

To apply, e-mail a cover letter, a résumé, and two letters of reference to recruiters@riversiders.com by September 16.

Visit www.riversiders.com and please refer to the specific information.

165. What is the purpose of the announcement?
 (A) To encourage residents to do outdoor activities
 (B) To recruit a new employee
 (C) To introduce a park to visitors
 (D) To help preserve the natural environment

166. The word "plus" in paragraph 2, line 5, is closest in meaning to
 (A) benefit
 (B) addition
 (C) extra
 (D) tip

167. How can additional information be obtained?
 (A) By sending an e-mail
 (B) By going on a field trip
 (C) By visiting a Web site
 (D) By reading a brochure

Questions 168-171 refer to the following contract.

Breeze Web Hosting Service Terms & Conditions

- Make a 30% down payment before we start the project. That amount is not refundable. You must pay the balance when all the work is done. The Web site will not run until all expenses are fully paid. Unless specified in the contract, the code and contents on the Web site are copyrighted by Breeze Web Hosting.

- Clients can request the modification of the Web site's content or design whenever necessary. However, in such cases, a fee may be charged.

- Once the Web site is built by Breeze Web Hosting, clients should register the completed site in the search engine either directly or through an agency. Breeze Web Hosting does not provide this service.

- Breeze Web Hosting will provide technical support until the contract is terminated.

- The contract is automatically renewed every year, and to stop it, you must contact us at least two weeks before the contract expires. Otherwise, it will be automatically extended.

By signing below, I acknowledge that I have read and understood the above terms and conditions.

Name: Alice Wood   Signature: *Alice Wood*

---

168. What type of service did Ms. Wood most likely request?

(A) Web server construction
(B) Automated payment
(C) Online advertising
(D) Internet access

169. According to the contract, why may an additional fee be charged?

(A) For using content on a Web site
(B) For making a payment late
(C) For modifying the terms of the contract
(D) For asking for changes on a Web site

170. What topic is NOT discussed in the contract?

(A) Content ownership
(B) Contract cancelation conditions
(C) Training courses for the client
(D) Technical support

171. The word "balance" in paragraph 1, line 2, is closest in meaning to

(A) stability
(B) evenness
(C) steadiness
(D) remainder

Questions 172-175 refer to the following online chat discussion.

Ian Cho — 2:05 P.M.
The Aki Clothing Company just sent us a message requesting technical support.

Betty Turner — 2:06 P.M.
Can you ask them if they can wait? We have a monthly inspection of them in two days.

Ian Cho — 2:12 P.M.
The message from the manager says it's an emergency.

Betty Turner — 2:16 P.M.
David, where are you now? Can you go to the Aki Clothing Company today?

David Roberts — 2:16 P.M.
Do you think the system is not working at all?

Ian Cho — 2:17 P.M.
I think so. It seems all the work is interrupted.

David Roberts — 2:18 P.M.
Okay. I can be there in about 30 minutes.

Betty Turner — 2:22 P.M.
Somebody should call Dennis Johnson at Aki Clothing so that he knows David is on his way.

Ian Cho — 2:22 P.M.
Okay, I'll do that right now.

172. What is the purpose of the online chat discussion?

(A) To discuss an urgent situation
(B) To request repairs
(C) To confirm a customer's information
(D) To replace a system

173. How often does a technician usually visit the Aki Clothing Company?

(A) Once a month
(B) Twice a month
(C) Once a week
(D) Once a year

174. At 2:17 P.M., what does Mr. Cho most likely mean when he writes, "I think so"?

(A) The customer sent the wrong message.
(B) A service engineer has already visited.
(C) Mr. Roberts has a good grasp of the situation.
(D) Some equipment must be replaced.

175. What will Mr. Cho do next?

(A) Contact a client
(B) Send a service engineer
(C) Help Mr. Roberts provide service
(D) Visit the Aki Clothing Company

GO ON TO THE NEXT PAGE

Questions 176-180 refer to the following Web page and e-mail.

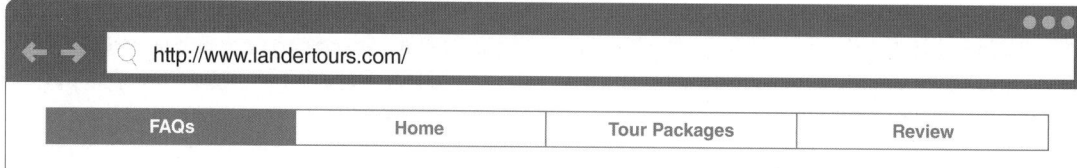

http://www.landertours.com/

| FAQs | Home | Tour Packages | Review |

Frequently Asked Questions about European Travel Package A

What documents do I need?

The European Union and our country have a visa waiver agreement. Therefore, be sure to have a valid passport before you go on a trip. If you are willing to drive, get an international driver's license. You must have them on the first day of the tour and on subsequent days at border crossings.

Is an airport pickup service available?

If you arrive at the airport by the scheduled time, we'll pick you up and then drop you off at the airport on the last day of your trip. Travelers, who are arriving or departing on other days not included in the package, need to arrange their own transportation.

What should I take to Northern Europe?

We suggest bringing a windbreaker. Some countries are relatively warm, but others are a bit cold. In addition, it can rain unexpectedly in the mountains, so you should bring appropriate outerwear.

What kind of information is provided before the tour?

You will receive an e-mail with a schedule and a description of the travel package you purchased. In it, you will find country descriptions, route information, hotel and restaurant information, and maps.

From:	kiki_1221@yaho.co.jp
To:	admin@landertours.com
Date:	June 8
Subject:	European Travel Package A

Dear Mr. Payne,

I recently booked a reservation for your European Travel Package A in September. I've been wanting to travel to Europe for a long time, but I'm finally going there for the first time. I really like the detailed terms and conditions of the package. However, I would like to extend my trip by five days to travel to Bulgaria and Albania, which are not included in the package. Could you make the necessary arrangements? In addition, since I don't have much information about travel destinations, I would appreciate it if you could provide me with data on some local tourist attractions. I assume that your package is the best choice I can make now.

Sincerely,

Masato Komuro

176. What is suggested about European Travel Package A?

(A) It goes to places with consistently warm weather.
(B) Its price is the most reasonable of all travel packages.
(C) It requires a person to have an international driver's license.
(D) It takes travelers to more than one country.

177. According to the Web page, what should travelers do before the tour begins?

(A) Submit a picture of their passport
(B) Apply for a visa
(C) Pack warm clothes
(D) Fill out some forms

178. What will Mr. Komuro most likely need to do?

(A) Pay extra money for his airline ticket
(B) Contact a hotel in advance
(C) Arrange his own transportation to the airport
(D) Present a list of the destinations he wants to go to

179. What is NOT true about Mr. Komuro?

(A) He has never been to Europe.
(B) He is going to visit every country in Europe.
(C) He wants to travel longer.
(D) He doesn't know much about tourist attractions in Europe.

180. In the e-mail, the word "assume" in line 6, is closest in meaning to

(A) believe
(B) accept
(C) take over
(D) simulate

Questions 181-185 refer to the following flyer and e-mail.

Visit Columbia Science Museum!

Welcome! If you haven't been to the Columbia Science Museum recently, you will notice some upgrades to our facilities upon your next visit. Located just minutes from Bernard Station in the metropolitan shopping district, the museum has expanded in size. Moreover, the lobby has been totally renovated. A new exhibition hall and a conference room have been added, and we have added a café. The parking lot has also been expanded so that it is twice as large as it was before, making it very convenient for drivers. And don't forget to visit the souvenir shop with its wide range of unique and interesting items.

Admission:

Ticket Type	Price	Provides
Basic	$12.00	Access to the museum's permanent exhibits
Basic Plus	$18.00	Basic benefits and access to all lectures
Prime	$25.00	Basic Plus benefits and 2 guest passes for museum admission
Prime Plus	$30.00	Prime benefits and access to all special exhibitions

Special Exhibition:
- Human World: Everything in the Human Body (January 1 – March 31)
- The Planets in the Solar System: Worlds of Infinite Possibilities (April 1 – June 30)
- Marine Resources: A Repository of Future Resources (July 1 – September 30)
- The Age of Artificial Intelligence: Breaking the Limits of Science and Technology (October 1 – December 31)

To: angels11@csmuseum.org
From: elevens@ingalaxy.com
Date: October 7
Subject: Upcoming excursion

Dear Ms. Lin,

I am writing to inquire about visiting the museum. I will go there with my family on October 14.

There are 3 people in my family, and we have decided to go there because we think we can learn a lot about science.

We don't need free museum tickets, but we're interested in this month's special exhibition. I wonder if there are tickets available for us now. If so, my son is 16 years old, and I wonder if he can get a discount. I would also appreciate it if you could tell me the opening and closing times of the museum.

Thank you in advance for your assistance.

Troye Walker

---

181. What is suggested about the Columbia Science Museum?

(A) It offers a discount to students.
(B) It is conveniently located.
(C) Its admission prices have been raised.
(D) It was closed to public during its renovations.

182. Why was the e-mail written?

(A) To find out how to get a free ticket
(B) To make a proposal for museum exhibitions
(C) To inquire about the museum's facilities
(D) To request information about a museum tour

183. According to the e-mail, what does Mr. Walker ask about?

(A) The lecture schedule
(B) How to buy tickets
(C) A discount for minors
(D) The prices of exhibits

184. What type of tickets will Mr. Walker most likely purchase?

(A) Basic
(B) Basic Plus
(C) Prime
(D) Prime Plus

185. What exhibition will Mr. Walker most likely visit?

(A) Human World
(B) The Planets in the Solar System
(C) Marine Resources
(D) The Age of Artificial Intelligence

Questions 186-190 refer to the following article, schedule, and e-mail.

Old Water Pipes Being Replaced throughout the City

(November 17)—During the month of December, the Federal Waterworks will be working on replacing most of the water pipes across the city of Dallas. Existing rusty iron pipes will be replaced with high-grade stainless steel pipes coated with plastic.

Arnold Bush, the president of the Broad Utilities Company, which will carry out the work, said, "By replacing old water pipes that have been used for more than 50 years with better ones, local residents will see improvements in the quality of the water they get." For instance, once all the replacements are completed, residents will be able to drink tap water without boiling it.

Some streets will be closed to traffic between 10:00 A.M. and 5:00 P.M. while the pipes are being replaced. The contractor is in constant discussions with city officials to set up a schedule that will minimize inconvenience to residents. The schedule will be announced on the city's and the contractor's Web site whenever it is updated. Those in urgent need of help can immediately call the contractor's at 088-9669-0482.

Pipe Replacement Work Schedule

Monday	Dec. 2	Sunset Avenue
Tuesday	Dec. 3	Gloria Street
Wednesday	Dec. 4	George Avenue
Thursday	Dec. 5	Stainwood Street
Friday	Dec. 6	Southwest Street

When work on your street has been completed, technicians from the Broad Utilities Company will come to your house to reconnect the water pipes.

To:	Joseph Greaves <joscorn@neit.com>
From:	Richard Anderson <nicer@broadutilities.com>
Re:	Service Information
Date:	November 28

Dear Mr. Greaves,

Your street is scheduled to have its water pipes replaced on Wednesday, December 4. Technicians will visit your home to reconnect your lines around 2:00 P.M. The work is expected to take about two hours if there are no problems. Work should be done during your stay at home. Please call us at 088-9669-0482 to confirm the schedule. In addition, while connecting the pipes, the water supply will be interrupted, so it is recommended that you store extra water in advance.

Thank you.

Richard Anderson

---

186. According to the article, what is true about the existing pipes?
  (A) They are made of plastic.
  (B) Water doesn't go through them properly.
  (C) They pollute the water.
  (D) They will be repaired.

187. What does the article indicate about the work schedule?
  (A) It was made by city officials.
  (B) It may be changed.
  (C) It has already been revised several times.
  (D) It is too complicated.

188. What will happen on December 5?
  (A) Road traffic will be blocked.
  (B) A new schedule will be released.
  (C) Customer feedback will be accepted.
  (D) City officials and local residents will meet.

189. What is suggested about Mr. Greaves?
  (A) He is supposed to come home in the afternoon.
  (B) He lives on George Avenue.
  (C) He will meet Mr. Bush soon.
  (D) He called the repairmen himself.

190. What did Mr. Anderson advise Mr. Greaves to do?
  (A) Inform him about any defects
  (B) Check some information online
  (C) Change a scheduled time
  (D) Keep enough water

Questions 191-195 refer to the following e-mails and information.

From:	Olive Gordon
To:	Anthony Renner
Date:	May 8
Subject:	Program copy
Attachment: June 8 event	

Hello, Mr. Renner,

Attached is a revised version of an event notice that needs to be printed. As we discussed yesterday, I think it would be better to apply white letters on blue paper. And the winners' names should be written in a decorative font to make them stand out. I did my best to make the contents of the notice as simple and noticeable as possible.

I've reviewed it several times, but I'd like you to take a look at it before the programs are printed. Could you give me your overall feedback on it by May 15?

Thank you.

Olive Gordon
Event Organizer

Giant Financial Company
21st Annual Celebration of the Best Employees

Paradise Hotel, Friday, June 8

6:00 P.M. – 7:00 P.M. Dinner
7:00 P.M. – 7:20 P.M. Keynote Address, Anna Kendrick, CEO
7:20 P.M. – 8:00 P.M. Presentations, Billy Burke, Senior Vice President

Business Performance – John Gere
Best Customer Management – Judy Pitt
Golden Decade Service – Mason Wells
Employee of the Year – Liam Mendelson

From:	Anthony Renner
To:	Olive Gordon
Date:	May 13
Subject:	Program for the upcoming event

Ms. Gordon,

Thank you for showing me this year's event notice. I think the poster has the best color combination. It is not very fancy, but it has a charm that catches people's attention. As a new organizer, you have tried a lot of new things.

I think it is very well-organized, but it was customary for the Golden Decade Service to be announced last. It is considered the most meaningful award at the event as it honors long-term employees who have worked for 10 years. I don't think that's going to be a problem, but you had better report it to Ms. Kendrick in advance. I would like to ask you to be careful not to make any mistakes in the time and the name of the winner.

Thank you.

Anthony Renner
Director of Human Resources

---

191. What will take place on June 8?

(A) A new employee orientation
(B) A retirement party
(C) An awards ceremony
(D) A board meeting

192. Whose name will most likely appear in a special style on the final version of the notice?

(A) Anthony Renner
(B) Judy Pitt
(C) Olive Gordon
(D) Anna Kendrick

193. What does Mr. Renner suggest Ms. Gordon do?

(A) Inform the CEO of a change
(B) Put more emphasis on long-term workers
(C) Print a poster in advance
(D) Include detailed information about the winners

194. What is indicated about Mr. Wells?

(A) He has been working at the company for ten years.
(B) He will make a presentation at an event.
(C) He was in charge of organizing the event last year.
(D) He is the most senior of the attendees.

195. What is implied about Ms. Gordon?

(A) She will give feedback on a poster.
(B) She has already won many awards.
(C) She is skilled at organizing events.
(D) She is in charge of new work this year.

Questions 196-200 refer to the following brochure and e-mails.

Ivy Event Hall

Located not far from the center of Seoul, the capital of Korea, Ivy Event Hall is the ideal venue for your reception, wedding ceremony, or business conference. It is in a peaceful place surrounded by bushes and other types of vegetation.

We have four rooms of different sizes. The Modern Room seats between 50 and 80 people comfortably, and the Special Room is perfect for up to 150 guests. The Executive Room can accommodate up to 200 guests, and the Exclusive Room with twice as much capacity as that is the largest room here. The Executive Room and the Exclusive Room have state-of-the-art presentation equipment, including a super-large screen and a projector.

Our restaurant offers a buffet with food prepared by the best chefs. You will be able to enjoy amazing dishes you've never experienced before!

For further information, call 242-555-0135 or visit www.ivyhall.net.

To	Emma Jeong
From	Tom McKellen
Date	April 6
Subject	Anniversary Planning

Dear Ms. Jeong,

I visited Ivy Event Hall and looked at all of the rooms there. Although the rent is a little high, the facilities were much better than I had expected. It might be just right for our company's anniversary celebration. The food served at the buffet is likely to be suitable for the wide variety of tastes of our 110 guests. By the way, we have to reserve a bigger room because we have to have a beam projector. That way, the attendees can be more comfortable since they will have a lot of room.

Let me know if I have your approval to book a room. We need to make a decision quickly. If we reserve at least two weeks before the event, we'll get a 20% discount. I think we had better make a reservation this month.

Tom McKellen
Head of the Planning Department
Kai Industries

To: Tom McKellen
From: Emma Jeong
Date: April 7
Subject: Re: Anniversary Planning

Dear Mr. McKellen,

Thanks for the information about the event hall. It is okay if the room is a little bigger than we need. In fact, some employees have not yet decided whether they will attend the event. We don't need to make a reservation right now, so do not worry.

Emma Jeong
Vice President
Kai Industries

---

196. According to the brochure, what is mentioned about Ivy Event Hall?

(A) It is used to hold events of various sizes.
(B) It is conveniently located downtown.
(C) It is more expensive than other venues.
(D) Its business center will be renovated.

197. What does Mr. McKellen indicate about the plans for the event?

(A) They require a lot of money to implement.
(B) They were proposed at the meeting.
(C) They need to be announced to all of the employees.
(D) They cannot be decided at once.

198. Where will the company's anniversary celebration most likely be held?

(A) In the Modern Room
(B) In the Special Room
(C) In the Executive Room
(D) In the Exclusive Room

199. Why does Mr. McKellen want to reserve a room this month?

(A) To complete the room condition report
(B) To install new equipment in advance
(C) To take advantage of the special offer
(D) To accommodate more guests

200. What does Ms. Jeong indicate about the event?

(A) There will be a shortage of seats.
(B) People can add seats to the room.
(C) More people may attend than expected.
(D) She prefers a larger room.

Stop! This is the end of the test. If you finish before time is called, you may go back to Parts 5, 6, and 7 and check your work.

MP3와 해설 파일은 온라인에서 제공됩니다.
▶ books.english.co.kr

TEST 03

test 03.mp3 | 정답 p.264

LISTENING TEST

In the Listening test, you will be asked to demonstrate how well you understand spoken English. The entire Listening test will last approximately 45 minutes. There are four parts, and directions are given for each part. You must mark your answers on the separate answer sheet.
Do not write your answers in your test book.

PART 1

Directions: For each question in this part, you will hear four statements about a picture in your test book. When you hear the statements, you must select the one statement that best describes what you see in the picture. Then find the number of the question on your answer sheet and mark your answer. The statements will not be printed in your test book and will be spoken only one time.

Statement (B), "They're shaking hands," is the best description of the picture, so you should select answer (B) and mark it on your answer sheet.

1.

2.

3.

4.

5.

6.

PART 2

Directions: You will hear a question or statement and three responses spoken in English. They will not be printed in your test book and will be spoken only one time. Select the best response to the question or statement and mark the letter (A), (B), or (C) on your answer sheet.

7. Mark your answer on your answer sheet.
8. Mark your answer on your answer sheet.
9. Mark your answer on your answer sheet.
10. Mark your answer on your answer sheet.
11. Mark your answer on your answer sheet.
12. Mark your answer on your answer sheet.
13. Mark your answer on your answer sheet.
14. Mark your answer on your answer sheet.
15. Mark your answer on your answer sheet.
16. Mark your answer on your answer sheet.
17. Mark your answer on your answer sheet.
18. Mark your answer on your answer sheet.
19. Mark your answer on your answer sheet.
20. Mark your answer on your answer sheet.
21. Mark your answer on your answer sheet.
22. Mark your answer on your answer sheet.
23. Mark your answer on your answer sheet.
24. Mark your answer on your answer sheet.
25. Mark your answer on your answer sheet.
26. Mark your answer on your answer sheet.
27. Mark your answer on your answer sheet.
28. Mark your answer on your answer sheet.
29. Mark your answer on your answer sheet.
30. Mark your answer on your answer sheet.
31. Mark your answer on your answer sheet.

PART 3

Directions: You will hear some conversations between two or more people. You will be asked to answer three questions about what the speakers say in each conversation. Select the best response to each question and mark the letter (A), (B), (C), or (D) on your answer sheet. The conversations will not be printed in your test book and will be spoken only one time.

32. Where does the man work?
    (A) At an employment agency
    (B) At a hotel
    (C) At a bookstore
    (D) At a bank

33. Why is the woman calling?
    (A) To reserve a room
    (B) To complain about a billing problem
    (C) To reject a position
    (D) To inquire about a job opening

34. What does the man say he will do next?
    (A) Schedule an interview
    (B) Talk with a coworker
    (C) Send an e-mail
    (D) Post a job opening

35. What does the man want to know about?
    (A) A meeting schedule
    (B) A woman's contact information
    (C) Other positions at the company
    (D) The location of the company's headquarters

36. What does the woman suggest the man do?
    (A) Check a bulletin board
    (B) Visit the company homepage
    (C) Fill out a request form
    (D) Speak with a marketing manager

37. What does the man ask the woman to do?
    (A) Review some documents
    (B) Look over a sales report
    (C) Fill out some paperwork
    (D) Find a new position

38. What product are the distributors coming to see?
    (A) A vehicle
    (B) A mobile phone
    (C) A computer
    (D) A home appliance

39. Why has the meeting been put off?
    (A) The prototype isn't finished yet.
    (B) A flight was postponed.
    (C) Some clients didn't take a plane.
    (D) Rooms are already fully booked.

40. What will the woman do next?
    (A) Contact a pickup service
    (B) Submit some paperwork
    (C) Hire some drivers
    (D) Pick up some clients

41. What does the woman want the man to do?
    (A) Review a sample
    (B) Change a color
    (C) Cancel an order
    (D) Print business cards

42. Why does the man say, "We actually created a new company logo"?
    (A) To reassure a client
    (B) To compliment a logo design
    (C) To express surprise at a decision
    (D) To request an update to an order

43. What does the man ask the woman to do?
    (A) Make a payment
    (B) Upgrade a credit card
    (C) Send a new logo
    (D) Arrange some files

GO ON TO THE NEXT PAGE

44. What do the women do at the art gallery?
(A) Display artwork
(B) Restore paintings
(C) Invite well-known painters
(D) Lead tours

45. Why have many people recently visited the art gallery?
(A) Tickets are inexpensive.
(B) There is an interesting display.
(C) It has extended its hours of operation.
(D) They received complimentary tickets.

46. According to the man, what will happen next Tuesday?
(A) A new exhibit will be opened.
(B) Some research results will be announced.
(C) Visitors will purchase tickets for an event.
(D) An expert will give a lecture.

47. Who most likely is the woman?
(A) A librarian
(B) A local resident
(C) A news reporter
(D) A constructor

48. What does the woman like the most about the new facility?
(A) Its modern appearance
(B) Its longer operating hours
(C) Its convenient location
(D) Its rare book collection

49. What advantage will members have?
(A) A free shuttle service
(B) Discounts on coffee and drinks
(C) Access to electronic reading material
(D) Tickets to special talks

50. What is the purpose of the woman's call?
(A) To purchase a television
(B) To complain about an air conditioner
(C) To schedule an appointment
(D) To place an order

51. What does the woman ask for?
(A) A telephone number
(B) A preferred model
(C) A delivery time
(D) A man's address

52. When will the item probably arrive?
(A) This evening
(B) Tomorrow afternoon
(C) In two days
(D) In a week

53. Where do the speakers most likely work?
(A) At a department store
(B) At an advertising agency
(C) At a bank
(D) At an accounting firm

54. Why does the woman say, "the Zahira Department Store account was the first project I worked on here"?
(A) To advertise a department store
(B) To explain why a proposal was rejected
(C) To complain about a client's mistake
(D) To express that she understands a problem

55. What does the woman suggest the man do?
(A) Reject a project
(B) Get help from a supervisor
(C) Prepare some samples
(D) Change a decision

56. What problem does the man have?

    (A) He was overcharged for an item.
    (B) He dropped his camera.
    (C) His device was delivered to the wrong place.
    (D) His device is defective.

57. What does the woman offer to do?

    (A) Provide technical support for free
    (B) Exchange the camera for a new one
    (C) Make a free delivery
    (D) File an insurance claim

58. What does the man want to do?

    (A) Increase insurance fee
    (B) Change his contact information
    (C) Look at some other items
    (D) Find a product warranty

---

59. Who most likely is the woman?

    (A) An athlete
    (B) An event planner
    (C) A sports coach
    (D) A clothing designer

60. Why does the man want to hire the woman?

    (A) To make her sell some T-shirts
    (B) To have her play a game
    (C) To have her design some merchandise
    (D) To organize some events

61. What does the woman request that the man do?

    (A) Fill out a questionnaire
    (B) Conduct a survey
    (C) Create a new design
    (D) Get a reimbursement

Interview Schedule		
Monday	10 A.M.	Room 201
Tuesday	1 P.M.	Room 205
Wednesday	3 P.M.	Room 302
Thursday	2 P.M.	Room 303

62. What kind of experience does the man have?

    (A) Sales
    (B) Car maintenance
    (C) Marketing
    (D) Delivery driving

63. Look at the graphic. What room will the man be interviewed in?

    (A) Room 201
    (B) Room 205
    (C) Room 302
    (D) Room 303

64. What should the man bring to the interview?

    (A) Recommendation letters
    (B) A driver license
    (C) A professional certificate
    (D) A list of addresses

Kim's Pizza
Always Fresh! Always Great!

Potato Pizza
$9.99

Made: October 10
Best before: October 15

Menu Options

Roast Chicken Sandwich	$7 per person
Grilled Chicken	$10 per person
Seafood Pasta	$12 per person
Beef Pizza	$13 per person

65. Look at the graphic. When does the conversation take place?
    (A) On October 10
    (B) On October 11
    (C) On October 13
    (D) On October 15

66. What does the man emphasize?
    (A) The price
    (B) The quality
    (C) The size
    (D) The packaging

67. What does the man say about the items?
    (A) A discount is available for frozen ones.
    (B) They are not refundable.
    (C) Their price will decrease in two weeks.
    (D) They are only available unfrozen.

68. What are the speakers talking about?
    (A) Throwing a farewell party
    (B) Leading a training session
    (C) Preparing for a visit
    (D) Celebrating an anniversary

69. Look at the graphic. How much will the speakers most likely spend per person?
    (A) $7
    (B) $10
    (C) $12
    (D) $13

70. What does the woman ask the man to do?
    (A) Reserve some hotel rooms
    (B) Cancel some accommodations
    (C) Order some food
    (D) Book a rental car

PART 4

Directions: You will hear some talks given by a single speaker. You will be asked to answer three questions about what the speaker says in each talk. Select the best response to each question and mark the letter (A), (B), (C), or (D) on your answer sheet. The talks will not be printed in your test book and will be spoken only one time.

71. What will be held on Friday?
    (A) An awards ceremony
    (B) A holiday parade
    (C) An anniversary celebration
    (D) A company retreat

72. What benefit will employees have if they work on Friday?
    (A) They can take a day off.
    (B) They can change shifts with someone else.
    (C) They can get paid more.
    (D) They can receive free parking.

73. What does the speaker recommend that the listeners do?
    (A) Take public transportation
    (B) Clean their uniforms
    (C) Pack a dinner
    (D) Use a parking lot

74. What is the main topic of the report?
    (A) Community activities
    (B) Sports news
    (C) Race rules
    (D) Traffic

75. What does the speaker recommend that the listeners do?
    (A) Upgrade a Web site
    (B) Check a map
    (C) Drive slowly
    (D) Visit a public museum

76. What does the speaker say will happen next week?
    (A) A winner will be announced.
    (B) A project will start.
    (C) Road construction will be completed.
    (D) A museum will officially open.

77. According to the speaker, what will take place on Monday?
    (A) An employee orientation
    (B) An interview
    (C) A workplace inspection
    (D) A job fair

78. What does the speaker imply when he says, "I don't have any appointments tomorrow"?
    (A) He can meet with a client.
    (B) He thinks a schedule is flexible.
    (C) He needs to work overtime tomorrow.
    (D) He has some time to review a task.

79. What does the speaker ask the listener to do?
    (A) Call him back
    (B) Check a calendar
    (C) Ask some questions
    (D) Cancel an appointment

80. What type of business does the speaker work for?
    (A) A clothing store
    (B) A design company
    (C) An employment agency
    (D) An antique store

81. What is a requirement for the position?
    (A) To be able to work on Saturdays
    (B) To have more than four years of work experience
    (C) To have a university degree in fashion
    (D) To have a background in fashion

82. What can listeners do to apply for the position?
    (A) Visit a company Web site
    (B) Call a store in person
    (C) Talk to a store manager
    (D) Send a résumé by e-mail

GO ON TO THE NEXT PAGE

83. Where does the speaker work?
    (A) At a national park
    (B) At a marine museum
    (C) At an aquarium
    (D) At a public library

84. What does the speaker imply when he says, "I can see that most of the seats are occupied"?
    (A) A talk is popular.
    (B) More people can participate.
    (C) The tickets are all sold out.
    (D) More chairs are needed.

85. What does the speaker ask the listeners to do?
    (A) Raise their hands to ask questions
    (B) Switch off their devices
    (C) Find their designated seats
    (D) Take some pictures

86. What is the broadcast mainly about?
    (A) Diet advice
    (B) Exercise tips
    (C) Useful recipes
    (D) Healthy fruits

87. Why does the speaker say he is surprised?
    (A) Sugar can be very harmful.
    (B) A popular view is incorrect.
    (C) Some fruit is high in sugar.
    (D) A task is time consuming.

88. What will be discussed on next week's broadcast?
    (A) Sugar-free food
    (B) The adverse effects of diets
    (C) Recipes using fruit
    (D) Sports news

89. Where most likely is the audience?
    (A) At a trade fair
    (B) At a professional conference
    (C) At a management meeting
    (D) At a university

90. What will Dr. Smith talk about?
    (A) Workplace stress
    (B) Corporate investments
    (C) Time management
    (D) Personality traits

91. What does the speaker recommend the listeners do?
    (A) Stay after the presentation
    (B) Submit questions
    (C) Fill out the form ahead of time
    (D) Issue a discount coupon

92. What news is the speaker talking about?
    (A) A renewed agreement
    (B) An extended deadline
    (C) A new employee
    (D) A garden party

93. What kind of business does the speaker work for?
    (A) A manufacturer
    (B) A landscape service
    (C) A botanical garden
    (D) A dry-cleaning service

94. What does the speaker mean when she says, "I've already ordered ten new machines"?
    (A) She wants to fix the machines.
    (B) She has extra time to help.
    (C) She wants to change an order.
    (D) She is addressing a problem.

Office 1	Office 3
Office 2	Staff Lounge
Meeting Room	Office 4

Time	Speaker	Subject
10:00 A.M.	Roger Rodriguez	Discussion: Future Goals
10:30 A.M.	Erin McGee	Last Month's Sales Figures
11:00 A.M.	Alex Delera	Marketing Strategies for This Month
11:30 A.M.	Helen Park	Last Quarter's Lessons

95. Which department does the speaker most likely work in?

(A) Maintenance
(B) Accounting
(C) Product Development
(D) Sales

96. Why does the speaker ask to meet with the listener?

(A) To get help increasing the budget
(B) To file a document
(C) To discuss a project
(D) To remodel the office

97. Look at the graphic. Where is the speaker's office?

(A) Office 1
(B) Office 2
(C) Office 3
(D) Office 4

98. What problem does the speaker mention?

(A) A conference will be delayed.
(B) A meeting room will be changed.
(C) A presenter will be late.
(D) A schedule is full.

99. Look at the graphic. At what time will Mr. Roger speak?

(A) 10:00 A.M.
(B) 10:30 A.M.
(C) 11:00 A.M.
(D) 11:30 A.M.

100. According to the speaker, what might be good about the change?

(A) The meeting time will be extended.
(B) The subjects will be in chronological order.
(C) The discussion will begin earlier.
(D) There will be more speakers.

This is the end of the Listening test. Turn to Part 5 in your test book.

READING TEST

In the Reading test, you will read a variety of texts and answer several different types of reading comprehension questions. The entire Reading test will last 75 minutes. There are three parts, and directions are given for each part. You are encouraged to answer as many questions as possible within the time allowed.

You must mark your answers on the separate answer sheet. Do not write your answers in the test book.

PART 5

Directions: A word or phrase is missing in each of the sentences below. Four answer choices are given below each sentence. Select the best answer to complete the sentence. Then mark the letter (A), (B), (C), or (D) on your answer sheet.

101. Compared with other electronic devices, ------- is much easier for beginners to operate.
    (A) ours
    (B) us
    (C) our
    (D) ourselves

102. In order to secure government funding, G&B Biz will cooperate with its ------- on the project this time.
    (A) compete
    (B) competitive
    (C) competition
    (D) competitor

103. Mr. Morgan should estimate the minimum required quantity before he ------- extra office furniture.
    (A) orders
    (B) measures
    (C) copies
    (D) stretches

104. Thanks to the detailed instructions in the manual, we can ------- replace consumable parts.
    (A) easy
    (B) easier
    (C) easily
    (D) ease

105. Because your baggage is overweight, you should pay an ------- charge of $20.
    (A) addition
    (B) additions
    (C) additional
    (D) additionally

106. The city government decided to set up a barrier ------- traffic accidents on King Road.
    (A) prevention
    (B) prevented
    (C) to prevent
    (D) is prevented

107. The movie has not been released in many theaters, but it received ------- reviews from a lot of people.
    (A) positive
    (B) eventual
    (C) suspicious
    (D) identical

108. According to the company accountant's report, current businesses dropped off ------- the restructuring issue.
    (A) when
    (B) after
    (C) because
    (D) along

109. During the last meeting, the department heads discussed how to boost customer ------- in the upcoming promotional event.
    (A) participate
    (B) participates
    (C) participated
    (D) participation

110. The scenic view of Busan ------- inspires Ms. Jane to paint.
    (A) continue
    (B) continued
    (C) continual
    (D) continually

111. When you visit our Web site, you can download the manual for the ------- of your computer.
    (A) vision
    (B) assembly
    (C) dedication
    (D) consequence

112. You can receive ------- information which is published in our periodical brochure through our Web site.
    (A) all
    (B) single
    (C) a few
    (D) many

113. Because of unexpected errors, we have decided to cease production ------- the cause is definitely identified.
    (A) prior to
    (B) during
    (C) until
    (D) with

114. If the design team ------- the project in time, we would have introduced our new vehicles at this auto fair.
    (A) finishes
    (B) will finish
    (C) has finished
    (D) had finished

115. We are confident of a return to normal production within a week, and delivery of ------- will occur at the earliest possible date.
    (A) replacements
    (B) replaces
    (C) replacing
    (D) replaced

116. In case the part you purchased does not work -------, you should have an extra storage drive for backup.
    (A) properly
    (B) considerably
    (C) surprisingly
    (D) restfully

117. An ------- must be accompanied by at least three letters of recommendation, which should be e-mailed to our HR manager.
    (A) indication
    (B) experience
    (C) application
    (D) obedience

118. A 20% discount on registration fees will be given to all customers ------- submit their forms before October 5.
    (A) whose
    (B) whom
    (C) who
    (D) which

119. One of our staff members in Newark mislabeled the tag, so your baggage was sent to Finland instead of your ------- in Switzerland.
    (A) ambition
    (B) destination
    (C) intention
    (D) signification

120. Mr. Simmons would like to work in an environment like the one at Gaza Global Publishing, which offers ------- freedom.
    (A) create
    (B) creation
    (C) creative
    (D) creatively

GO ON TO THE NEXT PAGE

121. Some promotional brochures are now posted on our Web site ------- attracting more customers.
    (A) for
    (B) around
    (C) since
    (D) from

122. ------- to expand Calvin Co.'s branches into Asian countries should be discussed at our regular general meeting of stockholders.
    (A) If
    (B) Whether
    (C) About
    (D) In order

123. Due to Mia's case analysis research, she was selected as the final candidate the most ------- for the state scholarship.
    (A) qualify
    (B) qualifying
    (C) qualified
    (D) qualification

124. Visitors need to be preregistered in the management system with their name and affiliation ------- the duration and purpose of their visit.
    (A) yet
    (B) as well as
    (C) so that
    (D) at the time

125. OG Gate's net profits have increased considerably since the company ------- its online shopping site.
    (A) launched
    (B) connected
    (C) persuaded
    (D) assumed

126. Our Internet search system's advertising revenue continues to grow ------- we have plans to expand into other business lines.
    (A) then
    (B) while
    (C) besides
    (D) in case of

127. The company asked you to submit the food safety and hygiene certificate ------- by the Penn Culinary Committee.
    (A) regarded
    (B) performed
    (C) constructed
    (D) issued

128. The board of directors considered the next stage of company's expansion program ------- interesting and challenging.
    (A) simultaneously
    (B) mutually
    (C) instinctively
    (D) collectively

129. The level of interest in the national retirement pension by the federal bank has declined ------- the last decade.
    (A) except
    (B) across
    (C) over
    (D) beyond

130. Before the contract ------- automatically, you are given the option to renew it without having to pay any fees.
    (A) expired
    (B) expires
    (C) will expire
    (D) was expired

PART 6

Directions: Read the texts that follow. A word, phrase, or sentence is missing in parts of each text. Four answer choices for each question are given below the text. Select the best answer to complete the text. Then mark the letter (A), (B), (C), or (D) on your answer sheet.

Questions 131-134 refer to the following Web page.

The Texas Cooking Association (TCA) is currently accepting entries for an upcoming event.

The TCA organizes trade fairs and conducts educational conferences and competitions ------- local food
131.
in Texas. The Texas government has officially proclaimed chili-based dishes as the state local food since 1977, and chili and tacos are very popular with the state's residents. Many of ------- are cooked
132.
by chefs at restaurants all over the world. The TCA holds its largest event every year in May by inviting chefs to participate in the TCA Grand Recipe Contest. -------. Last year, Kal Martinez got his name on
133.
the list of -------.
134.

131. (A) is advancing
(B) has advanced
(C) will advance
(D) to advance

132. (A) instead
(B) these
(C) each
(D) that

133. (A) Local companies will support the event financially.
(B) Participants should make hotel reservations in advance.
(C) A lot of cooks will gather to try to win first prize.
(D) New technology needs to be introduced for the issue.

134. (A) champions
(B) experts
(C) cookers
(D) speakers

Questions 135-138 refer to the following memo.

To: Bucks NET's Managers
Date: March 10
Re: Company Unity Day

Hello, everyone!

I am writing this memo to ------- you all to inform the members of your teams about our upcoming company retreat. -------.
135.   136.

I am responsible for planning and organizing a variety of group activities for us all to enjoy during that time. Detailed information about these activities ------- on the notice board in the staff cafeteria on March 20.
137.

Griffin Moth from the general affairs office is assisting me with the arrangements. If you have any questions about the event while I'm out of office, you can reach ------- at extension 701.
138.

Regards,

Kevin Durant
Manager, Human Resources Department

135. (A) reject
(B) respond
(C) remind
(D) recommend

136. (A) The retirement party has already held in the company's grand ballroom.
(B) Anyone who wants to help us should submit a volunteer request form.
(C) This is scheduled to take place at the Marine Tivoli Resort from March 27 to 30.
(D) Our company is proud that our newly launched products are highly rated by customers.

137. (A) was posted
(B) is posting
(C) would post
(D) will be posted

138. (A) she
(B) hers
(C) herself
(D) her

Questions 139-142 refer to the following advertisement.

The Safety and Security Agency of Detroit (SSAD) asks you to download our new security application (app) for your mobile device. It has been released in order to ------- information about the city's safety
139.
problems. In case you do not have access to information on what to do in emergencies, we are making the app available to all residents. -------. In addition, you can set up a variety of in-app functions such
140.
as on-screen alerts, links with city's news, and traffic conditions. When you just click on a button in the app, all the information will be transmitted ------- into your mobile phone or tablet PC. Now, turn on your
141.
mobile device and touch your Zetta Store ------- Gate Way icon to download this app.
142.

139. (A) supplement
(B) command
(C) demonstrate
(D) prohibit

140. (A) Using a cellphone while walking on the street is dangerous.
(B) The app is automatically updated with new data.
(C) Some of the app's function are subject to a service fee.
(D) The city government should check the status of the app download.

141. (A) directs
(B) directly
(C) directing
(D) direction

142. (A) rather
(B) well
(C) or
(D) only

Questions 143-146 refer to the following article.

Remington (December 20) — German pharmaceutical giant Meditech has been awarded the Year of Gold Humanity Award this week. -------. For example, the company has supported Carpe Foundation
                                                                                 143.
in order to build much-needed hospitals in the Remington area. To meet the expectations of its -------,
                                                                                               144.
a committee composed of regional leaders in social welfare has been commissioned to manage the hospitals.

Meditech is now one of Europe's largest pharmaceutical manufacturers, and it already has a foothold in eight countries, including Korea and Canada. -------, Mr. Ireland, a co-founder of Meditech, said that he
                                                               145.
intends to expand into the African continent, where people need better medical treatment, in his award acceptance speech. He said that people have to be ------- until the company achieves its own goals.
                                                                                            146.

143. (A) A lot of medical corporations from around the world participated in the ceremony.
(B) The company has continuously made considerable donations to local nonprofit organizations.
(C) The pharmaceutical companies at the conference decided to help lower-income groups together.
(D) By donating medical devices to public institutions, the firm has a chance to win the national project.

144. (A) contributes
(B) contribution
(C) contributing
(D) contributors

145. (A) For instance
(B) With that said
(C) In that case
(D) On the contrary

146. (A) definitive
(B) substantial
(C) cautious
(D) patient

PART 7

Directions: In this part you will read a selection of texts, such as magazine and newspaper articles, e-mails, and instant messages. Each text or set of texts is followed by several questions. Select the best answer for each question and mark the letter (A), (B), (C), or (D) on your answer sheet.

Questions 147-148 refer to the following ticket.

	**West Brook Transportation** Off-Season Value Ticket for Adults A passenger who has this ticket is eligible for an unlimited number of round trips. Because you might be inspected by a crew member on a ferry, you should hold on to your ticket until the end of your trip. **[NOTE]** This off-season-value ticket is available for travel from Monday through Thursday. (8:00 A.M. to 5:00 P.M.) If you want to travel at other times, you ought to upgrade to a regular ticket for an additional fee of $6.	Between West Brook Port and Erie Island
		Between West Brook Port and Yellow Creek Park

147. According to the ticket, what is true?
   (A) It requires a person to pay $6 for every trip.
   (B) It is valid for more than one trip.
   (C) It can be purchased at any time.
   (D) It is applicable to all trips.

148. What kind of transportation is the ticket for?
   (A) A train
   (B) A plane
   (C) A boat
   (D) A taxi

GO ON TO THE NEXT PAGE

Questions 149-150 refer to the following advertisement.

Wanted – Civil Engineer

The Kovalchuk Metro Development (KMD) is seeking a creative, passionate, and experienced person who can join our energetic project. The duties are to plan our new civil development project and to determine its business feasibility by assisting our project manager. Proficiency in office and design software is required, and at least two years of experience in the industry are needed. A variety of field experience is preferred. If you are interested in the position, pleased send your résumé with your work portfolio and two letters of recommendation to j_harman@kmd.net. For more information, you can visit our office in the morning from Monday to Friday.

---

149. What is a requirement of the job?
(A) Previous employment at a government agency
(B) Competency with graphic design software
(C) A graduate degree in a related field
(D) Sales experience in the targeted area

150. How can applicants get additional details?
(A) By stopping by the company
(B) By contacting their references
(C) By visiting the company's Web site
(D) By calling the manager

Questions 151-152 refer to the following memo.

MEMO

To: All Employees
From: Chris Paul, Director of General Affairs
Subject: Sakai Work and Office
Date: March 15

Thanks to a special affiliation with Sakai Work and Office, we will receive ten standing desks as a trial from March 20 to April 10. By using these desks, you can stand more comfortably while working in the office. The new Sakai 201 model will be introduced next week. The desk has a special function, so you can freely adjust its height as necessary. According to recent research, this kind of desk can relieve physical discomforts caused by sitting too long. If you want to take advantage of this opportunity, please feel free to contact me at c_paul@meviusco.com. In case there are too many applicants, we will choose only ten people on a first-come, first-served basis. Those who are selected to use a desk are required to take a survey afterward because we need to determine whether the desks are effective before purchasing them for all our employees.

151. What is the purpose of the memo?
    (A) To encourage employees to get regular medical checkups
    (B) To require employees to complete a survey about their work environment
    (C) To ask employees to move some furniture into a new office building
    (D) To give employees a chance to try some new furniture

152. What is implied about the Sakai 201 model?
    (A) It can enhance labor productivity.
    (B) Its height can be adjusted.
    (C) It is the most expensive of a company's newest items.
    (D) It will be chosen as the company's next item to sell.

Questions 153-154 refer to the following text-message chain.

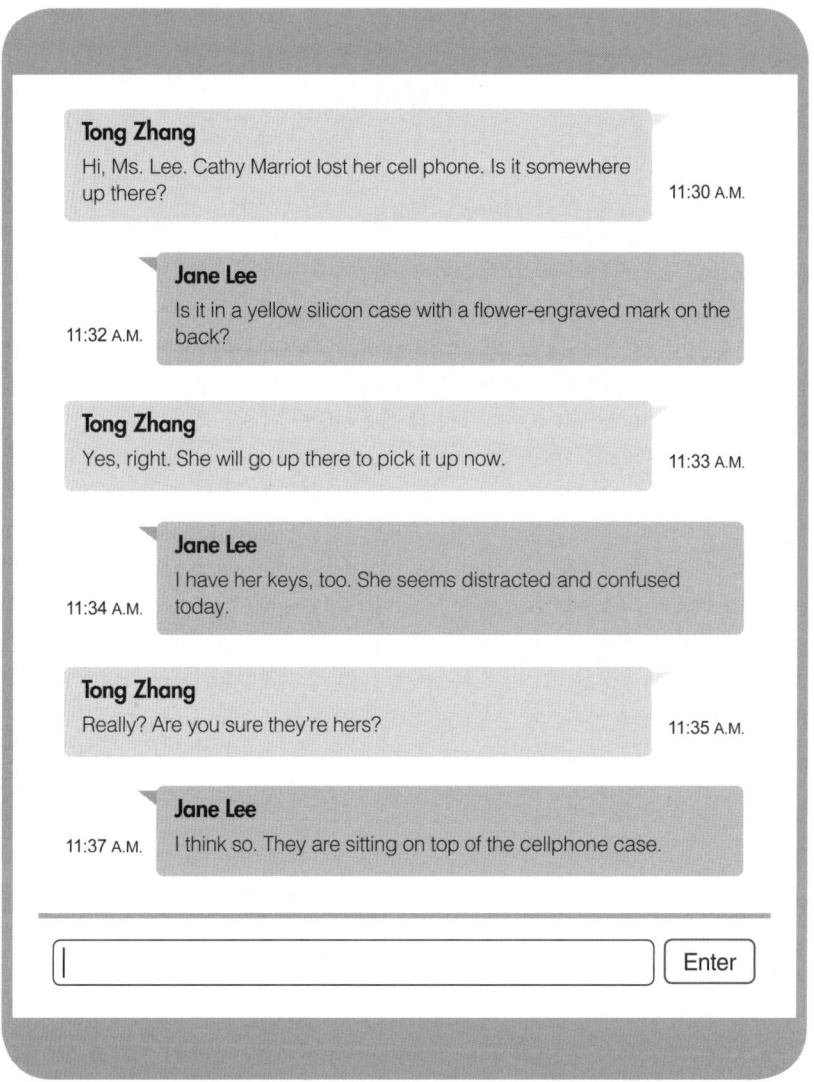

Tong Zhang 11:30 A.M.
Hi, Ms. Lee. Cathy Marriot lost her cell phone. Is it somewhere up there?

Jane Lee 11:32 A.M.
Is it in a yellow silicon case with a flower-engraved mark on the back?

Tong Zhang 11:33 A.M.
Yes, right. She will go up there to pick it up now.

Jane Lee 11:34 A.M.
I have her keys, too. She seems distracted and confused today.

Tong Zhang 11:35 A.M.
Really? Are you sure they're hers?

Jane Lee 11:37 A.M.
I think so. They are sitting on top of the cellphone case.

153. What will Ms. Marriot most likely do next?

(A) Go to get something
(B) Order a new phone accessory
(C) E-mail her cellphone service provider
(D) Borrow Mr. Zhang's cellphone

154. At 11:37 A.M., what does Ms. Lee mean when she writes, "I think so"?

(A) She assumes that Ms. Marriot is often forgetful.
(B) She thinks that the keys are part of Ms. Marriot's.
(C) She wants to know whether the keys are needed.
(D) She believes that Mr. Zhang has incorrect information.

Questions 155-157 refer to the following advertisement.

The best way to start your new business!

This new property includes an almost 2,500-square-meter office space, a 1,500-square-meter storage space, and a 2,000-square-meter garage space. —[1]—. This property is easily accessible to the downtown area of Pittsburgh, and there are a lot of restaurants and shopping complexes within 700 meters of it. —[2]—. Because the building consists of many big windows with its modernized exterior and interior design, heating costs will be cheaper than other properties by making the best use of natural lighting. —[3]—. The duration of a standard lease is twenty-four months, and it includes monthly payments and a security deposit. —[4]—. To apply for a lease or to tour the property, please contact Jessica Dorris at (710) 578-4813.

155. How large is the parking area?

(A) 700 square meters
(B) 1,500 square meters
(C) 2,000 square meters
(D) 2,500 square meters

156. What is NOT mentioned as an advantage of the property?

(A) It is within walking distance of the airport.
(B) It has a variety of spaces.
(C) It is near restaurants and shops.
(D) It can benefit from natural lighting.

157. In which of the positions marked [1], [2], [3], and [4] does the following sentence best belong?

"If you want to adjust the lease period, that can be negotiated."

(A) [1]
(B) [2]
(C) [3]
(D) [4]

Questions 158-160 refer to the following e-mail.

To: Benjamin Foster
From: Heesun Yoon
Subject: Information
Date: September 10

Dear Mr. Foster,

The opening of the Indiana branch has been delayed because of some problems regarding licensing procedures, so it is now scheduled to open on Friday, October 7. Next week, I will send an e-mail to you with more details, including a request that you join our team here. I would be grateful if you joined us from headquarters.

As we had planned, we will promote our relocation by offering customers special deals on all of our rental cars throughout the month. In addition, we have arranged a special partnership with the Indiana city government in order to publicize our affordable prices and services to visitors. Even though our existing customers are mainly business travelers, we should make every effort to attract tourists through this opportunity, too.

I look forward to meeting you soon.

Heesun Yoon

158. The word "scheduled" in paragraph 1, line 2, is closest in meaning to

(A) set
(B) trained
(C) extended
(D) discriminated

159. What is suggested about Ms. Yoon?

(A) She has met a lot of investors in her office.
(B) She is responsible for the relocation of an office.
(C) She decided to hire some new staff members.
(D) She is expected to transfer to the headquarters building.

160. What kind of business will open on October 7?

(A) A law firm
(B) A tourist agency
(C) A rental car office
(D) A development company

Questions 161-163 refer to the following letter.

University of Virginia Medical Center
3018 Washington Drive
Fairfax, Virginia 12301

June 10

Dear University of Virginia Medical Center Patients,

The University of Virginia Medical Center (UVMC) would like to extend our gratitude to all the patients who have chosen us as your healthcare provider. Over the past 40 years, we have successfully treated thousands of patients in the Fairfax area. Considering rapid changes in the medical field, we have always made every effort to provide the best medical service for you. To achieve this goal, we are pleased to announce that UVMC will be acquired by Progressive Health starting on July 1.

This does not mean that our current programs will change. Only our name will change; our current name will be changed to Virginia Progressive Health effective next month. Your existing medical teams will remain the same, and you can continue to see the doctors at our Fairfax location. However, you will be able to experience a wider range of treatments and medical devices from talented physicians and experts thanks to this acquisition. Progressive Health has consistently been rated at the top of the field of cutting-edge medical service.

To learn more about Progressive Health, visit their Web site at www.progressivehealth.com. If you want to see a doctor, use our current phone number.

We hope to continue to care for you.

Sincerely,

University of Virginia Medical Center

---

161. What is the purpose of the letter?

(A) To describe some new medical facilities
(B) To announce the grand opening of a new branch
(C) To notify patients of a takeover
(D) To express concern to patients

162. What can be inferred about UVMC?

(A) Its new location is far from its previous location.
(B) It will offer medical services it had previously not provided.
(C) Its patients' personal information will be shared with Progressive Health.
(D) It has been in business for a decade.

163. According to the letter, what should recipients do to schedule an appointment?

(A) Call the same number that they have used before
(B) Log into a new Web site
(C) Visit the medical center in person
(D) Send a request to the UVMC office by e-mail

GO ON TO THE NEXT PAGE

Questions 164-167 refer to the following online chat discussion.

Jerry Atkins 3:00 P.M.	Are the instructors whom we hired to teach our employees ready to start the Internet ethics session?
Dixie Lynn 3:02 P.M.	Yes, they are supposed to arrive at Zeta Web at 1 P.M. on Friday. I think someone will accompany them to get their security passes and guide them to the place they'll be teaching, right?
Jerry Atkins 3:03 P.M.	One of my team members can help with that.
Dixie Lynn 3:04 P.M.	Will equipment such as computers and whiteboards be provided for the upcoming event?
Den Bryant 3:04 P.M.	As mentioned above, I'll meet the instructors at the main entrance and distribute visitor passes to them.
Jerry Atkins 3:05 P.M.	Two large conference halls are already booked and equipped with everything they will require for the session.
Den Bryant 3:06 P.M.	The Web engineers will end their shifts right before 2 P.M., and then they will go to the session immediately.
Dixie Lynn 3:07 P.M.	Good. The lectures will finish at 4 P.M. Who will lock the rooms? Do the instructors need to do that themselves?
Jerry Atkins 3:08 P.M.	I'll be there to finalize everything after the session.
Dixie Lynn 3:09 P.M.	Great! That's it then.
Jerry Atkins 3:10 P.M.	I'll be here until 6 P.M. if you need anything else today.

164. Why did Mr. Atkins send a message?
  (A) To order new computers and supplies
  (B) To specify a company's security level
  (C) To inform employees about a changed schedule
  (D) To confirm the details of an event

165. When will Mr. Bryant be at the main entrance?
  (A) At 1:00 P.M.
  (B) At 2:00 P.M.
  (C) At 4:00 P.M.
  (D) At 6:00 P.M.

166. What is indicated about the Web engineers?
  (A) They were recently hired.
  (B) They need to have lunch between their shifts.
  (C) They will attend a lecture after work.
  (D) They should register for the class by tomorrow.

167. At 3:09 P.M., what does Ms. Lynn mean when she writes, "That's it then"?
  (A) She thinks that the doors need to be repaired.
  (B) She wants to help Mr. Atkins do his work.
  (C) She does not have any questions.
  (D) She would like to join the session.

Questions 168-171 refer to the following e-mail.

From	Bee Chamastri
To	Jane Bronte
Date	May 15
Subject	After-meeting Agenda

Dear Jane,

Since I heard your concerns about your workload at the last meeting, all of the department heads have been considering a solution to this issue. —[1]—. We have decided to divide all labor in accordance with company regulations. In doing so, our company can improve our productivity and the environment in many ways. —[2]—. In your case, we have made a decision to assign an assistant, Bertha Bennett, to you in order to complete our new Web site design successfully. —[3]—. You will supervise her work, which includes the basic levels of your design projects, such as posters, logos, and layouts.

You are asked to share the progress of existing projects including your current clients' information, detailed schedules, and your work methods, with her. You will also take responsibility for training her on our Web graphic tools as well as other programs that you are using next week.

If you have any problems, please feel free to share them with me. —[4]—.

Bee Chamastri
Director of Human Resources

168. Who most likely is Ms. Bronte?
(A) A computer programmer
(B) An electrical engineer
(C) A graphic designer
(D) A personnel manager

169. What issue did Ms. Bronte report?
(A) Too much work
(B) An outdated computer
(C) An inconvenient office environment
(D) Incompatible coworkers

170. What is Ms. Bronte required to do next week?
(A) Submit a report
(B) Share her concerns
(C) Meet her immediate boss
(D) Instruct a new staffer

171. In which of the positions marked [1], [2], [3], and [4] does the following sentence best belong?

"This new employee will assist you with most of your work."

(A) [1]
(B) [2]
(C) [3]
(D) [4]

Questions 172-175 refer to the following article.

Denver Gazette

Beyond the Brilliant Ridge

(October 1) If you want to know where James Milner is, you first need to look at some pictures of a mountain range. These dreamlike and exotic pictures are taken for his latest book of photography, *Beyond the Brilliant Ridge*.

Mr. Milner began to take photos about 20 years ago. When he was looking for his soccer ball, he came across his father's old camera on a shelf. After asking a favor of his father, he was allowed to fix and use it. However, he had no choice but to put his camera down in order to prepare for college and his future career to get a job in the field of journalism.

After graduation, he was employed as a full-time reporter by the *Denver Gazette*, so he had no time to take pictures as well. A few years later, forgetting his work activities, he spent his vacation in Kathmandu, Nepal. In that place, he got a chance to participate in a photography conference featuring scenic views of the Himalayas. Due to this conference, he decided to quit his job as a reporter and started concentrating on pictures.

Although he started by using an outdated camera, he now deals with advanced equipment such as wide-angle lenses and high-end cameras. Unexpected problems can occur in the mountains because of rapidly changing natural circumstances, so he has to replace or repurchase expensive equipment quite a lot. "Rugged cliffs and wild animals pose dangers to my technical equipment," he said.

Most of his photo artworks, including that in his newest book, feature a wide range of surroundings in the Rocky Mountains near the city of Denver. In addition, he is planning to travel to Peru to photograph the Andes Mountains soon, so he will show us the differences between the northern and southern mountain chains in his next book.

172. What is the main purpose of the article?
(A) To advertise Denver's tourism products
(B) To profile a former colleague
(C) To promote a newspaper's special deal
(D) To introduce new photographic equipment

173. What inspired Mr. Milner to take pictures again?
(A) A recommendation from his teammate
(B) A special workshop in Kathmandu
(C) A new journalist position in Nepal
(D) An advanced photography class in Denver

174. The word "pose" in paragraph 4, line 9, is closest in meaning to
(A) display
(B) monitor
(C) require
(D) present

175. What is indicated about Mr. Milner?
(A) He has taken pictures in Peru.
(B) He will soon release his first book.
(C) He runs a photo studio.
(D) He is an experienced mountaineer.

Questions 176-180 refer to the following brochure and article.

Spring Meadow Properties, CO.
Residential Development

Spring Meadow Properties (SMP) has two residential townhouse complexes in the city of Madison.

Nixon Mansion 1935 Merry Place Feature : • 2-and 3-bedroom units, including laundry facilities • Storage for each unit • Playground in the center of the complex • Fitness center only for residents • Ten minutes from the business district by car • Privileged schools nearby • Onsite maintenance and management	**Wayne Square** 657 Pratt Drive Feature : • Studio and 1-bedroom units, fully furnished • Utility fees included • Five minutes to college campus by bus • Various bus lines to the downtown area • Five minutes from the business district by car • Security cameras around the complex • Small library and work area only for residents

▶▶ If you want to check the floor plans, please visit our Web site at www.springmeadow.com. Or do not hesitate to contact us at 913-201-1394 to make an appointment to view these properties. Our real estate agents are available at our offices from Monday through Friday from 10 A.M. to 6 P.M. and from 1 P.M. to 4 P.M. on Saturday and Sunday, so you can discuss the lease during these times.

SMP Announcement

MADISON (April 20) — Spring Meadow Properties (SMP) has been closely associated with the city government. Thanks to this partnership, the company is scheduled to construct its third residential complex, Regency Town, after getting some investment from the Madison city government. This complex will consist of almost 200 single-family housing units.

Construction will begin in June, and it will take twenty-two months until new residents can move into Regency Town. 70 percent of the cost will be paid by SMP, and the rest will be provided by the city government.

SMP is well-known for providing people with comfortable and convenient houses at reasonable prices in our state. Its current properties, Nixon Mansion and Wayne Square, which were built 6 years ago, are in great demand with long waiting lists.

The planning director of SMP, Kevin Myer, said that Regency Town will be developed in an area within a twenty-five-minute drive of the city's business area. "Regency Town is the most suitable for people who are retired or in middle age and wish to get some good rest from their daily routines," he said.

176. What is true about Spring Meadow Properties?

(A) It is a part of the government.
(B) Its branches are located nationwide.
(C) It only lists available properties online.
(D) Its office is open on a daily basis.

177. What is NOT listed as a feature of the units at Wayne Square?

(A) They come with covered parking spaces.
(B) They are accessible to a local school.
(C) They are close to public transportation.
(D) They have furniture in each home.

178. What does the article suggest about the houses at Nixon Mansion and Wayne Square?

(A) Many people think they are more expensive than others.
(B) Many people would like to live there.
(C) They were constructed 22 months ago.
(D) They are too far from the city's downtown area.

179. What is mentioned about Regency Town?

(A) It will be affordable for local college students.
(B) The construction project is being led by Mr. Myer.
(C) SMP is focusing only on the real estate brokerage business in the complex.
(D) Its construction costs will be partly paid by the government.

180. How will Regency Town differ from the other two complexes?

(A) It will be strictly restricted to retirees.
(B) It will be farther from the business district.
(C) It will ask residents to pay rent once a year.
(D) It will be owned by the city government.

GO ON TO THE NEXT PAGE

Questions 181-185 refer to the following e-mails.

To:	Linda Park
From:	Jerry Gebhardt
Date:	Thursday, June 11, 11:00 A.M.
Subject:	Update

The directors of the Marketing and Distribution departments have submitted their reports about the finalists for the job openings in their divisions here at Neo-Altoona. Stephen Portman informed me that Brad Triana and David Harrelson will be invited to return for a final interview for the advertising position, and Jim Matthews asked to invite Karen Simon for a final interview for the position to manage our manufacturing process.

When calling these finalists, you need to arrange an interview time and date as well as luncheon arrangements. Please note that Ms. Portman will be out of the office next week for the upcoming woodworking fair.

Thank you for your help with the application procedure. I would particularly like to express my gratitude because you have carried out the initial mission successfully in spite of the tight deadline.

Regards,

Jerry Gebhardt
Director of Human Resources

To:	Jerry Gebhardt
From:	Linda Park
Date:	Friday, June 12, 3:00 P.M.
Subject:	RE: Update

Dear Gebhardt,

I contacted the three finalists you mentioned yesterday. When I checked their current situation, Karen Simon said that she had already accepted a job offer from Oak Furnishing, our competitor. I informed Jim of this, and he hoped to find a replacement for her as soon as possible.

I have confirmed an interview with Brad Triana at headquarters on Thursday, June 18, and we will also be having lunch with him at the restaurant Ruby Friday. However, Mr. Harrelson is on an overseas business trip until June 20, so I need to discuss this issue with you.

Linda Park
Business Support Team

181. What is the main purpose of the first e-mail?

(A) To post a company's new job openings
(B) To ask a person to contact job applicants
(C) To prepare for on-the-job training sessions
(D) To check a situation about the lack of staffers

182. What type of business most likely is Neo-Altoona?

(A) A furniture company
(B) An accounting firm
(C) A marketing agency
(D) A food retailer

183. What is implied about Mr. Harrelson?

(A) He would like to join the main office.
(B) He previously worked at Oak Furnishing.
(C) He has experience in the accounting field.
(D) He has visited Neo-Altoona before.

184. What will Mr. Matthews most likely do?

(A) Make a restaurant reservation
(B) Attend a furniture exhibition
(C) Choose a new candidate to interview
(D) Contact Mr. Triana in person

185. What was Ms. Park NOT able to do?

(A) Get in touch with Ms. Simon
(B) Schedule all the appointments she was asked to
(C) Report some changes to a department head
(D) Assist Mr. Gebhardt by arranging the previous procedures

Questions 186-190 refer to the following article, Web page, and online order form.

Liverpool (20 May) – A new local company has brought a mealtime revolution to Liverpool in the past few months. Metro F&B Co., which is a food delivery service, was founded by Susan Ariana 18 months ago. The company has provided customers with a variety of recipes on its Web site. After its customers choose their favorite recipes with ingredients, Metro F&B Co. delivers a meal package to them on a weekly basis.

The reason why Ms. Ariana started this service is that her friends were too busy to eat regular meals and were gradually losing their health. "I could not help but come up with a revolutionary idea for my friends, who lead hectic lives without taking care of their health," she said. "Because they don't have enough time to cook themselves and lack confidence in their cooking abilities, they mostly ate junk food or ordered takeout."

Ms. Ariana has struggled to make the delivery procedure simple so that her company offers quality meals to local customers at reasonable prices. To achieve her goal, she decided to form partnerships with local small farms and suppliers. By streamlining the distribution channel, Metro F&B Co. can maintain meals' freshness and even have competitive prices. Because of these factors, her business has become massively popular with Liverpool's citizens. Based on this success, she plans to expand her business into the Manchester area next year.

http://www.evertonfarm.uk

| HOME | PRODUCE | NEWS | CONTACT |

Everton Farm is working closely with Metro F&B Co.! In the last 20 years, we have consistently harvested high-quality fresh agricultural produce. We would like to continue to work in collaboration with Metro F&B Co. while supplying organic food to them.

You can purchase our fruits and vegetables at a booth of our farm every day from 10 A.M. to 4 P.M. In addition, our foods are sold at Giant Eagle Market on weekends and at Martin's Grocery on weekdays.

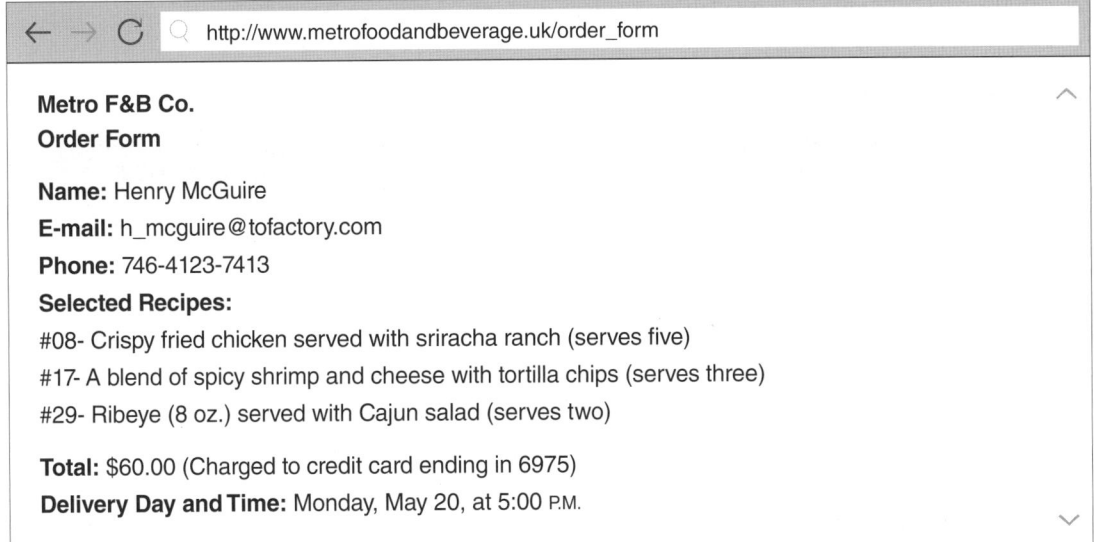

186. What is the purpose of the article?
    (A) To describe a place that sells delicious finger foods
    (B) To explain the reason for a local farm's popularity
    (C) To cover a person's intention in starting a new business
    (D) To discuss one way to find useful cooking classes

187. According to the article, what is one reason customers like Metro F&B Co.?
    (A) The employees are kind.
    (B) It has a convenient location.
    (C) Its prices are affordable.
    (D) It offers free delivery.

188. What is announced on the Everton Farm Web page?
    (A) A distribution process
    (B) A business partnership
    (C) A cultivation method
    (D) A job opportunity

189. What is most likely true about Everton Farm?
    (A) It grows organic food.
    (B) It sells produce only at local stores.
    (C) It is a family-owned business.
    (D) It will expand into other areas.

190. What can be inferred about Mr. McGuire?
    (A) He only eats vegetables.
    (B) He is associated with Everton Farm.
    (C) He is having a party on May 20.
    (D) He lives in Liverpool.

GO ON TO THE NEXT PAGE

Questions 191-195 refer to the following table of contents, article, and e-mail.

Worldwide News Magazine	March 20, Issue 250
Table of Contents	
Page 2	**Editor's Comment**
▸ Weekly News Update from all around the world	
Page 4	**COVER STORY**
▸ Is Your Personal Information Secure on the Web?	
Page 7	**On the Table**
▸ Two guests in the field of international affairs discuss a controversial issue.	
Page 10	**Business Insight**
▸ The Unexpected Growth of Hotels – Renovate Old-Fashioned Buildings!	
Page 15	**Food & Health**
▸ Super Food: Vegan Meat – You can enjoy delicious dishes made from vegetables.	
Page 21	**Sports**
▸ March Madness: the U.S. NCAA Basketball Tournament Finals	

Vegetable or Meat?

You can enjoy delicious dishes made from vegetables!

by Joshua Nelson

People enjoy eating a variety of meat, such as beef, pork, and chicken. However, consuming too much meat is threatening the health of people who have unbalanced diets. Nowadays, a lot of people are concerned about their health, so they are seeking nutritious food with lots of vegetables. Of course, eating only vegetables cannot satisfy the appetite. Solving the problem, a dish called soy meat, which is made of soybeans, is very popular with the public. Vegan Steak, a restaurant in the city of Atlanta, is enjoying an unprecedented boom. The owner and manager, Clara Kim, said that she had been diagnosed with diabetes 10 years ago. "By following a low-fat vegan diet, I had a chance to free myself from that disease," she added. At her restaurant, she likes to provide delicious vegetable dishes to people experiencing problems similar to her own. Fortunately, many residents of Atlanta enjoy her dishes and are staying healthy with her superfoods.

To: Clara Kim
From: Joshua Nelson
Date: March 27

Dear Ms. Kim,

Thanks for inviting me to your restaurant to taste some of your dishes last week. The vegan burger was so delicious and paired perfectly with the Mov Green Tea, which was my favorite of the teas you served me. I sincerely look forward to visiting your place again and hope that you liked my column in *Worldwide News Magazine*.

Best Wishes,

Nelson

191. What section of the magazine contains a debate?

(A) On the Table
(B) Business Insight
(C) Food & Health
(D) Sports

192. On what page of the magazine is the piece about Vegan Steak most likely found?

(A) Page 7
(B) Page 10
(C) Page 15
(D) Page 21

193. What is the main topic of the article?

(A) An upcoming cooking competition
(B) Recent trends in agriculture
(C) The success of a local business
(D) The recipes with vegetables

194. What can be inferred about Mr. Nelson?

(A) He will hold a cooking contest.
(B) He wants to know a recipe.
(C) He was just hired by a new company.
(D) He recently ate at Vegan Steak.

195. In the e-mail, the word "paired" in paragraph 1, line 2, is closest in meaning to

(A) oriented
(B) combined
(C) extended
(D) generated

Questions 196-200 refer to the following Web site, online review, and booking confirmation.

Za Za Guesthouse
SUNRISE ST. VILLA I SABANA CIR 161, 96932 Tamuning, Guam

Guam's Za Za Guesthouse offers you cozy accommodations in the Tamuning area. It is conveniently located within 5 minutes' walking distance of local restaurants and shopping complexes and is within 10 minutes of Tumon Beach on foot. Next to our building is Sandcastle Guam, which is attracting tourists with its magnificent and mysterious appearance.

Details:

- Each room comes with a private or shared bathroom with free toiletries.
- Shared kitchens are located at the center of each floor along with a living room.
- A free Guam local breakfast is given to all guests with local fruit juice.
- Offseason (Mar – Jun / Sep – Nov)
  Room for 2 ($60) / Room for 3 ($70_including extra bed) / Room for 4 ($80)
- Peak season (Jul – Aug / Dec – Feb)
  Room for 2 ($80) / Room for 3 ($90_including extra bed) / Room for 4 ($100)
- Check-in time: 2:00 P.M. / Checkout time: 11:00 A.M.
  (If you arrive after 6 P.M., you will be charged a late-check-in fee of $5.00 per person.)
- You are required to stay for at least 2 nights.

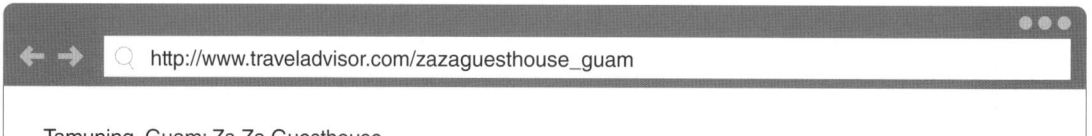

Tamuning, Guam: Za Za Guesthouse
Posted by Garry Hasselink on August 10

I stayed at the Za Za Guesthouse for four nights on March. There are a lot of hotels and shared houses in the Tamuning area, but I strongly believe that Za Za is the best place, considering its cost-effective services. This place provided me with a large, open living area and a fully equipped spacious kitchen, which were good for meeting the other guests and talking with one another even though they were from different countries and cultures. That was why I had a memorable experience in Guam. If you arrive after 6 P.M., please be aware that you should enter the code you received on the keypad by the front door. I forgot this, so I had to wait until someone opened the door for me. I really enjoyed my trip and stay except for this small issue.

http://www.guamzaza.net/confirmation_4810419

Thank you for your reservation!
Please print a copy of the confirmation details for your upcoming stay.

Guest Name: Victoria Brooks
Number of Guests: 1
Booking Number: 4810419
Check-In: May 7, 9:00 P.M.
Checkout: May 8, 11:00 A.M.
Amount Paid:
$20.00 Deposit
$5.00 Late Check-In Fee
$60.00 Room
Total: $85.00 (paid via card ending in -2348)

*****Security Code:** 7340

Please feel free to contact us at zazafront@guamzaza.com or at +01-471-3781 if you have questions at any time.
We hope to see you soon!

Guam Za Za Guesthouse

---

196. Where is the Za Za Guesthouse located?
   (A) Adjacent to a local attraction
   (B) In a new residential area
   (C) Near public transportation
   (D) Along a hill in Tamuning

197. What is indicated about the Za Za Guesthouse?
   (A) It officially organizes an association.
   (B) It offers guided tours to guests.
   (C) It provides a complimentary breakfast.
   (D) It requires a cash payment as a deposit.

198. What did Mr. Hasselink like the most about the Za Za Guesthouse?
   (A) Its proximity to attractions
   (B) Its comfortable space
   (C) Its attractive exterior
   (D) Its social atmosphere

199. How did the Za Za Guesthouse make an exception for Ms. Brooks?
   (A) By charging a lower price for her stay
   (B) By extending her checkout time
   (C) By allowing her to stay only one night
   (D) By exempting her from the late check-in fee

200. What is implied about Ms. Brooks?
   (A) She should remember the code to enter the guesthouse.
   (B) She asked the guesthouse to prepare her dinner.
   (C) She will visit Tumon Beach with a friend.
   (D) She requested a room with an ocean view.

Stop! This is the end of the test. If you finish before time is called, you may go back to Parts 5, 6, and 7 and check your work.

MP3와 해설 파일은 온라인에서 제공됩니다.
▶ books.english.co.kr

TEST 04

test 04.mp3 | 정답 p.280

LISTENING TEST

In the Listening test, you will be asked to demonstrate how well you understand spoken English. The entire Listening test will last approximately 45 minutes. There are four parts, and directions are given for each part. You must mark your answers on the separate answer sheet.
Do not write your answers in your test book.

PART 1

Directions: For each question in this part, you will hear four statements about a picture in your test book. When you hear the statements, you must select the one statement that best describes what you see in the picture. Then find the number of the question on your answer sheet and mark your answer. The statements will not be printed in your test book and will be spoken only one time.

Statement (B), "They're shaking hands," is the best description of the picture, so you should select answer (B) and mark it on your answer sheet.

1.

2.

3.

4.

5.

6.

PART 2

Directions: You will hear a question or statement and three responses spoken in English. They will not be printed in your test book and will be spoken only one time. Select the best response to the question or statement and mark the letter (A), (B), or (C) on your answer sheet.

7. Mark your answer on your answer sheet.
8. Mark your answer on your answer sheet.
9. Mark your answer on your answer sheet.
10. Mark your answer on your answer sheet.
11. Mark your answer on your answer sheet.
12. Mark your answer on your answer sheet.
13. Mark your answer on your answer sheet.
14. Mark your answer on your answer sheet.
15. Mark your answer on your answer sheet.
16. Mark your answer on your answer sheet.
17. Mark your answer on your answer sheet.
18. Mark your answer on your answer sheet.
19. Mark your answer on your answer sheet.
20. Mark your answer on your answer sheet.
21. Mark your answer on your answer sheet.
22. Mark your answer on your answer sheet.
23. Mark your answer on your answer sheet.
24. Mark your answer on your answer sheet.
25. Mark your answer on your answer sheet.
26. Mark your answer on your answer sheet.
27. Mark your answer on your answer sheet.
28. Mark your answer on your answer sheet.
29. Mark your answer on your answer sheet.
30. Mark your answer on your answer sheet.
31. Mark your answer on your answer sheet.

PART 3

Directions: You will hear some conversations between two or more people. You will be asked to answer three questions about what the speakers say in each conversation. Select the best response to each question and mark the letter (A), (B), (C), or (D) on your answer sheet. The conversations will not be printed in your test book and will be spoken only one time.

32. Who most likely is the woman?
    (A) A technician
    (B) A property manager
    (C) A tenant
    (D) A security guard

33. What problem does the man have?
    (A) There is a mistake in a contract.
    (B) He cannot drink cold water.
    (C) His apartment is too hot.
    (D) A device is malfunctioning.

34. What information does the woman ask for?
    (A) An address
    (B) A code number
    (C) A phone number
    (D) An appointment time

35. What is taking place next Tuesday?
    (A) The opening of a medical center
    (B) A professional convention
    (C) A festival in Canberra
    (D) A house party

36. What did the woman do last week?
    (A) She participated in a conference.
    (B) She talked with a doctor.
    (C) She reserved a hotel room.
    (D) She took a family vacation.

37. What is the man going to do most of his time in Canberra?
    (A) Go sightseeing
    (B) Stay at his hotel
    (C) See patients
    (D) Work on a new project

38. What most likely is the man's job?
    (A) Clerk
    (B) Patron
    (C) Author
    (D) Investor

39. What will happen next week?
    (A) A book signing will end.
    (B) A sale will begin.
    (C) A store will move.
    (D) A shipment will arrive.

40. What does the woman ask the man to do?
    (A) Make a copy
    (B) Exchange a book
    (C) Hold an item
    (D) Change a phone number

41. Where do the speakers most likely work?
    (A) At a car dealer
    (B) At a convention hall
    (C) At a restaurant
    (D) At a city hall

42. What is the woman's problem?
    (A) Her vehicle needs to be repaired.
    (B) She wants to borrow money to buy a car.
    (C) She has never worked an extra shift.
    (D) She recently sold her car.

43. What does the woman mean when she says, "Wednesday is my parents' wedding anniversary"?
    (A) She wants to invite her parents to a restaurant.
    (B) She has to buy a gift before Wednesday.
    (C) She is not available on Wednesday.
    (D) She can work anytime next week.

GO ON TO THE NEXT PAGE

44. Who most likely is Ms. Sato?

    (A) A real estate agent
    (B) An interior designer
    (C) A maintenance worker
    (D) A restaurant owner

45. What does Ms. Sato want to discuss first?

    (A) The costs of materials
    (B) A rental fee
    (C) Some flooring options
    (D) Some machinery upgrades

46. What will the speakers most likely do next?

    (A) Look at a catalog
    (B) Delay a meeting
    (C) Review some blueprints
    (D) Create an estimate

47. What is the man concerned about?

    (A) The size of some furniture
    (B) The quality of a sofa
    (C) The place some items will be delivered to
    (D) The construction of a living room

48. What does the woman say her team will do at the man's house?

    (A) Remove some furniture
    (B) Clean a living room
    (C) Measure some items
    (D) Assemble some items

49. What does the man ask the woman to do?

    (A) Revise a contract
    (B) Change a delivery date
    (C) Deliver an item tomorrow
    (D) Bring some samples

50. What problem does the woman mention?

    (A) A proposal was rejected.
    (B) A sales position was already filled.
    (C) Products are not selling well.
    (D) A sales report has incorrect information.

51. Why does the woman say, "this will be the first time he will give a presentation"?

    (A) To praise a new employee
    (B) To criticize a coworker
    (C) To offer a position
    (D) To express her concern

52. What does the man ask the woman to do next?

    (A) Transfer to the Sales Department
    (B) Speak with a coworker
    (C) Schedule a meeting
    (D) Make a presentation

53. What are the speakers talking about?

    (A) A security seminar
    (B) How to use some machines
    (C) A future inspection
    (D) Safety equipment

54. What aspect of the training does the woman disagree about?

    (A) Whether attendance should be compulsory
    (B) Whether refreshments should be served
    (C) How long it should last
    (D) When it should be announced

55. What does the woman want to distribute?

    (A) Employee directories
    (B) User manuals
    (C) Surveys
    (D) Some tools

56. What type of business do the speakers work for?

    (A) A hotel
    (B) A printing company
    (C) A travel agency
    (D) An airline

57. What is the woman concerned about?

    (A) The cost of a design for a Web site
    (B) A deadline for updating brochures
    (C) The inaccurate travel itinerary
    (D) The time required to complete some work

58. What does the man agree with the woman about?

    (A) An itinerary should be changed.
    (B) The travel packages should be worth more.
    (C) They should hire an expert.
    (D) A supervisor has provided valuable feedback.

59. Which industry do the speakers most likely work in?

    (A) Architecture
    (B) Furniture
    (C) Apparel
    (D) Tourism

60. What problem does the man mention?

    (A) The color of a product is too bright.
    (B) There aren't enough inside pockets.
    (C) A design should be completely changed.
    (D) A meeting should be delayed.

61. What will the woman most likely do next?

    (A) Contact her manager
    (B) Review some drawings
    (C) Distribute design samples
    (D) Change a color

1st Fitness Center Summer Activities 6:00 P.M. – 9:00 P.M.		
Monday Pilates	**Tuesday** Aerobics	**Wednesday** Swimming
Thursday Jazz Dance		**Friday** Yoga

62. Who most likely is the man?

    (A) A fitness trainer
    (B) An athlete
    (C) A medical doctor
    (D) A receptionist

63. What does the woman ask the man about?

    (A) A dietary regime
    (B) The operating hours of a center
    (C) Available class times
    (D) Alternative types of exercise

64. Look at the graphic. When will the woman probably go to the fitness center in the summer?

    (A) On Tuesdays
    (B) On Wednesdays
    (C) On Thursdays
    (D) On Fridays

GO ON TO THE NEXT PAGE

Destination	Departure	Status
Munich	9:30 A.M.	20-minute delay
Prague	10:00 A.M.	On time
Vienne	10:20 A.M.	35-minute delay
Budapest	11:00 A.M.	50-minute delay
Zagreb	11:30 A.M.	On time

Section	Location
Nonfiction	1F East
Novels & Poetry	1F West
Business & Travel	2F East
Foreign Language Books	2F West

65. What kind of company do the speakers work for?

(A) A wallpaper manufacturer
(B) A hardware store
(C) An interior decorating company
(D) An airline

66. Look at the graphic. What is the status of the woman's flight?

(A) 20-minute delay
(B) On time
(C) 35-minute delay
(D) 50-minute delay

67. Why does the man change the meeting time?

(A) A potential client will be late.
(B) The woman's flight was canceled.
(C) The woman has a tight schedule.
(D) He wants to review a contract.

68. Where is the conversation most likely taking place?

(A) At a library
(B) At a bookstore
(C) At a publishing company
(D) At a real estate agency

69. Look at the graphic. Where will the book signing be held?

(A) 1F East
(B) 1F West
(C) 2F East
(D) 2F West

70. What will the man do next?

(A) Clean some tables
(B) Move some shelves
(C) Display some books
(D) Go to the second floor

PART 4

Directions: You will hear some talks given by a single speaker. You will be asked to answer three questions about what the speaker says in each talk. Select the best response to each question and mark the letter (A), (B), (C), or (D) on your answer sheet. The talks will not be printed in your test book and will be spoken only one time.

71. What kind of event is the speaker talking about?
    (A) A race
    (B) A luncheon
    (C) A marathon
    (D) An orientation

72. What does the company most likely sell?
    (A) Beverages
    (B) Footwear
    (C) Clothing
    (D) Bicycles

73. What does the speaker ask Lucas to do?
    (A) Conduct a survey
    (B) Distribute some drinks
    (C) Visit a place
    (D) Manage some items

74. What is the broadcast about?
    (A) A new facility
    (B) A company acquisition
    (C) A fundraising initiative
    (D) A job fair

75. What advantage is expected for Charleston?
    (A) A public library will be built.
    (B) A hospital will provide more services.
    (C) Employment will increase.
    (D) Tourism will increase.

76. What will the listeners hear next?
    (A) An advertisement
    (B) An interview
    (C) A traffic report
    (D) A weather forecast

77. What does the company sell?
    (A) Home appliances
    (B) Medical equipment
    (C) Medicine
    (D) Experiment equipment

78. What does the speaker mean when she says, "I also went there last year"?
    (A) She does not want to go to the convention.
    (B) She cannot share any information.
    (C) She was disappointed by the convention.
    (D) She is willing to help her coworkers.

79. What does the speaker ask the listeners to do when they return from the convention?
    (A) Give a demonstration
    (B) Identify potential customers
    (C) Make a presentation
    (D) Speak to their supervisor

80. What type of event is the announcement about?
    (A) An art competition
    (B) A food festival
    (C) A local government election
    (D) A music event

81. Why does the speaker encourage the listeners to download an application?
    (A) To cast a vote
    (B) To look at a list of bands
    (C) To choose their favorite food
    (D) To check a schedule

82. What is a benefit for volunteers?
    (A) A complimentary ticket
    (B) A meal coupon
    (C) Free shuttle bus
    (D) Special seating

GO ON TO THE NEXT PAGE

83. What problem does the speaker mention?
    (A) Finding accommodations
    (B) Reserving tickets for the auto show
    (C) Booking a flight
    (D) Preparing for a presentation

84. Why does the speaker say, "there are some places to stay in Chatswood"?
    (A) To offer a solution
    (B) To cancel a booking
    (C) To change the schedule
    (D) To reject a recommendation

85. What requires a manager's approval?
    (A) Travel reimbursements
    (B) Registration for an event
    (C) Equipment purchases
    (D) A conference presentation

86. What is the purpose of the talk?
    (A) To assign a meeting room
    (B) To revise a manual
    (C) To provide some training
    (D) To introduce a new product

87. According to the speaker, what should the listeners remember to do?
    (A) Attend a demonstration
    (B) Fill out some paperwork
    (C) Save some data
    (D) Submit daily reports

88. Why does the speaker apologize?
    (A) Her computer didn't save some data.
    (B) Her device is malfunctioning.
    (C) The training is canceled.
    (D) A request has been denied.

89. What field does the speaker work in?
    (A) Agriculture
    (B) Education
    (C) Distribution
    (D) Medicine

90. What does the speaker remind the listeners to do?
    (A) Purchase hats and sunglasses
    (B) Use sun protection
    (C) Get some discount coupons
    (D) Put their belongings in a locker

91. What does the speaker mean when he says, "All of our products are up to 30 percent off for visitors"?
    (A) He wants to emphasize that there are not many products left.
    (B) He is surprised by a discount.
    (C) He is disappointed that the merchandise is not selling well.
    (D) He wants the listeners to buy some produce.

92. What is the purpose of the speech?
    (A) To welcome a new employee
    (B) To present an award
    (C) To describe a new advertisement
    (D) To plan a marketing strategy

93. What does the speaker say about Rosa Jimenez?
    (A) She has appeared on TV commercials.
    (B) She doesn't have any experience in the field.
    (C) She has won an award.
    (D) She has been an accountant for years.

94. What will most likely happen next?
    (A) The meeting will end.
    (B) A short video will be shown.
    (C) Refreshments will be served.
    (D) A speech will be made.

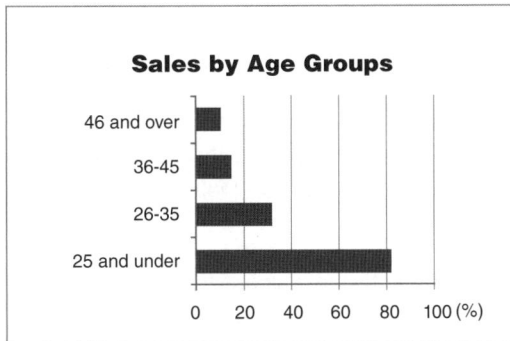

Pasta of the Day

Thursday	Bacon Cream
Friday	Seafood
Saturday	Meatball
Sunday	Tomato & Basil

95. Who most likely are the listeners?
    (A) Bookstore clerks
    (B) Magazine editors
    (C) Marketing employees
    (D) Fashion coordinators

96. Look at the graphic. Which group does the speaker suggest focusing on?
    (A) 25 and under
    (B) 26-35
    (C) 36-45
    (D) 46 and over

97. What does the speaker say he will do next?
    (A) Give his opinion
    (B) Listen to people's ideas
    (C) Contact a fashion coordinator
    (D) Receive funding for advertising

98. Look at the graphic. Which pasta does the speaker say will be served two days this week?
    (A) Bacon Cream
    (B) Seafood
    (C) Meatball
    (D) Tomato & Basil

99. Who is Peter Rauch?
    (A) A job applicant
    (B) A customer
    (C) A waiter
    (D) A chef

100. What did the speaker post on the bulletin board?
    (A) The restaurant's rules
    (B) A training timetable
    (C) A revised menu
    (D) The next meeting time

This is the end of the Listening test. Turn to Part 5 in your test book.

READING TEST

In the Reading test, you will read a variety of texts and answer several different types of reading comprehension questions. The entire Reading test will last 75 minutes. There are three parts, and directions are given for each part. You are encouraged to answer as many questions as possible within the time allowed.

You must mark your answers on the separate answer sheet. Do not write your answers in the test book.

PART 5

Directions: A word or phrase is missing in each of the sentences below. Four answer choices are given below each sentence. Select the best answer to complete the sentence. Then mark the letter (A), (B), (C), or (D) on your answer sheet.

101. In front of the hotel, you will find the kiosk between the fountain ------- the statue.
    (A) and
    (B) or
    (C) but
    (D) so

102. This is a reminder that you have an ------- soon with Clear Eyesight Clinic.
    (A) appoint
    (B) appointed
    (C) appointing
    (D) appointment

103. Ms. Jane started work as a researcher after receiving a degree at Bloomington State University, where ------- graduated from.
    (A) she
    (B) her
    (C) hers
    (D) herself

104. The Cultural District has some of the ------- and most interesting structures in the country, including Haein Temple.
    (A) local
    (B) urban
    (C) oldest
    (D) entire

105. Because of a lack of rooms in this building, the plan to expand our office has ------- options.
    (A) limit
    (B) limits
    (C) limited
    (D) limitation

106. Mr. Tyler has received ------- for the quality of his work in improving the way to deal with customer issues.
    (A) implementation
    (B) dedication
    (C) administration
    (D) recognition

107. *The Del Posta Tribune's* owners have already offered electronic versions of ------- articles on the Web since 2010.
    (A) they
    (B) their
    (C) theirs
    (D) them

108. You can pay at the reception desk or ------- using our wireless pay-by-phone system from your mobile device.
    (A) to
    (B) by
    (C) at
    (D) of

109. If our inspector discovers construction work being performed without the ------- permit, a fine will be issued.
(A) appropriate
(B) considerable
(C) unpleasant
(D) eloquent

110. We do not have enough educational materials, so please promptly return whichever ------- you borrowed.
(A) here
(B) ones
(C) every
(D) each

111. The reason why companies ask for help from us is to find a ------- for experienced employees.
(A) replace
(B) replaced
(C) replacing
(D) replacement

112. We always strive to make the most accurate ------- possible, but some shipments may take longer to be received.
(A) estimate
(B) competition
(C) transaction
(D) alternativeness

113. Airfares of Mevius Airlines are per person for economy flights ------- from New Orleans.
(A) depart
(B) departing
(C) departed
(D) departure

114. Since Mr. Choi restructured the customer service center, its annual revenue has risen -------.
(A) consider
(B) considerate
(C) considerable
(D) considerably

115. Available properties within the state of Indiana have ------- been identified for the new shopping complexes.
(A) already
(B) so that
(C) yet
(D) ever

116. Due to her urgent meeting, Ms. Sue asked whether the conference could ------- for tomorrow afternoon.
(A) reschedule
(B) have rescheduled
(C) be rescheduled
(D) be rescheduling

117. Some companies create an internship program to develop students' careers, ------- others use it in their recruiting.
(A) as if
(B) while
(C) therefore
(D) given

118. Charles Odell began to gain fame in the field of marketing ------- before his retirement.
(A) immediate
(B) more immediate
(C) immediately
(D) most immediately

119. ------- the old apartment is being inspected for its safety will all residents be required to go outside of their units.
(A) Whether
(B) Because
(C) Only if
(D) Although

120. The city officials have closely ------- the status of the Thames River in London to check its ecological pollution level.
(A) developed
(B) employed
(C) monitored
(D) purchased

GO ON TO THE NEXT PAGE

121. Our editor-in-chief announced that *London Post* will be ------- from a monthly to biweekly publishing schedule as of next month.

(A) switch
(B) to switched
(C) having switched
(D) switching

122. If you would like to get more detailed information, please feel free ------- our office.

(A) to call
(B) called
(C) calls
(D) is called

123. Clothing companies must comply with all ------- policies regarding this clearance sale at upcoming special events.

(A) apply
(B) applicator
(C) applicable
(D) applications

124. The national council has started to ------- a new law that regulates the import of foreign-made agricultural goods.

(A) instruct
(B) enforce
(C) gauge
(D) follow

125. Our store's E-coupon will allow our regular customers to buy groceries at half price ------- designated areas.

(A) except
(B) within
(C) during
(D) despite

126. Atlanta City has had a massive ------- of migrants seeking jobs, so the city has suffered from problems like a lack of housing.

(A) intrigue
(B) influx
(C) intuition
(D) indication

127. The upcoming renovation of the Kim-Hae International Airport will ------- traffic congestion and improve the facilities.

(A) easy
(B) easier
(C) ease
(D) eased

128. In order to ask for improvements to their houses' exterior, tenants of Westgate Apartment ------- delayed the payment of the rental fees.

(A) proficiently
(B) purposely
(C) precisely
(D) physically

129. College dorms in the Pennsylvania State are ------- to receive free recycling bins through the state-government funding.

(A) systematic
(B) eligible
(C) familiar
(D) successful

130. If you register for the Italian Cooking class in advance, the credit card fee will be -------.

(A) prohibited
(B) withdrawn
(C) waived
(D) reminded

PART 6

Directions: Read the texts that follow. A word, phrase, or sentence is missing in parts of each text. Four answer choices for each question are given below the text. Select the best answer to complete the text. Then mark the letter (A), (B), (C), or (D) on your answer sheet.

Questions 131-134 refer to the following article.

The Committee of Johnstown yesterday ------- its decision as to whether to restore the stream in its
131.
urban area. Committee member Brandon Cohen announced that an additional survey and study
should be considered ------- the committee approves it. -------. However, this type of venture needs
132. **133.**
to be assessed with a long-term point of view, considering the future urban ecological environment.
In response to this reason, the state government has tried to launch the Reproduction of Water
program. In addition, the public's demand for the plan ------- steadily for their urban environment and
134.
management.

131. (A) confirmed
(B) notified
(C) postponed
(D) demonstrated

132. (A) before
(B) as if
(C) since
(D) whether

133. (A) The protection of nature is very important for our future generation.
(B) Because of some viruses, updates will not be made until Friday.
(C) Only a few city councils have implemented this kind of project.
(D) In order to conduct the survey, we should collect personal information.

134. (A) has increased
(B) increase
(C) increasing
(D) will increase

157

GO ON TO THE NEXT PAGE

Questions 135-138 refer to the following e-mail.

To: Aaron Whitman <aaron_w@ylang.net>
From: Kazuki Burton <kazuki_burton@foxfirenet.com>
Date: August 14
Subject: Survey

Dear Mr. Whitman,

I am a staff member of Fox Fire Net Research, which is a widely recognized research institution in the U.S. We are ------- conducting an online survey to get information about bookstore and
　　　　　　　　　　　　　　　　　135.
online consumer behavior. This survey is to gather the right information about factors that affect

------- habits. You ------- because you are a regular subscriber of *American Society Journal*. -------.
136.　　　　　137.　　　　　　　　　　　　　　　　　　　　　　　　　　　　　138.
If you are willing to complete the survey, you can get a 10% discount that you can use through

the Public Journal Association Network. If you are interested in participating, please reply to this

e-mail, and I will send you the survey Web site link.

Best Wishes,

Kazuki Burton
Fox Fire Net Research

135. (A) presently
　　　(B) timely
　　　(C) increasingly
　　　(D) mutually

136. (A) purchasing
　　　(B) literacy
　　　(C) publishing
　　　(D) investment

137. (A) selects
　　　(B) will be selected
　　　(C) are selecting
　　　(D) have been selected

138. (A) The fees for your magazine and journals will rise as of next month.
　　　(B) The twenty questions on the survey form just take a few minutes to answer.
　　　(C) The publishing company tends to ask customers to submit book reviews.
　　　(D) Our select list of customers includes a diverse range of ages.

Questions 139-142 refer to the following letter.

Dear Reader,

Your subscription to *Monthly Design* magazine is about to -------. If you renew it this month, we will
139.
provide an annual subscription for the price of only ten issues. -------, you will receive the first issue of
140.
our latest home décor magazine free of charge.

If you do not renew the subscription, we will cease to provide issues of the magazine from the end of
next month. However, you ------- able to access most of our online contents without any extra fees.
141.
Subscribers can continue to view our excellent online contents for 12 months even if their subscription
ends. -------.
142.

Regards,

Eleanor Ricci
Monthly Design

139. (A) terminate
 (B) expire
 (C) finish
 (D) cancel

140. (A) In addition
 (B) For example
 (C) Finally
 (D) Nonetheless

141. (A) were
 (B) will be
 (C) have been
 (D) had been

142. (A) Therefore, make sure that you are aware of your username and password.
 (B) Accordingly, you can be paid for all articles you sent to us within a month.
 (C) Hence, you cannot log on to our Web site without permission in the future.
 (D) Meanwhile, there are no further printed editions anymore for your address.

Questions 143-146 refer to the following Web page.

Welcome to the International Literature Archives!

The International Literature Archives features a collection of literary works that span from the 1920s to the present day. Founded in 1970 as a section in the Museum of Public Literature, the Archives collects and ------- original copies along with literature in digital format.
143.

Most of the open novels are available to all registered users for one-week rentals. Please note that there is a limitation on the number of books you can rent at one time. -------, users can view open
144.
novels on the 2nd- and 3rd-floor shelves in the museum. Please review the recently updated terms and conditions posted on the bulletin board.

Original copies of our own literature are only available to approved users for research ------- academic
145.
purposes. -------.
146.

---

143. (A) develops
(B) stores
(C) borrows
(D) signs

144. (A) Even so
(B) Additionally
(C) Nevertheless
(D) As a result

145. (A) or
(B) more
(C) as
(D) yet

146. (A) We hope you will soon create your own archives.
(B) Unfortunately, we cannot allow users to borrow films.
(C) To register as a user, please sign up at the circulation desk.
(D) You can submit as many books as you like.

PART 7

Directions: In this part you will read a selection of texts, such as magazine and newspaper articles, e-mails, and instant messages. Each text or set of texts is followed by several questions. Select the best answer for each question and mark the letter (A), (B), (C), or (D) on your answer sheet.

Questions 147-148 refer to the following advertisement.

Butler Home Care Service

Landscape Service
- trimming and removing branches
- maintenance of lawn and landscape

Drainage Service
- drainage installation to correct any water collection issues

Irrigation System Repair
- repairing damaged lawn sprinklers and irrigation equipment

You can see the day and night appearance of your new landscape through our 3D virtual tour service on the Web, www.butlerhomecare.com/3dvirtual. Call us to make an appointment today!
(790) 891-9347

---

147. What type of business does the company operate?

(A) A home cleaning service
(B) Lawnmower sales
(C) A yard care service
(D) Computer graphic design

148. What can customers do on the company's Web site?

(A) Check other local stores
(B) Get a quote for the service
(C) Do a live chat for inquiries
(D) View samples of work

Questions 149-150 refer to the following flyer.

Petersburg Gym
Shape Your Perfect Body

Free for the first 30 who join [from May 20]!

Free personal training with your orientation and no joining fees

Membership Benefits

Buy 6 months, get 6 months Free!

Plus! One month of FREE training!

20% off – ends May 30

* If you sign up together with a friend, you both can get an additional 5% off.

WE OFFER

- Cardio Training
- Group / Personal Training
- Weight Training
- Diet Programs (Nutrition)
- Time Management

---

149. According to the flyer, what is the reason for joining the center?
(A) To get used to sporting equipment
(B) To experience outdoor activities
(C) To establish health habits
(D) To know how to buy sporting goods

150. How do customers get a discount?
(A) By training with a private instructor
(B) By registering with another person
(C) By joining the fitness center after May
(D) By purchasing a year membership

Questions 151-152 refer to the following text-message chain.

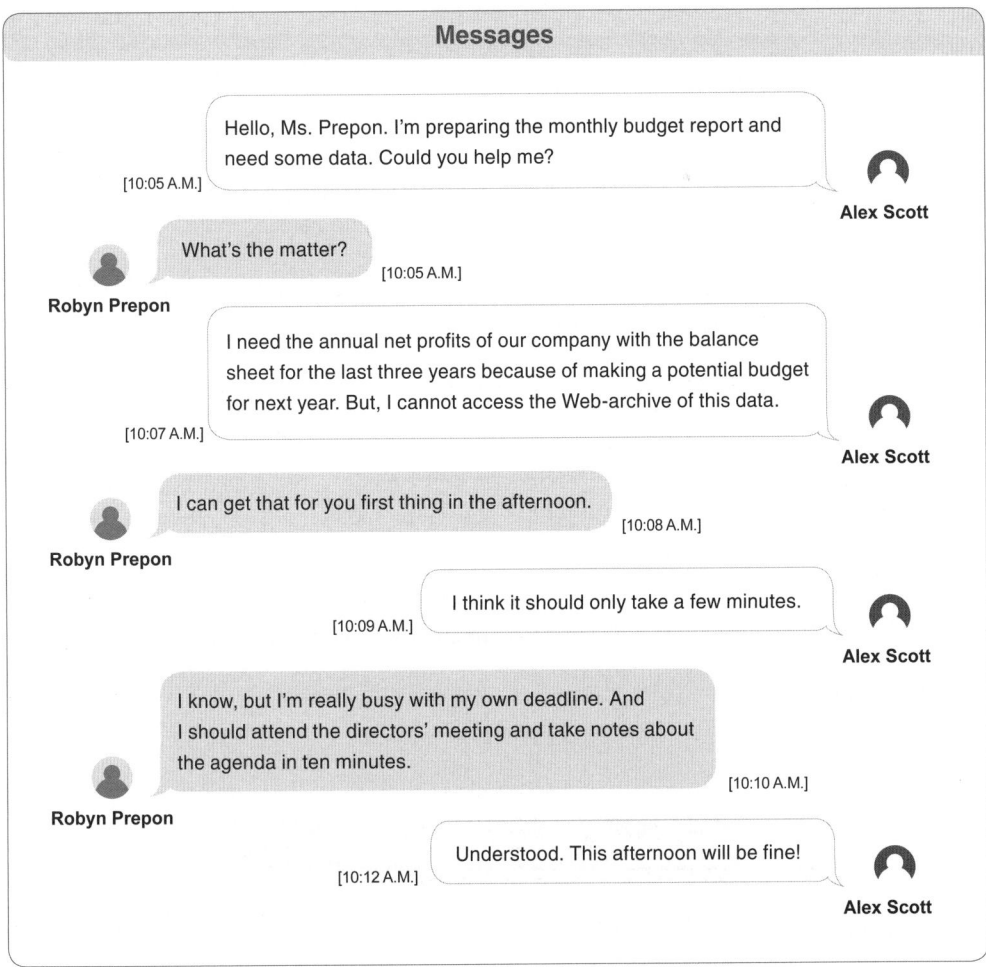

151. What most likely is Ms. Prepon's job?

(A) Sales representative
(B) Corporate accountant
(C) Administrative assistant
(D) Company Web master

152. At 10:12 A.M., what does Mr. Scott most likely mean when he writes, "This afternoon will be fine"?

(A) The afternoon is much better for meeting together.
(B) He will be out of the office in the afternoon.
(C) He has to participate in the afternoon meeting.
(D) He can wait for the information he needs.

Questions 153-154 refer to the following Web advertisement.

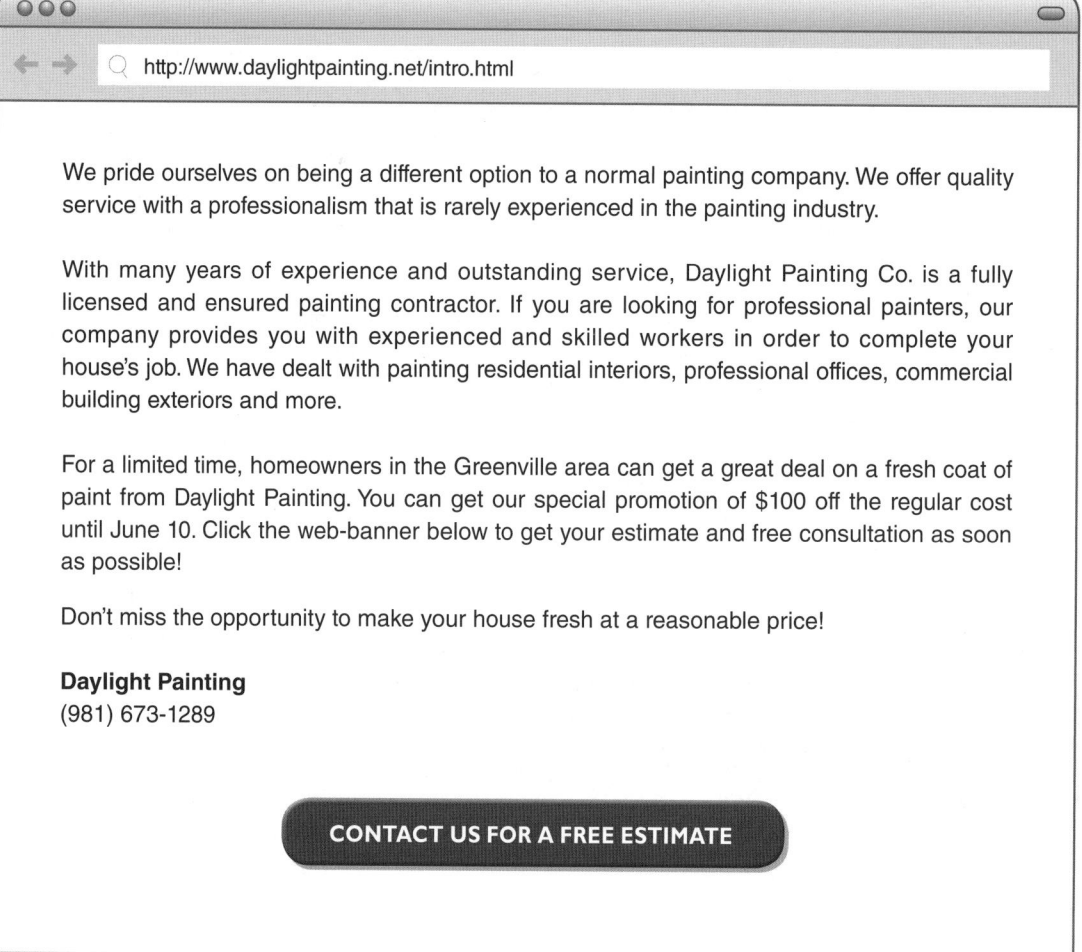

153. Who is the intended readers of the advertisement?

   (A) Local artists
   (B) House owners
   (C) Tenants in Greenville
   (D) Painting consultants

154. How can readers take advantage of the offer?

   (A) By accessing the company's Web site
   (B) By making a payment in full
   (C) By using a service before June 10
   (D) By visiting the company in person

Questions 155-157 refer to the following schedule.

10th Annual International Conference for Creative Writing
Edward Auditorium, Fordham College, New York City
April 13

* Event includes all activities listed in the schedule.

06:00 P.M. April 12 **Preliminary Convening**	Share and learn about local collaborations with NY Publishing: Murray-Weige Hall, 515 E Fordham Rd, The Bronx, NY 10458
10:00 A.M. **Opening Reception**	Location: Lobby, Edward Auditorium, 415 E Fordham Rd
11:00 A.M. **Keynote Speech**	Demonstration: Managing the work of collaboration with ASPECT (Heather Bryant, founder, Project Aspect)
12:00 P.M. **Lunch**	Aramak Cafeteria, Leonard Hall on Campus (A variety of dishes prepared)
01:00 P.M. **Lecture**	From competition to collaboration: How partnerships are changing local news in the eastern states of the U.S.A. (Danny Rivera, independent producer and adjunct journalism professor, Bronx College)
02:00 P.M. **Five Talks**	A lightning round of 10-minute presentations about collaborative projects around New York • "Stories of Oriental Cities" by Mike Piazza • "Philadelphia Journalism Cooperative" by Rebecca Beth • "How I Collaborated with College Students" by Andrew Tennent • "The Reentry Project Impact Report" by Maria Hill • "Granite State News Collaborative" by Nick Fury
03:00 P.M. **Break**	
03:30 P.M. **Outdoor Activity**	Explore New York's on-site reporting spots on foot with Nancy Gibbs, Blue Cap Trip Co.

155. For whom is the event most likely intended?

(A) University faculty
(B) Journalists
(C) Travel agents
(D) Community leaders

156. Whose presentation will most likely be related to undergraduates?

(A) Ms. Hill
(B) Mr. Piazza
(C) Mr. Tennent
(D) Ms. Bryant

157. What activity is included with the event?

(A) A city tour
(B) Career counseling
(C) A job experience program
(D) Visiting a high school

Questions 158-160 refer to the following memo.

MEMO

As you have been notified by your supervisors, construction for our parking area will begin as of Friday, April 10, and last until the end of the month. —[1]—. All employees will be allowed to park at Tan Storage's warehouse next to our building. Please be sure that your company identification is displayed on the windshield of your car. If not, the car will be towed without exception. —[2]—. In addition, you should park your vehicle in the designated area, the Blue Parking Lot, which is located behind the warehouse building. It seems that the distance between the parking lot and our office is a little bit far on foot, but it is just as well that we can use this space. —[3]—.

To thank you for your patience during this project, the company has a plan to reward each employee with a gift card for 20 dollars, which can be used in the Donatello Dining restaurant adjacent to our office building. —[4]—.

Thank you for your understanding and cooperation again.

Regards,

Kevin Caputo
Director of General Affairs, Terra System

---

158. What is mentioned about Terra System?

(A) It has a coffee kiosk in its parking area.
(B) It will use a temporary parking area.
(C) It provides towing services for users of its company cars.
(D) It is the owner of Tan Storage.

159. How will employees be thanked for their patience?

(A) They will be given priority parking spaces.
(B) They will receive a gift card.
(C) They will get an extra paid vacation day.
(D) They will be allowed to go home early.

160. In which of the positions marked [1], [2], [3], and [4] does the following sentence best belong?

"Additionally, your department head will distribute the vouchers for free coffee that can be used in our vending machine in the lobby."

(A) [1]
(B) [2]
(C) [3]
(D) [4]

Questions 161-163 refer to the following article.

Stout Global – Reach for your dreams!

Los Angeles (September 17)—Stout Global, the highly successful Internet portal company founded by two brothers, Eric Gardener and Henry Gardener, has launched its newest division, Stout Global Innovation. The division is to be led by Heather Lopez, a relatively unknown name among business leaders.

She would like to become a candidate for the managerial position herself. She has led Stout's research and development (R&D) department for the past three years, creating several innovative and successful products. She really wanted to join an environment like Stout Global Innovation, which offers greater creative research freedom.

That could be well appointed given its future because she has been assigned three ambitious projects to lead and a considerable budget for their accomplishment. Ms. Lopez explained that the division will work on the projects at once. The three projects include an innovative private means of transportation, a system to restore dry areas to grow a variety of plants, and e-learning networks which enable students to study all kinds of contents more effectively than before.

161. What is mentioned about Stout Global Innovation?

(A) It is a kind of secret agency.
(B) It uses a different building.
(C) It is a temporary division.
(D) It is well funded.

162. Which plan was most likely NOT adopted by Stout Global?

(A) Electric Personal Transportation
(B) Tidal Power Generators
(C) Anti-desertification Tech
(D) Advanced Learning Tools

163. What is indicated about Ms. Lopez?

(A) She was selected within her organization.
(B) She has a plan to retire from the company soon.
(C) She did not anticipate the success of the projects.
(D) She will assume all of the CEO's tasks in the future.

Questions 164-167 refer to the following e-mail.

To: Ken Hyland <k.hyland@oxbridge.edu>
From: Ian Raynold <i_raynold@bea.org>
Subject: Speech Proposal
Date: May 1

Dear Professor Hyland,

I am the director of the Bristol Enterprise Association (BEA). Last night, I attended your forum at Eberly Community Center with my colleagues. We were all impressed with your perspective and insight, and we would like to invite you to organize a similar forum at our association.

The BEA is one of the community groups in Bristol City. We have been associated with over 30 organizations and have almost 500 members, and these figures are gradually increasing. In order for us to provide a variety of information to our associates, we host career consulting and job fair events, and we operate our own employment bulletin on the Web. Could you present your journal article about career development on June 2? In general, we meet between 1 P.M. and 4 P.M. If you are interested in our proposal, please feel free to contact us before May 10.

I look forward to hearing from you soon.

Regards,

Ian Raynold
Director of Bristol Enterprise Association

---

164. Why did Mr. Raynold send the e-mail to Professor Hyland?

(A) To make an appointment for the general meeting
(B) To ask him to give a presentation
(C) To propose the publishing of his journal
(D) To suggest a position for a tenured professor

165. What is NOT mentioned as a service that the BEA provides to its members?

(A) Recruitment information
(B) Career counseling
(C) Socializing events
(D) Investing in a stock

166. What is suggested about the BEA?

(A) It has been in operation for 20 years.
(B) It offers regular courses for business.
(C) It convenes once a year.
(D) It holds its own talks for members.

167. The word "perspective" in paragraph 1, line 2, is closest in meaning to

(A) testing
(B) accounting
(C) processing
(D) understanding

Questions 168-171 refer to the following article.

However old you are, it's never too late!
– His adventure is not over yet –

(Wisconsin, Feb.20)—Chuck Franco has spent 25 years selling and repairing pianos in Madison City. Starting in April, he will regretfully stop his work and begin his new career at the Wisconsin College of Music and Art in Milwaukee. —[1]—. "I've loved my previous work, and now it's time for me to learn more specialized skills and share my field experiences," he said.

Although the residents within and around Madison City were sad because of his retirement, most of them sincerely supported his new challenge as a master artisan. Madison Tune UP was founded by Mr. Franco in 1994 and has had a good reputation in the state of Wisconsin and even outside of the U.S. —[2]—. His regular customers are afraid it is soon time to say good-bye to him.

The good news is that Mr. Franco wants to dispose of his stock to the public before he closes the store. On this occasion, people can get excellent instruments at highly discounted prices. —[3]—. Additional accessories for pianos will also be provided for sale. Anyone who is interested in this event can drop by his store and buy something at competitive prices. So, don't miss this opportunity to say goodbye to him there. —[4]—.

168. What is the purpose of the article?

(A) To promote Madison's prestigious university
(B) To introduce famous local musicians
(C) To profile a technician for musical instruments
(D) To notify customers of online promotional sales

169. What is suggested about Mr. Franco?

(A) He will resume his work in Madison as of April.
(B) He relocated from Milwaukee 25 years ago.
(C) He has a bachelor's degree in music.
(D) He already has a reputation for managing instruments.

170. What is indicted about the Madison Tune UP?

(A) The rental fees have risen considerably.
(B) The clearance sale will take place.
(C) Its products will be sold online.
(D) Traditional instruments is no longer available.

171. In which of the positions marked [1], [2], [3], and [4] does the following sentence best belong?

"Mr. Franco will take advanced courses about piano tuning and will be a teaching assistant."

(A) [1]
(B) [2]
(C) [3]
(D) [4]

Questions 172-175 refer to the following online chat discussion.

Bella Reynolds
As you know, I got promoted to editor-in-chief without much notice. Because this was expedited, I need to ask you to give me a lot of information. For boosting our sales, could you talk to me about what you are doing now?
10:15 A.M.

Karl Murphy
10:16 A.M. Well... I have updated revised user interface for our daily issues. We will publish an upgraded version electronically on March 1.

David Lennon
10:17 A.M. We are all very excited about this publication. It will be far easier for subscribers to find previous articles due to our improved online system. This is compatible with various mobile devices, and it's very user-friendly.

Bella Reynolds
It is essential for us to attract new subscribers. And we need to design more innovative ways to attract them.
10:18 A.M.

Terra Mitchell
10:20 A.M. Let me see... I am working on a new mobile application. The app can be customized to fit individual's needs. One of the functions is that subscribers can put an article they want on its first page.

Karl Murphy
10:21 A.M. Right! Terra told me that subscribers can choose stories through each category. For example, they can put certain articles on their first page, such as sports, entertainment, food, and so on.

Bella Reynolds
That sounds great! Keep me updated as more details emerge.
10:22 A.M.

Terra Mitchell
10:23 A.M. Okay, I'll prepare the outline of this application and its model no later than this Friday.

Bella Reynolds
Good. I would like to see these procedures in person. Tomorrow morning, all of you should see me in my office.
10:24 A.M.

170

172. Where do the writers most likely work?
(A) At a logistics corporation
(B) At an electronics company
(C) At a newspaper company
(D) At a travel agency

173. What is being improved?
(A) Electronic versions of newspapers
(B) Staffing procedures
(C) A building blueprint
(D) A travel package

174. At 10:22 A.M., what does Ms. Reynolds mean when she writes, "That sounds great"?
(A) She approves of Mr. Lennon's proposal of promotion.
(B) She likes the features that Ms. Mitchell is developing.
(C) She is pleased with learning about office processes.
(D) She is satisfied with the staff's current assignments.

175. What will most likely take place tomorrow?
(A) A mobile launch
(B) A customer survey
(C) A demonstration
(D) A marketing promotion

Questions 176-180 refer to the following notice and e-mail.

RETURN POLICY

In order to provide our customers with quality service, Penta Co. will allow them to exchange or get a full refund for all items purchased within 45 days. The amount of the refund or exchange will be equivalent to the original price. We just recommend that our customers comply with the rules below:

- You should bring and present your original receipt when asking for the return or exchange.
- If you do not have the receipt, please provide evidence of your credit card bill for your purchase.
- Defective items may be fully refunded by returning them within 60 days of purchase.
- If you return the defective items after 60 days of purchase, you may receive a refund or exchange for half of the item's original price.
- If you have any questions about store branches and our customer services, do not hesitate to contact us by e-mail, cs_managing@pentaco.com, or by phone, +1-800-381-1923, which is toll-free.

Thank you for your cooperation.

To: cs_managing@pentaco.com
From: julia_sonya@nmail.com

To Whom It May Concern:

My name is Julia Sonya, and I'm writing to inquire about your return policy. I have recently purchased some running shoes from your store in the Eagleville Mall. However, the sole of one of the sneakers fell off and the seams were all frayed just after a week of purchase. A floor salesperson said to me that the sneakers are much stronger and more comfortable than any other brands although they are more expensive. Because of his recommendation, I decided to buy them without hesitation. But, I was really surprised and disappointed by their durability. Of course, my left sneaker remains in good condition, and I would like to continue to wear the shoes by exchanging the right one.

However, I lost my original receipt, and I paid in cash at the time of purchase. How do I check my purchase history for this item? Could I exchange the right shoe only?

I look forward to your response as soon as possible.

Julia Sonya

176. According to the notice, what is mentioned about defective items?

(A) They may be exchanged for a similar item.
(B) They will be inspected for wear and tear.
(C) They may be refunded in full.
(D) They must be returned at a retail branch.

177. Why did Ms. Sonya write an e-mail to the company?

(A) She is disappointed with the customer service.
(B) She has a question about the return policy.
(C) She wants to know about the company's retail stores.
(D) She would like to confirm purchasing procedures.

178. What problem does Ms. Sonya discuss?

(A) An item wasn't discounted.
(B) An item is defective.
(C) An item was out of stock.
(D) The color of an item is wrong.

179. How would Ms. Sonya like to resolve her issue?

(A) By making an exchange
(B) By receiving a voucher
(C) By obtaining proof of purchase
(D) By talking to a manager

180. Why can Ms. Sonya NOT comply with the rules?

(A) She returned only an item without any packaging.
(B) She paid with a credit card that has since expired.
(C) She did not meet the store's returns deadline.
(D) She cannot present proof of payment.

Questions 181-185 refer to the following article and e-mail.

Never Stop Selling!

By Joe Klein, *Prime Magazine*, Chief Writer

March 20—Isabella Jermain watched the last few customers leave the store on February 24. She has been the manager of Giant Eagle Mart for over fifteen years, but the mart has been closed. Its store in Santa Barbara was a part of a family-owned chain that has been acquired by the Sheetz Corporation.

The Sheetz Corporation, based in San Francisco, has been buying stores throughout the western United States and rapidly converting them into Sheetz stores. It is hoped that the quick turnaround would prevent existing customers from taking their shopping to other markets. Ms. Jermain and most of her employees still remain at the store to work with the new company. Ms. Jermain had no idea exactly how sizable and complicated the acquisition would be. "I was amazed by its processing speed," she said. "A group of contractors, along with Sheetz's staff, descended upon our store on March 1. They worked night and day, removing refrigerator units and installing new ones, painting walls, and replacing flooring and shelves. The huge "Sheetz" sign in front of the store was installed by replacing the previous one, and it was changed in an instant."

Finally, all of the products and groceries were labeled and placed on the new shelves. On Sunday, March 12, tired but smiling Ms. Jermain was there to cut the ribbon and welcomed customers at the newest Sheetz.

From:	Arnold Kane <a_kane@sheetz.com>
To:	Isabella Jermain <i_jermain@sheetz.com>
Subject:	Progression
Date:	March 15

Dear Ms. Jermain,

I am so grateful that you were able to stay on as manager and that most of the existing staff have stayed together. I strongly believe that you were a very dedicated team, and it was a pleasure working with you there. I have assisted several stores in California—such as branches in Santa Barbara, Fresno, Palo Alto, and Long Beach—with their transitions, and none of them went as smoothly as yours did.

Thank you for your outstanding cooperation. I am confident that everything will continue to run well. Please do not hesitate to contact me with any questions or concerns.

Best regards,

Arnold Kane
General Manager of Department of Franchise Operations
Sheetz Corporation

181. What is indicated about Ms. Jermain?

(A) She has been promoted to the director of the headquarters.
(B) She has decided to resign from the new company.
(C) She has asked an executive to hire additional staff.
(D) She has held the same position for more than ten years.

182. When did the newest Sheetz store open?

(A) On February 24
(B) On March 10
(C) On March 12
(D) On March 15

183. Why did Mr. Kane send the e-mail?

(A) To express his appreciation
(B) To look for a new manager
(C) To request the store's sales report
(D) To announce the grand opening event

184. Where did Mr. Kane work with Ms. Jermain?

(A) San Francisco
(B) Santa Barbara
(C) Long Beach
(D) Palo Alto

185. In the e-mail, the word "run" in paragraph 2, line 1, is closest in meaning to

(A) understand
(B) race
(C) function
(D) open

Questions 186-190 refer to the following Web pages and review.

| Home | About Us | Property | Contact Us |

Delaney Realty

Greensburg's newest, most innovative property management group

Our goal is very simple!

To provide high-quality, amenity-rich houses at reasonable rental prices, we are now remodeling four old buildings in different areas. One-year leases on the new properties will be available beginning in September.

Click the property banner at the top of this page.

(When you click the building number, you can see its pictures and floor plans.)
- All of Delaney's apartment complexes have an on-site gym and extra storage rooms only for residents.
- Studio units start at $600 a month; 1 bedrooms start at $750 a month; 2 bedrooms start at $900 a month!

Need some short-term leases?

Click #606! – The first floor of this complex is the only short-term and fully-furnished rental space in the city.
(Rates start $70 a day — 10% discounts for a one-week lease)

NOTE: Units marked with " * " are affordable for college students, who may qualify for rental reduction under the city's Educational Financial Aid (EFA) — visit www.greensburg.org/EFA for details.

| Home | About Us | Property | Contact Us |

Freely Check the Below Properties.
Click the building number!

Building Number	Location	Adjacent Area	Date of Rentability
#120*	120 Fleming Ave.	Johns Town	September 20
#606	606 Courtland Rd.	Monroeville	September 10
#990*	990 Washington Drive	Indiana Valley	September 20
#428	428 Glendale St.	Altoona	September 1

If you want to know more information, please feel free to get in touch by clicking "Contact Us" at the top of the page.

Greensburg City Living

The latest updates about houses and apartments in our area

Look at a new property management group's renovated town houses.

Posted by Catherine James on October 5

With several other realty news articles and reviews on Web sites, I have been following the progress of Delaney's renovations for some time now. I have also been reading comments posted on the real estate group's newly introduced resident forum, and I've posted it on GREEN REALTY NEWS.

A few days ago, I had an opportunity to visit building #990 thanks to my acquaintance's invitation. It was a little small but impressive with a fully furnished kitchen including the newest home appliances. The complex's gym was well-equipped with excellent sporting equipment, but the extra storage room has been still under construction. My friend said that it will be finished next month. In addition, the eastern side of the complex has been undergoing repairs and upgrades. However, she said that the noise hasn't been a serious issue so far.

By all accounts, the building's apartments and town houses look very comfortable but are a little bit expensive, given the space offered. My current apartment on Oak Grove Avenue in the same area costs the same as a Delaney one but it is more spacious.

---

186. What information is NOT provided on the Web pages?

(A) Links to maps of city neighborhoods
(B) A real estate agency's mission statement
(C) Links to units' previews of each building
(D) The rental prices of complex units

187. Which building most likely would offer weekly rentals?

(A) #120
(B) #606
(C) #990
(D) #428

188. Where most likely was the review posted?

(A) On a Web site for tourists
(B) On a public bulletin board
(C) On an online real estate news site
(D) On a residents' discussion forum

189. According to the review, what most likely is true about Delaney Realty?

(A) It did not complete some renovations before the move-in date.
(B) It does not have any unoccupied units at present.
(C) It charges extra fees for the use of a fitness center.
(D) It is not related to the city's EFA program.

190. In which neighborhood does Ms. James live?

(A) Johns Town
(B) Monroeville
(C) Indiana Valley
(D) Altoona

Questions 191-195 refer to the following article, form, and e-mail.

Seattle Daily

Agencies' Support for Recruiting

by Serra Jones

Seattle (May 10)—It is hard for local companies to find good employees in many ways. In order to make their recruiting processes effective, some companies hire staffing agencies. Whether a company wants employees for a temporary or permanent job, or one that requires experience, subcontracting this process to the agencies can save time and money compared to doing it themselves.

"Companies can benefit from hiring competent employees for their part-time jobs," said Paul Kay, the general manager of SA Headhunter Co., which is one of the oldest staffing agencies in Seattle. In addition, he said that companies can solve some urgent and unexpected problems they face and even evaluate a prospective employee before offering a person a full-time job.

To give help to our local employers, we have posted a select list of staffing agencies on our Web site, www.seattledaily.com/job_bulletin.

SA Headhunter Co.

TEMPORARY EMPLOYEE REQUEST FORM

Employer Information

NAME	John Stockton
COMPANY	Three Rivers Accounting
INDUSTRY	Accounting & Finance
PHONE	702-183-1283
E-MAIL	j_stockton@threerivers.net

Assignment Information

Needed Number	5-6
Positions	Office Assistant
Working Duration	About a Month

Description
Recently, we have contracted several important audits with the state government and some other companies. Because of these tasks, we have to arrange and classify a wide range of documents. In compliance with our state law, we need to categorize the documents into each public and private section. The ideal candidate is someone who majored in Law or Administration and can review the documents meticulously.

How did you find out about us?
Saw the article in the 2nd Edition of May of *The Seattle Daily*

THANK YOU FOR YOUR SUBMISSION

** One of our agents will contact you within 24 hours.

From: John Stockton <j_stockton@threerivers.net>
To: Jane Fetterman <jane@saheadhunter.com>
Subject: RE: YOUR REQUEST
Date: May 23

Dear Ms. Fetterman,

I would like to extend my gratitude for your help. For the first time, I contacted a recruiting agency like your company, so I was not confident about hiring a good employee through that kind of service. Thanks to your support, it was no trouble to arrange for the temporary staff. You e-mailed me within only two hours after my online submission and listed qualified employees in the next correspondence within just eight hours. The employees you recommended to us are industrious, proficient, and passionate. As a matter of fact, our HR department has decided to offer three of the employees an interview for permanent jobs.

Regards,

John Stockton
Human Resources Department
Three Rivers Accounting

---

191. In the article, what benefit is NOT mentioned about the agencies' services?

(A) Saving a company money
(B) Helping to resolve a company's emergency
(C) Getting specialized assistance
(D) Making the hiring process easier

192. What is suggested about Mr. Stockton?

(A) He was interviewed by Ms. Jones.
(B) His company is listed on the *Seattle Daily's* Web site.
(C) His company is older than SA Headhunter Co.
(D) He read Ms. Jones's article.

193. On the form, the word "duration" in paragraph 2, line 3, is closest in meaning to

(A) amount
(B) urgency
(C) length
(D) estimate

194. What is the purpose of the e-mail?

(A) To express thanks for a service provided
(B) To voice a complaint about employee work habits
(C) To confirm a request for additional staff
(D) To inquire about positions at a staffing agency

195. Who most likely is Ms. Fetterman?

(A) A temporary employee
(B) An assistant of Mr. Stockton
(C) A staffing agent with SA Headhunter Co.
(D) A government official

Questions 196-200 refer to the following text message, schedule, and e-mail.

TO: Joshua Storm

FROM: Sophie Bell

SENT: August 15, 10:30 A.M.

JD Wave Band has unexpectedly had to cancel their performance at Georgia Festival next week. The Madison Square Stage at 6:30 P.M. is now available. If your group is still interested in the performance, please let me know as soon as possible. We should print out the brochure about the upcoming event tomorrow.

Georgia Festival

Performance Schedule
Friday, August 25

	4:30 P.M.	5:30 P.M.	6:30 P.M.	7:30 P.M.
Trevi Fountain Stage	Supersonic	Pirate Buccos	Cozy Comfy	
Penn Way Stage		Rising Sun		Lafayette Locals
Madison Square Stage	Bruno Brothers		Prism Band	

NOTE:

The first 50 people to arrive will receive a 20 percent discount on parking. Please note that outside food and beverages are not permitted, but complimentary refreshments will be provided. Participants are allowed to bring their own outdoor chairs and blankets because there are no seats available. There is no rain date for the festival; check the day of the event for weather updates through the Web site, www.georgiastate.org/stateweather.

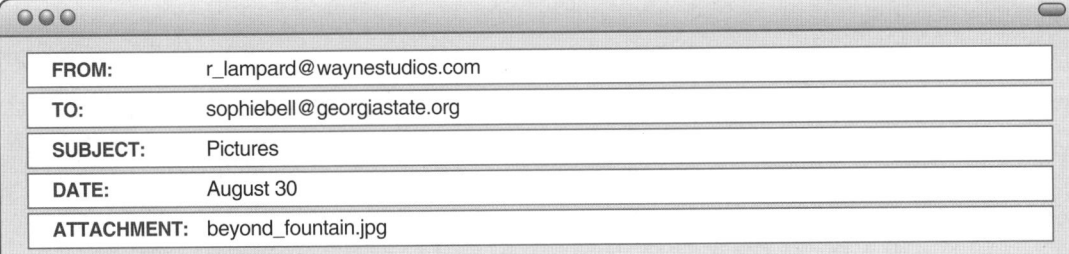

Dear Ms. Bell,

This festival was really great! Thanks to the ticket you sent to me, I fully enjoyed our state's proud event. Although I have not yet developed all of my pictures I took at the event, I have attached one picture that I think is really excellent. On the Trevi Fountain Stage, Cozy Comfy was taken in this photo, and the scenic view of the sunset beyond the stage was very beautiful. I strongly believe that this is a great one for posting on the festival's main page on the Web. After looking through all of the remaining pictures, I will make the list of outstanding pictures and send you the files by e-mail, which can be used for the next festival advertising materials.

Best wishes,

Ron Lampard
Wayne Studios

196. According to the text message, what will happen on August 16?

(A) Stages will be renovated.
(B) Mr. Storm will perform at a festival.
(C) A schedule will be published.
(D) JD Wave Band will begin a concert tour.

197. What is the name of Mr. Storm's group?

(A) Prism Band
(B) Rising Sun
(C) Supersonic
(D) Bruno Brothers

198. What is suggested about the event?

(A) Parking is free for all in-state residents.
(B) Free food will be available.
(C) Some seats incur additional fees.
(D) The activities will be rescheduled soon.

199. What is implied about Mr. Lampard's pictures?

(A) They will be exhibited in the state public gallery.
(B) They can be used in advertisements for the next event.
(C) They can be sold at a fundraising event for charity.
(D) They will be submitted for a photography contest.

200. When did Mr. Lampard most likely take the picture attached to the e-mail?

(A) At 4:30 P.M.
(B) At 5:30 P.M.
(C) At 6:30 P.M.
(D) At 7:30 P.M.

Stop! This is the end of the test. If you finish before time is called, you may go back to Parts 5, 6, and 7 and check your work.

MP3와 해설 파일은 온라인에서 제공됩니다.
▶▶ books.english.co.kr

TEST 05

test 05.mp3 | 정답 p.298

LISTENING TEST

In the Listening test, you will be asked to demonstrate how well you understand spoken English. The entire Listening test will last approximately 45 minutes. There are four parts, and directions are given for each part. You must mark your answers on the separate answer sheet.
Do not write your answers in your test book.

PART 1

Directions: For each question in this part, you will hear four statements about a picture in your test book. When you hear the statements, you must select the one statement that best describes what you see in the picture. Then find the number of the question on your answer sheet and mark your answer. The statements will not be printed in your test book and will be spoken only one time.

Statement (B), "They're shaking hands," is the best description of the picture, so you should select answer (B) and mark it on your answer sheet.

1.

2.

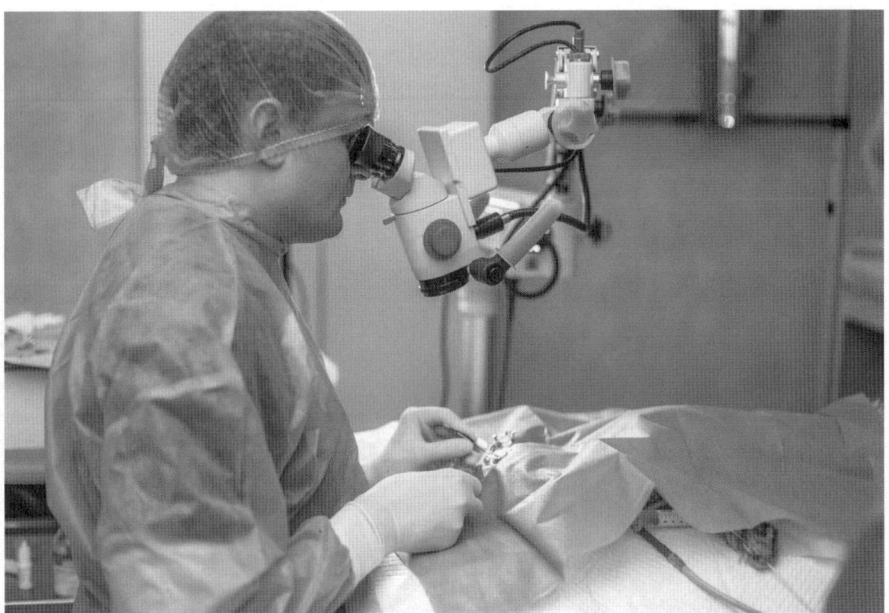

3.

4.

5.

6.

PART 2

Directions: You will hear a question or statement and three responses spoken in English. They will not be printed in your test book and will be spoken only one time. Select the best response to the question or statement and mark the letter (A), (B), or (C) on your answer sheet.

7. Mark your answer on your answer sheet.
8. Mark your answer on your answer sheet.
9. Mark your answer on your answer sheet.
10. Mark your answer on your answer sheet.
11. Mark your answer on your answer sheet.
12. Mark your answer on your answer sheet.
13. Mark your answer on your answer sheet.
14. Mark your answer on your answer sheet.
15. Mark your answer on your answer sheet.
16. Mark your answer on your answer sheet.
17. Mark your answer on your answer sheet.
18. Mark your answer on your answer sheet.
19. Mark your answer on your answer sheet.
20. Mark your answer on your answer sheet.
21. Mark your answer on your answer sheet.
22. Mark your answer on your answer sheet.
23. Mark your answer on your answer sheet.
24. Mark your answer on your answer sheet.
25. Mark your answer on your answer sheet.
26. Mark your answer on your answer sheet.
27. Mark your answer on your answer sheet.
28. Mark your answer on your answer sheet.
29. Mark your answer on your answer sheet.
30. Mark your answer on your answer sheet.
31. Mark your answer on your answer sheet.

PART 3

Directions: You will hear some conversations between two or more people. You will be asked to answer three questions about what the speakers say in each conversation. Select the best response to each question and mark the letter (A), (B), (C), or (D) on your answer sheet. The conversations will not be printed in your test book and will be spoken only one time.

32. Where does the man work?
    (A) At a restaurant
    (B) At a hotel
    (C) At a catering company
    (D) At a convention center

33. Why is the woman calling?
    (A) To alter a reservation
    (B) To rent a conference room
    (C) To purchase tickets
    (D) To order meals

34. What does the man suggest the woman do?
    (A) Change the booking time
    (B) Reserve a private room
    (C) Choose a different place
    (D) Cancel the reservation

35. What does the woman want to know?
    (A) The man's availability
    (B) The date of a workshop
    (C) The location of a function
    (D) The name of a product

36. What is the man most likely planning to do this week?
    (A) Drop by headquarters
    (B) Seek overseas markets
    (C) Open another branch
    (D) Prepare for an event

37. What is the man asked to do?
    (A) Provide a brief demonstration
    (B) Purchase additional equipment
    (C) Check his schedule
    (D) Explain his absence

38. What event does the man want to attend?
    (A) A celebration party
    (B) A press conference
    (C) The opening of a museum
    (D) A movie screening

39. According to the woman, what is the problem?
    (A) There was a problem with a Web site.
    (B) She cannot find her tickets.
    (C) The building is in need of renovations.
    (D) Free tickets are unavailable.

40. What information does the woman request?
    (A) Personal information
    (B) An address code
    (C) The method of payment
    (D) A preferred time

41. Where do the speakers most likely work?
    (A) At a packaging company
    (B) At a glass factory
    (C) At a logistics firm
    (D) At a real estate agency

42. What will take place in November?
    (A) A board of director's meeting
    (B) A opening of a new branch
    (C) A relocation of a facility
    (D) A corporate merger

43. What does the woman imply when she says, "we'll just wait and see what the board of directors decide"?
    (A) She is unsatisfied about the rent.
    (B) She believes the space is too small.
    (C) She disagrees with a colleague.
    (D) She thinks the facility requires refurbishment.

GO ON TO THE NEXT PAGE

44. What department does the woman work in?
    (A) Design
    (B) Sales
    (C) Quality Control
    (D) Advertising

45. How does the new program differ from the previous one?
    (A) It has a safer system.
    (B) It has more features.
    (C) It is more expensive.
    (D) It takes less time to use.

46. What does the man suggest the woman do?
    (A) Update some software
    (B) Speak to some of their co-workers
    (C) Take part in a training program
    (D) Demonstrate how to use some software

47. Where do the speakers most likely work?
    (A) At a gift shop
    (B) At a radio station
    (C) At a stationery store
    (D) At a gallery

48. Why does the man want to purchase boxes?
    (A) To place some items in
    (B) To organize his office
    (C) To send some packages
    (D) To pack his personal belongings

49. What will the man probably do next?
    (A) Make a phone call
    (B) Visit the woman's office
    (C) Make a list of necessary items
    (D) Distribute complimentary gifts

50. According to the woman, why do the speakers have to meet?
    (A) To modify some mistakes in a report
    (B) To make a budget for the current year
    (C) To give a product demonstration
    (D) To discuss a proposal

51. What problem do the men mention?
    (A) No room is available for a meeting.
    (B) A contract has expired.
    (C) Their availability is limited.
    (D) A request for leave was denied.

52. What will the woman arrange?
    (A) Free access to the office
    (B) More information on contractors
    (C) An orientation session for new employees
    (D) Precise budget allocations

53. What does the woman ask the man to do?
    (A) Go to the head office
    (B) Give her a ride to the office
    (C) Drop off the store key
    (D) Open a store

54. What does the man mean when he says, "As it happens, I am working this weekend"?
    (A) He cannot join the woman for lunch.
    (B) He accepts the woman's request.
    (C) He works every weekend.
    (D) He looks forward to working with the woman.

55. What does the woman say she will do?
    (A) Contact headquarters
    (B) Send a fax
    (C) Check her schedule
    (D) Put off an appointment

56. What are the speakers mainly discussing?
    (A) A reimbursement process
    (B) A cost of advertising
    (C) Some budget cuts
    (D) An advertising seminar

57. What information does the man ask the woman for?
    (A) The purpose of the advertisement
    (B) The period of the advertisement
    (C) The type of advertisement
    (D) The starting date of the advertisement

58. How can the woman get a discount?
    (A) By paying more than 100 pounds
    (B) By making a cash payment
    (C) By placing an ad for a certain period of time
    (D) By participating in a survey

59. What do the speakers sell?
    (A) DVDs
    (B) CD players
    (C) Books
    (D) Printers

60. What are the speakers concerned about?
    (A) Their business has been underperforming.
    (B) Their products are easily broken.
    (C) Their company's stock price has declined.
    (D) Other stores are selling the same products at cheaper prices.

61. What does the woman suggest?
    (A) Using discount coupons
    (B) Giving away new products
    (C) Thinking about a sales strategy
    (D) Asking for customers' feedback

Training Programs	
Class A	April 23 (Mon) / April 24 (Tue)
Class B	April 23 (Mon)
Class C	April 24 (Tue) / April 25 (Wed)
Class D	April 24 (Tue)

62. What is the man's problem?
    (A) He isn't interested in any classes.
    (B) He wasn't informed of the program.
    (C) He has a schedule conflict.
    (D) He forgot to organize a meeting.

63. What does the man say about the graphic software class?
    (A) It will only be offered one time.
    (B) It is offered every year.
    (C) No textbook is required for it.
    (D) He can take it online.

64. Look at the graphic. What class did the woman sign up for?
    (A) Class A
    (B) Class B
    (C) Class C
    (D) Class D

Meeting Schedule

10:00 – 11:00	New products education
11:00 – 12:00	Sales planning
01:00 – 02:00	Quarterly financial review
02:00 – 03:00	New employee orientation

65. What has the woman forgotten to bring?

(A) A key
(B) A phone
(C) A sample
(D) A computer

66. Look at the graphic. Which meeting will the woman attend?

(A) New products education
(B) Sales planning
(C) Quarterly financial review
(D) New employee orientation

67. What does the man say he will do?

(A) Send the woman an e-mail
(B) Stop by a computer repair shop
(C) Attend a meeting
(D) Head for headquarters

Cosmetic IZ-2 Rating

Quality	★ ★ ★ ★ ★
Price	★ ★ ★ ★
Quantity	★
Packaging	★ ★

68. Who did the woman meet this afternoon?

(A) Cosmetics manufacturers
(B) Marketing directors
(C) Retail representatives
(D) Customers

69. What does the man ask the woman to do?

(A) Send some information to another department
(B) Go to the Marketing Department
(C) Hold a press conference
(D) Test the company's new cosmetics

70. Look at the graphic. Which item will be discussed first?

(A) Quality
(B) Price
(C) Quantity
(D) Packaging

PART 4

Directions: You will hear some talks given by a single speaker. You will be asked to answer three questions about what the speaker says in each talk. Select the best response to each question and mark the letter (A), (B), (C), or (D) on your answer sheet. The talks will not be printed in your test book and will be spoken only one time.

71. Who is this announcement intended for?
    (A) Journalists
    (B) Ski instructors
    (C) Winter sports athletes
    (D) Newscasters

72. According to the speaker, what can listeners do on the Web site?
    (A) Check out entry requirements
    (B) Download an application form
    (C) Install new apps
    (D) Submit suggestions

73. What will happen at the end of the week?
    (A) The winners will be announced.
    (B) A competition will start.
    (C) The deadline for applications will end.
    (D) A sporting event will be officially held.

74. What kind of business is the speaker calling?
    (A) An insurance firm
    (B) A publishing company
    (C) A community center
    (D) A law firm

75. What is the speaker having trouble with?
    (A) Connecting to the Internet
    (B) Submitting a claim
    (C) Canceling a contract
    (D) Issuing a passport

76. What does the speaker ask the listener to do?
    (A) Reschedule an appointment
    (B) Send a reference letter
    (C) Resolve the problem
    (D) Transfer her some money

77. Who is the speaker?
    (A) A tour guide
    (B) A bus driver
    (C) A professor of zoology
    (D) A travel agent

78. What does the speaker imply when he says, "You're not aware of wild animals, aren't you"?
    (A) He wants the tour to be held more often.
    (B) He wants people to apply for an audio tour.
    (C) He wants to sign up for the tour for a cheap price.
    (D) He wants to meet a famous nature expert.

79. What will the listeners most likely do next?
    (A) Receive some audio players
    (B) Listen to an expert
    (C) Go around the area
    (D) Purchase tickets

80. What construction project is the speaker discussing?
    (A) A parking lot
    (B) A subway line
    (C) A highway
    (D) A bus terminal

81. Why has construction been suspended?
    (A) There was a blackout in the city.
    (B) There were inclement weather conditions.
    (C) The city has insufficient funds.
    (D) There is a lack of workers.

82. According to the speaker, what will be available after the project is completed?
    (A) Access to the main stations
    (B) Lower fares
    (C) Extended service hours
    (D) More Wall Street Station exits

GO ON TO THE NEXT PAGE

83. What is the speaker mainly discussing?
   (A) The types of projects assigned
   (B) Preparations for a company event
   (C) The status of some training materials
   (D) The location of a workshop

84. Why does the speaker say, "They're probably familiar with how to move those machines"?
   (A) To propose another option
   (B) To stress her dissatisfaction with a service
   (C) To give the reason for a choice
   (D) To agree with Mr. Perlman's opinion

85. What is the listener asked to do?
   (A) Book a flight
   (B) Rent some vehicles
   (C) Read some information
   (D) Invite some new employees

86. Who most likely is the speaker?
   (A) A tour conductor
   (B) A tourist
   (C) An artist
   (D) A product designer

87. According to the speaker, what kind of art did Mr. Adams create?
   (A) Murals
   (B) Abstract paintings
   (C) Portraits
   (D) Landscape paintings

88. What can the visitors do at the end of the tour?
   (A) Go to the souvenir shop
   (B) Take a picture with the tour guide
   (C) Meet with the head of the gallery
   (D) Listen to a lecture on art history

89. What happened last week?
   (A) New employees were hired.
   (B) An office was rented.
   (C) A company was relocated.
   (D) A property was shown.

90. What does the speaker inquire about?
   (A) Removing some furniture
   (B) Leasing a parking space
   (C) Examining a contract
   (D) Reconfirming a payment

91. What does the speaker ask the listener to do?
   (A) Explain a renovation plan
   (B) Give an estimated time for work
   (C) Renew a rental contract
   (D) Provide an accurate quotation

92. What is the news mainly about?
   (A) A merger between two firms
   (B) Projections of economic growth
   (C) Public opinions regarding a construction project
   (D) The construction of a business park

93. What are the residents worried about?
   (A) Pollution levels may increase.
   (B) There will be traffic problems.
   (C) Business will be depressed.
   (D) Property values will drop.

94. What will take place in two weeks?
   (A) Construction work will start.
   (B) Some information will be released.
   (C) The renovation will be completed.
   (D) A conflict between two companies will be resolved.

OPERATION HOURS	
Monday	8 A.M. – 6 P.M.
Tuesday	8 A.M. – 10 P.M.
Wednesday	8 A.M. – 6 P.M. (every other week)
Thursday	8 A.M. – 6 P.M.
Friday	8 A.M. – 7 P.M. (every other week)

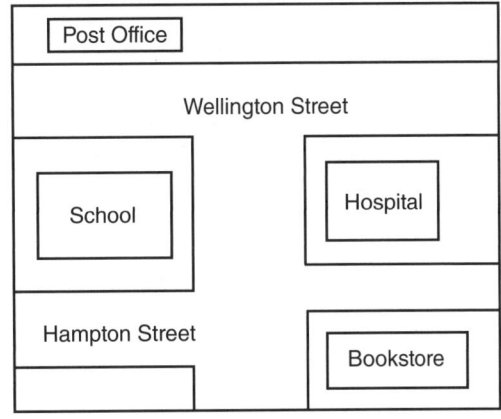

95. What kind of business is Alice's?
    (A) A clinic
    (B) An insurance agency
    (C) A counseling center
    (D) A pharmacy

96. Look at the graphic. Which day indicates the wrong business hours?
    (A) Monday
    (B) Tuesday
    (C) Wednesday
    (D) Friday

97. What does the speaker say is available on a Web site?
    (A) A sign-up sheet
    (B) A price list
    (C) A contact number
    (D) A map

98. Look at the graphic. Which building will be least affected by the festival?
    (A) The post office
    (B) The school
    (C) The hospital
    (D) The bookstore

99. According to the speaker, what will happen tomorrow?
    (A) A subway station will be closed.
    (B) There will be a restricted area.
    (C) New employees will be hired.
    (D) The furniture will be arranged.

100. What are the listeners asked to do to work extra hours?
    (A) Confirm a list
    (B) Write their names
    (C) Raise their hands
    (D) Attend an orientation session

This is the end of the Listening test. Turn to Part 5 in your test book.

READING TEST

In the Reading test, you will read a variety of texts and answer several different types of reading comprehension questions. The entire Reading test will last 75 minutes. There are three parts, and directions are given for each part. You are encouraged to answer as many questions as possible within the time allowed.

You must mark your answers on the separate answer sheet. Do not write your answers in the test book.

PART 5

Directions: A word or phrase is missing in each of the sentences below. Four answer choices are given below each sentence. Select the best answer to complete the sentence. Then mark the letter (A), (B), (C), or (D) on your answer sheet.

101. In light of the problems experienced with the Meteora project, Ms. Evans asked for an ------- of the deadline.
    (A) extensively
    (B) extend
    (C) extensive
    (D) extension

102. Please fill out all parts of the application forms, as only ------- forms will be considered.
    (A) complete
    (B) completes
    (C) completely
    (D) completing

103. As we were running short of time, Mr. Raymond had no choice but to work late -------.
    (A) he
    (B) his
    (C) himself
    (D) his own

104. Show schedules are adjusted and made ------- to current TD Broadband cable subscribers on a weekly basis.
    (A) convenient
    (B) potential
    (C) available
    (D) decisive

105. Ms. Semi will revise the data sheets ------- after the information comes in from Greensburg office.
    (A) immediate
    (B) immediately
    (C) immediacy
    (D) immediateness

106. Stock trading is ------- without analysts' help, but our new online system can do that easily.
    (A) generous
    (B) demonstrative
    (C) manageable
    (D) challenging

107. Implementing Mr. Berni's proposal was more complicated than everyone had -------.
    (A) anticipate
    (B) anticipating
    (C) anticipation
    (D) anticipated

108. The state's Education Department will present a ------- of hands-on art workshops.
    (A) safety
    (B) range
    (C) piece
    (D) matter

109. We wish to ------- your accomplishment at an award ceremony at the Apple Grand Ballroom on Friday, August 5.
(A) celebrate
(B) celebrating
(C) celebrated
(D) celebrity

110. The sales figures rose rapidly, pleasing staff at the headquarters, ------- Mr. James eventually landed the position of CEO.
(A) who
(B) what
(C) when
(D) where

111. Several one-of-a-kind devices will be available at ------- prices if you have this voucher.
(A) discounted
(B) generated
(C) experienced
(D) demonstrated

112. The company president required Ms. Jasmin ------- handle the contract negotiations in place of Mr. O'Reilly.
(A) at
(B) of
(C) for
(D) to

113. The consultant recommended ------- our company make a detailed employment manual for new recruits.
(A) what
(B) that
(C) when
(D) whether

114. In order to serve our patients as effectively and ------- as possible, we are offering appointment reminders.
(A) relying
(B) reliable
(C) reliably
(D) reliant

115. An employee in Personnel explained what new employees need to know ------- their employment package.
(A) concerning
(B) throughout
(C) in addition to
(D) in spite of

116. Thanks to the effort of the LEMI Group, ------- numbers at the Kovalchick Center have doubled.
(A) visit
(B) visits
(C) visitor
(D) visiting

117. All divisions must submit their orders to Mr. Harbour by the second Monday of each month to ------- with the new system.
(A) match
(B) comply
(C) maintain
(D) concentrate

118. The ------- of TP Distribution's branches in Busan could cause loss of productivity and efficiency in many ways.
(A) close
(B) closed
(C) closing
(D) closely

119. As of next Friday, the city government will enforce the safety regulations to limit the scale of building -------.
(A) expression
(B) application
(C) impression
(D) renovation

120. All the staff should obtain permission from their immediate boss ------- they need to remain in the building after normal working hours.
(A) whenever
(B) however
(C) whichever
(D) whatever

GO ON TO THE NEXT PAGE

121. Each vehicle produced by Autobahn Motors undergoes a variety of ------- before it is sent to local dealers.
    (A) tests
    (B) markets
    (C) trades
    (D) shares

122. You can work through the end of the business day or stop work at 5:00 P.M. tomorrow ------- originally planned.
    (A) because
    (B) in order that
    (C) since
    (D) as

123. Please be aware that returns of items are only accepted ------- fifteen days of purchase.
    (A) despite
    (B) beyond
    (C) along
    (D) within

124. The package containing your order will take about two or three days to reach you ------- mailed.
    (A) once
    (B) again
    (C) out of
    (D) now that

125. Our salary rates are ------- differently depending on the employee's previous experience in the related field.
    (A) calculate
    (B) calculated
    (C) calculation
    (D) calculating

126. Although residents ------- agree to the plan for boosting the city's economy, some oppose any commercial development of the area.
    (A) generally
    (B) precisely
    (C) roughly
    (D) fluently

127. This pass not only allows you ------- the exhibitions at half price, but also grants you access to our workshop free of charge.
    (A) attention
    (B) attending
    (C) to attend
    (D) attended

128. Our Asian and African markets have grown ------- strong since the company's branches expanded into those continents.
    (A) consideration
    (B) considerable
    (C) considerate
    (D) considerably

129. Packages that have not been picked up after one month should be kept wherever there is room in the ------- facility.
    (A) solution
    (B) storage
    (C) delivery
    (D) retail

130. The amount of $200 which you were overcharged has been automatically ------- to your account.
    (A) permitted
    (B) believed
    (C) credited
    (D) replied

PART 6

Directions: Read the texts that follow. A word, phrase, or sentence is missing in parts of each text. Four answer choices for each question are given below the text. Select the best answer to complete the text. Then mark the letter (A), (B), (C), or (D) on your answer sheet.

Questions 131-134 refer to the following memo.

To: Department Managers
From: Senior Designer, Kamil Graphic
Subject: Tech Today Magazine Review

A recent review in *Tech Today Magazine* highly praised our latest laptop computers. Both their design and performance ------- in particular, setting us apart from most of our competitors.
131.

However, the review was not entirely -------. There still remains an issue with its durability, which
132.
has been raised through the consumer report.

Our own research has indicated that some of the parts made of plastic are too vulnerable -------
133.
the internal heating system. It can cause some problems with other components inside the PC mainframe.

I recommend two solutions to this issue. First, we need to repair the damaged computers free of charge. Secondly, we should be sure to use more durable materials in our next products.

-------.
134.

131. (A) mentioned
     (B) are mentioning
     (C) were mentioned
     (D) will be mentioned

132. (A) relevant
     (B) positive
     (C) frustrated
     (D) essential

133. (A) since
     (B) upon
     (C) despite
     (D) due to

134. (A) I look forward to hearing your comments on these by Wednesday.
     (B) The publishing company will give you the editor's contact information soon.
     (C) All the supervisors are considering whether to update the system.
     (D) Please feel free to contact us to get new information.

Questions 135-138 refer to the following announcement.

All computers in our offices will receive notification messages this afternoon regarding updating an essential security software program.

-------. You can continue to use your computer during the installation of the set-up files, although you may ------- that your computer's speed is a bit slower than usual. After these security updates are in place, you need to restart your computer. -------, if you have urgent tasks, you can defer the installation until you have spare time for the update. We sincerely apologize for any ------- and inconvenience because of it and thank you for your understanding.

135. (A) Those updates are connected with other mobile devices.
(B) Do not hesitate to contact us about the questions.
(C) These updates will start automatically at 5 P.M.
(D) The latest model of computers is very popular with the public.

136. (A) notice
(B) convince
(C) enhance
(D) commence

137. (A) Similarly
(B) Rather
(C) However
(D) Besides

138. (A) disrupt
(B) disruptive
(C) disruption
(D) disruptively

Questions 139-142 refer to the following e-mail.

To: <j_wick@gammamail.com>
From: <customer@giantshopping.com>
Subject: Coms Sales for TFY members
Date: June 20

Dear Mr. Wick,

We believe that you would like to know that Coms is lowering its prices for many of our most popular ------- and accessories. In addition, Coms is giving TFY members exclusive access to its special
139.
promotional program for a limited time. -------. Up to a 35 percent discount can be applicable for
140.
products such as Coms desktops, laptops, and tablets. -------, customers who use this offer can get the
141.
extended warranty service and the technical service. If items TFY members purchased are sold at other stores at lower prices, you will ------- the difference.
142.

Click **here** to view special offers for our members.

139. (A) computers
 (B) furniture
 (C) stores
 (D) magazines

140. (A) Items can be purchased for personal use or sent as gifts.
 (B) You will find special offers not available to the public.
 (C) Action must be taken before the July 25 deadline.
 (D) TFY members report receiving the best customer service.

141. (A) Equally
 (B) For instance
 (C) Moreover
 (D) However

142. (A) complain
 (B) notify
 (C) pay
 (D) receive

Questions 143-146 refer to the following memo.

To: All Prudent Insurance Staff
From: Kathy Stella, CEO, Prudent Insurance
Subject: M&A Issue
Date: August 20

I am happy to notify all the staff that the merger between Prudent Insurance and Standard Bank will be finalized on August 30. From that date -------, the company's name will be Prudent Bancassurance Group. This merger will enable us to become one of the largest ------- of commercial banking and insurance in Europe.

143.
144.

Don't worry about your job status! Based on your current employment contract, your position, benefits package, and salaries will remain without any changes. -------.

145.

The merger will change some company policies in some areas. ------- will be shared during the formal company-wide conference on September 2 at 2 P.M. in the grand auditorium. If you have a question about the merger, please feel free to bring your inquiries there.

146.

143. (A) forward
(B) still
(C) besides
(D) last

144. (A) provide
(B) providers
(C) provided
(D) providing

145. (A) The modified rules will be under negotiation between Prudent and Standard.
(B) Our company needs more experienced staff in many departments.
(C) Please complete the formal document with three recommendation letters.
(D) In case some revisions are needed, look through your document thoroughly.

146. (A) Their
(B) Neither
(C) These
(D) Other

PART 7

Directions: In this part you will read a selection of texts, such as magazine and newspaper articles, e-mails, and instant messages. Each text or set of texts is followed by several questions. Select the best answer for each question and mark the letter (A), (B), (C), or (D) on your answer sheet.

Questions 147-148 refer to the following memo.

OFFICE MESSAGE

To: Chris Butterfield
From: Robert Dawson
Time: 11:25 A.M., Tuesday

Telephone    **Walk-in**

Message:
Your client Maria Hill came in and asked about your availability for an interior decorating project. Apparently, she has a friend who needs some work done. She showed me a picture of the space, and it looked like quite a big job. She asked that you call her as soon as possible.

Signed: *Robert Dawson*

147. Why most likely did Ms. Hill visit Mr. Butterfield?

(A) To refer business of a potential client
(B) To thank him for a project
(C) To confirm the meeting schedule
(D) To request photos of some work

148. What will Mr. Butterfield probably do after receiving the message?

(A) Start a project
(B) Visit a friend
(C) Make a phone call
(D) Take some pictures

Questions 149-150 refer to the following text-message chain.

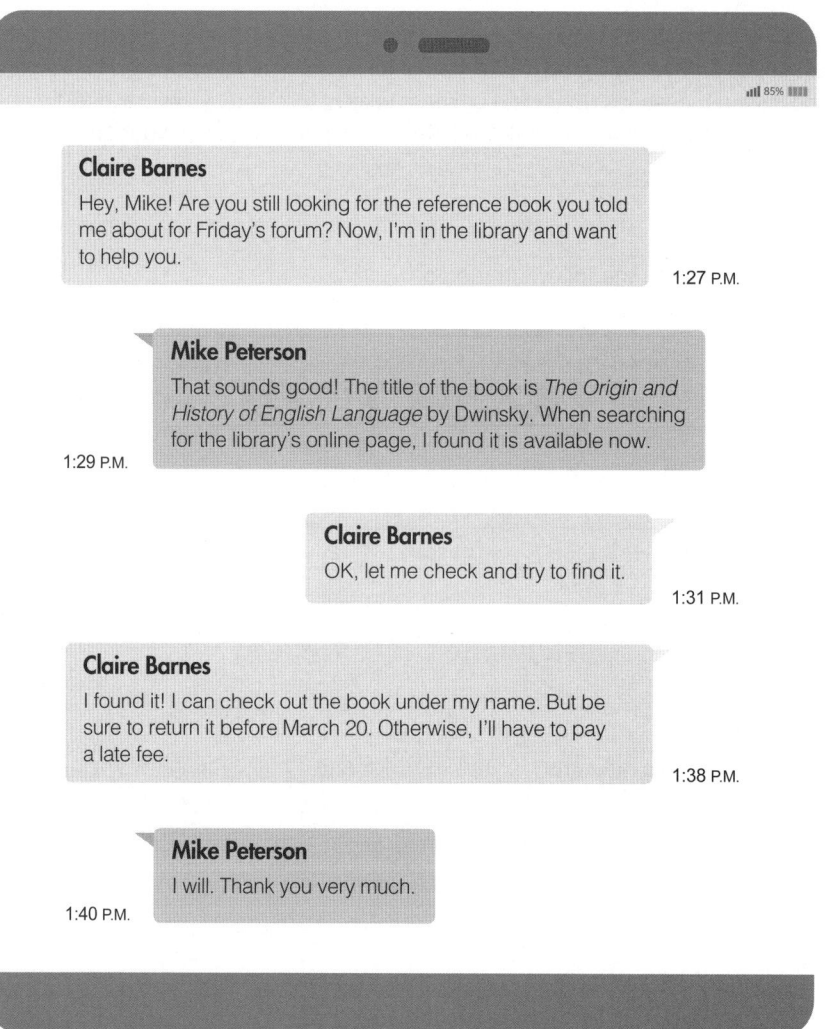

149. What is most likely true about *The Origin and History of English Language*?

(A) It is difficult to find in the library.
(B) It was written by a professor.
(C) It will be mentioned in a forum.
(D) It has been updated by the publishing company.

150. At 1:40 P.M., what does Mr. Peterson mean when he writes, "I will"?

(A) He will check out the book by himself.
(B) He will reserve the book on the Web site.
(C) He will be sent the book directly from the library.
(D) He will return the book on time.

Questions 151-152 refer to the following receipt.

FACTORY's Supplies

120 Fleming Avenue
Columbus, Ohio

Item Description	**Charges**
Electric drill	$40.00

Subtotal: $40.00
Coupon discount: 15%
Tax: $2.15
Total: $36.15

Thank you for making a purchase from FACTORY's, where you can find the best equipment and tools for your purposes.
Please note that returns are only accepted within two weeks of purchase. Make sure that the product you purchased comes with the original receipt and packaging together.
We are looking forward to seeing you in the near future again!

Date of receipt: November 20

151. What is indicated about the purchase?

(A) The purchased item was half price.
(B) A store coupon was applied.
(C) The shopper paid $40.00 in total.
(D) The customer was exempt from taxes.

152. What is implied about FACTORY's Supplies?

(A) It operates a variety of local branches.
(B) It discounted only a few items in November.
(C) It offers a customer buy-back programs.
(D) It does not accept returns after 14 days of purchase.

Questions 153-154 refer to the following advertisement.

Divine Memories Event Hall

6749 Winchester Rd, Memphis, TN 38115
Tel: 901-244-6488   E-mail: reservations@divinememories.net

September 1 is the grand opening of the Divine Memories Event Hall on Winchester Road in Memphis, and we are celebrating by opening up the rooms and halls to local businesses at no charge all week. Free rental is on a first-come, first-served basis, with up to four hours for the week.

All of our rooms are equipped with desks, chairs, air-conditioning, and the latest audio-visual equipment. Check out our Web site at www.divinememories.net to see room sizes and our competitive hourly rates. You can also find information about discounts available to our valuable members with our own MV User Program.

There is about a week left until the opening, but we are expecting a lot of interest. Businesses or individuals interested in taking advantage of this special offer should book a room in advance. Reservations can be made online or by calling our intelligent staff, who will be able to help you with any questions you may have.

153. What is the purpose of the advertisement?
 (A) To find staff for a new business
 (B) To confirm information on an event
 (C) To notify users of a policy change
 (D) To announce a special offer

154. What is indicated about the Divine Memories Event Hall?
 (A) It has already opened for business.
 (B) It has the largest rooms available.
 (C) It has knowledgeable employees.
 (D) It charges extra for the use of presentation equipment.

Questions 155-157 refer to the following notice.

NOTICE

To: All Residents at White Tower Square

This is just a reminder that the meeting for our tenants is scheduled for June 20th at 8 P.M. in the Ski-Hut Lodge next to the apartment's main entrance. We will discuss the issues related to the guidelines for our yard and watering. To be more specific, we will vote on whether or not to renew our contract with the current subcontracted company, TRES Cleaning & Landscaping, during the upcoming meeting.

At the moment, we have had just that issue for improving our living condition on the agenda, so please send your opinions and topics to Mr. Danny at www.whitetowersquare.net by June 12th.

Anyone who lives in our complex is welcome, and some finger foods will be available there.

Management Office
White Tower Square

155. What is the purpose of the notice?
(A) To explain a new regulation
(B) To notify tenants about an upcoming meeting
(C) To mention the opening of a new apartment
(D) To announce the results of a survey

156. What action has a deadline of June 12th?
(A) Moving in an apartment
(B) Voting on an issue
(C) Suggesting discussion topics
(D) Attending a meeting

157. What is suggested about TRES Cleaning & Landscaping?
(A) It owned the property of the White Tower Square.
(B) Its staff members will participate in the meeting.
(C) It provides only house cleaning services.
(D) Some residents in White Tower may be dissatisfied with its service.

Questions 158-160 refer to the following invitation.

In honor of Academic Achievements,
Cam Union University recognizes
Dr. Canale Swain

We sincerely invite you to celebrate Dr. Swain's retirement. He has been devoted to the educational field of Second Language Writing over the last 30 years. —[1]—. Please participate in this party on Friday, 17 March at 6:30 P.M., right after his final lecture. The event, including a meal, will be held in Leonard Hall in the Humanities Building on Rosewick Street. —[2]—.

At your discretion, you are welcome to bring a present as a surprise for Dr. Swain. —[3]—. Please note that any gifts will be sent to the charity Dr. Swain has contributed to, the State Literacy Foundation, in the form of donations. —[4]—.

158. Who most likely is Mr. Swain?

(A) A physician
(B) A university professor
(C) A chair of a charity
(D) A governmental official

159. What are the invitees asked to do?

(A) Keep the event a secret
(B) Bring a present for Mr. Swain
(C) Sign a special card
(D) Contribute to a potluck meal

160. In which of the positions marked [1], [2], [3], and [4] does the following sentence best belong?

"Free parking is available on-site."

(A) [1]
(B) [2]
(C) [3]
(D) [4]

Questions 161-163 refer to the following article.

Cal State Journal

California, April 10—The president of NMD Developments, Jerome Harts, has announced that his company had been selected to construct the L.A. Giant Mall, which will become the largest shopping center in the state. The L.A. Giant Mall will accommodate over 600 stores and shops, as well as indoor sports facilities and water parks.

This will be NMD's first time building a mega-shopping center, but it has previously achieved similar-scale building construction such as NFL football stadiums and various skyscrapers in San Francisco. The construction is set to begin on May 20, and the shopping complex and theme park will be opened to the public in the autumn of next year unless something comes up.

NMD Developments had one of the best years last year because it recorded one billion dollars in sales and associated with a lot of companies and governmental offices. Due to its rapid growth, the company has recently invited a lot of people in order to celebrate its achievement and opening of new branches throughout California. "Fortunately, we have been on a roll without stopping thanks to you," Mr. Harts remarked to his employees on the stage while at the new San Diego branch. "By winning this bid for the L.A. Giant Mall, we have a chance to become one of the nation's top companies and solidify our stance in the field of the construction industry," he added.

News of NMD's contract to construct the L.A. Giant Mall will have a strong, positive impact on its stock value increase. Some professionals expected that it could increase by almost 35% by next month. With this project, the company can establish its foundation to expand its operations into other states in the country.

161. What is mainly being discussed in the article?

(A) The merger of two construction firms
(B) The relocation of an office
(C) The securing of a business contract
(D) The opening event of a shopping center

162. What is true about the L.A. Giant Mall?

(A) Its construction will be completed on April 30.
(B) It will open for business this summer.
(C) It will contain a football stadium.
(D) It will be the largest shopping center in California.

163. The word "set" in paragraph 2, line 6, is closest in meaning to

(A) founded
(B) installed
(C) supposed
(D) assembled

Questions 164-167 refer to the following information.

Cox Net Co. is here to support your small business with all the computerized equipment you need. Cox Net Co. has been in operation for more than the last decade and has been selected by a lot of corporations within the state of Oregon whenever they have needed our computing assistance. We provide the best quality service and help to keep your business running smoothly and effectively for your customers and employees. We can help your company in a number of ways, including:

- Updating or installing the latest security software for detecting viruses
- Setting up a premium Internet networking station
- Giving a 2-year-warranty for free technical service
- Installing desktops and laptop computers
- Maintaining the equipment to keep it running in perfect condition

If you would like to know about the detailed services of our business, do not hesitate to contact us at 461-1893-1782 and talk with one of our licensed technicians. We are pleased to help fix your issues by phone or live chat on the Web, and we can even make arrangements for a full consultation with our specialist. We are available Monday through Friday from 6 A.M. to 8 P.M., Saturday from 9 A.M. to 5 P.M. with on-and off-line support, and Sunday from 10 A.M. to 4 P.M. only on the Web.

164. What type of business is being advertised?
  (A) Electrical engineering
  (B) Energy conservation
  (C) Financial consulting
  (D) Information technology

165. What is indicated about Cox Net Co.?
  (A) It has numerous stores around the country.
  (B) It was founded over ten years ago.
  (C) It is currently hiring new employees.
  (D) It has just released a new product line.

166. According to the information, what service is NOT provided?
  (A) An installation of electronic devices
  (B) An updated security program
  (C) A consultation with an expert
  (D) A remote support system

167. On which day does Cox Net Co. NOT offer consultations through the phone?
  (A) Sunday
  (B) Monday
  (C) Friday
  (D) Saturday

Questions 168-171 refer to the following online chat discussion.

George McGuire 5:10 P.M.		So, how are you doing today?
Jamie Chang 5:11 P.M.		Really good. Tommy sold three sedans. Twain and Matsuda each had one.
George McGuire 5:13 P.M.		Not bad for a Wednesday. Did any customers get a loan to buy their car?
Jamie Chang 5:15 P.M.		Yes, all of them. One customer also purchased an extended warranty. Tommy included two vouchers for an oil change.
George McGuire 5:17 P.M.		Good. How about in the mechanic area?
Kyrie Erving 5:20 P.M.		We did $65,000 worth of work today. Most of the maintenance was scheduled in advance. But some other people just showed up without an appointment.
Jamie Chang 5:21 P.M.		Oh! The mechanics must have been too busy to deal with them.
Kyrie Erving 5:24 P.M.		I had to call an employee to come in despite it being his day-off to help us.
George McGuire 5:26 P.M.		We should put 10 brand-new sedans and 20 new SUVs into our sales area tomorrow afternoon.
Kyrie Erving 5:30 P.M.		I'll ask three of my workers to inspect them as soon as they return from our mechanic area. We should get them out in the lot by the end of the day. Where do you want to park them?
George McGuire 5:32 P.M.		Right out in the front section just behind our main entrance where people can see them well while driving on the 39 Indi Highway. That's it now. Let's call it a day!
Jamie Chang 5:33 P.M.		Sounds good.

168. Where do the writers most likely work?

(A) At a taxi service
(B) At a car dealership
(C) At a parking garage
(D) At a bank

169. What is suggested about Mr. Erving?

(A) He purchased a new vehicle.
(B) He wasn't scheduled to work today.
(C) He supervises mechanics.
(D) He spent a lot of money.

170. What is mentioned about the place the writers work?

(A) It is located near a highway.
(B) It is usually closed on Mondays.
(C) It has dozens of employees.
(D) It will open early tomorrow.

171. At 5:32 P.M., what does Mr. McGuire mean when he writes, "Let's call it a day"?

(A) He needs to finish a few more activities.
(B) He thinks it is time to go home.
(C) He appreciates the work of his employees.
(D) He is very pleased with today's business.

Questions 172-175 refer to the following e-mail.

To	editor@albanytoday.com
From	gloria_h@honorsociety.org
Date	December 20
Subject	White Golden Award

Dear Editor,

I'm writing this e-mail because I'm concerned about Ronald Jackson's interview section in the December 19 issue of the *Albany Today's* newspaper. —[1]—. In his speech about last night's award ceremony, some mistakes could make the public confused, and we would like to correct the errors. Mr. Jackson explained the event as "an honor for organizations which have financially contributed to projects for the city's development." In addition, he mentioned our nonprofit organization, the Honor Society (HS), as the prize winner. —[2]—. His explanation was not clear as to why the award was presented. According to the article, it seemed that we have raised funds for some projects which are not related to our original mission.

The White Golden Award was not granted to the Honor Society, but to just a small community group of HS's staff who have been cleaning up the city's public areas in their spare time. Although the Honor Society sometimes requires our employees to do that kind of work, it was not implemented by our organization in this case. —[3]—.

Our generous contributors should be aware of the fact that we do not have any intention of getting financial aid or being nominated for some awards. Would you add clarifying information to Mr. Jackson's interview script? —[4]—. An immediate response could prevent more confusion regarding the event before it is introduced in local radio or television stations.

Gloria Han
Media Relations Manager
Honor Society

172. What is the purpose of the e-mail?
 (A) To decline an award
 (B) To invite the press to an event
 (C) To request a clarification
 (D) To thank staff for working extended hours

173. For what were some Honor Society employees recognized?
 (A) Their fundraising results
 (B) Their volunteer work
 (C) Their excellent presentations
 (D) Their improved performance

174. What is suggested about Mr. Jackson?
 (A) He has fully discussed the issue with Ms. Han.
 (B) He mistakenly nominated someone for an award.
 (C) He made a speech with inaccurate information.
 (D) He has worked for a charity foundation.

175. In which of the positions marked [1], [2], [3], and [4] does the following sentence best belong?

 "And I ask you to deal with this as soon as possible."

 (A) [1]
 (B) [2]
 (C) [3]
 (D) [4]

Questions 176-180 refer to the following schedule and article.

Thank you for visiting the Davenport Novel Society Homepage

Celebrate Davenport Novel Society's 45th anniversary with us!

Scholar Forum Night for Novels (July–August)
Plazma Auditorium, Iowa University

Updated on June 15

Novel	Date
The Kite Runner	Friday, July 5
Cleaning Out the Closet	Saturday, July 6
Faculty Room	Wednesday, July 10
The Shadow of America	Friday, July 12
Norwegian Forest	Friday, July 19
Beyond Atlantis	Friday, August 2
The Secret Life of Butterflies **(Only 20 seats available)**	Saturday, August 3
No Name Asian	Wednesday, August 7
For Banana Fish	Friday, August 9
The Others **(Only 30 seats available)**	Friday, August 16

There are only 50 seats available for each session, unless otherwise indicated, due to the auditorium's capacity. Monthly memberships and tickets for single attendance can be purchased from our Web site or at the reception desk of the auditorium. Monthly membership fees are $20, and single attendance ticket fees are $5. Monthly membership should be purchased no later than July 2.

CLICK HERE to purchase attendance passes.

The Iowa Times

Culture Section

The Davenport Novel Society Changes its 45th Anniversary Schedule

June 20—Story lovers across Iowa are looking forward to attending the special forums of the Davenport Novel Society (DNS)'s 45th anniversary. However, Plazma Auditorium, where the DNS's scholar forums have been held over the last twenty years, will be temporarily closed for renovation during the months of July and August. This means that the organization has no choice but to find an alternative venue and schedule, as well as change the host. The chairman of the novel society stated that the changes will be as follows:

Cleaning Out the Closet will be discussed on Saturday, July 20.

Norwegian Forest will be discussed on Wednesday, July 17.

No Name Asian will be discussed on Thursday, August 8.

For Banana Fish and its forum will be hosted by Charlotte Rivera.

* The seating capacity for each session will not be changed.

See you at the forums!

---

176. What is indicated about the Davenport Novel Society?

(A) It is commemorating its founding.
(B) It has recently reduced the number of members.
(C) It is accepting applications for a position.
(D) It is widely known throughout the world.

177. According to the schedule, what is true about the monthly membership?

(A) It costs five dollars per person.
(B) Its profits will be donated to a local charity.
(C) It can be obtained through the Web site.
(D) It will be available to purchase by June 15.

178. What is implied about Plazma Auditorium?

(A) It was constructed forty-five years ago.
(B) It has relocated to Davenport.
(C) It will undertake building repairs.
(D) It has recently been expanded.

179. What novel will be discussed at an earlier date than originally scheduled?

(A) *Cleaning Out the Closet*
(B) *Norwegian Forest*
(C) *No Name Asian*
(D) *For Banana Fish*

180. How many people will be allowed to attend the forum hosted by Ms. Rivera?

(A) 20
(B) 30
(C) 50
(D) 80

Questions 181-185 refer to the following e-mail and survey.

TO:	Sam Bryant <s_bryant@gsu.edu>
FROM:	Anna Theron <a_theron@hallnet.com>
DATE:	March 10
SUBJECT:	Winter Internship Program
ATTACHMENT:	📎 Program_Survey_Form.pdf

Dear Mr. Bryant,

Thank you for your participation in our winter internship program at the Ontario Tourism Board, Niagara Branch, this year. We really appreciate your contributions and hope that you found it helpful to your career.

We want you to give us your feedback in order to improve our program for upcoming seasons. Please download the file attached to this e-mail, fill out the form, and return it via this e-mail address. The completed surveys will assist us in improving this first program for prospective participants and will be returned to the department manager who worked with you. For those who worked in Marketing, that would be Christian Paul. For those who worked in Communication Service, that would be Dixie Lynn.

Now that we have already started the planning process for the next summer program, we hope to receive all surveys by March 30. If you have any questions, please feel free to contact us at 634-284-9123 or e-mail us at planning@hallnet.com. If I am not on duty, you can also talk with my assistant, Jerry Minnette, as he is very familiar with the program.

Thank you again for your devotion.

Sincerely,

Anna Theron
Program Director, Hallnet Co.

Survey for the Internship Program

Name: Sam Bryant
Duration: January 5 to February 20
Department: Translation Service

The meeting for the orientation was informative and helpful.	Yes [ ]	No [X]	N/A [ ]
I found my assignments interesting and satisfactory.	Yes [X]	No [ ]	N/A [ ]
I received responsive feedback from my manager.	Yes [X]	No [ ]	N/A [ ]
I was satisfied with the workload of my assignments.	Yes [X]	No [ ]	N/A [ ]
I would consider joining the program again.	Yes [X]	No [ ]	N/A [ ]

Additional Comments for Improvement

I am majoring in Linguistics at State University of Ontario and am always interested in practicing my language proficiency by meeting and talking with a lot of foreign tourists. I am confident that this experience was very helpful and encouraging for me to develop my career. The only suggestion I want to make for improvement is that you would extend the length of the orientation meeting. That session was so hectic and confusing because of its time pressure. If there had been more time for questions and answers with managers, it would have been very helpful for us to understand the job descriptions and your work environment.

---

181. What is the purpose of the e-mail?
(A) To ask about whether to hire new employees
(B) To obtain a recommendation letter
(C) To apply for a program
(D) To request information

182. What is suggested about the internship program?
(A) It was newly introduced.
(B) It required a bachelor's degree.
(C) It was just a one-time event.
(D) It was managed by the state government.

183. By when must the form be returned?
(A) January 5
(B) February 20
(C) March 10
(D) March 30

184. Who most likely did Mr. Bryant report to about the program?
(A) Anna Theron
(B) Christian Paul
(C) Dixie Lynn
(D) Jerry Minnette

185. What is indicated about Mr. Bryant?
(A) He is a student at present.
(B) He can accept a job offer.
(C) He is planning a trip.
(D) He is moving into Niagara.

Questions 186-190 refer to the following notice, e-mail, and bill.

Dr. Kevin Lopez's Office
6565 Fannin St., Houston, TX 77030, USA
+1 715-274-1284
kl_office@houstonmedic.com

Dear Sharon Monica,

Our priority is to maintain your health. That's why we would like to remind you about your appointment with us on

Thursday, June 10, at 10:00 A.M.

If you are visiting our clinic for the first time, please arrive twenty minutes before your doctor's appointment to complete our patient info form and payment-related form.

If you need help in changing or canceling your appointment, please contact us at least 36 hours in advance so as to avoid cancellation fee.

We hope to see you soon!

From:	s_monica@xmail.com
To:	kl_office@houstonmedic.com
Date:	June 5, 4:20 P.M.
Subject:	Appointment

Thank you for sending me the reminder. I had almost forgotten about my appointment because I have been very busy with a lot of work to do over the last few weeks. I am fully aware that it is very important for me to have regular checkups. However, I still have something to finish by the end of this week. Could I change my appointment to Tuesday, June 15? I am available anytime. I'll arrive twenty minutes ahead of time in order to fill out the paperwork.

Furthermore, another specialist told me that I would need additional endoscope procedures. I don't know how effective they are for me. I would like to discuss this issue with Dr. Lopez about whether to register for it or not.

Thanks,

Sharon Monica

Billing Statement for Patient

Sharon Monica
3891 Charlton Boulevard
Houston, TX 77030

Dr. Kevin Lopez
6565 Fannin St.
Houston, TX 77030

Service Summary

Physical Examination	$220.00
Endoscopy	$130.00

Account Summary

Account Number	3754901-12854912
Date of Service	June 15
Total Charges	$350.00
Payment Method	Insurance [Provider : **Newlife Health**]

NOTE

All fees billed to an insurance provider must be approved by its provider.
If the provider does not approve the charges, the patient will be responsible for the payment in full. Please check with your insurance provider before authorizing any services.

---

186. Which information is NOT provided in the notice?

(A) The time of the appointment
(B) The place of the appointment
(C) The deadline for the cancellation
(D) The charge for the appointment

187. What is suggested about Ms. Monica?

(A) She works near Dr. Lopez's office.
(B) She would like to receive the latest medicines.
(C) She is a new patient of Dr. Lopez's.
(D) She needs to pay the late cancellation fees.

188. Why did Ms. Monica write the e-mail?

(A) To change her appointment
(B) To request additional information
(C) To submit the patient survey form
(D) To make a new appointment

189. What is most likely true about Ms. Monica's visit?

(A) She arrived later than she reserved.
(B) It took place in the afternoon.
(C) It was on her preferred date.
(D) She did not need an additional checkup.

190. In the bill, the word "authorizing" in the Note section, line 3, is closest in meaning to

(A) confusing
(B) deducting
(C) rejecting
(D) allowing

Questions 191-195 refer to the following advertisement, e-mail, and letter.

Recommend Banka Asset to your friends and family, and get benefits together!

We would like to extend our appreciation for your trust in us. As a Platinum Member, you can access our high-quality financial plans and products, and get our best rates.

We want to give you $30 for each friend or family member you recommend us to who opens a new account. We will also give them $20 after making an initial deposit of over $300 into a Banka Asset Online Account or Banka Stock Trading Account. All they need to do is log on to www.bankaco.com and use the promotional code BAP2981.

This offer is exclusive to Platinum Members in good standing. Recommended acquaintances must be entirely new members. Existing members who have already had our Banka Group's account cannot participate.

To:	Lora Houston <l_houston@speednet.com>
From:	Jason Kid <j_kid@speednet.com>
Subject:	Banka Asset Service
Date:	January 10

Hi Lora,

I remember that you were discussing how to start your financial plans after retirement at lunch yesterday. Well, here is something that could give you some help in finance. Banka Asset will reward you $20 just for opening a new account.

I have used their services over the last three years, and I've been fully satisfied with them. They are secure, and it is easy for people to use their online banking and management systems.

I left a flyer which describes how to sign up in your mailbox.

Best wishes,

Jason Kid

Lora Houston
720 Queens Avenue
Indiana, PA 15701

January 17

Dear Ms. Houston,

Thank you for opening a Banka Group account. We have just opened your online savings account with your name. Please read the enclosed terms of the agreement and the payment schedule.

To express our gratitude for your new membership, we will deposit $20 into your online Banka Asset account. The amount of the deposit can be credited within two weeks of your account-opening date.

In addition, you can have access to your account through our Web site, www.banakagroup.com. First, you can use your identification numbers with the temporary password we provide below. As soon as you log into the site, please reset your username and password.

Account Number: 90342178023580
Temporary Password: tfc-ybm-1983-2019-zed

If you have any questions, feel free to call us at 1-729-1925-0183.

Sincerely,

Mark Tyler
Manager for New Customer's Accounts

---

191. For whom is the advertisement intended?

(A) Prospective customers
(B) Banka Group's employees
(C) Agents for stock trading
(D) Existing account holders

192. Why did Mr. Kid send the e-mail to Ms. Houston?

(A) To explain an investment method
(B) To confirm the amount of deposits
(C) To refer her to good banking services
(D) To introduce a local financial planner

193. What is most likely true about Mr. Kid?

(A) He is a Banka Asset Platinum member.
(B) He always meets Ms. Houston for lunch.
(C) He is recruited by Banka Stock Trading.
(D) He recently opened a new stock account.

194. In the e-mail, the word "flyer" in paragraph 3, line 1, is closest in meaning to

(A) application
(B) statement
(C) handout
(D) receipt

195. What is suggested about Ms. Houston?

(A) She is a previous Banka customer.
(B) She used to work with Mr. Tyler.
(C) She deposited more than $300 in her account.
(D) She is considering when she will retire.

Questions 196-200 refer to the following invoice and e-mails.

Order Confirmation
Edu Factory
4312 Butler St, Pittsburgh, PA 15201

Tel: +1 412-687-2965
Billing information: 533 Depot St, Latrobe, PA 15650, +1 724-537-5541
Shipping address: Same as billing address

Order date: April 20 (online order) **Shipping date:** April 25			**Order Number:** 218452185 **Estimated delivery date:** May 5		
Product Number	**Description**	**Unit Price**	**Qty**	**Amount**
BW 200	Wide Board - white	$450.00	1	$450.00
BW 220	Marker Sets - black with Storage Box - charcoal	$150.00	1	$150.00
BP 178	Tablet Charger - grey	$120.00	1	$120.00
BP 591	Bulletin Board, divided into 4 sections - beige	$200.00	1	$200.00
Payment: April 25 **Credit Card:** XXXX XXXX XXXX 2418			**Subtotal** $920.00 **Tax** $80.00 **Shipping** $100.00 **Total $1,100.00**		

TO: customerservice@edufactory.com
FROM: antoniomartial@comsmail.com
DATE: May 6
SUBJECT: Order #218452185

To Whom It May Concern:

My order was delivered to my home yesterday. I assembled everything except the item BW 200. However, I noticed when opening the package that the manual and the package of connecting parts did not come with the item. I was not able to assemble the piece. Could you please send the instructions and the tool to me right away? My home office needs to be set up as quickly as possible because I am planning to receive my students there as of next week.

Thank you.

Antonio Martial

To	antoniomartial@comsmail.com
From	customerservice@edufactory.com
Date	May 7
Subject	RE: Order #218452185

Dear Mr. Martial,

We have received your e-mail about the missing assembly instructions and connecting hardware. We have sent those to you today via express mail, and you should receive them tomorrow before noon. We sincerely apologize for the inconvenience caused to you. To show our devotion to excellent customer service, we would like to give you a reimbursement for the shipping cost of your order. It will be automatically deducted from your next credit card billing statement.

Please be aware that we have recently added online manuals to our Web site, www.edufactory.com/cs_manual. If you enter your model number, you can download its file. Please type the keyword "Assembly" in the search bar on the right side of the file. If you do so, you can see the instruction pictures and assemble the item easily.

Again, our sincere apologies,

Campbell Liu
Customer Service Manager

---

196. According to the invoice, when was Mr. Martial charged for his order?

(A) When he placed the order
(B) When the order was shipped
(C) When the items were received
(D) When he contacted customer service

197. What item was Mr. Martial unable to assemble?

(A) The wide board
(B) The storage box
(C) The tablet charger
(D) The bulletin board

198. What is true about Mr. Martial?

(A) He was not home at the time of a delivery.
(B) He damaged some office furniture.
(C) He does not own basic household tools.
(D) He will use his home office for teaching.

199. How much will Mr. Martial be refunded?

(A) $80
(B) $100
(C) $120
(D) $155

200. According to the second e-mail, what are customers now able to do online?

(A) Request a product refund
(B) Pay a bill
(C) Access some instructions
(D) Write a product review

Stop! This is the end of the test. If you finish before time is called, you may go back to Parts 5, 6, and 7 and check your work.

▸ 점수 환산표

LISTENING Raw Score (맞은 개수)	LISTENING Scaled Score (환산 점수)	READING Raw Score (맞은 개수)	READING Scaled Score (환산 점수)
96-100	475-495	96-100	460-495
91-95	435-495	91-95	425-490
86-90	405-475	86-90	395-465
81-85	370-450	81-85	370-440
76-80	345-420	76-80	335-415
71-75	320-390	71-75	310-390
66-70	290-360	66-70	280-365
61-65	265-335	61-65	250-335
56-60	235-310	56-60	220-305
51-55	210-280	51-55	195-270
46-50	180-255	46-50	165-240
41-45	155-230	41-45	140-215
36-40	125-205	36-40	115-180
31-35	105-175	31-35	95-145
26-30	85-145	26-30	75-120
21-25	60-115	21-25	60-95
16-20	30-90	16-20	45-75
11-15	5-70	11-15	30-55
6-10	5-60	6-10	10-40
1-5	5-50	1-5	5-30
0	5-35	0	5-15

※ 절대적인 기준이 아니므로 실제 토익 시험과 다소 차이가 있을 수 있습니다.

정답 및 스크립트

ANSWER Key

1회 | p.14

01	(A)	02	(A)	03	(D)	04	(A)	05	(D)
06	(C)	07	(A)	08	(A)	09	(B)	10	(B)
11	(A)	12	(C)	13	(C)	14	(B)	15	(A)
16	(B)	17	(C)	18	(C)	19	(B)	20	(A)
21	(A)	22	(C)	23	(C)	24	(C)	25	(B)
26	(A)	27	(C)	28	(C)	29	(C)	30	(A)
31	(B)	32	(B)	33	(A)	34	(A)	35	(D)
36	(D)	37	(B)	38	(B)	39	(C)	40	(A)
41	(C)	42	(B)	43	(C)	44	(A)	45	(A)
46	(B)	47	(C)	48	(D)	49	(A)	50	(D)
51	(C)	52	(B)	53	(B)	54	(C)	55	(A)
56	(B)	57	(C)	58	(B)	59	(C)	60	(B)
61	(D)	62	(D)	63	(C)	64	(D)	65	(A)
66	(C)	67	(B)	68	(A)	69	(A)	70	(C)
71	(D)	72	(C)	73	(D)	74	(B)	75	(A)
76	(C)	77	(A)	78	(C)	79	(B)	80	(D)
81	(B)	82	(A)	83	(A)	84	(B)	85	(C)
86	(D)	87	(B)	88	(C)	89	(A)	90	(C)
91	(D)	92	(C)	93	(D)	94	(B)	95	(C)
96	(C)	97	(B)	98	(B)	99	(D)	100	(C)
101	(C)	102	(B)	103	(C)	104	(A)	105	(B)
106	(D)	107	(A)	108	(C)	109	(B)	110	(D)
111	(B)	112	(D)	113	(B)	114	(C)	115	(D)
116	(B)	117	(A)	118	(C)	119	(D)	120	(A)
121	(D)	122	(B)	123	(D)	124	(D)	125	(D)
126	(B)	127	(A)	128	(A)	129	(C)	130	(D)
131	(C)	132	(B)	133	(D)	134	(D)	135	(A)
136	(B)	137	(C)	138	(B)	139	(A)	140	(C)
141	(D)	142	(B)	143	(C)	144	(B)	145	(A)
146	(B)	147	(D)	148	(C)	149	(B)	150	(C)
151	(D)	152	(D)	153	(B)	154	(A)	155	(A)
156	(D)	157	(B)	158	(C)	159	(C)	160	(A)
161	(D)	162	(C)	163	(C)	164	(C)	165	(B)
166	(C)	167	(B)	168	(C)	169	(B)	170	(B)
171	(A)	172	(C)	173	(D)	174	(B)	175	(A)
176	(D)	177	(A)	178	(C)	179	(B)	180	(B)
181	(D)	182	(A)	183	(C)	184	(C)	185	(B)
186	(D)	187	(C)	188	(C)	189	(C)	190	(A)
191	(C)	192	(A)	193	(C)	194	(D)	195	(B)
196	(C)	197	(B)	198	(D)	199	(A)	200	(D)

2회 | p.56

01	(C)	02	(B)	03	(A)	04	(D)	05	(B)
06	(D)	07	(B)	08	(B)	09	(C)	10	(A)
11	(C)	12	(A)	13	(A)	14	(B)	15	(B)
16	(B)	17	(C)	18	(A)	19	(C)	20	(B)
21	(A)	22	(A)	23	(B)	24	(C)	25	(A)
26	(A)	27	(C)	28	(B)	29	(C)	30	(B)
31	(A)	32	(C)	33	(D)	34	(A)	35	(B)
36	(D)	37	(A)	38	(D)	39	(B)	40	(A)
41	(A)	42	(B)	43	(C)	44	(B)	45	(C)
46	(D)	47	(A)	48	(D)	49	(A)	50	(C)
51	(D)	52	(B)	53	(A)	54	(C)	55	(B)
56	(D)	57	(C)	58	(D)	59	(B)	60	(B)
61	(D)	62	(A)	63	(C)	64	(D)	65	(C)
66	(D)	67	(A)	68	(D)	69	(B)	70	(C)
71	(B)	72	(D)	73	(D)	74	(B)	75	(C)
76	(D)	77	(C)	78	(C)	79	(C)	80	(A)
81	(D)	82	(C)	83	(A)	84	(B)	85	(C)
86	(A)	87	(C)	88	(D)	89	(C)	90	(B)
91	(D)	92	(D)	93	(C)	94	(D)	95	(C)
96	(B)	97	(A)	98	(C)	99	(C)	100	(B)
101	(A)	102	(A)	103	(D)	104	(D)	105	(D)
106	(D)	107	(B)	108	(D)	109	(D)	110	(D)
111	(C)	112	(A)	113	(D)	114	(D)	115	(B)
116	(D)	117	(A)	118	(B)	119	(D)	120	(D)
121	(C)	122	(B)	123	(C)	124	(B)	125	(A)
126	(A)	127	(C)	128	(B)	129	(D)	130	(C)
131	(C)	132	(C)	133	(A)	134	(D)	135	(C)
136	(A)	137	(D)	138	(C)	139	(C)	140	(C)
141	(D)	142	(C)	143	(C)	144	(D)	145	(A)
146	(A)	147	(C)	148	(A)	149	(C)	150	(C)
151	(C)	152	(B)	153	(A)	154	(C)	155	(D)
156	(B)	157	(C)	158	(D)	159	(A)	160	(B)
161	(B)	162	(D)	163	(C)	164	(D)	165	(B)
166	(A)	167	(C)	168	(A)	169	(D)	170	(C)
171	(D)	172	(A)	173	(A)	174	(C)	175	(A)
176	(D)	177	(C)	178	(C)	179	(B)	180	(A)
181	(B)	182	(C)	183	(C)	184	(D)	185	(D)
186	(C)	187	(C)	188	(A)	189	(B)	190	(D)
191	(C)	192	(B)	193	(A)	194	(A)	195	(D)
196	(A)	197	(D)	198	(C)	199	(C)	200	(C)

3회
p.98

#	Ans	#	Ans	#	Ans	#	Ans	#	Ans
01	(C)	02	(D)	03	(A)	04	(C)	05	(C)
06	(B)	07	(A)	08	(A)	09	(C)	10	(B)
11	(A)	12	(B)	13	(C)	14	(A)	15	(A)
16	(C)	17	(B)	18	(C)	19	(B)	20	(C)
21	(C)	22	(A)	23	(B)	24	(B)	25	(B)
26	(A)	27	(A)	28	(A)	29	(A)	30	(C)
31	(C)	32	(B)	33	(D)	34	(B)	35	(C)
36	(B)	37	(A)	38	(D)	39	(B)	40	(A)
41	(A)	42	(D)	43	(A)	44	(D)	45	(B)
46	(D)	47	(B)	48	(C)	49	(C)	50	(D)
51	(C)	52	(C)	53	(B)	54	(C)	55	(B)
56	(D)	57	(A)	58	(C)	59	(D)	60	(C)
61	(A)	62	(D)	63	(D)	64	(A)	65	(C)
66	(B)	67	(A)	68	(C)	69	(C)	70	(A)
71	(C)	72	(A)	73	(A)	74	(D)	75	(B)
76	(B)	77	(A)	78	(D)	79	(A)	80	(A)
81	(D)	82	(A)	83	(C)	84	(A)	85	(B)
86	(A)	87	(B)	88	(C)	89	(B)	90	(C)
91	(A)	92	(A)	93	(B)	94	(D)	95	(C)
96	(C)	97	(B)	98	(C)	99	(D)	100	(B)
101	(A)	102	(D)	103	(A)	104	(C)	105	(C)
106	(C)	107	(A)	108	(B)	109	(D)	110	(D)
111	(B)	112	(A)	113	(C)	114	(D)	115	(A)
116	(A)	117	(C)	118	(C)	119	(B)	120	(C)
121	(A)	122	(B)	123	(C)	124	(B)	125	(A)
126	(B)	127	(D)	128	(A)	129	(C)	130	(B)
131	(D)	132	(B)	133	(C)	134	(A)	135	(C)
136	(C)	137	(D)	138	(D)	139	(A)	140	(B)
141	(B)	142	(C)	143	(B)	144	(D)	145	(B)
146	(D)	147	(B)	148	(C)	149	(B)	150	(A)
151	(D)	152	(B)	153	(A)	154	(B)	155	(C)
156	(A)	157	(D)	158	(A)	159	(B)	160	(C)
161	(C)	162	(B)	163	(A)	164	(C)	165	(A)
166	(C)	167	(C)	168	(C)	169	(A)	170	(D)
171	(C)	172	(C)	173	(B)	174	(D)	175	(D)
176	(D)	177	(A)	178	(B)	179	(D)	180	(B)
181	(B)	182	(A)	183	(D)	184	(C)	185	(B)
186	(C)	187	(C)	188	(B)	189	(C)	190	(D)
191	(A)	192	(C)	193	(C)	194	(D)	195	(B)
196	(A)	197	(C)	198	(D)	199	(C)	200	(A)

4회
p.140

#	Ans	#	Ans	#	Ans	#	Ans	#	Ans
01	(A)	02	(C)	03	(C)	04	(B)	05	(B)
06	(D)	07	(A)	08	(C)	09	(C)	10	(C)
11	(A)	12	(B)	13	(A)	14	(B)	15	(C)
16	(B)	17	(A)	18	(A)	19	(A)	20	(A)
21	(B)	22	(C)	23	(B)	24	(C)	25	(B)
26	(A)	27	(B)	28	(B)	29	(A)	30	(A)
31	(A)	32	(B)	33	(D)	34	(C)	35	(B)
36	(B)	37	(A)	38	(A)	39	(D)	40	(C)
41	(C)	42	(A)	43	(C)	44	(D)	45	(A)
46	(A)	47	(C)	48	(D)	49	(B)	50	(C)
51	(D)	52	(B)	53	(C)	54	(A)	55	(B)
56	(C)	57	(D)	58	(C)	59	(C)	60	(B)
61	(B)	62	(A)	63	(D)	64	(B)	65	(A)
66	(D)	67	(C)	68	(B)	69	(A)	70	(C)
71	(A)	72	(C)	73	(D)	74	(A)	75	(C)
76	(A)	77	(C)	78	(B)	79	(C)	80	(D)
81	(A)	82	(D)	83	(B)	84	(A)	85	(D)
86	(C)	87	(C)	88	(B)	89	(A)	90	(B)
91	(D)	92	(A)	93	(C)	94	(D)	95	(C)
96	(D)	97	(B)	98	(A)	99	(C)	100	(B)
101	(A)	102	(D)	103	(A)	104	(C)	105	(C)
106	(D)	107	(B)	108	(B)	109	(A)	110	(B)
111	(D)	112	(A)	113	(B)	114	(D)	115	(A)
116	(C)	117	(B)	118	(C)	119	(C)	120	(C)
121	(D)	122	(A)	123	(C)	124	(B)	125	(B)
126	(B)	127	(C)	128	(B)	129	(B)	130	(C)
131	(C)	132	(C)	133	(C)	134	(A)	135	(A)
136	(A)	137	(D)	138	(B)	139	(B)	140	(A)
141	(B)	142	(A)	143	(B)	144	(B)	145	(A)
146	(C)	147	(C)	148	(D)	149	(C)	150	(B)
151	(C)	152	(D)	153	(C)	154	(C)	155	(B)
156	(C)	157	(A)	158	(B)	159	(B)	160	(D)
161	(D)	162	(B)	163	(A)	164	(B)	165	(D)
166	(D)	167	(D)	168	(C)	169	(D)	170	(B)
171	(A)	172	(C)	173	(A)	174	(B)	175	(C)
176	(C)	177	(B)	178	(B)	179	(A)	180	(D)
181	(D)	182	(C)	183	(A)	184	(B)	185	(C)
186	(A)	187	(B)	188	(C)	189	(A)	190	(C)
191	(C)	192	(D)	193	(C)	194	(A)	195	(C)
196	(C)	197	(A)	198	(B)	199	(B)	200	(C)

ANSWER Key

5회
p.182

01 (C)	02 (C)	03 (A)	04 (B)	05 (D)
06 (D)	07 (B)	08 (C)	09 (A)	10 (C)
11 (A)	12 (B)	13 (C)	14 (A)	15 (A)
16 (B)	17 (C)	18 (A)	19 (A)	20 (B)
21 (A)	22 (C)	23 (A)	24 (C)	25 (B)
26 (A)	27 (B)	28 (A)	29 (A)	30 (B)
31 (C)	32 (A)	33 (A)	34 (B)	35 (A)
36 (D)	37 (C)	38 (D)	39 (A)	40 (D)
41 (A)	42 (B)	43 (C)	44 (D)	45 (D)
46 (C)	47 (D)	48 (A)	49 (A)	50 (A)
51 (C)	52 (A)	53 (D)	54 (B)	55 (A)
56 (B)	57 (B)	58 (C)	59 (A)	60 (A)
61 (C)	62 (C)	63 (A)	64 (B)	65 (D)
66 (B)	67 (D)	68 (C)	69 (A)	70 (C)
71 (C)	72 (B)	73 (C)	74 (A)	75 (B)
76 (C)	77 (A)	78 (B)	79 (C)	80 (B)
81 (B)	82 (A)	83 (B)	84 (C)	85 (C)
86 (A)	87 (D)	88 (C)	89 (D)	90 (A)
91 (B)	92 (D)	93 (A)	94 (B)	95 (A)
96 (C)	97 (D)	98 (D)	99 (B)	100 (C)
101 (D)	102 (A)	103 (C)	104 (C)	105 (B)
106 (D)	107 (D)	108 (B)	109 (A)	110 (D)
111 (A)	112 (D)	113 (B)	114 (C)	115 (A)
116 (C)	117 (B)	118 (C)	119 (D)	120 (A)
121 (A)	122 (D)	123 (D)	124 (A)	125 (B)
126 (A)	127 (C)	128 (D)	129 (B)	130 (C)
131 (C)	132 (B)	133 (D)	134 (A)	135 (C)
136 (A)	137 (C)	138 (C)	139 (A)	140 (B)
141 (C)	142 (D)	143 (A)	144 (B)	145 (D)
146 (C)	147 (A)	148 (C)	149 (C)	150 (D)
151 (B)	152 (D)	153 (D)	154 (C)	155 (B)
156 (C)	157 (D)	158 (B)	159 (B)	160 (B)
161 (C)	162 (D)	163 (C)	164 (D)	165 (B)
166 (D)	167 (A)	168 (B)	169 (C)	170 (A)
171 (B)	172 (C)	173 (B)	174 (C)	175 (D)
176 (A)	177 (C)	178 (C)	179 (B)	180 (C)
181 (D)	182 (A)	183 (D)	184 (C)	185 (A)
186 (D)	187 (C)	188 (A)	189 (C)	190 (D)
191 (D)	192 (C)	193 (A)	194 (C)	195 (C)
196 (B)	197 (A)	198 (D)	199 (B)	200 (C)

1회

| p.14

01	(A)	02	(A)	03	(D)	04	(A)	05	(D)
06	(C)	07	(A)	08	(A)	09	(B)	10	(B)
11	(A)	12	(C)	13	(C)	14	(B)	15	(A)
16	(B)	17	(C)	18	(C)	19	(B)	20	(A)
21	(A)	22	(C)	23	(C)	24	(C)	25	(B)
26	(A)	27	(C)	28	(C)	29	(C)	30	(A)
31	(B)	32	(B)	33	(A)	34	(A)	35	(D)
36	(D)	37	(B)	38	(B)	39	(C)	40	(A)
41	(C)	42	(B)	43	(C)	44	(A)	45	(A)
46	(B)	47	(C)	48	(D)	49	(A)	50	(D)
51	(C)	52	(B)	53	(B)	54	(C)	55	(A)
56	(B)	57	(C)	58	(B)	59	(C)	60	(B)
61	(D)	62	(D)	63	(C)	64	(D)	65	(A)
66	(C)	67	(B)	68	(A)	69	(A)	70	(C)
71	(D)	72	(C)	73	(D)	74	(B)	75	(A)
76	(C)	77	(A)	78	(C)	79	(B)	80	(D)
81	(B)	82	(A)	83	(A)	84	(A)	85	(C)
86	(D)	87	(B)	88	(C)	89	(A)	90	(C)
91	(D)	92	(C)	93	(D)	94	(A)	95	(C)
96	(C)	97	(B)	98	(B)	99	(D)	100	(C)
101	(C)	102	(B)	103	(C)	104	(A)	105	(B)
106	(D)	107	(A)	108	(C)	109	(B)	110	(D)
111	(B)	112	(D)	113	(B)	114	(C)	115	(D)
116	(B)	117	(A)	118	(B)	119	(D)	120	(A)
121	(D)	122	(B)	123	(D)	124	(B)	125	(D)
126	(B)	127	(A)	128	(A)	129	(C)	130	(D)
131	(C)	132	(B)	133	(D)	134	(D)	135	(A)
136	(B)	137	(C)	138	(B)	139	(A)	140	(C)
141	(D)	142	(B)	143	(C)	144	(B)	145	(A)
146	(B)	147	(D)	148	(C)	149	(B)	150	(C)
151	(D)	152	(D)	153	(B)	154	(A)	155	(A)
156	(D)	157	(A)	158	(D)	159	(C)	160	(A)
161	(D)	162	(C)	163	(C)	164	(C)	165	(B)
166	(C)	167	(B)	168	(C)	169	(B)	170	(B)
171	(A)	172	(C)	173	(D)	174	(B)	175	(A)
176	(D)	177	(A)	178	(C)	179	(B)	180	(B)
181	(D)	182	(A)	183	(C)	184	(C)	185	(B)
186	(D)	187	(A)	188	(C)	189	(B)	190	(A)
191	(C)	192	(A)	193	(C)	194	(D)	195	(B)
196	(C)	197	(B)	198	(D)	199	(A)	200	(D)

Part 1

1   (A) He's wearing a hat.
    (B) He's enjoying the scenery.
    (C) He's riding a bike.
    (D) He's picking up a bag.

2   (A) A woman is grasping a book.
    (B) A woman is opening her handbag.
    (C) A man is reaching for an item.
    (D) They are facing each other.

3   (A) She's talking on the phone.
    (B) She's putting a bag on the sofa.
    (C) She's looking through a purse.
    (D) She's pulling her suitcase.

4   (A) A car is being cleaned.
    (B) A window is being installed.
    (C) A wall is being painted.
    (D) A man is moving a cart.

5   (A) The floor is being polished.
    (B) A man is leaning against a wall.
    (C) Some people are hanging up pictures.
    (D) Some people are appreciating some artwork.

6   (A) Some boxes are being assembled.
    (B) Some leaves have been raked into a pile.
    (C) Some fruit has been stacked on display tables.
    (D) Some products are being loaded into a box.

Part 2

7   Was it supposed to rain tomorrow?
    (A) Yes, probably.
    (B) Let me tell you the way.
    (C) No, I won't.

8   Who's the keynote speaker at this conference?
    (A) I'll look at the agenda.
    (B) I can attend the conference.
    (C) I need the key to the office.

9   Where can I eat dinner around here?
    (A) Let's go around this area once more.
    (B) The sandwich shop across the street.
    (C) At about 10 o'clock.

10 Won't the client attend the meeting?
    (A) He didn't attend meetings.
    (B) He is almost here.
    (C) A few years old.

11 Did we review all the customer accounts?
    (A) No, there are a couple more left.
    (B) We can enjoy a great view here.
    (C) I've never heard of that customer.

12 Why is the art museum so busy today?
    (A) He has exhibited his works.
    (B) I have some time in the afternoon.
    (C) Check the list of events over there.

13 You can join our movie club.
    (A) He's going to buy tickets for us.
    (B) They're filming in Vancouver now.
    (C) That sounds like something I'd enjoy!

14 Should we cancel the concert or go ahead with it as planned?
    (A) It's expected to be held on November 17.
    (B) Why don't we ask the director what he thinks?
    (C) No, we're planning to hold a conference next Wednesday.

ACTUAL TEST 1

15. Do you want to receive the weekly newsletter we provide?
    (A) Of course. That's what I want.
    (B) I have some surprising news.
    (C) Sure. I'll send you a discount coupon by this Friday.

16. Who should I call to repair the fax machine?
    (A) You should order more supplies.
    (B) There's a phone number on the right side of it.
    (C) The password isn't correct.

17. When are they going to hire a new employee to fill the vacancy?
    (A) Please explain the hiring process.
    (B) I enjoyed my vacation in Hawaii for a week.
    (C) They'll probably have an interview with three applicants next Monday.

18. How many people are supposed to participate in the workshop?
    (A) Two employees will be working overtime today.
    (B) The seminar provides useful information to many employees.
    (C) I think it has been canceled.

19. Which car would you recommend?
    (A) I had my car repaired.
    (B) I think a more economical one would be better.
    (C) Yes, you can order it.

20. Why don't we invite Ms. Lee to the banquet?
    (A) I do have her e-mail address.
    (B) I'm looking forward to the awards banquet.
    (C) She left the venue earlier than expected.

21. Could you help me revise this year's training materials?
    (A) Yes, when can we start?
    (B) No, the trainer isn't available now.
    (C) Thank you for attending the workshop.

22. I have no choice but to miss the meeting tomorrow.
    (A) Yes, you should come here by 3 o'clock.
    (B) There are more chairs to sit on.
    (C) Then who should take the minutes?

23. Can I install this program on a computer or on a phone?
    (A) You can use mine.
    (B) He called me this morning.
    (C) It's for PCs only.

24. Let's try the new restaurant downtown.
    (A) It was not easy to choose a menu.
    (B) The Italian restaurant.
    (C) I've been there two days ago.

25. Why won't William attend the reception next Monday?
    (A) That's because he's already had a meal.
    (B) He's probably on vacation until next Wednesday.
    (C) I think I'll have to leave a little early.

26. Do you want me to email the report to you?
    (A) I can't access my e-mail now.
    (B) Please wait a little longer for printing.
    (C) The reporter printed a lot of data yesterday.

27. I reserved a projector for my presentation yesterday.
    (A) You should be present at the meeting.
    (B) I think it was a great presentation.
    (C) May I have your name, please?

28. Have you finished designing the ad for the new line of smartphones?
    (A) I think advertising through social media will be effective.
    (B) Some new features have been added.
    (C) Not yet, but it's almost done.

29. The weather is really good today, isn't it?
    (A) I'm not sure whether it will be rainy tomorrow.
    (B) I didn't check the weather forecast.
    (C) Right. It's a great day to go on a picnic.

30. When will you arrive at the International Motor Show?
    (A) I'm leaving shortly.
    (B) Yes, I'll arrive there soon.
    (C) It's held in Busan.

31. Would you like to reschedule your appointment?
    (A) You should refer to the updated schedule.
    (B) Yes, how about Next Wednesday?
    (C) She'll be a little later than the doctor's appointment.

Part 3

Questions 32-34 refer to the following conversation.

M   Welcome to Glory Electronics. How can I help you?
W   I bought this tablet PC here last Tuesday, but it won't connect to the Internet well.
M   Okay. Can you show me the receipt? The product comes with a one-year warranty, so any repairs will be free of charge.
W   Great! Here you are.
M   Thanks. It will take more than 30 minutes to complete the repairs. First, please fill out this form and sign it.
W   Sure. Do you have a pen I can use?

32. Where is the conversation taking place?
    (A) At a library
    (B) At an electronics store
    (C) At an auto shop
    (D) At an Internet service company

33. What does the man want to check?
    (A) A receipt
    (B) A warranty period
    (C) A discounted price
    (D) A reservation time

34. What does the man ask the woman to do?
    (A) Complete a form
    (B) Visit again later
    (C) Pay for the repairs
    (D) Register the product

Questions 35-37 refer to the following conversation.

W Samuel, I need your help. I entered the password to get into the office, but I couldn't open the door.
M Oh, the security system was upgraded this morning. All employees must go to the security office and reset their passwords. The new password will take effect tomorrow.
W Thanks. Then how can I get into the office today?
M The security officer will give you a temporary password. You can use it today.

35 What is the woman's problem?
(A) She left some documents in the office.
(B) She forgot her password.
(C) She cannot change her password.
(D) She cannot access a room.

36 What does the man tell the woman to do?
(A) Get a key from the security office
(B) Install a new system
(C) Contact a security officer
(D) Change a secret code

37 How can the woman get into the office today?
(A) By changing her password
(B) By getting a different password
(C) By getting help from the man
(D) By signing up for a membership

Questions 38-40 refer to the following conversation.

M Thank you for calling the Global Advertising Company. How can I help you today?
W I ordered some flyers on your Web site to promote our newest restaurant branch. But there is a problem with the advertisement. Some of our menus are misspelled.
M Really? I'm sorry. We'll fix it for you as soon as possible. May I have your order number, please?
W It's 0808-16. When can I get the revised flyers?
M There isn't much to be fixed, so they should be done within three days.

38 What type of business is the woman calling?
(A) A publishing company
(B) An advertising office
(C) A food manufacturer
(D) A bistro

39 What problem are the speakers discussing?
(A) A service cost was overcharged.
(B) An order number was entered incorrectly.
(C) Some details are incorrect.
(D) The deadline for an advertisement was not met.

40 What does the man ask the woman to provide?
(A) An order number
(B) An order date
(C) A shipping date
(D) A menu

Questions 41-43 refer to the following conversation.

W Bryan, what brings you to this park? I never thought I'd see you here.
M Hi, Cindy. I often come here when the weather is nice. I came here to read instead of taking a walk.
W What kind of book do you have?
M This is Aron Kim's new novel *SAAD*, which was published about a month ago.
W Oh, I am very interested in the book, too. Has it been released yet?
M Maybe you don't have to buy it. If you wait three or four days, I'll probably finish reading the book. In addition, why don't you join the reading club I'm a member of? We share information about new books regularly.

41 Where are the speakers?
(A) At a bookstore
(B) At a library
(C) At a park
(D) At a book fair

42 What does the man imply when he says, "Maybe you don't have to buy it"?
(A) He will buy a new book.
(B) He will lend a book to the woman.
(C) He has two of the same books.
(D) He can get a book for free.

43 What does the man suggest the woman do?
(A) Recommend a book to read
(B) Order a book on the Internet
(C) Join a reading club
(D) Update some information regularly

Questions 44-46 refer to the following conversation with three speakers.

W1 Laura, I'm glad your teeth are in good condition. I think you can come back in three months. Pablo, please set a date for Laura's appointment in three months.
W2 Thank you for your help.
M   When do you want to come in next?
W2 I'm not sure how my schedule will change in the future. But I think after 4 P.M. on weekdays should be okay.
M   Okay. You can get treatment anytime in the fourth week of August.
W2 Then I'll be back on Wednesday, August 21.
M   Okay. I'll send you a text message one day before your appointment.
W2 Thank you. Have a nice day!

44 Where most likely are the speakers?
(A) At a dentist's office
(B) At a travel agency
(C) At a real estate agency

45. What does Laura request?
    (A) An afternoon appointment
    (B) A text message
    (C) A revised schedule
    (D) An informational booklet

46. When will the message be sent to Laura?
    (A) On May 20
    (B) On August 20
    (C) On August 21
    (D) On November 21

Questions 47-49 refer to the following conversation.

> W   Mr. Chomsky, I asked to see you because I want to know about your company's products. I'm a clothing designer, and I'd like to produce quality clothes to satisfy customers.
>
> M   As you know, we've been producing and supplying stores with quality clothing for more than 15 years, and we've never missed the number one market share.
>
> W   I'm well aware of that. However, since many people these days think raw materials are important, I hope you will supply those things to our store. Do you have any ideas for that?
>
> M   Sure, I'll come back tomorrow with some natural materials. They are ones that only our company handles in Australia.

47. What are the speakers talking about?
    (A) Newly designed equipment
    (B) An extended deadline
    (C) Product manufacturing
    (D) A product advertisement

48. What does the man say about his company?
    (A) It specializes in design.
    (B) It has many branches abroad.
    (C) It offers items at reasonable prices.
    (D) It has been in business for a long time.

49. What will the man do tomorrow?
    (A) Bring some items
    (B) Order new materials
    (C) Think of some ideas
    (D) Conduct a survey

Questions 50-52 refer to the following conversation.

> W   Do you carry *Independence Day*? I can't find the book anywhere.
>
> M   Yes, we have it. The book is selling very well. It's a bestseller, so there's only one book left.
>
> W   Really? I'm glad you have one left.
>
> M   The novels are in the fourth section of the K bookshelf. And the books are arranged in alphabetical order.
>
> W   Oh, I already checked that place many times, but (D) At a law firm I didn't see it.
>
> M   Maybe someone put it in another section. I'll check if the book is some where else around there.

50. Where is the conversation taking place?
    (A) At a publishing company
    (B) At a newsstand
    (C) At a library
    (D) At a bookstore

51. What does the woman imply when she says, "I didn't see it"?
    (A) She lost some goods.
    (B) Some data are missing.
    (C) She couldn't find an item.
    (D) A place has changed.

52. What is suggested about *Independence Day*?
    (A) It is no longer available.
    (B) It is very popular.
    (C) It is an old product.
    (D) It can be purchased online.

Questions 53-55 refer to the following conversation.

> M   Hi. I'm John. I called you yesterday.
>
> W   Yes, welcome to A-Plus Landscaping. You said you wanted to demolish the fountain in the middle of your lawn, right?
>
> M   That's right. It requires a lot of water, and these days, the water bill has gone up. It's too expensive for me. I'd like to replace it with a tree.
>
> W   I see. What kind of tree would you like?
>
> M   I want a tree that doesn't change with the seasons. Could you send me a list of recommendations?
>
> W   I'll ask another department for some information. It should be sent to you by e-mail this afternoon.

53. Where does the woman work?
    (A) At a public utility
    (B) At a landscaping company
    (C) At a construction company
    (D) At an interior design firm

54. Why does the man want to make a change?
    (A) To enlarge a space
    (B) To make a place clean
    (C) To save money
    (D) To create a safer environment

55. What does the woman say she will do?
    (A) Contact another department
    (B) Write an e-mail
    (C) Print some material
    (D) Prepare some paperwork

Questions 56-58 refer to the following conversation.

W	This is EM Technology. How can I help you?
M	Last year, I purchased some graphic cards for my office computers from you. I need more of the same product, but I can't find them listed in your catalog. The product number is VGA-G3000.
W	I'm sorry, but that model was discontinued several months ago. We are currently selling a new upgraded model. It will also be compatible with your system. The specifications for the new product can be found on our Web site.
M	Well, let me access your Web site first. I wonder if the price has gone up.

56 What does the man want to order?
(A) Furniture
(B) Computer parts
(C) A computer
(D) A printer

57 Why does the woman apologize?
(A) Some items are defective.
(B) The wrong number of products was delivered.
(C) Some items are no longer available.
(D) The customer was overcharged.

58 What will the man most likely do next?
(A) Inspect a system
(B) Look at a Web site
(C) Request a discount
(D) Speak with a service engineer

Questions 59-61 refer to the following conversation.

W	Thank you for accepting the invitation to appear on THBC Radio's business feature program. You run the first Vietnamese restaurant in this city, don't you? What is your biggest challenge?
M	Getting fresh ingredients and sauces. As there are many ingredients unavailable in the country, I had to choose a reliable supplier in Vietnam.
W	I see. You provide differentiated foods and services by using ingredients directly supplied from Vietnam. How's business these days?
M	Everything's going well. I'll open my tenth franchise next year. I'm planning a special event to celebrate it now.

59 Who most likely is the woman?
(A) A culinary expert
(B) A business consultant
(C) A business reporter
(D) A real estate agent

60 According to the man, what is the restaurant's biggest challenge?
(A) Hiring reliable employees
(B) Obtaining food materials
(C) Managing franchises
(D) Creating new menu items

61 What will the man do next year?
(A) Add a new menu item
(B) Make plans for an event
(C) Produce his own ingredients
(D) Expand his business

Questions 62-64 refer to the following conversation and graph.

M	Emma, are you still busy preparing tomorrow's orientation materials? Can I help you with the data classification work?
W	Thanks for offering, but there's not much left. You also had a hard time doing this last year, didn't you?
M	That's right. Last year, we had over 40 new employees, so I had a lot to prepare. Well, I have some free time now. Is there anything I can do to help?
W	Oh, I haven't asked to reserve a projector yet. Could you contact the Facilities Department?

62 What is the conversation about?
(A) A job interview
(B) An annual sales report
(C) A scheduling conflict
(D) An orientation session

63 Look at the graphic. In which year was the man in charge of the orientation preparation work?
(A) 2016
(B) 2017
(C) 2018
(D) 2019

64 What task does the woman ask for help with?
(A) Filing some documents
(B) Booking a venue
(C) Conducting a survey
(D) Reserving equipment

Questions 65-67 refer to the following conversation and sign.

W	It's good not to be crowded since we are taking the subway early. We can probably get very good seats to watch the magic show. Which station are we getting off at?
M	The show is being held in the Vancouver Art Theater. We're at Parker Avenue now. We have to go two more stops so that we can get there.
W	That's good! I'm looking forward to enjoying the show. I'm so happy to have an opportunity to see a magician in person whom I've only seen on TV.
M	Right. And after the performance, he's going to be signing autographs. Why don't we buy a notebook so that we can get his autograph?

65 What event are the speakers going to?
(A) A magic show
(B) A live concert
(C) A movie preview
(D) An art exhibition

66. Look at the graphic. At which stop will the speakers get off the train?
    (A) Parker Avenue
    (B) Robson Street
    (C) Robinson Street
    (D) Greenfield Avenue

67. What does the man suggest doing?
    (A) Touring some facilities later today
    (B) Preparing an item to get an autograph
    (C) Taking a subway earlier than usual
    (D) Watching a performance on TV

Questions 68-70 refer to the following conversation and map.

M	Hello and welcome to the Eastern Ocean Aquarium. Can I help you?
W	Yes, I have a problem. It's been a while since I've been here, and the structure has changed a lot. So I don't know where to get a parking ticket.
M	I see. After seeing everything, go into the exhibition hall directly opposite the exit. There is a small guide office where you can get a parking ticket issued.
W	Okay, thanks! How long is free parking available?
M	Well, free parking is only available for two hours on weekends, but there is no time limit on weekdays. You don't have to hurry today.

68. What problem does the woman mention?
    (A) She is having difficulty finding a location.
    (B) She parked in the wrong parking lot.
    (C) She lost her admission ticket.
    (D) She was overcharged for parking.

69. Look at the graphic. Which hall will the woman go to?
    (A) Hall 1
    (B) Hall 2
    (C) Hall 3
    (D) Hall 4

70. Why does the man tell the woman not to rush?
    (A) There are still two hours left.
    (B) There are few cars in the parking lot.
    (C) She doesn't need to pay for parking.
    (D) A staff member will wait for her.

Part 4

Questions 71-73 refer to the following news report.

Welcome to KBC News. The mayor of Canberra announced plans to renovate the bus terminal. The purpose of the renovations is to connect the terminal to the nearby subway station and to install various amenities. There is always heavy traffic around the terminal due to the various entertainment establishments located nearby. So many residents have long wanted to be able to get to the terminal by subway. Construction is scheduled to begin on April 6 and will be completed before November, said the city's transportation director. To hear more about the project, stay tuned. We'll be talking with him after the commercial break.

71. What will be renovated?
    (A) A subway station
    (B) A shopping complex
    (C) Some amenities
    (D) A bus terminal

72. What problem does the speaker mention about the structure?
    (A) It is always crowded with people.
    (B) It is located on the outskirts of the city.
    (C) It is difficult to get there by public transportation.
    (D) It has some old facilities.

73. What will happen after the commercial break?
    (A) Some residents will ask questions.
    (B) The mayor will give details about a project.
    (C) There will be information on the use of some facilities.
    (D) A senior official will be interviewed.

Questions 74-76 refer to the following advertisement.

Are you having a lot of trouble with your computer getting slower and slower? DoctorCom specializes in maintaining computers at many businesses. We offer high-end antivirus programs for free, so our customers are very satisfied. We regularly check the computers in your office to make sure they stay the same as the new ones. You can sign a contract with us for at least one year. If you sign a contract for three or more years, we will give you a 20% discount on the service fee. You can apply online for a consultation right away.

74. What kind of service is being advertised?
    (A) Computer classes
    (B) Computer maintenance
    (C) Internet service
    (D) Online advertisements

75. According to the speaker, what do customers like about the service?
    (A) It provides a useful program for free.
    (B) It always takes care of problems quickly.
    (C) It often offers discounts.
    (D) It provides new products every year.

76. How can customers get a discount?
    (A) By applying for a service online
    (B) By purchasing new software
    (C) By making a contract for a certain period of time
    (D) By ordering multiple products

Questions 77-79 refer to the following talk.

Before we wrap up this seminar for aspiring power bloggers, I want to summarize some important points. The competition is really fierce because so many people want to be power bloggers. As you know, there are countless blogs that introduce tourist attractions, great restaurants, and a variety of products. In order for you to succeed, you have to keep blogging. It's also important for you to have a variety of experiences. Last, but not least, you have to post accurate and reliable information. I think that is the most important part of all. Before we finish, does anyone have any questions?

77 What is the talk mainly about?
    (A) How to run a blog successfully
    (B) Why blogs are so popular
    (C) Effective online marketing methods
    (D) Various topics of blogs

78 What does the speaker mention about power bloggers?
    (A) They don't need a lot of experience.
    (B) They should provide a variety of information.
    (C) They should write blog posts consistently.
    (D) They have to update only useful information.

79 What does the speaker recommend doing?
    (A) Looking at various blogs
    (B) Posting reliable content
    (C) Taking frequent trips
    (D) Collecting a lot of data

Questions 80-82 refer to the following telephone message.

Hi, Patrick. I'm calling to see when we can discuss our travel agency's future operation plans. I remember you once suggested that I coordinate more activities for our travelers, but I'm in charge of overall management. I think we'd better hire a guide who specializes in entertainment. Of course, we'll need extra funding to do that. I'd like to talk to you about that in more depth. I can't decide by myself whether it will be worth the extra cost. Please give me a call at your earliest convenience.

80 Where does the speaker work?
    (A) At a restaurant
    (B) At an amusement park
    (C) At a fitness center
    (D) At a travel agency

81 What does the speaker mean when she says, "I'm in charge of overall management"?
    (A) She wants more funding.
    (B) She can't do another job.
    (C) She can handle anything.
    (D) She can control labor costs.

82 What does the speaker want to discuss with the listener?
    (A) The value of an additional expenditure
    (B) The details of some expected costs
    (C) Current trends in tourism
    (D) Types of recreational programs

Questions 83-85 refer to the following tour information.

Welcome to the Victoria Art Gallery. On today's tour, we will get to appreciate new works by renowned portrait photographer Matt Carter. Originally, sixteen people signed up for this tour, but four are not here now. It's almost ten o'clock, and we should start the tour without them. They'll probably have to come to the exhibition next time. Before we start, I'd like to remind you that taking photographs is strictly prohibited. You also need to keep your phone in silent or vibrate mode to hear the descriptions of the photos. Now, let's move on to the first one!

83 What type of art will the listeners see?
    (A) Photography
    (B) Sculptures
    (C) Craftworks
    (D) Paintings

84 What does the speaker imply when she says, "They'll probably have to come to the exhibition next time"?
    (A) There is no time to wait any longer.
    (B) The tickets are all sold out.
    (C) There are no additional vacancies.
    (D) Some people have changed their reservations.

85 What does the speaker ask the listeners to do?
    (A) Move quickly
    (B) Wait a little longer
    (C) Turn off the ringers on their phones
    (D) Speak quietly

Questions 86-88 refer to the following announcement.

Before starting work today, I want to let you know something. The number of products produced during the past quarter surpassed our target, and management will pay a special bonus in appreciation of your hard work. Starting now, the bonus that used to be given twice a year will be given every quarter. In addition, the winner of the employee-of-the-quarter award will be announced next Monday. Since we have not yet determined a winner, I hope you will recommend someone this week.

86 Where do the listeners most likely work?
    (A) At an electronics shop
    (B) At a hospital
    (C) At a restaurant
    (D) At a factory

87 What type of policy has changed?
    (A) Vacation periods
    (B) Bonus payments
    (C) Working hours
    (D) Production goals

88 What does the speaker ask the listeners to do?
    (A) Work overtime
    (B) Submit sales reports
    (C) Make recommendations
    (D) Contact the winner

Questions 89-91 refer to the following introduction.

Hi, everyone. As you know, you will be getting one week of training on the use of our new accounting software next month. Jessica Page, who will be responsible for your training, won the Presidential Award for developing a lot of excellent software for government agencies last year. Ms. Page is an expert on Web site development as well as software. In fact, she has led the development of some top companies' Web sites. I'm sure you'll obtain a large amount of knowledge from her.

89. What will the listeners do next month?
 (A) Receive some training
 (B) Develop a Web site
 (C) Get an award
 (D) Purchase new software

90. According to the speaker, what field is Ms. Page an expert in?
 (A) Education
 (B) Politics
 (C) Web programming
 (D) Accounting

91. Why did Ms. Page win an award last year?
 (A) She taught quality classes.
 (B) She improved an educational environment.
 (C) She created an innovative Web site.
 (D) She developed some software.

Questions 92-94 refer to the following excerpt from a workshop.

As demand for the low-end smartphones we produce is exploding, the number of products you have to produce per day has also increased significantly. Today, I'm going to teach you a new production strategy to make production more efficient. For our first training activity, you will be divided into groups of five, and every group will receive the same product one by one. Then, you and your group members can come up with the production procedure of the product and write a report on it. Once your report is complete, review it carefully and submit it. I'll give you three days to review it. Members of the group who devise the most efficient method will be given a week off.

92. What is the purpose of the workshop?
 (A) To strengthen the bond between employees
 (B) To come up with an efficient way to negotiate
 (C) To learn how to meet demand efficiently
 (D) To study how to make up for the shortcomings of a product

93. What kind of documents does the speaker ask the listeners to submit?
 (A) A training plan
 (B) A catalog of products
 (C) A product performance report
 (D) A team report

94. What will be given to the winning team?
 (A) Vacation time
 (B) A bonus
 (C) Gift certificates
 (D) New products

Questions 95-97 refer to the following telephone message and receipt.

Hello. This is Kyle Johnson. I work at the Special Movement Center. I'm calling to confirm the details of your move in three days. The workers were scheduled to arrive at your house early in the morning that day, but due to equipment problems, the arrival time will be delayed until noon. I beg your pardon for that. Upon arriving there, they'll start packing and moving. All of your items will be moved to 406 Granville Street, and all work will be completed by 7 P.M. As an apology for the delay in the appointment, we'll clean your house for free. We'll do our best to make sure you don't have any problems moving into your new house.

95. What is the purpose of the message?
 (A) To ask for a payment
 (B) To change a moving date
 (C) To confirm the details of a contract
 (D) To inform the listener of the price of a service

96. Look at the graphic. What information has changed?
 (A) Daniel Antonio
 (B) 86 North Hills Avenue
 (C) 8:00 A.M.
 (D) $1,640

97. What does the speaker offer to do?
 (A) Finish the work quickly
 (B) Provide a free service
 (C) Send more staff members
 (D) Give a discount

Questions 98-100 refer to the following tour information and map.

Welcome to the North Edmonton Island tour. In a few minutes, we'll start our walk in Golden Forest. On today's tour, you will see a variety of animals, such as raccoons and squirrels. Some wild animals may be sensitive to camera flashes. Therefore, please refrain from taking pictures except for in the designated areas. It will take about an hour and a half to get to our destination. You'll probably need some water and snacks. You had also better buy animal food from the vending machine next to the park management office so that you can have a more interesting experience.

98. Look at the graphic. Which route will the listeners take?
 (A) Peace Line
 (B) Banff Line
 (C) Jasper Line
 (D) Sunshine Line

99. According to the speaker, why should the listeners refrain from taking pictures?
 (A) They don't have enough time.

(B) It could cause an accident.
(C) It's too dark there.
(D) It may have a bad effect on wild animals.

100 What does the speaker suggest the listeners do?
(A) Get enough rest
(B) Buy some souvenirs
(C) Get some animal food
(D) Drink enough water

Part 5

101 소비자 설문 조사는 Golden Planet의 최신 휴대폰이 너무 비싸다는 것을 보여 준다.

102 당신은 사원증을 항상 지참해야 합니다.

103 300달러 이상 사용하는 사람들은 20% 할인을 받을 것이다.

104 추가적인 설명을 보시려면 그냥 저희 웹 사이트에서 Customer 링크로 접속하시면 됩니다.

105 Fresh Life 사의 공기 청정기는 3년간 유효한 품질 보증이 따라온다.

106 Richard Business Consulting은 직원들에게 가치 있는 업무 현장과 관련된 제안을 하는 것에 대해 보상을 해 준다.

107 SJ Communications가 이전할 새 사무실을 물색할 때 대중교통에 대한 접근성은 큰 고려 사항이었다.

108 Clinton 씨는 배송품이 경비실 안에 놓여야 한다고 조언했다.

109 Dragons Motors는 더 이상 세단형 자동차를 생산하지 않을 것이라고 발표했다.

110 Washington에 본사를 두고 있는 Komerican Group은 계열사들의 지속적인 혁신을 효율적으로 지원한다.

111 회의에도 불구하고 두 회사의 대표들은 여전히 계약 조건에 대해 합의에 도달하지 못했다.

112 Ventors Broadband의 환불은 서비스 취소로부터 2주 이내에 이루어진다.

113 저희는 고객들의 편의를 위해 사용자가 스마트폰으로 메뉴를 확인하고 주문할 수 있는 애플리케이션을 개발하고 있습니다.

114 Kim 씨는 지난 10월의 누락된 매출 정보를 포함해서 보고서를 다시 제출하라는 요청을 받았다.

115 워크숍 주최자들은 원래 야외에서 행사를 개최하려고 했지만 좋지 않은 날씨로 인해 그렇게 하지 못했다.

116 내일 연회에서 지난 한 해 동안 회사의 기록적인 매출을 달성하는 데 기여한 모든 사람들에게 상이 수여될 겁니다.

117 내일 시카고로 출장 가는 팀원들은 예정된 출발 시간보다 2시간 일찍 공항에 도착해야 합니다.

118 3일 전에 주문한 사무용품이 직원들이 막 퇴근하려고 할 때 배송되었다.

119 잡지사가 시장과 인터뷰할 시간이 충분하지 않아서 이번 호를 발행하는 데 문제가 있었다.

120 World Travel 사의 영업 사원이 되기 위해서는 창의성과 적극적인 성격이 필수이다.

121 Current Economics 사는 올해 2분기에 역대 가장 높은 실업률을 기록했다고 보도했다.

122 United Insurance Company에서 정규직이 되려면 1년 간의 수습 기간을 거쳐야 합니다.

123 사고를 예방하기 위해서 모든 기술자들은 발전기를 점검할 때 조심해야 한다.

124 Linda Sives는 학창 시절에 외국어 공부를 즐겼지만, 그녀가 프랑스어를 가르치는 직업을 가지게 될 거라고 결코 생각하지 못했다.

125 우리는 새로운 복사기가 도착할 때까지 인사부 사무실에 있는 것을 사용할 겁니다.

126 Kenzi 씨는 뭐든 자신이 가장 좋아한다고 생각하는 것을 선택하라는 이야기를 들었다.

127 Pitt 씨와 Roberts 씨에게 연락해서 4월 6일에 면접을 볼 수 있는지 물어보세요.

128 내일 아침에 지하 주차장이 폐쇄되어 있을 경우 사무실 건물 건너편의 도로에 주차하세요.

129 Hofmann 씨는 우수한 관리 능력으로 인해 다음 달 승진 대상자로 선정되었습니다.

130 우리는 원자재 공급업체를 변경함으로써 최대 30%의 비용을 절약할 수 있을 것이다.

Part 6

Questions 131-134 refer to the following announcement.

다가오는 새해부터 휴가 정책이 일부 변경될 겁니다. 휴가를 가려고 하는 날보다 최소 2주 전에 저희에게 알려 주셔야 합니다. 여태껏 여러분은 양식을 작성해서 신청했지만 내년부터는 회사 홈페이지에서 신청해야 할 겁니다. 그렇게 함으로써 휴가 신청 절차는 분명히 간단해질 겁니다.

뿐만 아니라 가장 중요한 것은, 8월과 12월을 제외하고 팀에서 최대 3명까지만 동시에 휴가를 갈 수 있도록 허용할 겁니다. 이는 저희 회사가 계속 원활하게 운영되도록 할 겁니다. 물론 예전에도 그랬듯이 갑작스러운 병가는 언제든 신청할 수 있습니다. 그것은 일반적인 휴가 정책과는 다른 별도의 규정을 적용 받을 겁니다.

만약 더 궁금한 점이나 제안 사항이 있으시면 인사부로 연락 주세요.

132 (A) 저는 많은 직원들이 함께 휴가를 즐길 수 있기를 바랍니다.
(B) 이는 저희 회사가 계속 원활하게 운영되도록 할 겁니다.
(C) 여러분은 여행사를 신중하게 선택하는 게 좋을 겁니다.
(D) 여러분은 웹 사이트 게시판에서 구체적인 일정표를 보실 수 있습니다.

Questions 135-138 refer to the following article.

캘거리 (2월 18일)—미국의 거대 식품 기업인 Star Grocery Factories가 오늘 캐나다의 캘거리에 진입할 계획을 발표했다. 그 회사는 캘거리에서 최초의 캐나다 지점을 오픈할 것이다. 그 지점은 다음 달 1일에 오픈할 예정이다. 더욱이 올해 두 번째와 세 번째 매장들이 Victoria와 Edmonton에 차례대로 오픈할 것이다. "우리는 최고의 과일과 야채를 포함한 모든 종류의 식품을 합리적인 가격에 제공할 목표를 가지고 있습니다. 이것들은 북미 지역의 모든 소비자들이 이용할 수 있습니다."라고 회사의 부회장 Michael Jonadan이 말했다.

136 (A) 그 도시의 많은 기업들이 해외로 진출했다.
(B) 그 지점은 다음 달 1일에 오픈할 예정이다.
(C) 그들은 이미 많은 명성을 얻었다.
(D) Star Grocery Factories는 국제적인 기업이다.

Questions 139-142 refer to the following e-mail.

수신: 모든 고객
발신: Asiana Electronics Service Center
날짜: 6월 8일
제목: 새로운 사무 공간

고객님들께,

Asiana Electronics Service Center가 더 큰 시설로 이전했다는 것을 알리게 되어 아주 기쁩니다. Riverside Building에 있는 저희 새로운 시설은 더 넓은 접수처와 다양한 편의 시설을 제공합니다. 이것들을 통해 우리 직원들이 여러분들에게 훨씬 더 효율적으로 서비스를 제공해 드릴 수 있을 겁니다. 사실 저희가 같은 건물의 다른 층으로만 이전했기 때문에 큰 혼란은 없을 거라고 생각합니다. 6층 엘리베이터에서 내리면 오른쪽에 저희 사무실이 보일 겁니다.

저희 주소를 제외한 모든 연락처 정보는 계속 변경되지 않을 겁니다. 더 나은 환경에서 여러분을 뵙기를 기대하고 있습니다. 감사합니다.

진심으로,

Asiana Electronics Service Center

140 (A) 저희는 높은 임대료 때문에 계약 취소를 검토 중입니다.
(B) 예산 문제 때문에 작은 공간을 선택할 수밖에 없었습니다.
(C) 이것들을 통해 우리 직원들이 여러분들에게 훨씬 더 효율적으로 서비스를 제공해 드릴 수 있을 겁니다.
(D) 일부 배송품이 아직 도착하지 않았습니다.

Questions 143-146 refer to the following e-mail.

날짜: 11월 17일
수신: 운영팀의 모든 직원들
발신: Raymond Smith
회신: Grace White 떠남

동료 직원들에게,

우리와 함께 오랫동안 근무해 온 Grace White 씨가 회사를 떠납니다. 그녀가 근무하는 마지막 날은 12월 30일 월요일이 될 겁니다.

그녀는 지난 8년 동안 우리 회사에 근무하면서 아주 다재다능한 직원으로서 인정 받아 왔습니다. 지난 8년간 그녀는 동료들간의 강한 업무 관계가 형성되는 데 기여했고, 다른 사람들이 업무 통찰력을 가지는 데 도움을 주었습니다. 우리는 그녀가 여태껏 보여준 직업 의식과 인간미를 잊지 못할 겁니다. 그것들이 항상 감사히 여겨질 겁니다.

이번 주 금요일 저녁에 그녀의 지속적인 성공을 기원하기 위한 송별회를 개최할 겁니다. 많은 분들이 오셔서 저희와 함께 축하해 주시기 바랍니다.

안부를 전하며,

Raymond Smith
운영부 부장
운영팀

145 (A) 우리는 그녀가 여태껏 보여준 직업 의식과 인간미를 잊지 못할 겁니다.
(B) 그녀는 항상 업무 관련 세미나에 참석했습니다.
(C) 그녀를 대체할 직원은 한 달 전에 이미 채용되었습니다.

(D) 여러분은 더 이상 그녀에게 의존하면 안 됩니다.

Part 7

Questions 147-148 refer to the following coupon.

다음 주 토요일, 7월 6일에 수제 피자를 전문적으로 하는 Super Pizza가 두 번째 매장을 드디어 오픈합니다. 이 쿠폰을 가지고 저희 새로운 곳을 방문하세요. 오픈 당일날, 여러분은 10가지 이상의 다양한 피자와 음료들을 50% 할인된 가격에 즐기실 수 있습니다. 1인당 쿠폰 한 장만 사용할 수 있습니다.

Super Pizza

매장 위치를 확인하시려면 쿠폰 뒷면의 약도를 참조하세요.

147 Super Pizza에 대해 암시되는 것은?
(A) 10년 넘게 사업을 했다.
(B) 정기적인 할인 행사를 개최한다.
(C) 새로운 매장을 계속 열 것이다.
(D) 다양한 피자를 제공한다.

148 쿠폰에 대해 사실인 것은?
(A) 모든 지점에서 사용될 수 있다.
(B) 고객들은 쿠폰을 이용해서 무료 음료를 받을 수 있다.
(C) 단 하루 동안만 사용될 수 있다.
(D) 유효 기간이 지정되지 않았다.

Questions 149-150 refer to the following advertisement.

하와이의 선택

여러분의 분주한 일상에서 벗어나 휴식을 취하러 파라다이스로 가세요. 하와이에 새로 생긴 고급 저택에서 멋진 추억을 만드세요. 그림 같은 풍경을 즐기면서 태양의 기운을 느끼실 수 있습니다. 다양하고 신선한 해산물로 구성된 저녁 식사와 하와이 최고의 와인을 음미할 기회를 놓치지 마세요. 낮에는 파도 타기나 스노클링과 같은 다양한 활동에 참여할 수 있습니다. 더 구체적인 사항은 저희 웹 사이트 www.tourmanias.com에서 확인하실 수 있습니다.

Hawaiian Crystal Villa
1-689-555-0088

149 광고의 목적은 무엇인가?
(A) 지역 특산물을 홍보하기 위해
(B) 휴양지를 홍보하기 위해
(C) 스포츠 활동 참여를 독려하기 위해
(D) 거주지를 추천하기 위해

150 광고되지 않은 특징은 무엇인가?
(A) 멋진 경치
(B) 질 좋은 음식
(C) 진열된 그림
(D) 다양한 활동

Questions 151-152 refer to the following e-mail.

수신: plannings1@smmotors.com
발신: gmanager1@publics.org
날짜: 6월 6일
제목: 주차 공지

모터쇼 참가자들에게,

다음 주 토요일에 국제모터쇼를 개최할 Jexpo Center의 주차장에서 누수를 발견했습니다. 그날, 그 옆에 있는 Galleria Mart가 영업을 하지 않기 때문에 그곳 주차장을 사용하도록 허가 받았습니다. 그래서 기업 관계자들과 참여자 및 행사 방문객들은 주차하는 데 문제가 없을 겁니다. 여러분은 지상에 있는 주차 공간을 이용하게 될 것입니다. 3일 이내에 여러분의 휴대폰으로 승인 바코드를 보내 드릴 겁니다. 주차장 입구에서 그걸 스캔하시면 차단기가 열릴 거예요. 궁금한 점이 있으시면 이메일로 연락 주시길 바랍니다.

Graham Wilson

151 Wilson 씨는 누구일 것 같은가?
(A) 기술자
(B) 유지보수 직원
(C) 경비원
(D) 행사 준비자

152 방문객들은 어떻게 주차장에 진입할 수 있는가?
(A) 경비원에게 문자메시지를 보여 줌으로써
(B) 차량 번호를 등록함으로써
(C) 암호를 입력함으로써
(D) 특정 이미지를 스캔함으로써

Questions 153-154 refer to the following form.

Oasis Hotel Restaurant

당신의 소중한 식사 시간을 책임지게 된 것을 아주 기쁘게 생각합니다. 잠깐만 시간을 내셔서 아래 설문 조사를 작성해 주세요. 그리고 식사 비용을 지불하실 때 계산대 직원에게 제출해 주세요. 설문지를 제출하신 분들은 매월 1일에 추첨을 통해 무료 식사 쿠폰을 받을 기회를 얻으실 수 있습니다.

	전적으로 동의	동의	보통	동의 안 함	전혀 동의 안 함
메뉴가 아주 다양하다.		V			
음식의 양이 충분했다.				V	
가격 대비 음식의 질이 좋았다.	V				
서빙 직원들의 서비스가 만족스러웠다.			V		
주문한 음식이 제때 제공되었다.	V				

의견:
서빙 직원들은 때때로 바빴지만 아주 친절하고 세심했습니다. 음식의 질은 아주 좋았는데, 한 끼 식사로는 양이 충분하지 않았습니다.

이름: Olive Beck   이메일: younger01@kanmail.net

153 Beck 씨가 가장 불만족스러워하는 것은 무엇인가?
(A) 선택의 다양성
(B) 음식의 양
(C) 대기 시간
(D) 직원들의 태도

154 Oasis Hotel Restaurant에 대해 나타난 것은?
(A) 고객들은 한 달에 한 번 상품권을 받을 수 있다.
(B) 가격이 저렴하다.
(C) 그 지역에서 아주 유명하다.
(D) 항상 사람들로 붐빈다.

Questions 155-157 refer to the following e-mail.

발신: David Sanders <vidds@irtca.net>
수신: 모든 발표자들 <수신자 비공개>
제목: 컨퍼런스 참가 공지
날짜: 10월 7일

국제 로봇 기술 학회에 오신 걸 환영합니다. 10월 25일 행사 장소인 미래 기술 연구 센터에 도착하면 반드시 1층 로비에서 등록하셔야 합니다. 등록 절차가 끝나면 기념 선물과 안내 자료들을 받으실 겁니다.

발표는 2층에 있는 A-1 홀에서 열릴 예정이고, 각 회사의 출품작들은 A-3 홀에 전시될 겁니다. 프로젝터를 포함한 발표 장비는 A-1홀에 다 갖춰져 있습니다. 여러분은 발표 자료를 USB에 저장해서 가지고 오시면 됩니다. 발표 전에 보안 담당자가 별도의 노트북 컴퓨터로 USB를 검사할 겁니다.

참여 기업 목록이 발표된 직후에 등록한 회사들이 좀 있습니다. 참가 상태를 조정해야 한다면 10월 15일까지 저희 웹 사이트에서 신청해 주세요.

진심으로,

David Sanders
컨퍼런스 주최자

155 행사 참가자들은 어디서 등록 절차를 해야 하는가?
(A) 1층 로비에서
(B) A-1 홀에서
(C) A-3 홀에서
(D) 웹 사이트에서

156 발표 전에 행해져야 하는 것은 무엇인가?
(A) 새로운 장비를 준비하기
(B) 자료를 검토하기
(C) 일정을 확인하기
(D) 기기를 검사하기

157 웹 사이트를 통해 참가자들이 무엇을 할 수 있는가?
(A) 참석 취소하기
(B) 장비 요청하기
(C) 발표 자료 등록하기
(D) 출품작 미리 보기

Questions 158-160 refer to the following online chat discussion.

Pablo Antonio [오전 09:16]	Brown 씨와 Roberts 씨, 안녕하세요. 제가 드디어 다음 달 세미나의 주제에 관한 전문가를 확정했습니다.
Elle Brown [오전 09:17]	좋아요. 누군데요? 유명한 사람인가요?
Pablo Antonio [오전 09:18]	소셜 미디어 마케팅 분야에서 아주 인정 받는 Kenneth Jones라고 합니다. 그분에 대해 아세요? 그는 웹 디자인에도 능숙해서 세미나에서 그 부분에 대한 내용도 포함할 것 같아요.
Terry Roberts [오전 09:21]	반가운 소식이네요. 저는 그 분야에 아주 관심이 많습니다.
Elle Brown [오전 09:22]	그분에 대해 들은 적 있어요. 아마 소셜 미디어와 웹에 관한 베스트셀러 책을 집필하신 분일 거예요.
Terry Roberts [오전 09:25]	그렇군요. 그럼 제가 오늘 세미나에 관해 부서 직원들에게 이메일을 발송하겠습니다.
Pablo Antonio [오전 09:29]	세미나가 끝난 후에 우리 모두가 그 발표자와 함께 저녁 식사를 할 거라는 내용을 이메일에 꼭 포함하세요.
Terry Roberts [오전 09:30]	알겠습니다. 잊지 않을게요.

Elle Brown [오전 09:33]	우리 각자 질문할 수 있는 기회도 있는 거죠?
Pablo Antonio [오전 09:36]	물론이죠. Terry, 모든 참석자들은 질문을 미리 준비해야 한다는 내용을 이메일에 추가하세요. 저는 오후 2시에 세미나 장소에 오는 방법에 대해 알려 주기 위해 Jones 씨에게 전화할 겁니다.

158 Antonio 씨가 동료들에게 메시지를 보낸 이유는 무엇인가?
 (A) 회의 일정을 변경하기 위해서
 (B) 신입 사원을 소개하기 위해서
 (C) 세미나에 관한 아이디어를 얻기 위해서
 (D) 동료들에게 초빙 강사에 대해 알려 주기 위해서

159 오전 9시 21분에, Roberts 씨가 "반가운 소식이네요"라고 말한 것은 무슨 의미인 것 같은가?
 (A) 그는 Jones 씨를 만나고 싶었다.
 (B) 그는 Jones 씨가 집필한 책을 이미 읽었다.
 (C) 그는 다가올 강의가 재미있을 거라고 예상한다.
 (D) 그는 많은 직원이 웹 디자인 분야에 관심이 있다고 생각한다.

160 Antonio 씨는 오후에 무엇을 할 것인가?
 (A) 강사에게 행사 장소로 가는 길을 알려준다
 (B) 직원들에게 이메일을 보낸다
 (C) 회의에 참석한다
 (D) 직원들의 의견을 묻는다

Questions 161-163 refer to the following announcement.

> **시청 개조 공사**
>
> Glasgow 시에서 시청 개조 공사를 위한 업체를 물색하고 있다. 업체는 공개 입찰을 통해 선정될 것이라고 James Denver 시장이 말했다. 일단 계약업체로 선정되고 나면 해당 회사는 2년간 시청의 개조 공사와 수리를 담당할 것이다.
>
> 최소 10년 이상 건설 업계에 종사한 기업들만 입찰에 지원할 수 있다. 게다가 필요한 자료들은 미리 준비되어 있어야 한다. 입찰을 위해 요구되는 서류의 목록은 시청 웹 사이트의 공지 게시판에서 확인할 수 있다.
>
> 만약 프로젝트가 잘 마무리된다면 시에서 추진하는 건축이나 토목 공사에 대한 입찰에 참여할 때 가산점이 주어질 수 있다.

161 발표문의 목적은 무엇인가?
 (A) 시청에 직원들을 채용하기 위해
 (B) 우수한 회사에 상을 수여하기 위해
 (C) 새 건물을 건설하기 위한 업체를 발표하기 위해
 (D) 프로젝트를 위한 업체를 찾기 위해

162 기업들이 입찰에 관한 세부 내용을 어떻게 알 수 있는가?
 (A) 시 공무원에게 연락함으로써
 (B) 시청을 방문함으로써
 (C) 인터넷에서 정보를 확인함으로써
 (D) 견적을 제시함으로써

163 [1], [2], [3] 그리고 [4]로 표시된 곳 중에 다음 문장이 들어가기에 가장 적합한 위치는 어디인가?
 "게다가 필요한 자료들은 미리 준비되어 있어야 한다."
 (A) [1]
 (B) [2]
 (C) [3]
 (D) [4]

Questions 164-167 refer to the following article.

> **British Daily**
>
> 그림즈비 (7월 6일)—세계적인 호텔 체인인 Emerald Hotel Group이 휴양 분양 아파트 사업에 진출한다. 영국 런던에 본사를 두고 있지만 그 그룹의 첫 번째 분양 아파트는 대한민국의 남해에 열 예정이다. 그곳은 세계 최대의 휴양지가 될 것이고, 자동 주차 안내 시스템을 포함한 최첨단 편의 시설을 보유할 것이다.
>
> 고객들은 1년 단위로 회원권을 구입할 수 있고, 원하면 객실의 소유권을 구매할 수도 있다. 이례적으로 우수한 시설물이기 때문에 구입하려는 사람들이 많이 몰릴 것으로 예상된다. 실제로 한국에서 유명한 부동산 투자자들과 기업가들이 이미 많은 관심을 보이고 있다고 전해진다.
>
> 또 다른 주목할 만한 점은 레스토랑이 아시아 최고의 요리 전문가인 김세준에 의해 운영될 것이라는 점이다. 그곳에 머무르는 관광객들은 아시아의 아주 다양한 대표 메뉴들을 즐길 기회가 있을 것이다.
>
> 엄청난 휴양 시설이 생겨나면서 그 지역의 고용률뿐만 아니라 전반적인 경제도 상당히 개선될 것으로 예상된다. 반면에 일부 전문가들은 해당 지역의 부동산 가격이 너무 많이 상승할 수 있다고 우려하기도 한다.
>
> 지역 주민들은 오랜 기간 변화가 없었던 지역에 생겨날 변화에 대해 대체적으로 매우 긍정적이다.
>
> – Anne Louis, 한국 특파원

164 기사의 목적은 무엇인가?
 (A) 아시아의 관광 경향을 설명하기 위해
 (B) 독자들에게 호텔 보수 공사에 대해 알려 주기 위해
 (C) 사업의 확장을 알리기 위해
 (D) 프로젝트에 투자자들을 유치하기 위해

165 분양 아파트에 대해 암시되는 것은?
 (A) 남해 시민들의 투자금으로 지어질 것이다.
 (B) 다양한 첨단 시설물들이 포함될 것이다.
 (C) 회원권은 비싼 가격에 거래될 것이다.
 (D) 유명 인사가 일부 시설물을 소유할 것이다.

166 Emerald Hotel Group의 본사는 어디에 있는가?
 (A) 홍콩에
 (B) 한국에
 (C) 영국에
 (D) 일본에

167 [1], [2], [3] 그리고 [4]로 표시된 곳 중에 다음 문장이 들어가기에 가장 적합한 위치는 어디인가?
 "이례적으로 우수한 시설물이기 때문에 구입하려는 사람들이 많이 몰릴 것으로 예상된다."
 (A) [1]
 (B) [2]
 (C) [3]
 (D) [4]

Questions 168-171 refer to the following text-message chain.

Rebecca Taylor	[오후 2:11]
안녕하세요, Carol. 홍보부의 Rebecca입니다. 지금 바쁘세요?	
Carol Thompson	**[오후 2:14]**
아뇨, 무슨 일 있어요?	
Rebecca Taylor	**[오후 2:15]**
고객 정보를 확인해야 하는데 전산망에 로그인할 수 없습니다.	

Carol Thompson	[오후 2:18]
잘못된 암호를 입력했나요?	

Rebecca Taylor	[오후 2:19]
그럴 리가 없습니다. 당신 팀의 Jim이 오늘 아침에 이미 제 암호를 재설정해 줬어요.	

Carol Thompson	[오후 2:20]
알겠습니다. 제가 당신의 컴퓨터를 한번 봐야겠어요. 지금 당신 사무실로 갈게요.	

Rebecca Taylor	[오후 2:22]
알겠습니다, 기다릴게요.	

168 Thompson 씨는 어느 부서에 근무할 것 같은가?
(A) 마케팅
(B) 인사
(C) 정보 기술
(D) 경영

169 Taylor 씨에 대해 암시되는 것은 무엇인가?
(A) 그녀는 암호를 자주 잊어버린다.
(B) 그녀의 로그인 정보가 변경됐다.
(C) 그녀의 컴퓨터가 제대로 작동되지 않는다.
(D) 그녀는 컴퓨터를 다루는 데 익숙하지 않다.

170 오후 2시 19분에, Taylor 씨가 "그럴 리가 없습니다"라고 쓴 의도는 무엇인가?
(A) 컴퓨터가 고장 났다.
(B) 그녀는 정확한 암호를 안다.
(C) 네트워크가 정상화될 수 없다.
(D) 프로젝트가 완료되지 않았다.

171 Thompson 씨는 다음에 무엇을 할 것인가?
(A) Taylor 씨의 업무 현장으로 간다
(B) 암호를 변경한다
(C) 소프트웨어를 확인한다
(D) 기술자를 보낸다

Questions 172-175 refer to the following article.

비즈니스 뉴스

EDINBURGH (11월 1일) — Kings Networks를 영국 3대 기업 중 하나로 성장시킨 Roy Smith가 10월 31일에 은퇴를 발표했다.

그는 미국에서 뉴욕대학교를 졸업한 직후, Kings Networks의 Manchester 지점에 입사했다. 그는 고객 서비스 담당자로서 짧은 기간에 매우 평판이 좋은 직원이 되었다. 그의 우수한 능력으로 그는 빠르게 승진해서 입사 4년 만에 Edinburgh 본사의 CFO 직책을 맡게 되었다.

그는 새로운 경영 정책을 도입함으로써 CFO로 임명된 지 10년이 되지 않아서 회사 순수익을 두 배가 넘게 만들었다. 결국 그는 43살의 나이에 Kings Networks의 역대 최연소 CEO가 되었다.

결과적으로 그의 후임자를 찾을 때까지 London 지점에서 온 Victoria Camden이 지난 30년 동안 회사의 귀중한 자산이었던 Roy Smith를 임시로 대신하는 데 선정되었다. 하지만 그녀만큼 적합한 후보자가 없기 때문에 대부분의 직원들은 Camden 씨가 최고경영자의 직책을 계속 수행할 것으로 예상한다.

Smith 씨가 은퇴한 후에도 본사가 있는 도시에 계속 거주할 것이기 때문에 회사는 그에게 고문직을 맡기기로 결정했다.

172 기사의 목적은 무엇인가?
(A) 사업의 폐업을 알리기 위해
(B) 회사 정책을 홍보하기 위해
(C) 임원의 은퇴를 알리기 위해
(D) 회사의 실적을 설명하기 위해

173 두 번째 문단의 여덟 번째 줄에 있는 단어 "landed"와 가장 의미가 가까운 것은?
(A) 찾았다
(B) 도착했다
(C) 사퇴했다
(D) 맡았다

174 Camden 씨에 대해 암시되는 것은?
(A) 회사에 거의 30년 동안 헌신했다.
(B) 회사의 리더로서 계속 남을 것 같다.
(C) 빠르게 진급했다.
(D) 회사의 고문이었다.

175 Smith 씨는 현재 어디에 거주하는가?
(A) Edinburgh에
(B) Manchester에
(C) London에
(D) New York에

Questions 176-180 refer to the following flyer and e-mail.

Grand Photo Festival

제8회 Grand Photo Fair가 7월 6일부터 8일까지 3일 동안 Stainley Art & Culture Center에서 개최됩니다. 이 박람회에 지원하려면 예선에 먼저 참여해야 합니다. 예선은 6월 8일부터 12일까지 진행되며 누구나 참여할 수 있습니다. 최대 500명까지 선착순으로 작품을 제출할 수 있습니다. 제출된 것들 중에 100개의 작품이 전시될 겁니다. 작년에는 Rotterdam 지역 출신의 사진작가들만 초대했지만 이번에는 지역 제한을 폐지했습니다. 각 참가자는 최대 두 개의 작품을 제출할 수 있습니다.

지원하시려면 다음의 단계를 따라 주세요.

1. 등록 양식을 www.artfestival.org.ca에서 다운로드하세요. 그러고 나서 양식을 작성해서 웹 사이트의 'Application' 링크에 접속해서 올려 주세요.

2. 작품을 우편을 통해 Rotterdam Photography Association으로 보내세요. 주소는 신청서 양식에 있습니다.

3. 마지막으로, 양식에 명시된 계좌 번호로 30달러를 송금하세요. 만약 두 작품을 제출하신다면 45달러를 납부해야 합니다.

신청 마감기한은 6월 1일입니다. 예선에서는 심사위원들의 평가 점수와 인터넷 설문 조사 점수를 합산하여 작품이 선정될 겁니다. 참가자들은 7월 1일에 작품이 전시용으로 선정되었는지 여부에 관해 개별적으로 통보 받을 겁니다.

수신: nice_world@artfestival.org.ca
발신: ken11@sepmail.com
날짜: 5월 16일
제목: 다가올 사진 전시회

저는 각 참가자가 두 개의 작품을 제출할 수 있다는 것을 알고 있습니다. 저는 지난 금요일에 사진 하나와 등록비를 보냈습니다. 그런데 지금 하나 더 보내도 될까요? 물론, 15달러의 추가 비용도 지불할 겁니다. 사실 제가 새로운 사진을 하나 찍었는데 그게 아주 마음에 들어서 제출하고 싶습니다.

그렇게 해도 되는지 알려 주세요.

감사합니다.
Rayleigh Bryk

수신: Leila Lütjens <lutjens_ace@naite.com>
발신: Brigham Heyes <bh_ok@oceanworlds.com>
회신: 정보
날짜: 3월 16일

Lütjens 씨에게,

지난 금요일에 호텔에서 당신과 대화하게 되어서 즐거웠습니다. 저는 당신에게 호텔 구매부의 일자리를 제안하려고 합니다. 구매부장과 저는 당신의 이력서를 검토한 후 당신이 그 부서에 아주 적합하다는 결론을 내렸습니다. 추가적으로 논의하기 위해 호텔로 다시 와 주시길 바랍니다.

3월 21일 수요일 오전 10시에 시간이 괜찮으신가요? 그 시간에 가능하지 않다면 언제가 당신에게 편한지 알려 주시겠어요?

당신을 다시 뵙길 기대합니다.

진심으로,

Brigham Heyes

176 전단지에 따르면, Grand Photo Festival에 대해 알 수 있는 것은?
(A) 한 달에 한 번 개최된다.
(B) 전문 사진작가들만 참여할 수 있다.
(C) 작품들은 온라인으로 전시될 것이다.
(D) 참가 조건이 변경되었다.

177 전단지의 여섯 번째 문단, 두 번째 줄에 있는 단어 "points"와 가장 의미가 가까운 것은?
(A) 점수
(B) 지점
(C) 단계
(D) 의미

178 참가자들은 예선 결과를 언제 알 수 있는가?
(A) 5월 16일에
(B) 6월 12일에
(C) 7월 1일에
(D) 7월 8일에

179 Bryk 씨는 등록비로 얼마를 지불했는가?
(A) 15달러
(B) 30달러
(C) 45달러
(D) 60달러

180 이메일에 따르면, Bryk 씨는 무엇에 대해 물어보는가?
(A) 지불 금액
(B) 추가 제출
(C) 비용 환불
(D) 작품의 수

181 보도 자료에 따르면, Ocean Worlds Hotel Group에 무슨 일이 생길 것인가?
(A) 새로운 지점 오픈하기
(B) 새로운 정책 시행하기
(C) 고객들을 행사에 초대하기
(D) 신입 사원을 대규모로 채용하기

182 Ocean Worlds Hotel Group에 대해 언급된 것은 무엇인가?
(A) 어린이들을 위한 사업을 하고 있다.
(B) 업계 최대의 기업이다.
(C) 임시직 근로자를 채용하고 있다.
(D) 새로 설립된 기업이다.

183 오픈 하우스에 대해 사실인 것은 무엇인가?
(A) 참가자들에게 식사가 제공될 것이다.
(B) 모든 구직자들은 참석해야 한다.
(C) 3월에 매주 한 번씩 열린다.
(D) 최대 300명까지 수용할 수 있다.

184 Heyes 씨가 이메일을 보낸 이유는 무엇인가?
(A) 특별한 선물을 주기 위해서
(B) 관리자를 소개하기 위해서
(C) 일자리를 제안하기 위해서
(D) 약속을 연기하기 위해서

185 Heyes 씨에 대해 암시되는 것은 무엇인가?
(A) 그는 기업의 회장이다.
(B) 그는 지점 관리자이다.
(C) 그는 인사부에서 근무한다.
(D) 그는 신입 사원이다.

Questions 181-185 refer to the following press release and e-mail.

For Immediate Release
연락처: media_team@oceanworlds.com

Sydney, 2월 16일—일류 호텔 기업 중의 하나인 Ocean Worlds Hotel Group이 올해 상반기에 대규모의 신입 사원 채용을 실시합니다. 지원서는 3월 6일부터 4월 6일까지 받을 것입니다. 호주에 있는 본사 외에도 스위스, 프랑스, 독일, 그리고 네덜란드를 포함한 유럽 주요 국가에 있는 호텔 지점에서 근무할 300명을 모집하고 있습니다. 저희 회사는 업계 최고의 급여와 넉넉한 복리후생제도를 제공하는 것으로 잘 알려져 있습니다.

오픈 하우스 행사가 유럽의 각 지점에서 개최될 겁니다. 지점장으로부터 잠재적인 직원들은 저희 회사에 관한 많은 정보를 얻을 수 있을 뿐만 아니라 회사 주요 시설을 둘러보는 좋은 기회도 가질 수 있습니다. 오픈 하우스 행사는 3월 매주 금요일에 열릴 것입니다. 금요일 오픈 하우스에 참석하고 싶은 분들은 3월 3일까지 www.oceanworlds.com에서 등록해야 합니다. 지원 가능한 일자리에 관한 정보도 얻을 수 있습니다.

Ocean Worlds Hotel Group은 1945년에 설립되어서 현재 전 세계의 16개국에 33개의 지점을 보유하고 있습니다. 게다가 호주, 프랑스 그리고 영국에서 어린이들을 위한 대형 놀이공원을 운영하고 있습니다.

Questions 186-190 refer to the following article, e-mail, and online review.

Karlstad Weekly

2월 18일—Karlstad의 외곽에 Green City Park로 가는 모든 길에 연결되는 새로운 자전거 도로가 건설되고 있다. Riverside Trail에 대한 작업은 약 두 달 전에 시작되었다. 스웨덴 기업인 Concord Industries의 Karlstad 지점에서 근무하는 Harald Albinson이 그 길을 설계했다. 그는 토목 설계 분야에서 15년 이상의 경력을 보유한 전문가이다.

Concord Industries는 영국과 프랑스를 포함한 많은 유럽 국가에서 차도와 자전거 도로 작업에 참여했다. 새로운 자전거 도로에 맞게 주변 도로도 일부 개조되어야 할 필요가 있기 때문에 이 일은 역대 가장 큰 프로젝트이다. 그러므로 만약 그것이 잘 마무리된다면 그 작업에 참여한 Albinson 씨와 모든 직원들은 특별 보너스와 추가적인 유급 휴가를 받을 것이다. 그 프로젝트는 올해 10월까지 완료될 것으로 예상된다.

많은 지역 주민들이 그 프로젝트가 가져올 고용과 관광에 대한 지원에 매우 좋아하고 있다. Concord Industries는 도로에서 일할 수백 명의 지역 주민들을 고용했다. Karlstad의 관광 행정 담당관은 새로운 자전거 도로가 많은 서비스 부문의 활동을 늘려서 결국 지역 경제를 활성화시킬 거라고 기대한다. 일단 공사가 끝나고 나면 완공을 기념하기 위한 마라톤이 11월에 열릴 예정이다.

수신: Harald Albinson <ha_smile@concordindustries.se>
발신: Hanna Vinter <hannavinter@concordindustries.se>
날짜: 10월 30일
제목: 당신의 성과

Albinson 씨에게,

Riverside Trail과 주변 시설물을 잘 완성한 것에 대해 축하 드리기 위해 메일을 보냅니다. 이번 작업이 Karlstad에서 우리 회사의 입지를 더욱 굳히게 해 줬습니다. 당신의 엄청난 업적을 기념하기 위해 Karlstad 시장님이 이번 주 목요일에 당신에게 감사패와 기념 선물을 전달할 예정입니다. 생각지도 못했던 일이죠? 게다가 당신은 함께 일했던 동료들과 다음 달에 한 달간 휴가를 즐기게 될 겁니다.

Hanna Vinter
관리부, Concord Industries

http://www.karlstadhotels.co.se/
| 홈 | 서비스 | 예약 | **후기** |

Berta Riverside Hotel

11월 18일 Viola Strand 작성

제 이름은 Viola이고 저는 Stockholm에 살고 있습니다. 일주일 전에 저는 두 명의 친구들과 함께 Karlstad에서 열린 마라톤 경기에 참여했습니다. 정말 멋진 행사였어요! 행사도 당연히 재미있었지만 우리가 달렸던 도로는 특히 인상 깊었습니다. 주변의 경치가 아주 좋았기 때문에 Berta Riverside Hotel에서 이틀을 머물렀습니다. 호텔도 역시 주변 풍경과 조화가 잘 되는 멋진 장소였습니다. 편안한 객실부터 무료 무선 인터넷까지 모든 편의 시설이 제공되었습니다. 아침 식사 뷔페는 제가 여태껏 먹어 본 것 중 최고였습니다. 하지만 호텔방에서 그 아름다운 길을 조금도 볼 수 없었다는 것이 아쉬웠습니다.

186 기사의 목적은 무엇인가?
(A) 지역 행사를 홍보하기 위해
(B) 지역 교통 문제를 설명하기 위해
(C) 사람들에게 경주에 참여하도록 권장하기 위해
(D) 건설 프로젝트에 대해 보고하기 위해

187 Albinson 씨에 대해 암시되는 것은?
(A) 추가 상여금을 받을 것이다.
(B) 마라톤 대회에서 상을 받았다.
(C) 호텔 경영 분야의 전문가다.
(D) 더 큰 프로젝트를 맡게 될 것이다.

188 이메일에 나타난 내용은 무엇인가?
(A) Albinson 씨는 Karlstad로 여행을 갈 것이다.
(B) Albinson 씨는 휴가를 가고 싶어 한다.
(C) Albinson 씨는 예상치 못했던 소식을 들을 것이다.

(D) Concord Industries는 Karlstad에 본사를 두고 있다.

189 Strand 씨에 대해 사실인 것은 무엇인가?
(A) 그녀는 Concord Industries에서 일하고 싶어 한다.
(B) 그녀는 호텔의 전망에 대해 만족하지 않았다.
(C) 그녀는 Stockholm에서 Karlstad로 이사했다.
(D) 그녀는 Karlstad에 친구들이 있다.

190 Strand 씨가 호텔에 대해 가장 좋아했던 것은 무엇인가?
(A) 아침 식사
(B) 무료 인터넷 서비스
(C) 직원들의 친절함
(D) 청소 서비스

Questions 191-195 refer to the following advertisement and e-mails.

Top Smart Case

Top Smart Case는 한국에서 가장 오랜 기간 동안 휴대폰 보호 케이스 생산 및 공급을 전문적으로 하고 있습니다. 우리 제품은 여러분들이 한번도 본 적 없는 혁신적인 재료로 만들어집니다. 케이스를 선택하기 전에 아래의 특징들을 확인하세요.

1. **부드러움** - Top Smart Case에서 생산된 모든 제품은 끼워진 휴대폰에 전혀 손상을 입히지 않습니다. 케이스를 휴대폰에 쉽게 씌우고 벗길 수 있습니다.

2. **스며들지 않음** - 케이스 내부로 공기나 물이 들어가지 않습니다. 케이스에 보관된 제품은 잘 보호되며 먼지 하나도 들어가지 않는 상태로 유지됩니다.

3. **인체에 무해** - 저희 제품은 100% 고급 실리콘으로 만들어져서 인체에 나쁜 영향을 끼치지 않습니다.

4. **편리** - 깨끗한 물로 씻기만 주면 케이스는 항상 새것처럼 보일 겁니다.

5. **스타일** - 저희 웹 사이트 www.topsmart.com에서 다양한 제품 디자인들을 보실 수 있습니다. 저희는 고객들을 위해 디자인을 주문 제작하기도 합니다.

수신: Paul Staunton
발신: Nancy Harris
날짜: 6월 1일
제목: 판촉용 물품

Staunton 씨에게,

저희 판촉 물품용 케이스의 디자인에 관한 친절한 설명에 감사 드립니다. 당신이 말씀하신 대로 케이스 뒷면에 저희 회사 로고가 너무 크면 안 될 것 같습니다.

그리고 저희 팀원들과 논의한 후, 로고가 케이스에 인쇄되는 것보다 새겨지는 게 더 나을 것 같습니다. 귀사의 제품은 깨끗하게 유지하기 쉬워서 고객들이 오랜 기간 사용할 겁니다. 그런데 제 생각엔 인쇄된 로고는 시간이 지나면서 지워질 것 같아요. 만약 로고를 새긴다면 시간과 비용이 얼마나 소요될지 궁금합니다. 또한 혹시 더 좋은 방법이나 아이디어를 알려 주신다면 감사하겠습니다.

안부를 전하며,

Nancy Harris
Tanny Life Insurance

수신: Nancy Harris
발신: Paul Staunton
날짜: 6월 5일
제목: 로고 작업

Harris 씨에게,

당신이 보내 주신 이메일을 신중하게 검토해 봤습니다. 물론 대부분의 사람들은 휴대폰 케이스를 며칠만 사용하고 버리지는 않습니다. 당신이 언급한 대로, 인쇄된 로고는 그렇게 오래 유지되지 않을 겁니다. 만약 케이스 표면에 로고를 그리려고 레이저 기법을 사용한다면 꽤 오랜 기간 유지될 수 있지만 비용이 더 비쌉니다. 만약 당신이 얘기한 대로 저희가 새겨진 제품을 제작한다면 아마 원래 예정된 일정보다 약 5일 정도 더 걸리겠지만 추가적인 비용은 발생하지 않을 것 같아요. 최종 결정이 나오면 연락해 주세요. 고품질의 제품을 제공해 드리기 위해 최선을 다하겠습니다.

안부를 전하며,
Paul Staunton
Top Smart Case

191 Top Smart Case에 대해 알 수 있는 것은 무엇인가?
(A) 새로 생긴 기업이다.
(B) 포장용 상자를 생산한다.
(C) 상품을 맞춤 제작할 수 있다.
(D) 한국에서만 제품을 판매한다.

192 Harris 씨가 이메일을 보낸 이유는 무엇인가?
(A) 조언을 구하기 위해
(B) 할인을 요청하기 위해
(C) 문제점을 알리기 위해
(D) 제조업체를 추천하기 위해

193 왜 Harris 씨는 각인된 휴대폰 케이스를 원하는가?
(A) 가격이 싸다.
(B) 희귀한 물건이다.
(C) 사람들이 오래 사용할 수 있다.
(D) 고급 재료가 사용된다.

194 첫 번째 이메일에 따르면, Top Smart Case의 어떤 특징이 고객들에게 영향을 미칠 것인가?
(A) 부드러움
(B) 스며들지 않음
(C) 인체에 무해
(D) 편리

195 Staunton 씨는 자신의 이메일에서 무엇을 인정하는가?
(A) 인쇄 기술이 많이 발전했다.
(B) 인쇄물은 수명이 길지 않다.
(C) 로고를 만드는 것은 비용이 많이 든다.
(D) 레이저 기법이 가장 효율적이다.

Questions 196-200 refer to the following article, schedule, and e-mail.

지역 회사들이 운영하는 무료 강의

Jenny Houston 작성

(2월 16일)—Boston에 있는 몇몇 기업들은 지역 주민들을 위해 다양한 교육 프로그램들을 제공하고 있습니다. 그들은 지역 주민들에게 혜택을 주면서 동시에 홍보를 극대화하고 있습니다.

모든 무료 교육 과정은 정규 운영 시간 동안에 진행되고, 장소는 지역 주민센터에서 제공됩니다. 각 기업의 담당자들이 수강 신청자들을 관심 분야에 맞는 교육 과정에 배정될 수 있도록 안내해 드립니다.

지역 주민들과 기업체 모두에게 유익한 이 행사는 실질적으로 취업에 도움이 되는 과정들을 다룹니다. 이 무료 교육 과정을 이수한 많은 구직자들이 원하는 직업을 구하는 데 성공했습니다. 게다가 많은 기업들이 더 숙련된 직원을 채용했기 때문에 이 프로그램에 더 관심을 가지게 되었습니다. Wells Bank의 인사부장인 Martin Greaves는 "이 교육 프로그램 덕분에 저희는 신입 사원들을 별도로 교육시킬 필요가 없어서 매우 만족스럽습니다"라고 말했습니다.

Howard 주민센터의 주간 교육 프로그램 일정표

시간대	월	화	수	목	금
오전 10시-오후 12시	오피스 프로그램 실습 (Bill Anderson)	기본 웹 디자인 (John Stevens)	오피스 프로그램 실습 (Bill Anderson)	기본 웹 디자인 (John Stevens)	오피스 프로그램 실습 (Bill Anderson)
오후 1시-오후 3시	현대의 조경 (Sam Stimson)	미정	현대의 조경 (Sam Stimson)	발표 기술 (Sara Jeong)	기본 웹 디자인 (John Stevens)
오후 4시-오후 6시	발표 기술 (Sara Jeong)	미정	발표 기술 (Sara Jeong)	미정	현대의 조경 (Sam Stimson)

※모든 강의는 주 3회 열립니다.

수신: Peter Mendes
발신: Jiyeon Lee
날짜: 3월 16일
제목: 회신: 교육 프로그램

Mendes 씨께,

지역 기업들에 의해 운영되는 교육 프로그램에 대해 저희 주민센터에 연락해 주셔서 감사 드립니다. 그 교육 과정은 4년 동안 운영되었고, 많은 주민들이 직업을 구하기 위한 유용한 전문 지식을 배웠습니다. 사람들은 무료 강의이기 때문에 정말 유용한지 의문을 가지시는 경우가 종종 있습니다.

이 프로그램들은 Planting Industries와 같은 저희 지역을 대표하는 기업들의 후원을 받기 때문에 모든 수업은 명성 있는 강사들이 진행합니다. 물론, 지난달의 기사에 보도된 것처럼 당신의 구직 활동에도 매우 유익할 겁니다.

하지만 당신이 관심 있는 교육 과정의 일정 중, 금요일 오후 4시 수업은 목요일 같은 시간대로 변경될 겁니다.

안부를 전하며,

Jiyeon Lee

196 기사문에서 무료 교육 과정에 대해서 언급된 것은 무엇인가?
(A) 인기가 많아지고 있다.
(B) 구직자들만 수업에 참석할 수 있다.
(C) 고용과 연관되어 있다.
(D) 주민들이 지역 사회에서 인맥을 형성하는 데 도움이 된다.

197 일정표에서 알 수 있는 것은 무엇인가?
(A) 모든 웹 디자인 수업은 아침에 열린다.
(B) 일부 시간대는 아직 정해지지 않았다.
(C) 과목별로 수업의 횟수는 다르다.
(D) 모든 학생들은 매일 아침에 출석해야 한다.

198. 이메일에 따르면, 모든 프로그램의 장점은 무엇인가?
    (A) 수업 시간이 유동적이다.
    (B) 무료 자료들이 우편으로 제공된다.
    (C) 학생들은 장학금을 받을 수 있다.
    (D) 믿을 만한 강사들이 강의를 한다.

199. 이메일에 따르면, 주민들이 프로그램에 대해 염려하는 것은 무엇인가?
    (A) 강의의 질
    (B) 강의를 위한 준비
    (C) 일정 겹침
    (D) 수업의 난이도

200. Mendes 씨에 대해 암시되는 것은?
    (A) 예전에 수업에 참석한 적이 있다.
    (B) 오후에는 시간이 없다.
    (C) 금요일 오후에 강의를 들어야 한다.
    (D) 입사 후에 교육이 필요하지 않을 수도 있다.

2회

| p.56

01 (C)	02 (B)	03 (A)	04 (D)	05 (B)
06 (D)	07 (B)	08 (B)	09 (C)	10 (A)
11 (C)	12 (A)	13 (A)	14 (B)	15 (B)
16 (B)	17 (C)	18 (A)	19 (C)	20 (B)
21 (A)	22 (A)	23 (B)	24 (C)	25 (A)
26 (A)	27 (C)	28 (B)	29 (C)	30 (B)
31 (A)	32 (C)	33 (D)	34 (A)	35 (B)
36 (D)	37 (A)	38 (D)	39 (B)	40 (A)
41 (A)	42 (C)	43 (C)	44 (B)	45 (C)
46 (D)	47 (A)	48 (D)	49 (A)	50 (C)
51 (D)	52 (B)	53 (A)	54 (C)	55 (C)
56 (D)	57 (C)	58 (D)	59 (B)	60 (B)
61 (C)	62 (A)	63 (C)	64 (D)	65 (C)
66 (D)	67 (D)	68 (D)	69 (B)	70 (C)
71 (B)	72 (C)	73 (C)	74 (B)	75 (C)
76 (D)	77 (A)	78 (C)	79 (C)	80 (A)
81 (D)	82 (C)	83 (A)	84 (B)	85 (C)
86 (A)	87 (C)	88 (C)	89 (C)	90 (B)
91 (D)	92 (D)	93 (C)	94 (D)	95 (C)
96 (B)	97 (A)	98 (C)	99 (C)	100 (B)
101 (A)	102 (A)	103 (D)	104 (D)	105 (D)
106 (D)	107 (B)	108 (D)	109 (D)	110 (D)
111 (C)	112 (A)	113 (D)	114 (D)	115 (B)
116 (D)	117 (A)	118 (B)	119 (D)	120 (D)
121 (C)	122 (B)	123 (C)	124 (B)	125 (A)
126 (A)	127 (C)	128 (B)	129 (D)	130 (C)
131 (A)	132 (C)	133 (A)	134 (C)	135 (C)
136 (A)	137 (D)	138 (C)	139 (C)	140 (C)
141 (D)	142 (C)	143 (A)	144 (C)	145 (A)
146 (A)	147 (C)	148 (A)	149 (C)	150 (C)
151 (C)	152 (B)	153 (A)	154 (C)	155 (D)
156 (B)	157 (C)	158 (D)	159 (A)	160 (B)
161 (C)	162 (D)	163 (C)	164 (D)	165 (B)
166 (A)	167 (C)	168 (A)	169 (D)	170 (C)
171 (D)	172 (A)	173 (A)	174 (C)	175 (A)
176 (D)	177 (C)	178 (C)	179 (B)	180 (D)
181 (B)	182 (D)	183 (C)	184 (D)	185 (D)
186 (C)	187 (B)	188 (A)	189 (B)	190 (D)
191 (C)	192 (B)	193 (A)	194 (A)	195 (D)
196 (A)	197 (D)	198 (C)	199 (C)	200 (C)

Part 1

1. (A) He's putting down his briefcase.
   (B) He's fixing the railing.
   (C) He's walking down some steps.
   (D) He's putting on his jacket.

2. (A) They are writing on the paper.
   (B) They are looking at a screen.
   (C) They are assembling a monitor.
   (D) They are painting some seats.

3   (A) She's mopping the floor.
    (B) She's placing a sofa against a wall.
    (C) She's ironing her shirt.
    (D) She's holding the curtain.

4   (A) Some boxes are being closed on shelves.
    (B) Some suitcases are being wrapped.
    (C) Some employees are unloading a shipment of boxes.
    (D) Some boxes are stacked in a warehouse.

5   (A) A camera is being moved onto a table.
    (B) One of the men is adjusting some equipment.
    (C) One of the men is installing a machine.
    (D) One of the men is dusting a camera lens.

6   (A) People are swimming in the sea.
    (B) Some people are fishing on a ship.
    (C) A flag is fluttering in the wind.
    (D) Some boats are docked at a pier.

Part 2

7   What's the new manager's name?
    (A) In the Sales Department.
    (B) It's Gilbert.
    (C) Before 10 A.M.

8   Where did you find the folder?
    (A) Yes, you can use it.
    (B) I ordered it online.
    (C) Some papers are in it.

9   Are the landscapers planting flowers or trees in the company garden?
    (A) You should call the power plant.
    (B) My office is on the second floor.
    (C) That hasn't been decided yet.

10 How often do you go to the fitness club?
    (A) Three times a week.
    (B) It's really good for your health.
    (C) It is located behind the museum.

11 I went to Seattle to see a rock concert.
    (A) I can reserve tickets for you.
    (B) The seating position was very good.
    (C) Really? It must have been exciting.

12 Who's going to teach you how to play the piano?
    (A) Mr. Favreau is.
    (B) It was a wonderful performance.
    (C) It will be $200 per month.

13 Does your store sell gift certificates?
    (A) Sure, we do.
    (B) Please sign on the bottom of the form.
    (C) Thank you for the unexpected gift.

14 I don't know what the error message on my computer means.
    (A) Have you checked attendance?
    (B) Mr. Rogen is good at using computers.
    (C) She is very kind.

15 Would you like to go to lunch with us?
    (A) A table for 4.
    (B) That sounds good.
    (C) Well done, please.

16 Is Dr. Kim available, or is there someone else I can see now?
    (A) Your appointment is confirmed.
    (B) Could you come back around 4 P.M.?
    (C) The office will be closed tomorrow.

17 The sales seminar for managers isn't full yet, is it?
    (A) Some sales assistants will attend the seminar.
    (B) The community center closes at five.
    (C) I can put you on the waiting list.

18 Don't you have a meeting at three?
    (A) Only Human Resources staffers can attend.
    (B) The files are in the cabinet.
    (C) He will make a presentation.

19 Have you finished planning the foundation celebration event?
    (A) I am planning to order a new one.
    (B) The report was found in the drawer.
    (C) It's not for another few months.

20 Could you return the rental car by next Tuesday?
    (A) I've already signed the rental agreement.
    (B) Do I have to refuel it?
    (C) Turn left at the second intersection.

21 The bus will arrive within the next half hour, right?
    (A) I think so.
    (B) The ticket is three dollars.
    (C) A monthly pass is much more economical.

22 Did you remember to renew your subscription?
    (A) I already paid for next year's subscription.
    (B) He signed the new contract.
    (C) You can get it at the seminar.

23 Weren't you supposed to send out the memo to all of the members?
    (A) Everyone, this is Janet, a new employee.
    (B) It has to be partially modified.
    (C) I haven't read it yet.

24 Why don't we close the restaurant early?
    (A) How about having lunch there?
    (B) It is always crowded with diners.
    (C) Someone made a reservation for later.

25 The warranty is for one year, isn't it?
    (A) I'll check it out. Hold on, please.
    (B) We are offering a special discount today.
    (C) No, I've lived in this town for two years.

26 I noticed that you majored in English literature as an undergraduate.
    (A) Yes, I was very interested in American literature.
    (B) No, my graduation is next month.
    (C) I revised the document several times.

27 How did you like the new movie theater?
    (A) I went there by taxi.
    (B) I'm sorry, but I can't go to see a movie.

(C) It was amazing!

28. Did the office supplies we ordered last week arrive yesterday afternoon?
    (A) The train arrives at seven o'clock.
    (B) I left work early yesterday.
    (C) There are many old supplies.

29. How can I request that the air conditioner be repaired?
    (A) You don't have to turn it off.
    (B) I'm going on vacation tomorrow.
    (C) I'll give you a form to fill out.

30. Which advertising agency do you recommend?
    (A) I think TV commercials will be more effective.
    (B) We're looking for one, too.
    (C) Could you write me a letter of recommendation?

31. When will the post office open tomorrow?
    (A) At 9 A.M.
    (B) It's on Parker Street.
    (C) By express mail, please.

Part 3

Questions 32-34 refer to the following conversation.

> M: Jessy, did you know that the trade show will be held in September?
> W: I read the news in the newspaper. It will be held for a week starting on September 12, right?
> M: Yes, why don't we take this opportunity to make our washing machines go beyond Asia and into Europe?
> W: That's a good idea. Our product is competitive enough. Could you find out what we need to do to attend the fair?

32. What is the conversation about?
    (A) A new product
    (B) A sporting competition
    (C) A business-related event
    (D) Business travel

33. Where do the speakers most likely work?
    (A) At a travel agency
    (B) At a publishing company
    (C) At an advertising agency
    (D) At a home appliance company

34. What does the woman suggest the man do?
    (A) Check out what they need to do for an event
    (B) Present an idea to promote a product
    (C) Analyze European market trends
    (D) Register for an event in advance

Questions 35-37 refer to the following conversation.

> W: Nolan, I just talked to the Goldman Trading Company about the design of its headquarters building. The people there responded very favorably to our plans to use rather expensive but environmentally friendly construction materials and to install roofs with solar panels that save energy.
> M: If the proposal's carried out, we're going to make a really good building. By the way, the demand for solar panels has skyrocketed these days, so their prices have gone up even more. Do you think that's okay?
> W: Yes, they said they don't really care about the cost. I'll ask Mr. McKay, the head of the material purchase team, to provide us with an estimate.

35. What type of company do the speakers most likely work for?
    (A) A real estate agency
    (B) An architectural firm
    (C) An interior design company
    (D) A trading company

36. Why have the prices of solar panels gone up?
    (A) The cost of materials is high.
    (B) They take a long time to produce.
    (C) They do not consume much electricity.
    (D) They have become more popular.

37. What will the woman most likely do next?
    (A) Contact a colleague
    (B) Cancel a contract
    (C) Ask for funding
    (D) Send out an estimate

Questions 38-40 refer to the following conversation.

> W: Thank you for calling Sunshine Cleaning. How may I help you?
> M: Hello. My name's Donald Nair, and I'm going to move into my new apartment on Wednesday, August 8.
> W: Congratulations! I'm sure you are very happy.
> M: Thank you. I'm looking for a company to clean up my place before I move there and my neighbor recommended you. Do you clean residential spaces?
> W: I'm so glad to hear that, Mr. Nair. We clean all kinds of buildings. Would you like to make a reservation now?
> M: Yes, how about at 9 A.M. on August 6? How long will it take to finish the work?
> W: It will take about eight hours, including one hour for lunch. I think the crew will be finished around 5 P.M. Please tell me the address of your current residence.

38. What kind of company does the woman work for?
    (A) A marketing firm
    (B) A construction company
    (C) A moving company
    (D) A cleaning service

39. How did the man know about the service provider?
    (A) He did a search on the Internet.
    (B) His acquaintance gave him some information.
    (C) He saw an ad near an apartment complex.
    (D) A moving company told him about it.

40 What information does the woman ask the man for?
(A) The location of his residence
(B) His preferred payment plan
(C) His e-mail address
(D) His appointment time

Questions 41-43 refer to the following conversation.

W	Hi. I'm calling to see if you have a large private room available at your restaurant on April 24. I'm planning a dinner for 12 employees in my department.
M	Yes, we have enough room for 12 people. What time would you like to make a reservation?
W	I'd like to make it for 6:30 P.M.
M	Okay. I think the Topaz Room will be suitable for you. It is very quiet because it is located in the innermost part of our restaurant.
W	Perfect! Do you also serve vegetarian dishes? Two of our employees need them.
M	Yes, you can access our Web site and look at all the food options. Just tell me a day in advance, and we can prepare special dishes for those with dietary restrictions.

41 What event is the woman planning?
(A) A departmental meeting
(B) A retirement party
(C) A charity event
(D) A cooking seminar

42 What does the man ask about?
(A) Preferred dishes
(B) A reservation time
(C) A mailing address
(D) The number of attendees

43 What is suggested about the Topaz Room?
(A) It is already booked.
(B) It can accommodate more than 12 people.
(C) It is a completely independent space.
(D) It is equipped with amenities.

Questions 44-46 refer to the following conversation.

W	This is Dr. Harris's office. You have an appointment with the doctor tomorrow afternoon at three o'clock. I'm afraid that Dr. Harris says he has to leave work earlier than usual tomorrow, so your appointment needs to be rescheduled. How about next Tuesday?
M	Well, I'm supposed to go on a business trip next week. I won't be back for about 10 days starting next Monday. Is there any possibility I can see him before I leave?
W	Let me check. Hmm... Can you come tomorrow at 9 A.M.? Dr. Harris will be here an hour earlier than usual.
M	Okay. I'll be there then. Thank you.
W	I'll enter the change in the system right now. I apologize for the inconvenience.

44 Why is the woman calling?
(A) To suggest a medical examination
(B) To reschedule an appointment
(C) To confirm a reservation
(D) To report a system error

45 What time does Dr. Harris usually start working?
(A) At 8:00 A.M.
(B) At 9:00 A.M.
(C) At 10:00 A.M.
(D) At 11:00 A.M.

46 What does the man say he has to do next week?
(A) Visit another hospital
(B) Apply for sick leave
(C) Enter some new information
(D) Go on a business trip

Questions 47-49 refer to the following conversation with three speakers.

W1	Hello. We booked the Venable Convention Center for a new smartphone demonstration. We're here to get a brochure with detailed instructions for the event.
M	I see. Here's a brochure for the event organizers. The event will be held in the Grand Performance Hall. It's on the second floor.
W1	Thanks. Oh, we brought some shelves and equipment to be preinstalled today, and I think we should use the elevator.
W2	Yes, and not only is that necessary, but we'd like to have a cart that can be used to move the equipment easily.
M	Okay. I'll show you where the freight elevator is. There are several carts.

47 What event are the women organizing?
(A) A product demonstration
(B) A trade fair
(C) A sports competition
(D) A grand opening

48 What do the women ask about?
(A) Checking some equipment
(B) Putting products on display
(C) Promoting the details of an event
(D) Using an elevator

49 What will the man do next?
(A) Show the women to a place
(B) Help the women carry some goods
(C) Ask the women for a guidebook
(D) Inspect a machine

Questions 50-52 refer to the following conversation.

M	Hi, Rumi. We need to finalize the details of this year's company anniversary celebration.
W	I think we need some volunteers to help out with setting up the room and cleaning up afterward. As I said last Wednesday, let's have a meeting about the arrangements, including ways to recruit volunteers.

M   I just checked the schedule you e-mailed. <u>Will the meeting be held for only one hour tomorrow afternoon?</u> There are many things to talk about.

W   Oh, I must have written it wrong. I'd like to discuss it from 3 P.M. to 6 P.M. tomorrow. Please make some volunteer application forms to distribute tomorrow.

M   Okay. Before then, I'll have to notify the staff of the correct schedule.

W   All right. And I'll ask the manager where we can hold the meeting.

50 What are the speakers mainly discussing?
    (A) Launching a new product
    (B) Correcting some wrong information
    (C) Preparing for an upcoming event
    (D) Recruiting new employees

51 What does the man imply when he says, "Will the meeting be held for only one hour tomorrow afternoon"?
    (A) The meeting should not take a long time.
    (B) The discussion will end earlier than scheduled.
    (C) The man doesn't have any time to spare.
    (D) The meeting should be extended.

52 What does the woman ask the man to do?
    (A) Call a manager
    (B) Make a document
    (C) Do volunteer work
    (D) Contact all employees

Questions 53-55 refer to the following conversation.

M   Ms. Lee, you asked all employees this morning to come up with ideas to effectively promote our insurance products, didn't you?

W   Sure, what's your suggestion?

M   Since most people use social network services on smartphones these days, it would be the most realistic promotional tool.

W   I see what you mean. However, <u>there are so many ads on SNS.</u>

M   I understand. How about hiring some SNS experts and content creation specialists? Then, we could produce ads that get the attention of consumers.

W   I'm not sure if we have enough money in the budget to do that, but could you write me a detailed report for now? I'll look it over and discuss it with the managers.

M   Thank you. I'll get started on that right now.

53 Where is the conversation taking place?
    (A) At an insurance company
    (B) At an Internet service provider
    (C) At an electronics company
    (D) At an advertising agency

54 What does the woman mean when she says, "there are so many ads on SNS"?
    (A) Everyone has a smartphone.
    (B) Many people do not use other forms of media.
    (C) Consumers will not be interested in advertisements.
    (D) SNS advertising is essential.

55 What is the woman concerned about?
    (A) Recruiting the right person
    (B) Expenses for advertising
    (C) A deadline for a report
    (D) Additional public expenditures

Questions 56-58 refer to the following conversation.

M   We're back at SJB Radio after that short commercial break, and we're talking with Sheryl Taylor about her 5-city concert tour. Can you tell us about it?

W   I will be performing with my band in 5 big cities from October to November this year.

M   I see. I'm really looking forward to it.

W   In addition to my previous hits, the show will include several songs to be released in January next year. I've never sung an unreleased song at a performance. In addition, for the first time, this concert will be broadcast live on the Internet.

M   I think it's going to be great. Is there anything you want to ask your fans?

W   Umm… As I'll be performing during a time when there's little rain, I'll be putting on outdoor performances. However, due to unexpected weather conditions, the performances may be postponed or canceled, so please be sure to check the weather forecast.

56 What are the speakers discussing?
    (A) A new album
    (B) A TV program
    (C) An Internet broadcast
    (D) A musical performance

57 According to the woman, what is new about the event?
    (A) The length of a performance
    (B) The prices of tickets
    (C) Livestreaming
    (D) The number of songs

58 What does the woman suggest doing?
    (A) Buying tickets as soon as possible
    (B) Arriving earlier than the starting time
    (C) Finding more information on the Internet
    (D) Paying attention to the weather

Questions 59-61 refer to the following conversation.

M   I've been informed that Flight UK360 will arrive about 30 minutes later than its scheduled landing time. I'm sure there are passengers who will be changing planes.

W   Okay. Then I'll ask Justin on the service support team to prepare some shuttles for passengers.

M   Good idea. Oh, wait! We also need to send out an announcement for the passengers who will board Flight UK360 this evening. Umm, I'll do that now.

W	It's a flight to L.A., right? Marina's already on the announcement. Instead, please check the remaining flight schedules again.

59 What problem does the man mention?
(A) Some wrong information was announced.
(B) A flight will not arrive on time.
(C) Several passengers missed a connecting flight.
(D) The staff did not remember the schedule properly.

60 Why will the woman contact Justin?
(A) To change a plane reservation
(B) To ask for transportation
(C) To ask him to help carry baggage
(D) To report an arrival time

61 What does the woman ask the man to do?
(A) Call a coworker on the service support team
(B) Announce a schedule again
(C) Check some schedules
(D) Reset the landing time

Questions 62-64 refer to the following conversation and sign.

M	The parking lot in front of the concert hall is full of cars, so I'd better park in this parking lot instead.
W	It has limited parking times. I don't think you're allowed to park there now. It's 6:50 P.M.
M	Oh, you're right. Then we'll have to park in a parking structure a little away from the concert hall. It will take about five minutes to walk to the concert hall from there. Except for that, there won't be any problems.
W	I think it's a privately owned facility, so the parking fee will be more expensive. Anyway, it's time for the performance to start, so we have to hurry.
M	Okay. Then could you pick up the tickets at the ticket office while I park?

62 What problem are the speakers discussing?
(A) They need to find an alternative parking space.
(B) The man lost his parking ticket.
(C) They are not allowed to enter the concert hall.
(D) They arrived too late for the concert.

63 Look at the graphic. What day is it today?
(A) Monday
(B) Wednesday
(C) Friday
(D) Saturday

64 What does the man ask the woman to do?
(A) Pay a bill
(B) Book seats
(C) Confirm a charge
(D) Get tickets

Questions 65-67 refer to the following conversation and class schedule.

W	Our employees seem to be very happy with the company's new policy to pay the cost of foreign language courses.
M	Yes, as our company is engaged in the trading business, it would be a very good program for our employees.
W	I have a list of courses at the most prestigious language institute in our city. Here's the class schedule.
M	Are you saying that the company will pay for any of these courses I take?
W	Exactly, I'll have to enroll in the German class as I get off work almost every day after seven.
M	I usually get off work earlier than you do, but there's only one thing I can choose because I have a book discussion meeting every Thursday.

65 What are the speakers mainly discussing?
(A) Waiting lists for courses
(B) Preparations for a business trip
(C) A company-sponsored program
(D) An orientation session

66 According to the man, why is the company policy good for employees?
(A) They often go on business trips.
(B) They can make good use of their spare time.
(C) They can leave work earlier.
(D) They do a lot of business with foreign companies.

67 Look at the graphic. Which class will the man most likely take?
(A) Russian
(B) Spanish
(C) German
(D) French

Questions 68-70 refer to the following conversation and directory.

W	Hi. This is Emma calling from Sun Electronics. I'm calling to let you know that your air conditioner has been completely repaired.
M	It took longer than I had expected. Was it difficult to repair?
W	It wasn't particularly hard work. As summer is approaching, we get a lot of requests for air-conditioning maintenance.
M	I see. Please let me know how much I owe and when it can be installed in my house.
W	The price is $82, and our installer will take it to your home by 4 P.M. today. Is your address apartment number 1500 at 1160 Haro Street?
M	I'm in apartment 1506, not 1500. There's a directory in the administration office, so tell the installer to refer to it.

68. Where does the woman most likely work?
    (A) At a department store
    (B) At a car repair shop
    (C) At an electric company
    (D) At a customer service center

69. Why did the work take a long time?
    (A) There was an unexpected difficulty.
    (B) The demand for services has increased a lot.
    (C) There was a serious defect in the product.
    (D) Core parts were not supplied on time.

70. Look at the graphic. What is the man's name?
    (A) Roy Smith
    (B) Robert Walker
    (C) Kenneth Jones
    (D) Frank Evans

Part 4

Questions 71-73 refer to the following broadcast.

Hello. This is *Today's Focus* on THBC FM Radio. In today's news, a city official announced that the 6th annual drama festival scheduled for March 31 will be postponed until April 6. The schedule was changed suddenly since unprecedented heavy rain has been predicted for the day that it was originally scheduled for. Organizers of the event said this year's event will be very special with not only local actors but also famous French actors attending. Furthermore, Tommy Holland, the pop singer with the current number-one hit on the Billboard chart, is supposed to give a performance.

71. According to the speaker, why will the event be delayed?
    (A) To meet the schedules of some participants
    (B) To avoid inclement weather
    (C) To prevent scheduling conflicts
    (D) To make further preparations

72. Why do organizers say the event will be special?
    (A) It will be broadcast on the radio.
    (B) People can listen to new songs.
    (C) It will run late into the evening.
    (D) Celebrities from abroad will be there.

73. Who is Tommy Holland?
    (A) An event organizer
    (B) An actor
    (C) A broadcaster
    (D) A musician

Questions 74-76 refer to the following telephone message.

Good afternoon. My name is Shirley Hall. I booked a dinner for five people today, but I think two more people need to be added. The time won't change. We'll arrive there together at 6 P.M. I'm sorry to call you on such short notice, but be sure to let me know if it is possible to change my reservation. If I don't answer the phone, please send me a text message. I'll call you back as soon as I check it. Thank you.

74. Where does the listener work?
    (A) At a hotel
    (B) At a restaurant
    (C) At a library
    (D) At a theater

75. Why is the speaker calling?
    (A) To check a reservation time
    (B) To get information about a menu
    (C) To request a change in a reservation
    (D) To cancel a reservation

76. What is the speaker apologizing for?
    (A) She gave the wrong information.
    (B) She didn't answer the phone.
    (C) She arrived behind schedule.
    (D) She should have called earlier.

Questions 77-79 refer to the following advertisement.

We at Tech World are very proud to announce the release of our new high-performance laptop. This product currently performs the best of any product on the market in the country. The product looks very soft and light, but it is durable and will not break even if it falls 5 meters to the ground. The hard drive, the most vulnerable part of a computer, is also well protected. The warranty period is one year, but if you pay an extra $30, it will increase to three years. And for those who purchase laptops within the next week, we'll double the memory to 16 gigabytes.

77. What is being advertised?
    (A) A laptop computer
    (B) A hard drive
    (C) A camera
    (D) A mobile phone

78. What is suggested about the product?
    (A) It is inexpensive.
    (B) It is the lightest product.
    (C) Its memory is originally 8 gigabytes.
    (D) It is well packaged.

79. What should customers do to extend the warranty period?
    (A) Buy a memory chip
    (B) Register a product
    (C) Pay extra
    (D) Order an item within a week

Questions 80-82 refer to the following talk.

Congratulations on working for the Smart Engineering Company. Before we start work today, I have a few things to tell you. You should always wear work clothes at the factory. Your work clothes should be kept in your locker, and you can keep all your belongings there, too. There are more rules that you should follow. First, the most important thing is that information about our technology must not be leaked. Next, you must comply with the safety regulations at our company. I'm going to give you some documents that contain details about those two things right now. Please sign them and turn them in at the end of the meeting. There is a drop box next to the exit in this conference room. Let me know if you have any questions. Thank you.

80. Where does the talk most likely take place?
   (A) At a manufacturing plant
   (B) At a clothing company
   (C) At a construction company
   (D) At a hardware store

81. What does the speaker say the most important thing for the listeners to do is?
   (A) Wear working clothes
   (B) Follow safety regulations
   (C) Comply with working hours
   (D) Protect information security

82. What does the speaker mean when she says, "There is a drop box next to the exit in this conference room"?
   (A) Listeners should not throw away garbage.
   (B) The box should be moved to another room.
   (C) Papers should be dropped into the box.
   (D) Personal belongings should be kept in the box.

Questions 83-85 refer to the following telephone message.

Hi, Mr. Peterson. I'm calling from the store to give you the update you requested. Did the product demonstration go well? Customer responses to today's event were very enthusiastic. Your idea of offering discounts on computers for the graduation season was perfect. Today's computer sales were a complete success. The Vivace-6000 model is sold out, but many customers had difficulty installing the new operating system. We need to make a manual. Anyway, I should call the supplier right away to order additional products.

83. Where is the speaker calling from?
   (A) An electronics store
   (B) A software company
   (C) A gift shop
   (D) A furniture store

84. What does the speaker imply when she says, "We need to make a manual"?
   (A) More detailed information should be provided to the supplier.
   (B) Many people find it difficult to install a program.
   (C) She wants to run a different operating system.
   (D) She needs a strategy to increase product sales.

85. What is the speaker going to do next?
   (A) Send some products
   (B) Revise a manual
   (C) Contact a supplier
   (D) Assist customers

Questions 86-88 refer to the following talk.

I hope guest speaker Alan Windsor's lecture at this workshop will be beneficial to all of you. He has been teaching marketing for more than 15 years. Since he usually teaches in England, you have a very rare opportunity today. Moreover, it is a field that is directly related to your work, so be sure to ask him for a lot of advice. At noon, he'll be joining us for lunch. After that, Mr. Windsor's book, *The Essentials of Online Marketing*, will be distributed to all of you, and he will brief you on it. Please come to the seminar room about ten minutes before the beginning of the lecture to receive the wonderful gift he has for you.

86. What event is taking place?
   (A) A workshop
   (B) A company tour
   (C) A press conference
   (D) An anniversary celebration

87. What are the listeners advised to do?
   (A) Come up with ideas
   (B) Make presentations
   (C) Consult with a lecturer
   (D) Work overtime

88. What will happen in the afternoon?
   (A) Opinions will be exchanged.
   (B) A public hearing will be held.
   (C) Practical training will be implemented.
   (D) A publication will be introduced.

Questions 89-91 refer to the following introduction.

Hi, everyone. As you know, you'll be starting an onsite training session in Web programming technology for practical applications beginning on August 8. I will introduce you to Web programming expert Hassid Jung, who will be in charge of your training. He is an internationally renowned Web programmer and has been responsible for building the Web sites of major companies and organizations in Korea, Japan, and Australia. Furthermore, Mr. Jung teaches advanced Web programming theory at Stanford University. He says he is greatly rewarded by fostering as many excellent students as possible. He will surely be a great teacher for you.

89. Where do the listeners most likely work?
   (A) At a telecom company
   (B) At an educational institution
   (C) At a Web design company
   (D) At an online shopping mall

90. According to the speaker, what is Mr. Jung an expert in?
   (A) Business management
   (B) Web site construction
   (C) International trade
   (D) Public relations

91. What does Mr. Jung say about teaching students?
    (A) It is not an easy task.
    (B) It requires thorough preparation.
    (C) It costs him a lot of money.
    (D) It makes him feel fulfilled.

Questions 92-94 refer to the following excerpt from a meeting.

Klein Street, which is connected to Brown University, has heavy traffic these days. Because of that, many residents complain to the city's Transportation Department almost every day. It's a very old road. It's almost 30 years old. Compared to when the road was first completed, the number of cars has increased more than five times, so we need to find a way to solve this problem. Edward Jones, a member of the Transportation Department, suggested designating bus-only lanes during times when people commute to and from work and developing policies that actively encourage carpooling. And the Transportation Department manager advised us to expand the road while considering places to build additional roads nearby.

92. What problem is being discussed?
    (A) Noise from vehicles
    (B) Some damaged roads
    (C) A reduction in public transportation
    (D) Traffic congestion

93. Why is the problem occurring?
    (A) Some roads were repaired poorly.
    (B) The number of buses has increased in a city.
    (C) There are too many cars on a road.
    (D) Public transportation is not available to residents.

94. What does Mr. Jones suggest?
    (A) Expanding existing roads
    (B) Restricting traffic to certain vehicles
    (C) Adjusting commuting times
    (D) Creating bus-only lanes

Questions 95-97 refer to the following telephone message and schedule.

Hello, Dr. Baker. This is Catherine Wright. I'm calling to confirm your participation in the annual high-tech industry conference. Attendees in various fields are supposed to come to hear your presentation. I've already sent you the agenda for the conference and the presentation schedule, but some changes have been made. From 8 A.M. to 8:50 A.M., there will be some equipment tests. Thus, all presentations will be delayed by 30 minutes from the original schedule. As always, please respond to the survey that will be sent to your mobile phone at the end of the event. Thank you.

95. What is the purpose of the message?
    (A) To send some materials
    (B) To apologize for an inconvenience
    (C) To confirm participation in an event
    (D) To inform the listener about the attendees

96. Look at the graphic. At what time is the listener's presentation?
    (A) 8:30 A.M.
    (B) 9:00 A.M.
    (C) 10:00 A.M.
    (D) 12:00 P.M.

97. What is implied about the event?
    (A) The survey is conducted every year.
    (B) The presenter must arrive half an hour early.
    (C) It is only for engineers.
    (D) Attendees must register in advance.

Questions 98-100 refer to the following excerpt from a meeting and agenda.

Welcome to our monthly meeting. As you know, during the past week, we conducted a customer survey on our recently reorganized Internet shopping mall. What we learned from the survey is that our customers are satisfied with our overall products, but the problem is that errors often occur when they make online payments. In addition, sometimes it is not possible to track products being delivered. We have to fix all the problems as soon as possible. I'll contact the Web site's creator right away, and all of you should check for any other problems.

98. Look at the graphic. In which month is the staff meeting taking place?
    (A) March
    (B) April
    (C) May
    (D) June

99. What problem does the speaker mention?
    (A) A Web site connection is not smooth.
    (B) Some product pictures do not appear on screens.
    (C) There are problems locating products.
    (D) Deliveries are not being made on time.

100. What will the listeners most likely do after the meeting?
    (A) Inspect some machinery
    (B) Check a Web site
    (C) Call a specialist
    (D) Ship some orders

Part 5

101. 인터넷 서비스 업체는 일부 고객들에게 매주 컴퓨터 사용 횟수에 대한 설문에 답변해 주길 요청했다.

102. Culture & Entertainment는 기업 정책을 홍보하는 데 자주 사용되는, 눈을 뗄 수 없는 영상물을 주로 제작한다.

103. 비록 영업 프레젠테이션은 간략했지만 Prime Accounting Company는 그들을 전속 회계사로 채용하기로 즉시 결정했다.

104. 마케팅 부장은 정보를 더 효과적으로 전달하기 위해 프로젝터를 급히 사용해야 한다.

105. 여러분은 뮤지컬 공연 티켓을 온라인이나 전화로 구매할 수 있습니다.

106. 우리는 Bryan Dylan이 주문한 새 프린터와 두 개의 컬러 잉크 카트리지를 방금 받았다.

107 경리부는 전 직원들에게 모든 업무 관련 영수증을 내일 오후 5시까지 제출하라고 요청했다.

108 SH Technology 사는 현재 고등 교육 학위의 취득에 관심이 있는 직원들의 교육비를 상환해 준다.

109 많은 주간 교대 근무자들은 날씨가 좋을 때 야외에서 점심 먹는 것을 선호한다.

110 Ella Bush는 지난 10년간 스트레스를 없애는 법을 포함해서, 건강에 관련된 다양한 주제들에 대한 많은 책을 썼다.

111 비품 주문 양식이 어제 오후에 제출되었고, 주문품들은 내일 오후 2시까지 도착하기로 예정되어 있습니다.

112 새로운 정책은 기존 직원들뿐만 아니라 신입 사원들에게도 유익해야 한다.

113 Graham 씨는 계약 조건 중 일부를 수정해야 하기 때문에 계약서를 그에게 즉시 보내라고 요청했다.

114 Swift 씨는 잃어버린 자신의 지갑을 누가 우편으로 보냈는지 모른다.

115 영업 부장은 자신이 주문한 상품을 복사기 옆에 두라고 요청했다.

116 사장님은 저에게 쇼핑 센터 건축 과정을 주기적으로 보고하라고 말했습니다.

117 인사부의 모든 직원들은 내일 세미나에 참석하는 것이 중요하다.

118 Kistar Construction 사는 아주 경쟁력 있는 제안을 했지만 수주하는 데 실패했다.

119 자전거 타기가 시드니에서 인기가 매우 많아서 시의회가 모든 주요 도로에 자전거 도로를 추가한다는 계획을 승인했다.

120 최신 고속버스에 있는 뒤로 젖힐 수 있는 좌석으로 인해 승객들은 아주 편안하게 몸을 뻗고 누울 수 있다.

121 서류상에 표시된 금액은 견적일 뿐이며, 추가 선택 사항에 따라 달라질 수 있습니다.

122 양질의 식재료를 공급하는 Rich Mart는 다음 주 내내 고객들에게 30% 할인을 제공할 것이다.

123 대중에게 널리 알려진 바이올리니스트 이수미의 공연이 점점 많은 사람들을 끌어들이고 있습니다.

124 London Museum of Art는 방문객들이 전시물을 사진 촬영하는 것을 허용하지 않습니다.

125 Charles의 책상을 옮기는 과정에서 서랍 속에 있는 그의 모든 서류가 뒤섞였다.

126 모든 음식점 업주들은 음식물 쓰레기를 처리할 때 해당되는 모든 주 법규를 준수하기로 되어 있습니다.

127 인사부 직원들은 신입 사원들과 회의를 하기 위해 내일 모일 겁니다.

128 당신이 편할 때 등록 양식 한 부를 제게 보내 주세요.

129 저희는 고객의 동의 없이 개인 연락 정보를 어느 누구에게도 공개하지 않습니다.

130 대부분의 사람들은 시상식 결과가 나오기 전의 지연 시간을 참기 어렵다고 생각한다.

Part 6

Questions 131-134 refer to the following press release.

민감한 물건을 위한 케이스

가방 전문 브랜드 Mandelisa의 수석 디자이너 Frank Robinson은 깨지기 쉬운 물건들을 위한 케이스를 고안했다고 발표했다. 이 제품은 여행 시 충격에 취약한 물품들을 보호하기 위해 개발되었다. Robinson 씨는 장기 여행을 위해 특별히 설계된 혁신적인 여행 가방을 개발하여 인정 받았다. 하지만 민감한 물건을 운반하는 데 여전히 문제가 있었다. "여행 가방의 공간이 넉넉하다 하더라도, 여행자들은 짐 가방에 딱 맞게 들어갈 수 있도록 소지품에 더 많은 신경을 써야 합니다. 이 케이스의 표면은 매우 단단하지만 여행하는 데 가볍고 이상적입니다"라고 Robinson 씨가 말했다.

133 (A) 하지만 민감한 물건을 운반하는 데 여전히 문제가 있었다.
(B) 그것들은 추가적인 장비를 필요로 하지 않았다.
(C) 오늘날, 여행자들은 많은 소지품을 가지고 다니지 않는다.
(D) 장기 여행을 위해서는 큰 여행 가방이 필요하다.

Questions 135-138 refer to the following notice.

Centum Premium Shopping Mall이 쇼핑객들을 위한 셔틀 버스 서비스 개시를 알리게 되어 기쁩니다. 이 서비스는 쇼핑몰을 방문하는 누구에게나 제공될 것입니다. 장애가 있는 분들을 위해 버스는 휠체어에 앉은 승객들이 탑승할 수 있게 설계되었습니다. 차량 운행은 버스를 타는 장소에서 반경 3km 이내에 제공됩니다. 서비스는 화요일부터 일요일까지, 오전 11시에서 저녁 8시까지 이용 가능합니다.

차량을 이용하기 위해서 저희가 그에 맞게 계획을 할 수 있도록 최소 30분 미리 예약하셔야 합니다. 셔틀 서비스는 무료이지만, 자발적인 기부는 환영합니다. 기부금은 뛰어난 서비스를 유지하는 데 큰 도움이 될 겁니다. 운전석 옆에 있는 상자에 기부금을 넣어 주시면 됩니다.

136 (A) 차량 운행은 버스를 타는 장소에서 반경 3km 이내에 제공됩니다.
(B) 운전자는 10분 후에 출발할 준비가 될 겁니다.
(C) 많은 쇼핑객들은 자신의 차를 운전할 겁니다.
(D) 버스는 저렴하고 실속 있는 이동 수단입니다.

Questions 139-142 refer to the following e-mail.

수신: Cliff Clapton <cliff2@kitchensupplies.site>
발신: Chris Stevens <stevenstar@skrestaurant.com>
날짜: 5월 22일
제목: 계약 갱신

Clapton 씨에게,

지난 8년간, 귀사는 저희에게 식기와 용기들을 공급해 왔습니다.

저는 저희의 관계가 앞으로도 계속 되길 바랍니다. 저희 사이의 계약은 3년마다 자동으로 갱신되도록 되어 있습니다. 저는 다음 갱신 날짜가 되기 전에 계약서에 일부를 변경하고 싶어요.

요즘 정부는 자영업자들에게 일회용 제품을 사용하지 말라고 요구하고 있습니다. 저희도 친환경 제품의 비율을 늘리기로 결정했어요. 플라스틱 식기를 대체할 만한 것들을 추천해 주시겠어요? 예전에 당신의 카탈로그에서 재활용이 가능한 제품들을 본 적이 있는데, 샘플들을 좀 보내 주시겠습니까? 자연분해되는 제품들을 추천해 주셔도 좋아요.

제가 제품을 검토할 충분한 시간을 가질 수 있도록 가능한 한 빨리 샘플을 보내주세요.

안부를 전하며,
Chris

139 (A) 대부분의 고객들은 저희가 제공하는 점심 식사를 선호합니다.
(B) 수리 작업은 저희 매장에서 진행될 겁니다.
(C) 저는 저희의 관계가 앞으로도 계속 되길 바랍니다.
(D) 최근에 많은 경쟁업체들이 생겼습니다.

Questions 143-146 refer to the following memo.

수신: 모든 직원들
발신: William Jones
날짜: 9월 26일

안녕하세요,

Richard Scott이 독일 최고의 자동차 제조업체인 Vents에서 그의 꿈을 추구하기 위해 Instar Electronics를 떠나기로 결정했다는 것을 알려 드리게 되어 슬픔과 자랑스러움이 교차합니다. 그가 우리와 함께하는 마지막 날은 11월 28일 금요일이 될 겁니다.

그는 여기서 근무를 시작했을 때부터 우리의 모든 제품에 첨단 기능을 적용하는 데 핵심적인 역할을 했습니다. 게다가 Scott 씨는 더 비용 효율적이고, 생산적인 업무 체계를 직접 조직하기도 했죠. 그 과정에서 직원들의 결속력을 더욱 단단하게 만들었습니다. 그가 우리 회사의 전반적인 문화의 개선에 크게 기여했다는 것은 확실합니다.

Richard의 직장에서의 행운과 계속되는 성공을 기원하는 자리에 함께해 주시길 바랍니다.

안부를 전하며,
William Jones,
차장, 연구개발 부서

145 (A) 그가 우리 회사의 전반적인 문화의 개선에 크게 기여했다는 것은 확실합니다.
(B) 그는 뉴욕에서 우수한 성적으로 대학을 졸업했습니다.
(C) 그는 작년에 3개월간 아시아 시장을 연구했습니다.
(D) 그는 내일부터 연구개발부 부장으로 근무할 겁니다.

Part 7

Questions 147-148 refer to the following advertisement.

Perosque의 Symbolic 컬렉션

100년이 넘는 기간 동안 전 세계의 패션 애호가들은 Perosque의 독특하고 고전적인 가방들의 진가를 인정했습니다. 저희는 기존 상품들에 추가하기 위한 신상품을 소개하게 되어 기쁩니다. 저희 전통적인 스타일의 핸드백과 모든 종류의 가방들은 인증 받은 장인들에 의해 수작업으로 만들어지며 모든 상품들은 최고급의 천연 가죽으로 제작됩니다. 대량 주문도 가능하지만 수제품이기 때문에 완성되는 데 예상보다 더 오래 걸릴 수도 있다는 점을 알아 두시길 바랍니다. 그리고 저희는 유럽과 미국 전 지역에 상품을 공급할 수 있습니다. 저희 웹 사이트 www.perosque.com에서 상품들을 둘러보시길 바랍니다.

147 누구를 대상으로 하는 광고인가?
(A) 관광객들
(B) 의류 제조업체들
(C) 양품점 주인들
(D) 제품 디자이너들

148 Perosque에 대해 암시되는 것은?
(A) 다양한 나라에 상품을 수출한다.
(B) 가죽 공예 전문가를 찾고 있다.
(C) 미국으로 사업을 확장할 계획이다.
(D) 같은 상품만을 계속 판매할 것이다.

Questions 149-150 refer to the following information.

FRESH WORLD 식당

월요일-토요일
점심 식사: 오전 11시 - 오후 3시
저녁 식사: 오후 5시 30분 - 오후 9시

일요일
아침 식사: 오전 8시 - 오후 3시
저녁 식사: 오후 4시 - 오후 9시

일반 메뉴 외에도 단돈 12달러에 다음과 같은 오늘의 특별 요리를 제공합니다:

월요일: 라자냐
화요일: 라비올리
수요일: 리소토
목요일: 브루스케타
금요일: 해물 스튜

금요일과 토요일 저녁에는 라이브 공연이 있습니다.
금요일과 토요일 저녁은 예약을 권장합니다.

149 화요일에 저녁 식사는 언제 시작하는가?
(A) 오후 3시에
(B) 오후 4시 30분에
(C) 오후 5시 30분에
(D) 오후 9시에

150 금요일에 대해 언급된 것은?
(A) 예약이 필수이다.
(B) 아침 식사는 오전 9시부터 가능하다.
(C) 라이브 공연이 있다.
(D) 리소토가 특별 메뉴로 제공된다.

Questions 151-152 refer to the following text-message chain.

John Breedlove [오후 4:56]	Clara, 아직 사무실인가요?
Clara Jones [오후 4:58]	네, 막 퇴근하려던 참이었어요. 무슨 일이에요?
John Breedlove [오후 5:01]	원격 컴퓨터 시스템에 접속하기 위한 제 새로운 비밀번호가 기억이 안 납니다. 회사가 긴 암호를 설정하라고 해서 기억하기 어렵네요.
Clara Jones [오후 5:02]	제가 도와드릴 수 있는 방법이 있을까요?
John Breedlove [오후 5:06]	네, 제 책상 위에 보시면 암호가 적힌 종이가 있을 겁니다.
Clara Jones [오후 5:08]	당신 책상 위에는 많은 서류들이 있어요.
John Breedlove [오후 5:11]	미안해요! 녹색 종이에 적혀 있어요. 아마 흰색 표지의 책 속에 있을 거예요.
Clara Jones [오후 5:12]	알겠습니다. 이건가 보네요. 당신이 알아야 하는 암호는 aux1020855입니다.

| John Breedlove [오후 5:15] | 네, 정말 고마워요, Clara. 내일 봅시다. |

151 Breedlove 씨의 문제점은 무엇인가?
(A) 그는 사무실 문을 열 수 없다.
(B) 그는 중요한 서류를 분실했다.
(C) 그는 시스템에 접속할 수 없다.
(D) 그의 컴퓨터에 있던 일부 정보가 삭제됐다.

152 오후 5시 8분에, Jones 씨가 "당신 책상 위에는 많은 서류들이 있어요"라고 쓴 것은 무슨 의미인가?
(A) 그녀는 Breedlove 씨가 업무를 미루지 않기를 원한다.
(B) 그녀는 찾으려는 것을 발견할 수 없다.
(C) 그녀는 오늘 저녁에 늦게까지 일해야 한다.
(D) 그녀는 청소가 필요하다고 생각한다.

Questions 153-154 refer to the following e-mail.

발신: Jonny McFerrin
수신: Gloria Jackson
날짜: 3월 16일
제목: 정보
첨부: 편지

Jackson 씨에게,

다음 달 당신의 괌 여행에 관한 세부 사항을 이 이메일에 첨부했습니다. 여행 일정표와 호텔 확인 내용도 포함되어 있습니다. 물론, 여행 경비의 세부 내용이 기록된 문서도 있어요. 확인해 보시고 문제가 없으면 동의서 양식을 출력하셔서, 서명하신 후 저희에게 보내주시길 바랍니다. 그것은 당신이 정보를 확인했다는 것을 인정하는 역할을 할 겁니다. 당신도 한 부를 보관해야 한다는 것을 기억해 주세요.

궁금한 점이 있으시면 저에게 알려주세요.

안부를 전하며,

Jonny McFerrin
Ace Travel Agency

153 이메일의 목적은 무엇인가?
(A) 여행 준비에 대해 알리기 위해
(B) 판매 세부 내용을 보고하기 위해
(C) 서류 복사본을 요청하기 위해
(D) 예산에 대한 승인을 요청하기 위해

154 Jackson 씨는 무엇을 하라고 조언 받는가?
(A) 양식을 작성할 것
(B) 미리 예약할 것
(C) 문서를 보관할 것
(D) 추가적인 정보를 제공할 것

Questions 155-158 refer to the following article.

Angelina Hale은 독특한 이력을 가지고 있는 음식점 주인이다. 그녀는 10년 전까지만 해도 촉망 받는 펀드 매니저였다. 그녀는 많은 돈을 벌었지만 바쁜 삶을 살았다. 그 결과로 그녀는 규칙적인 식사를 하지 못했고 패스트푸드와 같은 건강에 좋지 않은 음식을 많이 먹어야 했다. 결국 그녀는 심각한 건강 문제로 인해 직장을 그만뒀다. 그때 그녀는 자신의 음식점인 Home Cook에 대한 아이디어를 떠올렸다.

고향에서 작은 음식점으로 시작했을 때부터 그녀는 직접 재배한 야채뿐만 아니라 믿을 만한 농부들로부터 받은 유기농 재료만으로 요리를 했다. 처음엔 다소 특징 없는 맛으로 인해 대중의 관심을 끌지 못했다. 하지만 점차 현지 풍미를 가미해 가면서 그녀는 맛도 좋고 영양가도 있는 요리법을 개발하기 위해 끊임없이 노력해 왔다. "저희 지역이 건강에 관심을 갖는 것을 보면 행복해요"라고 Angelina Hale은 말했다. 이제, 그녀의 사업은 더욱 성장할 전망이다.

실제로 몇몇 지역 어린이집 원장들은 최근에 아이들에게 Home Cook의 요리를 제공하기로 결정했다.

155 Hale 씨는 원래 어디에서 일했는가?
(A) 식품 회사에서
(B) 병원에서
(C) 여행사에서
(D) 금융 기관에서

156 Hale 씨는 자신의 지역 사회에서 무슨 변화를 봤는가?
(A) 야채의 부족
(B) 건강한 식습관에 관한 관심 증가
(C) 요식업의 호황
(D) 유기농 농장 수의 증가

157 Home Cook에 대해 사실인 것은?
(A) 그곳의 요리사들이 재료를 자체적으로 제공한다.
(B) 채식주의자 요리만 제공한다.
(C) 식품 생산량이 증가할 것이다.
(D) 곧 새로운 지점을 열 것이다.

158 [1], [2], [3] 그리고 [4]로 표시된 곳 중에 다음 문장이 들어가기에 가장 적합한 위치는 어디인가?
"이제, 그녀의 사업은 더욱 성장할 전망이다."
(A) [1]
(B) [2]
(C) [3]
(D) [4]

Questions 159-161 refer to the following press release.

부산 공공 수영장 6월 재개장

5월 30일 — 부산시 보건부는 도시 공용 수영장 두 군데에 대한 보수 작업이 곧 완료될 것이라고 발표했다. 두 수영장 모두 6월에 재개장될 예정이다.

작년에 분기별 수질 검사에 통과하지 못한 후, 그 수영장들은 약 10개월간 폐쇄된 상태로 있었다. Southern Pool은 물 필터링 장비만 교체되어야 했기 때문에 이틀 후에 재개장할 것이다. 그 수영장은 6월 1일부터 대중이 이용할 수 있을 것이다. 하지만 Centum Swimming Pool은 수영장 바닥이 수리되어야 하기 때문에 조금 더 오래 걸릴 것이다. 또한 국내에서 가장 큰 수영장이고, 아주 많은 사람들이 이용하기 때문에 필요한 모든 안전 예방조치가 행해져야 한다. 이와 같이 실내 수영장들은 정기적으로 점검을 받고 유지보수가 수시로 실행되어야 한다.

159 보도 자료의 주요 내용은 무엇인가?
(A) 일부 도시 시설의 정비
(B) 수영장의 확장
(C) 일부 보건 규정의 개정
(D) 낡은 수영장의 폐쇄

160 Southern Pool의 문제점은 무엇인가?
(A) 바닥에 물이 새는 곳이 있었다.
(B) 물이 제대로 여과되지 않았다.

(C) 국내에서 인기가 없다.
(D) 그곳에서 안전사고가 자주 발생한다.

161 Centum Swimming Pool에 대해 알려진 것은 무엇인가?
(A) 피트니스 센터를 특징으로 한다.
(B) 안전 점검이 항상 철저하게 이루어졌다.
(C) 실내에 있는 시설물이다.
(D) 올해 규모가 커졌다.

Questions 162-164 refer to the following advertisement.

연락처: Bobby Petrov, bobbyp16@pacificcompany.com

Pacific Development Company는 최신 프로젝트인 Ocean View Apartment의 완공을 발표하게 되어 기쁩니다. 그 복합 단지에는 160개의 주택이 아직 남아 있습니다. 모델 하우스가 대중에게 공개되자마자 대부분의 가구가 사전 매각되었습니다.

각 가구는 설비가 잘 갖춰진 주방, 세 개의 넓은 침실, 그리고 두 개의 욕실을 포함하고 있습니다. 각 방에는 큰 유리창이 있어서 거주자들은 훌륭한 경치를 즐길 수 있습니다. 모든 가구는 중앙 에어컨, 에너지 효율적인 오븐, 식기세척기, 세탁기 및 건조기와 같은 현대식 편의 시설도 갖추고 있습니다. 모든 가전제품은 스마트폰으로 작동시킬 수 있습니다.

Ocean View Apartment 단지는 각종 정부 기관, 쇼핑센터, 그리고 대형 할인 매장 주변의 편리한 곳에 위치해 있습니다. 게다가 모든 주민들은 아파트 부지 내에 있는 피트니스 센터와 도서관을 이용할 수 있습니다.

만약 입주 가능한 매물을 방문하고 싶다면 051-008-8949로 미리 전화 주셔서 방문 시간을 잡아 주세요. 월요일부터 토요일까지 오전 11시부터 오후 8시까지 구경할 수 있도록 개방됩니다.

162 Pacific Development Company는 무엇일 것 같은가?
(A) 인테리어 디자인 회사
(B) 주택 임대 업체
(C) 주택 대출 제공업체
(D) 주택 건설업체

163 타운 하우스에 대해 알려진 것은 무엇인가?
(A) 모든 주택이 아직 비어 있다.
(B) 모든 가구를 갖추고 있다.
(C) 일부 가전제품들을 포함한다.
(D) 각 가구마다 3대씩 주차할 수 있다.

164 [1], [2], [3] 그리고 [4]로 표시된 곳 중에 다음 문장이 들어가기에 가장 적합한 위치는 어디인가?
"월요일부터 토요일까지 오전 11시부터 오후 8시까지 구경할 수 있도록 개방됩니다."
(A) [1]
(B) [2]
(C) [3]
(D) [4]

Questions 165-167 refer to the following announcement.

현장 학습 진행자 모집

Emerald Riverside Park에서 환경 교육 프로그램을 이끌어 줄 견학 가이드를 찾고 있습니다. 직무 내용에는 현장 학습 준비하기, 방문자들에게 공원의 자연환경과 생태계 설명하기, 현장 학습 단체의 일정 잡기가 포함됩니다.

자격 제한이 약간 있습니다. 적격의 지원자는 팀을 관리하고 이끈 이전의 경험이 있어야 하며, 도시 내의 공원과 환경 자원에 대해 잘 알아야 합니다. 생물학이나 환경학 전공자는 우대됩니다. 스페인어나 프랑스어와 같은 외국어 구사 능력도 가산점의 요인이 됩니다.

지원하려면 자기소개서, 이력서 그리고 추천서 두 장을 9월 16일까지 recruiters@riversiders.com으로 이메일을 보내주세요.

www.riversiders.com을 방문하셔서 구체적인 정보를 참조하세요.

165 발표문의 목적은 무엇인가?
(A) 주민들에게 야외 활동을 하라고 권장하기 위해서
(B) 신입 사원을 모집하기 위해서
(C) 방문자들에게 공원을 소개하기 위해서
(D) 자연 환경을 보존하는 데 도움을 주기 위해서

166 두 번째 문단의 다섯 번째 줄에 있는 단어 "plus"와 가장 가까운 의미는?
(A) 이득
(B) 추가
(C) 여분
(D) 조언, 팁, 봉사료

167 추가 정보를 어떻게 얻을 수 있는가?
(A) 이메일을 보냄으로써
(B) 현장 학습에 감으로써
(C) 웹 사이트를 방문함으로써
(D) 안내 책자를 읽음으로써

Questions 168-171 refer to the following contract.

Breeze Web Hosting 서비스 계약 조건

● 저희가 프로젝트에 착수하기 전에 30%의 계약금을 지불하세요. 그 금액은 환불되지 않습니다. 잔액은 모든 작업이 끝났을 때 지불해야 합니다. 모든 비용이 지불될 때까지 웹 사이트는 가동되지 않을 것입니다. 계약서에 명시되지 않은 한, 웹 사이트의 소스코드와 내용물에 대한 소유권은 Breeze Web Hosting에게 있습니다.

● 고객은 필요한 경우 웹 사이트의 내용이나 디자인에 대한 수정을 요청할 수 있습니다. 하지만 그런 경우에는 비용이 청구될 수도 있습니다.

● 일단 웹 사이트가 Breeze Web Hosting에 의해 구축되면 고객은 완성된 사이트를 직접 혹은 대행사를 통해서 검색 엔진에 등록하셔야 합니다. Breeze Web Hosting은 이 서비스를 제공하지 않습니다.

● Breeze Web Hosting은 계약이 만료될 때까지 기술 지원을 제공합니다.

● 계약은 매년 자동 갱신되며, 계약을 중단하시려면 계약 만기 최소 2주 전에 저희에게 연락을 주셔야 합니다. 그렇지 않을 경우 자동으로 연장됩니다.

아래에 서명함으로써 저는 위의 조건을 읽고 이해했다는 것을 인정합니다.

이름: Alice Wood   서명: *Alice Wood*

168 Wood 씨는 어떤 종류의 서비스를 요청했을 것 같은가?
(A) 웹 서버 구축
(B) 자동 결제
(C) 온라인 광고
(D) 인터넷 연결

169 계약서에 따르면, 왜 추가 요금이 청구될 수도 있는가?
(A) 웹 사이트의 내용물을 사용하는 것 때문에
(B) 요금을 늦게 지불하는 것 때문에
(C) 계약 조건을 수정하는 것 때문에
(D) 웹 사이트에 변경을 요청하는 것 때문에

170 계약서에 논의되지 않은 주제는 무엇인가?
  (A) 내용물 소유권
  (B) 계약 취소 조건
  (C) 고객을 위한 교육 과정
  (D) 기술적인 지원

171 첫 번째 문단의 두 번째 줄에 있는 단어 "balance"와 의미가 가장 가까운 것은?
  (A) 안정성
  (B) 균등성
  (C) 견실함
  (D) 나머지

Questions 172-175 refer to the following online chat discussion.

Ian Cho [오후 2시 5분]	Aki Clothing Company에서 기술 지원을 요청하는 메시지를 막 보냈어요.
Betty Turner [오후 2시 6분]	그들에게 기다릴 수 있는지 물어볼래요? 어차피 이틀 후에 월간 점검이 있거든요.
Ian Cho [오후 2시 12분]	그쪽 부장님이 보낸 메시지에 긴급 상황이라고 표시되어 있습니다.
Betty Turner [오후 2시 16분]	David, 지금 어디예요? 오늘 Aki Clothing Company에 갈 수 있을까요?
David Roberts [오후 2시 16분]	시스템이 전혀 작동되지 않는 것 같나요?
Ian Cho [오후 2시 17분]	그런 거 같아요. 모든 업무가 중단된 것 같습니다.
David Roberts [오후 2시 18분]	알겠어요. 제가 약 30분 후에 거기로 갈게요.
Betty Turner [오후 2시 22분]	누군가가 Aki Clothing에 근무하는 Dennis Johnson에게 전화해서 David가 가고 있다고 알려 줘야 해요.
Ian Cho [오후 2시 22분]	알겠습니다. 제가 당장 연락할게요.

172 온라인 채팅의 목적은 무엇인가?
  (A) 긴급한 상황에 대해 논의하기 위해서
  (B) 수리를 요청하기 위해서
  (C) 고객 정보를 확인하기 위해서
  (D) 시스템을 교체하기 위해서

173 기술자는 보통 Aki Clothing Company를 얼마나 자주 방문하는가?
  (A) 한 달에 한 번
  (B) 한 달에 두 번
  (C) 일주일에 한 번
  (D) 일 년에 한 번

174 오후 2시 17분에, Cho 씨가 "그런 거 같아요"라고 쓴 의도는 무엇일 것 같은가?
  (A) 고객이 메시지를 잘못 보냈다.
  (B) 서비스 기사가 이미 방문했다.
  (C) Roberts 씨가 상황을 잘 파악하고 있다.
  (D) 일부 장비가 교체되어야 한다.

175 Cho 씨가 다음에 무엇을 할 것인가?
  (A) 고객에게 연락한다
  (B) 서비스 기사를 보낸다
  (C) Roberts 씨가 서비스를 제공하도록 돕는다
  (D) Aki Clothing Company에 방문한다

Questions 176-180 refer to the following Web page and e-mail.

http://www.landertours.com/

| 자주 묻는 질문 | 홈 | 여행 패키지 | 후기 |

European Travel Package A에 대해 자주 묻는 질문들

어떤 서류가 필요합니까?
유럽 연합과 우리나라는 비자 면제 협정이 체결되어 있습니다. 그러므로 여행을 가기 전에 유효한 여권을 반드시 챙기세요. 만약 운전을 하시려면 국제 운전면허증을 발급 받으세요. 그것들은 관광 첫날과 그 후 국경을 넘을 때 소지하고 있어야 합니다.

공항 픽업 서비스가 제공되나요?
만약 여러분이 예정된 시간까지 공항에 도착하시면 저희가 여러분을 픽업해 드리고 여행 마지막 날에는 공항에 데려다 드립니다. 패키지에 포함되지 않은 다른 날에 도착하거나 떠나는 여행객들은 스스로 이동 수단을 마련하셔야 합니다.

북유럽을 여행하기 위해 챙겨야 하는 건 뭐가 있을까요?
저희는 바람막이 재킷을 가져올 것을 제안합니다. 일부 나라들은 비교적 따뜻하지만 다른 곳들은 다소 춥습니다. 뿐만 아니라 산악 지역에서는 갑자기 비가 내릴 수도 있으므로 적절한 외투를 가져오시는 게 좋습니다.

여행 전에 어떤 정보가 제공되나요?
여러분이 구매한 여행 상품의 일정표와 설명이 있는 이메일을 받으실 것입니다. 그 안에는 나라에 관한 설명, 경로 정보, 호텔과 음식점에 관한 정보와 지도가 포함되어 있을 겁니다.

발신: kiki_1221@yaho.co.jp
수신: admin@landertours.com
날짜: 6월 8일
제목: European Travel Package A

Payne 씨에게,

저는 최근 9월에 가는 귀사의 European Travel Package A를 예약했습니다. 저는 유럽 여행을 오랜 기간 동안 갈망해 왔는데 마침내 처음으로 가게 됐습니다. 저는 이 패키지의 상세한 계약 조건이 정말 마음에 듭니다. 하지만 패키지에 포함되지 않은 불가리아와 알바니아를 여행하기 위해 여행 기간을 5일 정도 연장하고 싶습니다. 필요한 준비를 해 주실 수 있을까요? 또한 저는 여행지에 관한 많은 정보를 가지고 있지 않기 때문에 만약 지역의 관광 명소에 관련된 정보도 제공해 주시면 감사하겠습니다. 저는 당신의 패키지가 제가 지금 할 수 있는 최선의 선택이라 믿습니다.

진심으로,

Masato Komuro

176 European Travel Package A에 대해 암시되는 것은?
  (A) 날씨가 지속적으로 따뜻한 곳들을 간다.
  (B) 모든 여행 상품들 중 가격이 가장 합리적이다.
  (C) 국제 운전면허증을 소지할 것을 요구한다.
  (D) 여행객은 한 국가 이상 여행하게 한다.

177 웹 페이지에 따르면, 여행자들은 관광을 시작하기 전에 무엇을 해야 하는가?
  (A) 여권의 사진을 제출한다
  (B) 비자를 신청한다
  (C) 따뜻한 옷을 챙긴다
  (D) 몇 가지 양식을 작성한다

178 Komuro 씨가 무엇을 해야 할 것 같은가?
 (A) 항공권에 대한 추가 비용을 지불한다
 (B) 호텔에 미리 연락한다
 (C) 공항으로 가는 이동 수단을 직접 마련한다
 (D) 가고 싶은 행선지의 목록을 제시한다

179 Komuro 씨에 대해 사실이 아닌 것은?
 (A) 그는 유럽에 가 본 적이 없다.
 (B) 그는 유럽에 있는 모든 나라를 관광할 것이다.
 (C) 그는 더 오래 여행하고 싶어 한다.
 (D) 그는 유럽에 있는 관광지에 대해 잘 모른다.

180 이메일에서, 여섯 번째 줄에 있는 단어 "assume"과 의미상 가장 가까운 것은?
 (A) 믿다
 (B) 받아들이다
 (C) 물려받다, 떠맡다
 (D) 흉내 내다, 가장하다

Questions 181-185 refer to the following flyer and e-mail.

Columbia Science Museum에 방문하세요!

환영합니다! 만약 Columbia Science Museum을 최근에 방문해 보신 적이 없다면, 여러분은 다음 방문 때 저희 시설이 업그레이드 되었다는 것을 알게 될 겁니다. 대도시 쇼핑 구역에 있는 Bernard Station에서 불과 몇 분 거리에 위치해 있으며, 박물관의 규모가 더 확장되었습니다. 게다가, 로비는 완전히 개조되었습니다. 새로운 전시관과 회의실이 추가되었고, 카페도 하나 추가했습니다. 주차장도 과거보다 두 배로 확장되었기 때문에 차량 운전자들을 아주 편리하게 해 드릴 겁니다. 그리고 아주 다양하고 독특하면서 흥미로운 물품들이 있는 기념품점에 오시는 걸 잊지 마세요.

입장료:

티켓 종류	가격	제공되는 것들
Basic	12달러	박물관 상설 전시물 관람 가능
Basic Plus	18달러	Basic 혜택 포함 및 모든 강의에 참석 가능
Prime	25달러	Basic Plus 혜택 포함 및 박물관 2인 입장권
Prime Plus	30달러	Prime 혜택 포함 및 모든 특별 전시회 관람 가능

특별 전시회:
- 인간계: 인체의 모든 것 (1월 1일 ~ 3월 31일)
- 태양계의 행성들: 무한한 가능성의 세계 (4월 1일 ~ 6월 30일)
- 해양 자원: 미래 자원의 보고 (7월 1일 ~ 9월 30일)
- 인공 지능의 시대: 과학 기술의 한계를 깨기 (10월 1일 ~ 12월 31일)

수신: angels11@csmuseum.org
발신: elevens@ingalaxy.com
날짜: 10월 7일
제목: 앞으로의 방문

Lin 씨에게,

저는 박물관 방문에 관하여 문의하려고 이메일을 씁니다. 저는 가족들과 함께 10월 14일에 그곳을 방문할 예정입니다.

저희 가족은 3명이며, 과학에 관해 많은 정보를 얻을 수 있을 거라는 생각에 그곳을 방문하기로 결정했습니다.

저희는 무료 박물관 입장권은 필요하지 않지만 이번 달의 특별 전시회에는 관심이 있습니다. 지금 저희가 사용할 수 있는 티켓이 있는지 궁금합니다. 만약 있다면, 제 아들이 16살인데 그가 할인을 받을 수 있는지 알고 싶어요. 또한, 박물관 개장 시간과 폐장 시간을 알려 주시면 감사하겠습니다.

당신의 도움에 미리 감사드립니다.

Troye Walker

---

181 Columbia Science Museum에 대해 암시되는 것은 무엇인가?
 (A) 학생들에게 할인을 제공한다.
 (B) 편리한 곳에 위치해 있다.
 (C) 입장료가 인상되었다.
 (D) 개조하는 동안 대중에게 폐쇄되었다.

182 왜 이메일은 작성되었는가?
 (A) 무료 티켓을 구하는 방법을 알아내기 위해
 (B) 박물관 전시회에 관한 제안을 하기 위해
 (C) 박물관의 시설물에 대해 문의하기 위해
 (D) 박물관 관람에 관한 정보를 요청하기 위해

183 이메일에 따르면, Walker 씨는 무엇에 관해 문의하는가?
 (A) 강의 일정
 (B) 티켓을 구매하는 방법
 (C) 미성년자를 위한 할인
 (D) 전시물의 가격

184 Walker 씨는 어떤 종류의 티켓을 구매할 것 같은가?
 (A) Basic
 (B) Basic Plus
 (C) Prime
 (D) Prime Plus

185 Walker 씨는 무슨 전시회를 보러 갈 것 같은가?
 (A) 인간계
 (B) 태양계의 행성들
 (C) 해양 자원
 (D) 인공 지능의 시대

Questions 186-190 refer to the following article, schedule, and e-mail.

도시 전역의 낡은 수도관 교체

(11월 17일) — 12월 한 달 동안, 연방 수도공사가 Dallas시 전역에 걸쳐 대부분의 수도관을 교체하는 작업에 착수할 예정이다. 기존의 녹슨 철 파이프들은 플라스틱으로 코팅된 고급의 스테인리스 스틸 파이프로 교체될 예정이다.

공사를 시행할 Broad Utilities Company의 회장 Arnold Bush는 "50년이 넘는 기간 동안 사용되어 온 낡은 수도관을 더 나은 것으로 교체함으로써 지역 주민들은 자신들이 사용하는 물이 개선된 것을 볼 수 있을 것입니다"라고 말했다. 이를테면 모든 교체 작업이 완료되기만 하면 주민들은 수돗물을 끓이지 않아도 마실 수 있을 것이다.

일부 거리들은 파이프가 교체되는 동안 오전 10시에서 오후 5시 사이에 교통이 통제될 것이다. 시행사는 주민들의 불편을 최소화할 수 있는 일정을 짜기 위해 시 관계자들과 지속적으로 논의 중이다. 일정은 업데이트될 때마다 시청과 시행사의 웹 사이트에 발표될 것이다. 긴급히 도움이 필요한 사람들은 즉시 시행사에 088-9669-0482로 전화하면 된다.

배관 교체 작업 일정

월요일	12월 2일	Sunset Avenue
화요일	12월 3일	Gloria Street
수요일	12월 4일	George Avenue
목요일	12월 5일	Stainwood Street
금요일	12월 6일	Southwest Street

여러분의 거리에서 작업이 완료되면 Broad Utilities Company의 기술자들이 수도관을 다시 연결하기 위해 여러분의 집으로 갈 겁니다.

수신: Joseph Greaves <joscorn@neit.com>
발신: Richard Anderson <nicer@broadutilities.com>
회신: 서비스 정보
날짜: 11월 28일

Greaves 씨에게,

귀하의 거리는 12월 4일 수요일에 수도관을 교체할 예정입니다. 기술자들이 오후 2시쯤 배관을 다시 연결하기 위해 당신의 집에 방문할 겁니다. 그 작업은 문제가 없으면 약 2시간 정도 걸릴 것으로 예상됩니다. 작업은 당신이 집에 계시는 동안 진행되어야 합니다. 일정을 확정 짓기 위해 088-9669-0482로 전화해 주세요. 또한 배관을 연결하는 동안 물 공급이 중단될 것이므로 미리 여러분의 물을 저장해 두실 것을 권장합니다.

감사합니다.

Richard Anderson

---

186 기사에 따르면, 기존의 파이프에 대해 사실인 것은 무엇인가?
(A) 플라스틱으로 만들어졌다.
(B) 물이 파이프를 제대로 통과하지 않는다.
(C) 물을 오염시킨다.
(D) 수리될 것이다.

187 기사문에서 작업 일정에 대해 무엇을 알 수 있는가?
(A) 시 공무원들에 의해 짜여졌다.
(B) 변경될 수도 있다.
(C) 이미 여러 번 수정되었다.
(D) 너무 복잡하다.

188 12월 5일에는 무슨 일이 일어날 것인가?
(A) 도로 교통이 차단될 것이다.
(B) 새로운 일정이 공개될 것이다.
(C) 고객의 의견을 받을 것이다.
(D) 시 공무원들과 지역 주민들이 만날 것이다.

189 Greaves 씨에 대해 암시되는 것은?
(A) 그는 오후에 귀가하기로 되어 있다.
(B) 그는 George Avenue에 거주한다.
(C) 그는 곧 Bush 씨를 만날 것이다.
(D) 그는 수리공을 직접 불렀다.

190 Anderson 씨는 Greaves 씨에게 무엇을 하라고 조언하는가?
(A) 그에게 결함에 대해 알려줄 것
(B) 온라인에서 정보를 확인할 것
(C) 예정된 시간을 변경할 것
(D) 충분한 물을 보관할 것

Questions 191-195 refer to the following e-mails and information.

발신	Olive Gordon
수신	Anthony Renner
날짜	5월 8일
제목	프로그램 복사본
첨부	6월 8일 행사

안녕하세요, Renner 씨,

인쇄해야 할 행사 공지의 수정본을 첨부했습니다. 어제 우리가 논의한 대로, 저는 푸른색 용지에 흰색 글씨를 적용하는 게 좋을 거 같아요. 그리고 수상자들의 이름은 부각될 수 있도록 장식용 폰트를 써야겠어요. 저는 공지 내용이 가능한 한 간단하면서도 눈에 띄게 만들기 위해 최선을 다했습니다.

제가 여러 번 검토했지만 프로그램을 출력하기 전에 당신이 한번 봐 주시면 좋겠습니다. 5월 15일까지 전반적인 피드백을 주실 수 있을까요?

감사합니다.

Olive Gordon
행사 기획자

Giant Financial Company
제21회 연례 우수 직원 기념식

6월 8일 금요일, Paradise 호텔

저녁 6시 ~ 7시   저녁 식사
저녁 7시 ~ 7시 20분 기조 연설, Anna Kendrick, 최고경영자
저녁 7시 20분 ~ 8시 발표, Billy Burke, 수석 부회장

업무 성과 - John Gere
최고의 고객 관리 - Judy Pitt
특별한 10년 근무 - Mason Wells
올해의 직원 - Liam Mendelson

발신: Anthony Renner
수신: Olive Gordon
날짜: 5월 13일
제목: 앞으로의 행사를 위한 프로그램

Gordon 씨에게,

저에게 올해의 행사 공지를 보여 줘서 고맙습니다. 포스터는 색상 조합이 가장 잘 된 것 같아요. 그것은 그렇게 화려하진 않지만 사람들의 주목을 끄는 매력이 있습니다. 당신은 새로운 기획자로서 새로운 것들을 많이 시도했네요.

제 생각엔 아주 잘 구성된 것 같지만, Golden Decade Service는 마지막에 발표되는 것이 관례였습니다. 그것은 10년 동안 근무한 장기 근무자를 기리는 것이기 때문에 이 행사에서 가장 의미 있는 상으로 여겨집니다. 저는 그게 문제가 될 거라고 생각하진 않지만 Kendrick 씨에게 미리 보고하는 게 좋겠습니다. 저는 당신에게 시간과 수상자 이름에 실수하지 않게 주의하라고 요청 드리고 싶어요.

감사합니다.

Anthony Renner
인사부 부장

191 6월 8일에 무슨 일이 일어날 것인가?
(A) 신입 사원 오리엔테이션
(B) 은퇴 기념 파티
(C) 시상식
(D) 이사회

192 누구의 이름이 공지의 최종본에 특별한 스타일로 나타날 것 같은가?
(A) Anthony Renner
(B) Judy Pitt
(C) Olive Gordon
(D) Anna Kendrick

193 Renner 씨는 Gordon 씨에게 무엇을 하라고 제안하는가?
(A) 최고경영자에게 변경 사항에 대해 알릴 것
(B) 장기 근무자를 더 강조할 것
(C) 포스터를 미리 인쇄할 것
(D) 수상자에 대한 구체적인 정보를 포함할 것

194 Wells 씨에 대해 알 수 있는 것은 무엇인가?
(A) 그 회사에서 10년 동안 일했다.
(B) 행사에서 발표할 것이다.
(C) 작년에 행사 준비를 담당했다.
(D) 참석자들 중 가장 선배이다.

195 Gordon 씨에 대해 암시되는 것은?
(A) 포스터에 피드백을 줄 것이다.
(B) 이미 많은 상을 받았다.
(C) 행사를 준비하는 데 능숙하다.
(D) 올해 새로운 일을 맡았다.

Questions 196-200 refer to the following brochure and e-mails.

Ivy Event Hall

한국의 수도인 서울 중심부에서 멀지 않은 곳에 위치한 Ivy Event Hall은 여러분의 연회, 결혼식 혹은 비즈니스 컨퍼런스를 위한 이상적인 장소이고, 수풀과 초목으로 둘러싸인 평화로운 곳에 있습니다.

저희는 다양한 크기의 방이 4개 있습니다. Modern Room은 50명에서 80명 정도가 편안하게 앉을 수 있고, Special Room은 최대 150명의 손님들에게 안성맞춤입니다. Executive Room은 최대 200명의 손님을 수용할 수 있고 그 방보다 두 배 더 큰 수용량의 Exclusive Room은 여기서 가장 큰 방입니다. Executive Room과 Exclusive Room에는 초대형 스크린과 프로젝터를 포함한 최신식 발표 장비들이 갖춰져 있습니다.

저희 식당은 최고의 요리사들이 준비한 음식이 있는 뷔페를 제공합니다. 여러분은 전에 경험해 본 적이 없는 놀라운 요리들을 즐길 수 있을 겁니다!

추가적인 정보가 필요하면 242-555-0135번으로 전화하시거나 www.ivyhall.net에 접속하세요.

수신 Emma Jeong
발신 Tom McKellen
날짜 4월 6일
제목 기념일 계획

Jeong 씨께,

저는 Ivy Event Hall에 가서 그곳의 모든 방을 봤습니다. 임대료가 약간 비싸긴 하지만 시설은 예상보다 훨씬 더 좋았습니다. 우리 회사의 기념 행사를 위해 딱 알맞을 것 같습니다. 뷔페에서 제공하는 음식도 110명의 손님들의 다양한 취향에 적합할 것 같습니다. 그런데 빔 프로젝터가 필요하기 때문에 더 큰 방을 예약해야 할 것 같습니다. 그렇게 하면 공간이 더 많

을 것이기 때문에 참가자들은 더 편안하게 있을 수 있습니다.

방 예약을 승인하실 건지 여부를 알려 주세요. 빨리 결정해야 합니다. 우리가 최소 행사 2주 전에 예약을 한다면 20% 할인을 받을 겁니다. 제 생각엔 이번 달에 예약을 하는 것이 나을 것 같습니다.

Tom McKellen
기획 부장
Kai Industries

수신: Tom McKellen
발신: Emma Jeong
날짜: 4월 7일
제목: 회신: 기념일 계획

McKellen 씨께,

그 행사장에 관한 정보를 알려 주셔서 감사드려요. 방이 필요한 것보다 조금 큰 것은 괜찮습니다. 사실, 일부 직원들은 행사에 참석할지 여부를 아직 결정하지 못했어요. 우리는 지금 당장 예약할 필요가 없으니 걱정하지 마세요.

Emma Jeong
부사장
Kai Industries

---

196 안내 책자에 따르면, Ivy Event Hall에 대해 뭐라고 언급되어 있는가?
(A) 다양한 규모의 행사를 개최하는 데 사용된다.
(B) 도심에 편리하게 위치해 있다.
(C) 다른 행사 장소들보다 더 비싸다.
(D) 그곳의 비즈니스 센터가 개조될 것이다.

197 McKellen 씨가 행사 계획에 대해 무엇을 이야기하는가?
(A) 구현하는 데 많은 돈이 든다.
(B) 회의에서 제안되었다.
(C) 전 직원들에게 알려져야 한다.
(D) 당장 결정할 수 없다.

198 회사 기념일 행사는 어디에서 열릴 가능성이 가장 큰가?
(A) Modern Room에서
(B) Special Room에서
(C) Executive Room에서
(D) Exclusive Room에서

199 McKellen 씨는 왜 이번 달에 방을 예약하고 싶어 하는가?
(A) 방 상태 보고서를 작성하기 위해
(B) 새 장비를 미리 설치하기 위해
(C) 특별 할인을 이용하기 위해
(D) 더 많은 손님을 수용하기 위해

200 Jeong 씨는 행사에 대해서 뭐라고 말하는가?
(A) 좌석이 부족할 것이다.
(B) 사람들은 방에 좌석을 추가할 수 있다.
(C) 예상보다 더 많은 사람들이 참석할 수도 있다.
(D) 그녀는 더 큰 방을 선호한다.

3회

01	(C)	02	(D)	03	(A)	04	(C)	05	(C)
06	(B)	07	(A)	08	(A)	09	(C)	10	(B)
11	(A)	12	(B)	13	(C)	14	(A)	15	(A)
16	(C)	17	(B)	18	(C)	19	(B)	20	(C)
21	(C)	22	(A)	23	(B)	24	(B)	25	(B)
26	(A)	27	(A)	28	(A)	29	(A)	30	(C)
31	(C)	32	(B)	33	(D)	34	(B)	35	(C)
36	(B)	37	(A)	38	(D)	39	(B)	40	(A)
41	(A)	42	(D)	43	(A)	44	(D)	45	(B)
46	(D)	47	(B)	48	(C)	49	(C)	50	(D)
51	(C)	52	(C)	53	(B)	54	(D)	55	(B)
56	(D)	57	(A)	58	(C)	59	(D)	60	(C)
61	(A)	62	(D)	63	(D)	64	(A)	65	(C)
66	(B)	67	(A)	68	(C)	69	(C)	70	(A)
71	(C)	72	(C)	73	(A)	74	(D)	75	(B)
76	(B)	77	(A)	78	(D)	79	(A)	80	(A)
81	(D)	82	(A)	83	(C)	84	(A)	85	(B)
86	(A)	87	(B)	88	(C)	89	(B)	90	(C)
91	(A)	92	(A)	93	(B)	94	(D)	95	(C)
96	(C)	97	(B)	98	(C)	99	(D)	100	(B)
101	(A)	102	(D)	103	(A)	104	(C)	105	(C)
106	(C)	107	(A)	108	(B)	109	(D)	110	(D)
111	(B)	112	(A)	113	(C)	114	(D)	115	(A)
116	(A)	117	(C)	118	(C)	119	(B)	120	(C)
121	(A)	122	(B)	123	(C)	124	(B)	125	(A)
126	(B)	127	(D)	128	(A)	129	(C)	130	(B)
131	(D)	132	(B)	133	(C)	134	(A)	135	(C)
136	(C)	137	(D)	138	(D)	139	(A)	140	(B)
141	(B)	142	(C)	143	(B)	144	(D)	145	(B)
146	(D)	147	(B)	148	(C)	149	(B)	150	(A)
151	(D)	152	(B)	153	(A)	154	(B)	155	(C)
156	(A)	157	(D)	158	(A)	159	(B)	160	(C)
161	(C)	162	(B)	163	(A)	164	(D)	165	(A)
166	(C)	167	(C)	168	(C)	169	(A)	170	(D)
171	(C)	172	(B)	173	(B)	174	(D)	175	(D)
176	(D)	177	(A)	178	(B)	179	(D)	180	(B)
181	(B)	182	(A)	183	(D)	184	(C)	185	(B)
186	(C)	187	(C)	188	(B)	189	(A)	190	(D)
191	(A)	192	(C)	193	(C)	194	(D)	195	(B)
196	(A)	197	(C)	198	(D)	199	(C)	200	(A)

Part 1

1. (A) He's wearing a backpack.
   (B) He's setting his watch.
   (C) He's examining a timetable.
   (D) He's holding a cup of coffee.

2. (A) A clerk is folding a shirt on the shelf.
   (B) A jacket is being hung on the rack.
   (C) They are shopping outdoors.
   (D) Some garments are on display.

3. (A) Lighting fixtures are hanging from the ceiling.
   (B) One of the men is pouring water into a glass.
   (C) All the people are having a meal.
   (D) One of the men is taking off his glasses.

4. (A) Grass is being trimmed with a lawnmower.
   (B) Wastebaskets are filled with trash.
   (C) Some signs are attached on the pole.
   (D) A tree is being planted on the roadside.

5. (A) A woman is reaching for a drink.
   (B) A woman is placing a plant behind the desk.
   (C) Papers are spread out on the table.
   (D) Folders are stacked beside the laptop.

6. (A) A lamp is being turned on.
   (B) Some pillows have been arranged on the beds.
   (C) There are some pictures on the wall.
   (D) A chair is being placed by the table.

Part 2

7. Do you think it will rain this afternoon?
   (A) Check the weather forecast.
   (B) I'll show you where the umbrella is.
   (C) No, he won't.

8. Why is the museum closed?
   (A) It's being renovated.
   (B) At 9 o'clock.
   (C) Several exhibitions.

9. When will the new plant be completed?
   (A) Across from the library.
   (B) I knew that.
   (C) Soon, I hope.

10. How was the annual banquet yesterday?
    (A) By subway.
    (B) Actually, I couldn't make it.
    (C) The Paradise Hotel.

11. Didn't you read Mr. Park's e-mail?
    (A) I read it this morning.
    (B) Send it by post.
    (C) He used to live near the park.

12. Where can I eat a quick lunch?
    (A) At noon.
    (B) Are you in a hurry?
    (C) Three sandwiches, please.

13. You submitted the travel reimbursement form, didn't you?
    (A) That sounds interesting.
    (B) Yes, probably tomorrow.
    (C) Yes, this morning.

14. Would you like me to call you a taxi?
    (A) My car is behind the building.
    (B) About 20 miles.
    (C) Thank you for calling.

15. Shouldn't we change our company uniforms?
    (A) We'll have to get approval first.
    (B) That schedule is more convenient.

(C) I'll accompany you to the station.

16. Why is the conference center locked today?
(A) Of course, I have some time.
(B) He got a ticket for the special exhibit.
(C) I haven't been told yet.

17. What maintenance work needs to be done on this building?
(A) Sure, I can walk.
(B) I haven't finished checking it.
(C) The heater works well.

18. Why don't you check the price range at a different office supplier?
(A) Order ten boxes of paper.
(B) Sure, it's enough.
(C) Please recommend one.

19. How many cups of coffee should I buy for the staff meeting?
(A) Okay, I'll take the receipt.
(B) Everyone from the department is attending.
(C) We need five more chairs.

20. Who approved that order?
(A) An hour ago.
(B) Mark will check the budget.
(C) John authorized it.

21. Should I show the figures on a chart or on a table?
(A) The number is accurate.
(B) No, that's not proper.
(C) A chart would be better.

22. Tom placed the lunch order.
(A) What kind of food did he order?
(B) The product is launching next week.
(C) He will pay for it.

23. When are you showing your clients the office in the Pitt Mall?
(A) On the tenth floor.
(B) They've just canceled.
(C) The theater is located downtown.

24. I'm sorry I won't be able to lead the workshop next week.
(A) I left it for you by the flower shop.
(B) Thanks for letting me know.
(C) No, maybe just a quick update.

25. Which box should I use to mail these items?
(A) They are too heavy to carry.
(B) Do you want to send them by express mail?
(C) Next to the post office.

26. The inspectors are coming to the factory soon, right?
(A) Everything is ready.
(B) No, they didn't.
(C) On the assembly line.

27. We have to purchase a new coffeemaker.
(A) Let me check our budget.
(B) With more milk and sugar.
(C) No, the copier is broken.

28. Where's the nearest train station?
(A) I'm going there now.
(B) The training starts at 2 P.M.
(C) At the bus stop.

29. Is there a fitting room where I can try this shirt on?
(A) Sure, follow me.
(B) This is too small for me.
(C) Sorry. They're out of stock.

30. Would you like to meet on Thursday or Friday?
(A) Actually, I did like it.
(B) How about my office?
(C) I don't have my appointment book with me now.

31. Should I bring my portfolio to the job interview?
(A) She is highly qualified.
(B) I already applied for it.
(C) I've seen it online.

Part 3

Questions 32-34 refer to the following conversation.

M Good afternoon. You've reached the Concord Hotel. How can I help you?

W Hello. My name is Kimberly. I've been told that your hotel is looking for a receptionist. So I'd like to apply for the position if it is still available.

M Let me ask the HR manager, Oliver Hooper, first. He'll know if the position has been filled yet. I'll get back to you at this phone number.

32. Where does the man work?
(A) At an employment agency
(B) At a hotel
(C) At a bookstore
(D) At a bank

33. Why is the woman calling?
(A) To reserve a room
(B) To complain about a billing problem
(C) To reject a position
(D) To inquire about a job opening

34. What does the man say he will do next?
(A) Schedule an interview
(B) Talk with a coworker
(C) Send an e-mail
(D) Post a job opening

Questions 35-37 refer to the following conversation.

W Robert, it's been a long time. How have you been?

M Hi, Joanne. I'm great. Thanks. I heard at the general meeting yesterday that we're opening a branch office in Denver next year. I wonder what kinds of jobs are going to be available there. Do you know anything?

W Have you checked the company Web site? I noticed several internal postings for the Marketing and Sales departments this morning.

M	Okay. I'll check them out. One more thing: if you have time, would you mind looking over my résumé and cover letter?

35 What does the man want to know about?
 (A) A meeting schedule
 (B) A woman's contact information
 (C) Other positions at the company
 (D) The location of the company's headquarters

36 What does the woman suggest the man do?
 (A) Check a bulletin board
 (B) Visit the company homepage
 (C) Fill out a request form
 (D) Speak with a marketing manager

37 What does the man ask the woman to do?
 (A) Review some documents
 (B) Look over a sales report
 (C) Fill out some paperwork
 (D) Find a new position

Questions 38-40 refer to the following conversation.

W	We're ready to show the prototype for our new washing machine to our appliance distributors from Singapore today, right?
M	Oh, actually, we had to reschedule the meeting about the product because their plane was delayed. So their plane won't be arriving until tonight.
W	All right. I think when they arrive here, they'll be going straight to their hotel. So should I arrange for a car to pick them up in the morning?
M	Good thinking. Around ten o'clock would be great.
W	Okay, I'll do that right now.

38 What product are the distributors coming to see?
 (A) A vehicle
 (B) A mobile phone
 (C) A computer
 (D) A home appliance

39 Why has the meeting been put off?
 (A) The prototype isn't finished yet.
 (B) A flight was postponed.
 (C) Some clients didn't take a plane.
 (D) Rooms are already fully booked.

40 What will the woman do next?
 (A) Contact a pickup service
 (B) Submit some paperwork
 (C) Hire some drivers
 (D) Pick up some clients

Questions 41-43 refer to the following conversation.

W	Hello. This is Barbara from CM Printing Press. I just e-mailed you the sample of your company's business cards. Do you have time to look it over?
M	Oh, I just saw your draft and was about to call you myself. We actually created a new company logo.
W	Okay, no problem. Could you send it to me before 2 P.M. so that I can be sure to finish the print job by the end of day as promised?
M	Sure, I'll e-mail you right now. In addition, please charge the order to the credit card you have on file.

41 What does the woman want the man to do?
 (A) Review a sample
 (B) Change a color
 (C) Cancel an order
 (D) Print business cards

42 Why does the man say, "We actually created a new company logo"?
 (A) To reassure a client
 (B) To compliment a logo design
 (C) To express surprise at a decision
 (D) To request an update to an order

43 What does the man ask the woman to do?
 (A) Make a payment
 (B) Upgrade a credit card
 (C) Send a new logo
 (D) Arrange some files

Questions 44-46 refer to the following conversation with three speakers.

W1	More and more people have been visiting the art gallery lately. So my tours this month have been completely full. How about yours, Yujin?
W2	Mine, too. I think it's due to the Impressionist paintings on loan from the National Gallery. It would be interesting to know about Impressionist art.
M	Well, I just heard that Dr. Ciara, who has researched Impressionist art for several years, will be here to talk about the exhibit next Tuesday afternoon. I'm sure that will be a great opportunity to ask many questions.
W2	That's good to know. Are there the tickets to that event? If so, how much are they?
M	Oh, you don't need to pay. All employees who work at the gallery can get in free of charge.

44 What do the women do at the art gallery?
 (A) Display artwork
 (B) Restore paintings
 (C) Invite well-known painters
 (D) Lead tours

45 Why have many people recently visited the art gallery?
 (A) Tickets are inexpensive.
 (B) There is an interesting display.
 (C) It has extended its hours of operation.
 (D) They received complimentary tickets.

46 According to the man, what will happen next Tuesday?
 (A) A new exhibit will be opened.
 (B) Some research results will be announced.
 (C) Visitors will purchase tickets for an event.

(D) An expert will give a lecture.

Questions 47-49 refer to the following conversation.

M I'm Samuel Ferguson with Eastwood TV, your local news station, broadcasting from the new Eastwood Public Library. Construction will be complete next March, so local residents are excited about the library's opening. Let's talk to someone now. Excuse me, ma'am. Do you live in the neighborhood?

W Yes, and I'm so pleased to have a library in this area because I always have to take the bus across town to borrow books. That is really inconvenient. However, starting next year, I can check out books anytime I want.

M Right, and it has a digital system for borrowing electronic books online when you apply for a library card. That will be especially easy for members to borrow books. It will also have a café, a small hall, and some other places.

47 Who most likely is the woman?
(A) A librarian
(B) A local resident
(C) A news reporter
(D) A constructor

48 What does the woman like the most about the new facility?
(A) Its modern appearance
(B) Its longer operating hours
(C) Its convenient location
(D) Its rare book collection

49 What advantage will members have?
(A) A free shuttle service
(B) Discounts on coffee and drinks
(C) Access to electronic reading material
(D) Tickets to special talks

Questions 50-52 refer to the following conversation.

W Hello. I'd like to order one of your new energy-saving air conditioners that you're advertising on TV.

M Certainly. May I ask which model you'd like, the standard or the deluxe, and in which color, silver or white?

W White and the deluxe model, please. How soon can I get it? I live in Sydney.

M If you place an order right now, it'll be shipped from our warehouse in Melbourne tomorrow.

W So when will it be delivered here?

M It should arrive in the evening of the following day.

50 What is the purpose of the woman's call?
(A) To purchase a television
(B) To complain about an air conditioner
(C) To schedule an appointment
(D) To place an order

51 What does the woman ask for?
(A) A telephone number
(B) A preferred model
(C) A delivery time
(D) A man's address

52 When will the item probably arrive?
(A) This evening
(B) Tomorrow afternoon
(C) In two days
(D) In a week

Questions 53-55 refer to the following conversation.

M I'm so upset about this project. Do you have time to talk?

W Sure, Benjamin. What's the matter?

M Well, I've been working on the Zahira Department Store account. Whenever I send them an advertisement that they've requested, they turn it down! That's happened three times this week. Can you believe it?

W Actually, the Zahira Department Store account was the first project I worked on here, and it doesn't sound like they've changed much.

M Really? It's too bad they haven't changed over time.

W Some clients have difficulty making decisions. I think you should ask your manager to help with the problem.

53 Where do the speakers most likely work?
(A) At a department store
(B) At an advertising agency
(C) At a bank
(D) At an accounting firm

54 Why does the woman say, "the Zahira Department Store account was the first project I worked on here"?
(A) To advertise a department store
(B) To explain why a proposal was rejected
(C) To complain about a client's mistake
(D) To express that she understands a problem

55 What does the woman suggest the man do?
(A) Reject a project
(B) Get help from a supervisor
(C) Prepare some samples
(D) Change a decision

Questions 56-58 refer to the following conversation.

M Hello. I purchased this camera here last week, but I think it has a problem. Several times when I have taken a photo, the screen has frozen. I tried to turn it off and then turn it back on, but it hasn't worked properly.

W I'm sorry to hear that. This model sometimes has that problem. It's easy to fix though. I can fix it for you for free.

M Thank you, but I'd like to swap it for a new one because I feel uncomfortable using this one again.

W	Okay, do you want a different model or the same one? The warranty period depends on the models.
M	I'm not sure yet. Can I look at the other cameras first?

56 What problem does the man have?
(A) He was overcharged for an item.
(B) He dropped his camera.
(C) His device was delivered to the wrong place.
(D) His device is defective.

57 What does the woman offer to do?
(A) Provide technical support for free
(B) Exchange the camera for a new one
(C) Make a free delivery
(D) File an insurance claim

58 What does the man want to do?
(A) Increase insurance fee
(B) Change his contact information
(C) Look at some other items
(D) Find a product warranty

Questions 59-61 refer to the following conversation.

M	Thanks for your time. Things have been so hectic with training for our new game next month.
W	No problem. I understand completely.
M	We love the imagery you created for our team the last time, and we'd like to have a new T-shirt design to sell our fans for the season.
W	Oh, I appreciate the business, and I'm looking forward to this.
M	Could you make sure the design fits on our caps, too?
W	Absolutely. Now, before designing anything, we always give clients a questionnaire to get a sense of their style. So after I get your responses, I can start drawing.

59 Who most likely is the woman?
(A) An athlete
(B) An event planner
(C) A sports coach
(D) A clothing designer

60 Why does the man want to hire the woman?
(A) To make her sell some T-shirts
(B) To have her play a game
(C) To have her design some merchandise
(D) To organize some events

61 What does the woman request that the man do?
(A) Fill out a questionnaire
(B) Conduct a survey
(C) Create a new design
(D) Get a reimbursement

Questions 62-64 refer to the following conversation and schedule.

W	Hi. This is Yoko from MR Express Logistics. I reviewed your résumé. You have a lot of experience as a driver. I was very impressed by that.
M	Sure, I've driven a delivery truck for over a decade.
W	Good, I'd like to arrange an interview for next week. I know that you are available on Wednesday morning. Unfortunately, there are no open interview times that morning. Could you come in on Thursday at 2 P.M.?
M	Let me check my schedule… Yes, I can meet you then.
W	Okay. Now, I already have your application, so please bring a cover letter and at least two references, including the names of your previous managers and their phone numbers.
M	All right, I'll bring the documents to the interview. Thanks.

62 What kind of experience does the man have?
(A) Sales
(B) Car maintenance
(C) Marketing
(D) Delivery driving

63 Look at the graphic. What room will the man be interviewed in?
(A) Room 201
(B) Room 205
(C) Room 302
(D) Room 303

64 What should the man bring to the interview?
(A) Recommendation letters
(B) A driver license
(C) A professional certificate
(D) A list of addresses

Questions 65-67 refer to the following conversation and label.

W	Excuse me. This label has the expiration date, but does that mean this pizza is only good for two more days?
M	Oh, that's only if you buy pizzas before they're frozen.
W	Are they sold unfrozen?
M	Yes. Many of our customers purchase them that way, but we freeze some of them right after we make them. As long as they stay frozen, our pizzas last for at least two weeks past the marked date. We're proud of the freshness of our pizzas, however, which is why we discount our frozen items.

65 Look at the graphic. When does the conversation take place?
(A) On October 10
(B) On October 11
(C) On October 13

(D) On October 15

66 What does the man emphasize?
(A) The price
(B) The quality
(C) The size
(D) The packaging

67 What does the man say about the items?
(A) A discount is available for frozen ones.
(B) They are not refundable.
(C) Their price will decrease in two weeks.
(D) They are only available unfrozen.

Questions 68-70 refer to the following conversation and menu.

W Hi, Dan. Our investors are coming from overseas next week, so we need to order some food for the welcome party. What kinds of dishes do you think we should order? Do you have any ideas?
M Well, we ordered roast chicken sandwiches for our clients the last time. Everyone was really satisfied with them.
W Yes, I know. But we received enough funds this time, so I'd like to order something special.
M Why don't we order pasta or pizza?
W Pasta would be good. Also, we still have to arrange accommodations for our clients. Could you do that?

68 What are the speakers talking about?
(A) Throwing a farewell party
(B) Leading a training session
(C) Preparing for a visit
(D) Celebrating an anniversary

69 Look at the graphic. How much will the speakers most likely spend per person?
(A) $7
(B) $10
(C) $12
(D) $13

70 What does the woman ask the man to do?
(A) Reserve some hotel rooms
(B) Cancel some accommodations
(C) Order some food
(D) Book a rental car

Part 4

Questions 71-73 refer to the following excerpt from a meeting.

Let's start the weekly staff meeting. First of all, this Friday evening is the Mildton Company's 10th anniversary party at our restaurant. As many of you know, Friday evening is one of our busiest times. Not only will the people attending the event come, but many regular diners will also stop by for dinner, and the line may get quite long. So we'll need a few extra cooks and servers, and everyone who works that day will get double their hourly rate. If you are available that day, please let me know as soon as possible. I also highly suggest taking the bus or train here because it will be very difficult to park in the lot during the event.

71 What will be held on Friday?
(A) An awards ceremony
(B) A holiday parade
(C) An anniversary celebration
(D) A company retreat

72 What benefit will employees have if they work on Friday?
(A) They can take a day off
(B) They can change shifts with someone else.
(C) They can get paid more.
(D) They can receive free parking.

73 What does the speaker recommend that the listeners do?
(A) Take public transportation
(B) Clean their uniforms
(C) Pack a dinner
(D) Use a parking lot

Questions 74-76 refer to the following news report.

You are listening to the hourly traffic report. I'm Sam Dier. There is traffic congestion on the Oxford Bridge because of the marathon that's taking place until 5 P.M. So drivers who want to find alternate routes should take a look at the transit map on our Web site. In addition, remember that construction of the public museum will begin in the downtown area early next week, so some parts of George Street will likely be closed. We'll be sure to let you know as soon as the construction project is complete. Thanks for listening and enjoy your drive.

74 What is the main topic of the report?
(A) Community activities
(B) Sports news
(C) Race rules
(D) Traffic

75 What does the speaker recommend that the listeners do?
(A) Upgrade a Web site
(B) Check a map
(C) Drive slowly
(D) Visit a public museum

76 What does the speaker say will happen next week?
(A) A winner will be announced.
(B) A project will start.
(C) Road construction will be completed.
(D) A museum will officially open.

Questions 77-79 refer to the following telephone message.

Hi, Reilly. I don't want to disturb you since you've already left the office for the day, but I just looked over the materials for the new employee orientation on Monday morning. Actually, Andy was supposed to prepare the health insurance packets, but he's been out sick, so they're not finished. I know you have a lot of tasks to do, but I need your help. I don't have any appointments tomorrow. Can you meet me for a while tomorrow? I have some important questions about some of the material. Please get back to me. Thanks.

77 According to the speaker, what will take place on Monday?
   (A) An employee orientation
   (B) An interview
   (C) A workplace inspection
   (D) A job fair

78 What does the speaker imply when he says, "I don't have any appointments tomorrow"?
   (A) He can meet with a client.
   (B) He thinks a schedule is flexible.
   (C) He needs to work overtime tomorrow.
   (D) He has some time to review a task.

79 What does the speaker ask the listener to do?
   (A) Call him back
   (B) Check a calendar
   (C) Ask some questions
   (D) Cancel an appointment

Questions 80-82 refer to the following advertisement.

Are you interested in fashion? Tandy offers the latest clothing fashions and top brands as well as the highest quality of service. We are looking for a talented and motivated person to be a shop manager at our new Westminster store, which is opening at the beginning of April. Applicants should be qualified with one to two years' experience in a similar role in the fashion industry and have the ability to inspire and manage a sales team. If you want to apply for the job, bring your application in person or apply online at our Web site, www.tandy.com.

80 What type of business does the speaker work for?
   (A) A clothing store
   (B) A design company
   (C) An employment agency
   (D) An antique store

81 What is a requirement for the position?
   (A) To be able to work on Saturdays
   (B) To have more than four years of work experience
   (C) To have a university degree in fashion
   (D) To have a background in fashion

82 What can listeners do to apply for the position?
   (A) Visit a company Web site
   (B) Call a store in person
   (C) Talk to a store manager
   (D) Send a résumé by e-mail

Questions 83-85 refer to the following introduction.

Good morning. I'm Gary Cooper, the head manager at the Codex Public Aquarium. I'm so pleased that many of you are visiting the aquarium to see many kinds of sea creatures. Tonight, we're happy to be hosting our first annual marine biology lecture, which will give you the opportunity to learn about marine life in the ocean. Actually, when we talked about having a lecture series in a meeting, we weren't sure the people would be interested in it. However, I can see that most of the seats are occupied. Now, let's watch a short video about beautiful sea life. But before we begin, please turn off your mobile phones and avoid taking pictures during the talk since the light can disturb your visibility.

83 Where does the speaker work?
   (A) At a national park
   (B) At a marine museum
   (C) At an aquarium
   (D) At a public library

84 What does the speaker imply when he says, "I can see that most of the seats are occupied"?
   (A) A talk is popular.
   (B) More people can participate.
   (C) The tickets are all sold out.
   (D) More chairs are needed.

85 What does the speaker ask the listeners to do?
   (A) Raise their hands to ask questions
   (B) Switch off their devices
   (C) Find their designated seats
   (D) Take some pictures

Questions 86-88 refer to the following broadcast.

Good evening. This is *Lead a Healthy Life*, a weekly radio broadcast that gives you useful tips on eating habits. Today, we're talking about sugar. Most people know that sugar is not good for your health. Well, it is surprising that this negative view of sugar is simply not true. You actually need sugar in your diet to remain healthy. But remember that most foods naturally contain sugar, so you don't need to add extra sugar to all your diet. In fact, even fruit contains sugar. I know you're all interested in trying more recipes that use fruits. We'll be talking about that on next week's broadcast. Stay tuned for sports news after this commercial break.

86 What is the broadcast mainly about?
   (A) Diet advice
   (B) Exercise tips
   (C) Useful recipes
   (D) Healthy fruits

87 Why does the speaker say he is surprised?
   (A) Sugar can be very harmful.
   (B) A popular view is incorrect.
   (C) Some fruit is high in sugar.
   (D) A task is time consuming.

88 What will be discussed on next week's broadcast?
(A) Sugar-free food
(B) The adverse effects of diets
(C) Recipes using fruit
(D) Sports news

Questions 89-91 refer to the following introduction.

Ladies and gentlemen, may I have your attention, please? We're so pleased to see such a large number of attendees at this year's time management conference. I'd like to take this opportunity to introduce our keynote speaker, Professor Eleanor Smith. Dr. Smith will be presenting her research on time management to improve productivity. Since all of you have important roles in your departments, I think you'll find this conference very informative. Before I hand the microphone over to Dr. Smith, I'd like to encourage you to stay afterward for a question-and-answer session. You can also register for next year's conference on our Web site in advance to receive a discount on the registration fee.

89 Where most likely is the audience?
(A) At a trade fair
(B) At a professional conference
(C) At a management meeting
(D) At a university

90 What will Dr. Smith talk about?
(A) Workplace stress
(B) Corporate investments
(C) Time management
(D) Personality traits

91 What does the speaker recommend the listeners do?
(A) Stay after the presentation
(B) Submit questions
(C) Fill out the form ahead of time
(D) Issue a discount coupon

Questions 92-94 refer to the following excerpt from a meeting.

Let's start our meeting. I'd like to share some good news with you all. We've just renewed our contract with the Aquatic Botanical Garden. We'll continue trimming all the plants and mowing the grass there for the next three years. I know we're all happy to hear that. Next, several of you have complained that some of the blades in the lawnmowers are becoming dull and that it's taking longer to cut trees and bushes. Don't worry. I've already ordered ten new machines, which will be arriving within a week. And now, Jason will talk about the next item on the agenda.

92 What news is the speaker talking about?
(A) A renewed agreement
(B) An extended deadline
(C) A new employee
(D) A garden party

93 What kind of business does the speaker work for?
(A) A manufacturer
(B) A landscape service
(C) A botanical garden
(D) A dry-cleaning service

94 What does the speaker mean when she says, "I've already ordered ten new machines"?
(A) She wants to fix the machines.
(B) She has extra time to help.
(C) She wants to change an order.
(D) She is addressing a problem.

Questions 95-97 refer to the following telephone message and floor plan.

Hello, David. This is Amiko. I was just told I'm being assigned to be the team manager for the project to develop our newest mobile phone. I'm working on the budget for the development of the new product and have been going over the expenses from the previous model. I have a couple of questions that I'd like to ask you because you worked on a similar project last year. Would you mind stopping by my office when you have time today? Oh, I moved to the office on the third floor which is located directly across from the staff lounge. Thank you.

95 Which department does the speaker most likely work in?
(A) Maintenance
(B) Accounting
(C) Product Development
(D) Sales

96 Why does the speaker ask to meet with the listener?
(A) To get help increasing the budget
(B) To file a document
(C) To discuss a project
(D) To remodel the office

97 Look at the graphic. Where is the speaker's office?
(A) Office 1
(B) Office 2
(C) Office 3
(D) Office 4

Questions 98-100 refer to the following excerpt from a meeting and schedule.

Good morning, everyone. Could I have your attention, please? We're just about to begin our monthly meeting. First of all, please take a look at the schedule on the paper in front of you. As you can see, we have four speakers lined up. However, ten minutes ago, Roger, who is one of the speakers, called me. He said he was stuck in traffic on the highway due to road construction. He wants to switch speaking times with Helen. I think that is fine. So we'll talk about what happened in the past at first and end with a talk about the future. Okay. Helen, are you ready?

98 What problem does the speaker mention?
(A) A conference will be delayed.
(B) A meeting room will be changed.
(C) A presenter will be late.

(D) A schedule is full.

99 Look at the graphic. At what time will Mr. Roger speak?
    (A) 10:00 A.M.
    (B) 10:30 A.M.
    (C) 11:00 A.M.
    (D) 11:30 A.M.

100 According to the speaker, what might be good about the change?
    (A) The meeting time will be extended.
    (B) The subjects will be in chronological order.
    (C) The discussion will begin earlier.
    (D) There will be more speakers.

Part 5

101 다른 전자 장비들과 비교해 보았을 때 우리의 것이 초보자들이 작동하기에 훨씬 더 쉽습니다.

102 정부 자금을 확보하기 위해서 G&B Biz 사는 이번에 프로젝트를 경쟁사와 협업할 것입니다.

103 Morgan 씨는 추가적인 사무용 가구를 주문하기 전에 최소한의 필요한 수량을 추정해야 합니다.

104 사용 설명서의 상세한 지시 사항 덕분에 우리는 소모품들을 쉽게 교체할 수 있습니다.

105 당신의 수화물의 중량이 초과되었기 때문에 20달러의 추가 비용을 지불하셔야 합니다.

106 시 정부는 King Road에 교통사고를 예방하기 위해 방벽을 설치하기로 결정했습니다.

107 그 영화는 많은 극장에서 개봉되지는 않았지만 많은 관중들로부터 긍정적인 평가를 받았습니다.

108 회사 회계사의 보고서에 따르면 현재 사업들이 구조조정 논란 이후 하락세를 보였습니다.

109 지난 회의 동안에 부서장들은 다가오는 판촉 행사에서 고객들의 참여를 증진시킬 방법을 논의했습니다.

110 부산의 멋진 전망은 Jane 씨가 그림을 그리는 데 지속적으로 영감을 주었습니다.

111 여러분이 저희 웹 사이트에 방문하면, 컴퓨터 조립에 대한 설명서를 다운로드 받을 수 있습니다.

112 여러분들은 웹 사이트를 통해 저희 정기 간행물에 게재된 모든 정보를 받아 볼 수 있습니다.

113 예상치 못한 오류들로 인해 우리는 원인이 명확히 규명될 때까지 생산을 중단하기로 결정했습니다.

114 디자인팀이 그 프로젝트를 제때 마쳤다면 우리는 이번 자동차 박람회에서 새로운 차량들을 선보일 수 있었을 것입니다.

115 우리는 일주일 이내에 정상적인 생산으로 돌아올 것이라 확신하며, 교체품들의 배송은 가장 빠른 시일에 이루어질 것입니다.

116 당신이 구매하신 부품이 적절하게 작동하지 않을 경우에 대비하여 백업용 추가 저장 드라이브를 보유하고 있어야 합니다.

117 지원서는 반드시 적어도 3장의 추천서와 함께 첨부되어야 하고, 이는 인사과 부장에게 이메일로 보내져야 합니다.

118 10월 5일 전에 양식을 제출하는 모든 고객들에게 20퍼센트의 등록비 할인이 주어질 것입니다.

119 Newark의 우리 직원들 중 한 명이 꼬리표를 잘못 붙여서 당신의 수화물이 목적지인 스위스 대신 핀란드로 보내졌습니다.

120 Simmons 씨는 창작의 자유를 제공하는 Gaza Global Publishing 사와 같은 환경에서 일하고 싶어 합니다.

121 더 많은 고객들을 끌어들이기 위해 판촉 책자들이 현재 우리 웹 사이트에 게시되어 있습니다.

122 Calvin 사의 지점들을 아시아 지역으로 확장할 것인지 여부는 우리의 정기 주주총회에서 논의되어야 합니다.

123 Mia의 사례 분석 연구 때문에 그녀는 국가 장학금에 가장 적합한 최종 후보자로 선정되었습니다.

124 방문자들은 방문 기간과 목적뿐만 아니라 그들의 이름 및 소속과 함께 운영 시스템에 사전 등록되어야 합니다.

125 OG Gate 사의 순수익이 온라인 쇼핑 사이트를 시작한 이래로 상당히 증가했습니다.

126 우리가 다른 사업 분야로의 확장을 계획하는 동안 우리 인터넷 검색 시스템의 광고 수익이 계속 증가하고 있습니다.

127 그 회사는 당신에게 Penn Culinary 위원회에서 발급된 식품 안전 및 위생 인증서를 제출하도록 요구했습니다.

128 이사회는 회사의 확장 프로그램의 다음 단계가 흥미로운 동시에 도전적이라고 간주했습니다.

129 지난 10년 이상 동안 연방 은행에 의한 국가 퇴직 연금에 대한 관심도가 떨어지고 있습니다.

130 계약이 자동으로 만료되기 전에 여러분은 어떤 비용을 지불할 필요 없이 그 계약을 갱신할 수 있는 선택권을 받습니다.

Part 6

Questions 131-134 refer to the following Web page.

텍사스 요리 협회(TCA)는 현재 다가오는 행사를 위한 참가자를 모집하고 있습니다.
TCA는 텍사스의 지역 음식들을 발전시키기 위하여 무역 박람회를 준비하고 교육적인 컨퍼런스와 경연들을 실시합니다. 텍사스 정부는 1977년 이래로 칠리 기반의 음식들을 주 지역 음식으로 공식적으로 선언하였고, 주민들에게 칠리와 타코는 매우 인기가 있습니다. 이러한 것들 중 많은 음식들이 전 세계에 있는 식당의 요리사들에 의해 조리됩니다. TCA는 매년 5월 요리사들에게 TCA Grand Recipe 경연에 참가를 권유함으로써 가장 큰 규모의 행사를 개최하고 있습니다. 많은 요리사들이 1등상을 타기 위해 모일 것입니다. 작년에는 Kal Martinez가 그의 이름을 우승자 명단에 올렸습니다.

133 (A) 지역 기업들이 그 행사를 재정적으로 도울 것입니다.
    (B) 참가자들은 사전에 호텔 예약을 해야 합니다.
    (C) 많은 요리사들이 1등상을 타기 위해 모일 것입니다.
    (D) 신기술이 이 문제를 위해 도입되어야 합니다.

Questions 135-138 refer to the following memo.

수신: Bucks NET의 부장들
날짜: 3월 10일
회신: 회사 단합일

안녕하세요, 여러분!

저는 귀하가 팀원들에게 다가오는 회사 단합 대회에 관하여 알릴 것을 다시 상기시키고자 이 메모를 씁니다. 이것은 Marine Tivoli Resort에서 3월 27일부터 30일까지 열릴 예정입니다.

저는 그 시기에 우리 모두가 즐길 다양한 단체 활동들을 기획하고 조직하는 일을 맡았습니다. 이 활동들의 세부적인 정보는 3월 20일에 직원 식당의 공지판에 게시될 것입니다.

총무과의 Griffin Moth 씨가 제가 준비하는 것을 돕고 있습니다. 제가 부재중인 동안 그 행사에 관한 문의가 있으시면 그녀에게 내선 번호 701로 연락하세요.

그럼 이만,

Kevin Durant
인사과 부장

136. (A) 퇴임식은 이미 회사의 대연회장에서 열렸습니다.
 (B) 저희를 돕고자 하는 분은 자원봉사 신청서를 제출하셔야 합니다.
 (C) 이것은 Marine Tivoli Resort에서 3월 27일부터 30일까지 열릴 예정입니다.
 (D) 우리 회사는 새로 출시된 제품들이 고객들에게 높은 평가를 받아 자랑스럽습니다.

Questions 139-142 refer to the following advertisement.

디트로이트 안전 및 보안국(SSAD)은 여러분들이 저희의 새로운 보안 애플리케이션(앱)을 휴대폰에 다운로드하시길 요청합니다. 이것은 도시의 안전 문제에 관한 정보를 보완하고자 출시되었습니다. 여러분이 비상시 해야 할 일에 관한 정보를 접하지 못할 경우에 대비하여, 저희는 모든 주민들이 이 앱을 사용할 수 있도록 만듭니다. 이 앱은 새로운 데이터로 자동으로 업데이트됩니다. 게다가 여러분은 화면상 알림, 도시 뉴스의 링크 그리고 교통 상황과 같은 다양한 앱 안의 기능들을 설치하실 수 있습니다. 여러분이 앱에서 버튼을 클릭만 하면 모든 정보들이 휴대폰 또는 태블릿 PC로 바로 전송될 것입니다. 지금 휴대폰을 켜시고, Zetta Store 또는 Gate Way 아이콘을 터치하셔서 이 앱을 다운로드 받으세요.

140. (A) 길을 걸으면서 휴대폰을 사용하는 것은 위험합니다.
 (B) 이 앱은 새로운 데이터로 자동으로 업데이트됩니다.
 (C) 이 앱의 일부 기능들은 서비스 요금이 부과될 수 있습니다.
 (D) 시 정부는 앱 다운로드의 상태를 확인해야 합니다.

Questions 143-146 refer to the following article.

Remington (12월 20일) — 독일의 거대 제약회사 Meditech는 이번 주에 올해의 Gold Humanity 상을 수상했습니다. 이 회사는 지역의 비영리 기관들에 지속적으로 상당한 기부를 했습니다. 예를 들어 이 회사는 Remington 지역에 절실히 필요한 병원들을 짓기 위해 Carpe Foundation을 후원했습니다. 사회 복지 분야의 지역 지도자들로 구성된 위원회는 기부자들의 기대에 부응하기 위해 병원 운영을 위임하고 있습니다.

Meditech 사는 현재 유럽의 가장 큰 제약 제조업체들 중 하나이고, 이미 한국과 캐나다를 포함한 8개국에 기반을 확보하고 있습니다. 그렇기는 하지만 Meditech 사의 공동 창업자인 Ireland 씨는 수상 연설에서 더 나은 의료적 치료를 필요로 하는 아프리카 대륙으로도 확장할 의향이 있다고 말했습니다. 그는 사람들에게 회사가 목표를 달성할 때까지 인내심을 가져 달라고 말했습니다.

143. (A) 전 세계의 많은 의료 회사들이 이 행사에 참여했습니다.
 (B) 이 회사는 지역의 비영리 기관들에 지속적으로 상당한 기부를 했습니다.
 (C) 컨퍼런스의 제약 회사들은 함께 저소득층을 돕기로 결정했습니다.
 (D) 공공기관에 의료 장비들을 기부함으로써 그 회사는 국책 사업을 따낼 수 있습니다.

Part 7

Questions 147-148 refer to the following ticket.

West Brook 교통	
비수기 가격의 성인용 티켓	
이 티켓을 소지하신 승객은 무제한으로 왕복하실 수 있습니다.	West Brook Port와 Erie Island 사이
선박의 승무원이 검사할 수 있기 때문에 여러분은 이동을 마칠 때까지 이 티켓을 소지하고 있으셔야 합니다.	
[주의]	
이 비수기 가격의 티켓은 월요일부터 목요일까지의 이동에만 유효합니다. (오전 8시부터 오후 5시까지)	West Brook Port와 Yellow Creek Park 사이
다른 시간대에 여행하고 싶으시면 추가 금액 6달러로 일반 티켓으로 업그레이드하셔야 합니다.	

147. 이 표에 따르면, 맞는 것은 무엇인가?
 (A) 한 사람당 모든 이동에 6달러를 지불해야 한다.
 (B) 한 번 이상의 이동에 대해 유효하다.
 (C) 언제든지 구매할 수 있다.
 (D) 모든 이동에 적용된다.

148. 이 티켓은 어떤 종류의 교통수단을 위한 것인가?
 (A) 기차
 (B) 비행기
 (C) 배
 (D) 택시

Questions 149-150 refer to the following advertisement.

토목 기사 구함

Kovalchuk Metro Development (KMD) 사는 우리의 활동적인 프로젝트에 합류할 창의적이고 열정적이며 경험 있는 사람을 구하고 있습니다. 업무는 프로젝트 관리자를 도움으로써 우리의 새로운 도시 개발 프로젝트를 기획하고, 사업 타당성을 알아내는 것입니다. 사무용 및 디자인용 소프트웨어의 능숙함이 요구되고, 그 분야에서 최소 2년의 경력이 필요합니다. 다양한 현장 경험도 선호됩니다. 이 직책에 관심이 있으시다면 당신의 작업 포트폴리오 및 두 장의 추천서와 함께 이력서를 j_harman@kmd.net으로 보내주세요. 추가 정보를 위해 월요일부터 금요일 오전에 저희 사무실을 방문하셔도 됩니다.

149. 그 직책에 요구되는 것은 무엇인가?
 (A) 정부 기관에서의 이전 경력
 (B) 그래픽 디자인 소프트웨어에 대한 능력
 (C) 관련 분야의 대학원 학위
 (D) 목표 지역에서의 판매 경력

150 지원자들은 어떻게 추가적인 세부 사항을 얻을 수 있는가?
(A) 회사에 들름으로써
(B) 그들의 추천인들에게 연락함으로써
(C) 회사의 웹 사이트에 방문함으로써
(D) 관리자에게 전화함으로써

Questions 151-152 refer to the following memo.

[메모]

수신: 전 직원
발신: Chris Paul, 총무과 과장
제목: Sakai Work and Office
날짜: 3월 15일

Sakai Work and Office 사와의 특별한 제휴 덕분에 우리는 3월 20일부터 4월 10일까지 10개의 입식 책상을 시범적으로 받을 것입니다. 이 책상들을 사용함으로써 여러분은 사무실에서 일하는 동안 더 편안하게 서 있을 수 있습니다. 신제품인 Sakai 201 모델이 다음 주에 출시됩니다. 이 책상은 특별한 기능을 가지고 있어서 필요에 따라 책상의 높이를 자유롭게 조절할 수 있습니다. 최근 연구에 따르면, 이런 종류의 책상은 너무 오래 앉아서 생기는 신체적인 불편을 해소할 수 있을 것이라고 합니다. 이 기회를 잡고 싶으시다면 c_paul@meviusco.com으로 저에게 편히 연락 주세요. 지원자들이 너무 많을 경우에 대비하여 선착순으로 10명만 선정하겠습니다. 전 직원들을 위해 구매하기 전에 이 책상들이 효율적인지 결정해야 하기 때문에 이 책상을 사용하는 데 선정되신 분들은 사용한 후 설문 조사에 응해 주셔야 합니다.

151 이 메모의 목적은 무엇인가?
(A) 직원들에게 정기 건강 검진을 받으라고 장려하기 위해
(B) 직원들에게 근무 환경에 대한 설문 조사를 작성하라고 요구하기 위해
(C) 직원들에게 새로운 사무실 건물로 가구를 옮기라고 요청하기 위해
(D) 직원들에게 새로 출시되는 가구를 사용해 볼 기회를 주기 위해

152 Sakai 201 모델에 대하여 암시되는 것은?
(A) 노동 생산성을 높일 수 있다.
(B) 높이를 조절할 수 있다.
(C) 회사의 신제품들 중에서 가장 비싸다.
(D) 회사의 다음 판매 품목으로 선정될 것이다.

Questions 153-154 refer to the following text-message chain.

Tong Zhang [오전 11:30]	안녕하세요, Lee 씨. Cathy Marriot이 휴대폰을 잃어버렸어요. 혹시 거기 어딘가에 있나요?
Jane Lee [오전 11:32]	뒷면에 꽃 그림이 각인되어 있는 노란색 실리콘 케이스인가요?
Tong Zhang [오전 11:33]	네, 맞아요. 지금 그녀가 가지러 올라갈 거예요.
Jane Lee [오전 11:34]	여기에 그녀의 열쇠들도 있어요. 그녀는 오늘 산만하고 정신 없나 봐요.
Tong Zhang [오전 11:35]	정말요? 그녀의 것이 맞나요?
Jane Lee [오전 11:37]	그런 것 같아요. 휴대폰 케이스 위에 놓여 있거든요.

153 Marriot 씨는 다음에 무엇을 할 것 같은가?
(A) 무언가를 가지러 간다
(B) 새로운 휴대폰 액세서리를 주문한다
(C) 휴대폰 서비스 제공업체에게 이메일을 보낸다
(D) Zhang 씨의 휴대폰을 빌린다

154 오전 11시 37분에, Lee 씨가 "그런 것 같아요"라고 쓴 의도는 무엇인가?
(A) 그녀는 Marriot 씨가 자주 잊어버린다고 가정한다.
(B) 그녀는 열쇠들이 Marriot 씨의 것이라고 생각한다.
(C) 그녀는 열쇠들이 필요한지 알고 싶어 한다.
(D) 그녀는 Zhang 씨가 잘못된 정보를 갖고 있다고 믿는다.

Questions 155-157 refer to the following advertisement.

당신의 신규 사업을 시작하는 최고의 방법!

이 새로운 매물에는 약 2,500 평방미터의 사무 공간과 1,500 평방미터의 저장 공간, 2,000 평방미터의 주차 공간을 포함되어 있습니다. 이 매물은 피츠버그 도심 지역에 쉽게 접근할 수 있고, 여기서 700 미터 이내에 많은 식당들과 쇼핑 단지들이 있습니다. 이 건물은 현대적인 내외관 디자인과 함께 많은 큰 창문들로 구성되어 있기 때문에 자연 채광을 최대한 활용함으로써 다른 매물들에 비해 난방비가 더 쌀 것입니다. 기본 임대 기간은 24개월이며, 월세와 보증금을 포함합니다. 임대 기간을 조정하고 싶으시다면 협의 가능합니다. 임대하거나 매물을 둘러보고 싶으시다면 Jessica Dorris에게 (710) 578-4813으로 연락 주세요.

155 주차 공간은 얼마나 넓은가?
(A) 700 평방미터
(B) 1,500 평방미터
(C) 2,000 평방미터
(D) 2,500 평방미터

156 이 매물의 장점으로 언급되지 않은 것은?
(A) 공항에서 걸어갈 수 있는 거리이다.
(B) 다양한 공간이 있다.
(C) 식당들과 가게들에 인접해 있다.
(D) 자연 채광의 이점을 볼 수 있다.

157 [1], [2], [3] 그리고 [4]로 표시된 곳 중에 다음 문장이 들어가기에 가장 적합한 위치는 어디인가?
"임대 기간을 조정하고 싶으시다면 협의 가능합니다."
(A) [1]
(B) [2]
(C) [3]
(D) [4]

Questions 158-160 refer to the following e-mail.

수신: Benjamin Foster
발신: Heesun Yoon
제목: 정보
날짜: 9월 10일

Foster 씨에게,

허가 절차에 관한 몇 가지 문제들 때문에 Indiana 지점의 개업이 지연되었고, 그래서 현재 10월 7일 금요일에 오픈할 예정입니다. 다음 주에 제가 여기 우리 팀에 당신이 합류하는 것에 관한 요청서를 포함하여 추가적인 세부 사항들을 당신 이메일로 보내 드리겠습니다. 본사에 있다가 저희와 합류해 주신다면 감사 드리겠습니다.

저희가 계획한 대로 한달 내내 모든 렌터카에 대한 특가 상품을 고객들에게 제공함으로써 이전을 홍보할 것입니다. 이에 더하여, 방문객들에게 저희의 저렴한 가격과 서비스를 알리기 위해 Indiana 시 정부와 특별 제휴를 맺었습니다. 비록 기존 고객들이 주로 출장 오시는 분들이긴 하지만 우리는 이 기회를 통해 관광객들도 끌어모으는 데 만전을 기해야 합니다.

당신을 곧 만나기를 기대합니다.

Heesun Yoon

158 첫 문단, 두 번째 줄의 단어 "scheduled"와 의미상 가장 가까운 것은?
(A) 예정된
(B) 훈련된
(C) 연장된
(D) 차별된

159 Yoon 씨에 관해 무엇이 암시되는가?
(A) 그녀는 사무실에서 많은 투자자들을 만났다.
(B) 그녀는 사무실 이전을 담당하고 있다.
(C) 그녀는 신규 직원을 채용하기로 결정했다.
(D) 그녀는 본사로 이전할 예정이다.

160 10월 7일에 어떤 종류의 회사가 개업할 것인가?
(A) 법률 사무소
(B) 관광 회사
(C) 렌터카 업체
(D) 개발 회사

Questions 161-163 refer to the following letter.

버지니아 대학 의료 센터
3018 워싱턴 드라이브
페어팩스, 버지니아 12301

6월 10일

버지니아 대학 의료 센터 환자분들께,

버지니아 대학 의료 센터(UVMC)는 여러분의 의료 기관으로 저희를 선택해 주신 모든 환자분들께 감사를 전하고자 합니다. 지난 40여년 동안 저희는 페어팩스 지역의 수천 명의 환자분들을 성공적으로 치료했습니다. 의료 분야의 급격한 변화를 고려해 볼 때 저희는 항상 여러분들을 위한 최상의 의료 서비스를 제공하고자 최선의 노력을 다했습니다. 이러한 목표를 달성하기 위해 7월 1일부터 Progressive Health가 UVMC를 인수할 것임을 발표하게 되어 기쁩니다.

이것은 저희 현재 프로그램들이 변화한다는 걸 의미하지 않습니다. 오직 저희 이름만 바뀝니다; 다음 달에 저희의 현재 이름은 Virginia Progressive Health로 변경될 것입니다. 여러분의 기존 의료진들은 그대로일 것이며, 페어팩스 지역에서 여러분의 의사 선생님들에게 진찰을 계속 받으실 수 있습니다. 그러나 이번 인수 덕분에 재능있는 의사들과 전문가들을 통해 더욱더 폭넓은 치료법들과 의료 장비들을 경험하실 수 있을 겁니다. Progressive Health는 최신 의료 서비스 분야에서 항상 상위권을 유지하고 있습니다.

Progressive Health에 대해 더 많은 것을 알고 싶다면 그들의 웹 사이트인 www.progressivehealth.com을 방문해 보세요. 진료 예약을 하고 싶으시면 저희 현재 전화번호를 사용하시면 됩니다.

당신을 지속적으로 보살펴 드리기를 희망합니다.

진심으로,
버지니아 대학 의료 센터

161 이 편지의 목적은 무엇인가?
(A) 새로운 의료 시설을 설명하기 위해
(B) 새 지점의 개점을 알리기 위해
(C) 환자들에게 기업 인수를 알리기 위해
(D) 환자들에게 우려를 표하기 위해

162 UVMC에 대하여 추론할 수 있는 것은?
(A) 새로운 위치가 이전의 위치로부터 멀리 있다.
(B) 이전에 제공하지 않았던 의료 서비스를 제공할 것이다.
(C) 환자들의 개인 정보가 Progressive Health와 공유될 것이다.
(D) 10년 동안 운영되었다.

163 편지에 따르면, 수신인들은 진료 예약을 위해 무엇을 해야 하는가?
(A) 그들이 전에 사용했던 동일 번호로 전화한다
(B) 새로 만들어진 웹 사이트에 로그인한다
(C) 직접 의료 센터에 방문한다
(D) 이메일로 UVMC 사무실에 요청서를 보낸다

Questions 164-167 refer to the following online chat discussion.

Jerry Atkins [오후 3:00]	직원들 교육을 위해 고용한 강사들이 인터넷 윤리 강의를 시작할 준비가 되었나요?
Dixie Lynn [오후 3:02]	네, 그들은 금요일 오후 1시에 Zeta Web에 도착할 예정입니다. 제 생각에는 누군가 그들과 동행해서 보안 통행권을 받게 하고 강의할 곳으로 안내해야 할 것 같은데요, 그렇죠?
Jerry Atkins [오후 3:03]	제 팀원들 중 한 명이 도와줄 수 있어요.
Dixie Lynn [오후 3:04]	다가오는 행사를 위해 컴퓨터나 칠판 같은 장비들이 제공되나요?
Den Bryant [오후 3:04]	위에서 언급하신 것처럼 제가 정문에서 강사분들을 만나서 방문자 통행권을 나눠 드리겠습니다.
Jerry Atkins [오후 3:05]	두 개의 대형 컨퍼런스 홀이 이미 예약되어 있고, 강사들이 강의하는 데 필요한 모든 것들이 갖춰져 있습니다.
Den Bryant [오후 3:06]	웹 기술자들은 오후 2시 직전에 근무 교대가 끝날 예정이므로 바로 수업에 가도록 하겠습니다.
Dixie Lynn [오후 3:07]	좋아요. 강연은 오후 4시에 끝날 겁니다. 누가 문을 잠그실 건가요? 강사들이 직접 잠가야 하나요?
Jerry Atkins [오후 3:08]	제가 강의가 끝난 이후 모든 것을 정리하기 위해 거기에 있을게요.
Dixie Lynn [오후 3:09]	좋아요! 그러면 됐습니다.
Jerry Atkins [오후 3:10]	여러분들이 오늘 다른 필요한 게 있을 경우, 제가 여기서 오후 6시까지 있을게요.

164 Atkins 씨가 메시지를 보낸 이유는 무엇인가?
(A) 새로운 컴퓨터들과 사무용품을 주문하기 위해
(B) 회사의 보안 등급을 명시하기 위해
(C) 직원들에게 변경된 스케줄을 알리기 위해
(D) 행사의 세부 사항들을 확인하기 위해

165 Bryant 씨는 언제 정문에 있을 것인가?
(A) 오후 1시에
(B) 오후 2시에
(C) 오후 4시에
(D) 오후 6시에

166 웹 기술자들에 대하여 알 수 있는 것은?
(A) 그들은 최근에 고용되었다.
(B) 그들은 근무 교대 시간 사이에 점심 식사를 해야 한다.
(C) 그들은 일이 끝나고 강의에 참석할 것이다.
(D) 그들은 내일까지 강의에 등록해야 한다.

167 오후 3시 9분에, Lynn 씨가 "그러면 됐습니다"라고 쓴 의도는 무엇인가?
(A) 그녀는 문들이 수리되어야 한다고 생각한다.
(B) 그녀는 Atkins 씨의 일을 돕고자 한다.
(C) 그녀는 더 이상의 질문이 없다.
(D) 그녀는 그 교육에 합류하고자 한다.

Questions 168-171 refer to the following e-mail.

발신: Bee Chamastri
수신: Jane Bronte
날짜: 5월 15일
제목: 회의 후속 안건

Jane 씨에게,

지난 회의에서 당신의 업무량에 대한 걱정을 듣고, 모든 부서장이 이 문제의 해결책을 고민하고 있습니다. 우리는 회사 내규에 따라 모든 업무를 분담하기로 결정했습니다. 그렇게 함으로써 우리 회사는 여러 측면에서 생산성과 작업 환경을 개선할 수 있을 것입니다. 당신의 경우 우리의 새로운 웹 사이트 디자인을 성공적으로 완수하기 위해 당신에게 Bertha Bennett 이라는 조수를 배치하기로 결정했습니다. 이 신입 직원은 당신의 일 대부분을 도와줄 것입니다. 당신은 포스터, 로고 그리고 배치 같은 당신의 디자인 프로젝트의 기본 수준을 포함한 그녀의 일을 감독할 것입니다.

당신은 현재 고객들의 정보, 세부적인 일정, 작업 방식을 포함한 기존 프로젝트의 진행 사항을 그녀와 공유하셔야 합니다. 또한 다음 주에 당신이 사용하고 있는 다른 프로그램뿐만 아니라 웹 그래픽 도구에 대해 그녀를 훈련시키는 일을 맡을 것입니다.

혹시 다른 문제 있으시면, 저와 언제든지 공유합시다.

Bee Chamastri
인사부장

168 Bronte 씨는 누구일 것 같은가?
(A) 컴퓨터 프로그래머
(B) 전기 기술자
(C) 그래픽 디자이너
(D) 인사과 관리자

169 Bronte 씨는 어떤 문제를 보고했는가?
(A) 너무 많은 작업
(B) 구식 컴퓨터
(C) 불편한 사무 환경
(D) 맞지 않는 동료들

170 Bronte 씨는 다음 주에 무엇을 하라고 요구 받는가?
(A) 보고서를 제출한다
(B) 그녀의 걱정거리를 공유한다
(C) 그녀의 직속 상관을 만난다
(D) 신입 직원을 교육한다

171 [1], [2], [3] 그리고 [4]로 표시된 곳 중에 다음 문장이 들어가기에 가장 적합한 위치는 어디인가?
"이 신입 직원은 당신의 일 대부분을 도와줄 것입니다."
(A) [1]
(B) [2]
(C) [3]
(D) [4]

Questions 172-175 refer to the following article.

Denver Gazette
눈부신 능선을 넘어

(10월 1일) 여러분이 James Milner 씨가 어디에 있는지 알고 싶다면, 먼저 산맥의 사진들을 보셔야 합니다. 이러한 꿈같고 이국적인 사진들은 그의 사진 촬영에 관한 최신 책 <눈부신 능선을 넘어>를 위해 찍은 것입니다.

Milner 씨는 약 20년 전에 사진을 찍기 시작했습니다. 그는 자신의 축구공을 찾고 있을 때 선반 위에서 아버지의 오래된 카메라를 우연히 발견하였습니다. 그의 아버지에게 동의를 구하고, 그것을 고쳐 쓰도록 허락 받았습니다. 그러나 그는 대학을 준비하고, 언론 분야의 일자리를 얻기 위해 진로를 준비해야 했기 때문에 카메라를 내려 놓을 수밖에 없었습니다.

졸업하고 <Denver Gazette>에 정규 기자로 채용되었지만 역사나 사진을 찍을 시간이 없었습니다. 몇 년이 지나 그의 작업 활동을 잊은 채 네팔의 카트만두에서 휴가를 보냈습니다. 그곳에서 그는 히말라야의 멋진 풍경들에 관한 사진 촬영 컨퍼런스에 참여할 기회가 있었습니다. 이 컨퍼런스 때문에 그는 기자를 그만두고 사진에 집중하기 시작했습니다.

비록 그는 구식 카메라를 사용하는 것으로 시작했지만 현재는 광각 렌즈, 고급 카메라와 같은 첨단 장비를 다루고 있습니다. 급격히 변화하는 자연 환경으로 인해 산에는 의도치 않은 문제들이 발생할 수 있기 때문에 그는 고가 장비를 꽤 자주 교체하거나 재구매해야 합니다. 그는 "험한 절벽이나 야생 동물들은 제 기술 장비에 위험을 야기합니다."라고 말했습니다.

그의 신간 도서에 있는 작품을 포함하여 그의 사진 작품들의 대부분은 Denver시 근처에 있는 로키 산맥의 다양한 주변 환경들을 담고 있습니다. 게다가 그는 곧 안데스 산맥의 사진을 찍으러 페루로 떠날 예정이며, 다음 책을 통해 우리에게 북쪽과 남쪽 산맥들의 차이점을 보여 줄 것입니다.

172 이 기사문의 주된 목적은 무엇인가?
(A) Denver의 관광 상품들을 광고하기 위해
(B) 이전 동료의 프로필을 알려 주기 위해
(C) 신문의 특가 상품을 홍보하기 위해
(D) 새로운 사진 장비를 소개하기 위해

173 무엇이 Milner 씨가 다시 사진을 찍도록 고취시켰는가?
(A) 그의 팀 동료의 조언
(B) 카트만두에서의 특별한 워크숍
(C) 네팔에서의 새로운 기자 직업
(D) 덴버에서의 고급 사진 강의

174 네 번째 문단, 아홉 번째 줄의 단어 "pose"와 의미상 가장 가까운 것은?
(A) 보여 주다
(B) 감사하다
(C) 요구하다
(D) 나타내다

175 Milner 씨에 대하여 알 수 있는 것은?
(A) 그는 페루에서 사진을 찍었다.
(B) 그는 곧 첫 번째 책을 출간할 것이다.
(C) 그는 사진관을 운영하고 있다.
(D) 그는 숙련된 산악인이다.

Questions 176-180 refer to the following brochure and article.

Spring Meadow Properties 사

주거 단지

Spring Meadow Properties(SMP)는 Madison시에 두 개의 주거 타운 하우스 단지들을 보유하고 있습니다.

Nixon Mansion	Wayne Square
1935 Merry Place	657 Pratt Drive
특징:	특징:
• 세탁 시설이 포함된 침실 2-3개의 유닛	• 가구가 완비된 원룸과 침실 1개의 유닛

- 각 유닛당 창고 있음
- 단지 중앙에 위치한 놀이터
- 거주자만 이용 가능한 피트니스 센터
- 상업 지역으로부터 차로 10분 거리
- 인근에 명문 학교들 있음
- 현장 유지 및 관리

- 공과금 포함
- 버스로 대학교 캠퍼스까지 5분 거리
- 도심 지역까지 가는 다양한 버스 노선
- 상업 지역으로부터 차로 5분 거리
- 단지 주위의 보안 카메라
- 거주자만 이용 가능한 작은 도서관과 작업 장소

▶ 평면도를 확인하고 싶으시면 웹 사이트 www.springmeadow.com을 방문해 보세요. 아니면 이 매물들을 보기 위한 약속을 잡기 위해 913-201-1394로 저희에게 주저 말고 연락주세요. 우리 부동산 직원들이 월요일부터 금요일까지는 오전 10시부터 오후 6시까지, 토요일과 일요일에는 오후 1시부터 오후 4시까지 사무실에 있기 때문에 여러분은 이 시간대에 임대에 관하여 상담 받으실 수 있습니다.

SMP의 발표

MADISON (4월 20일) — Spring Meadow Properties(SMP)는 시 정부와 긴밀히 협력하고 있습니다. 이러한 파트너십 덕분에 이 회사는 Madison 시 정부로부터 일부 투자를 받아 Regency Town이라는 세 번째 주거 단지를 건설할 예정입니다. 이 단지는 약 200개의 단독 주택 유닛들로 구성될 것입니다.

공사는 6월에 시작할 것이며, 새로운 거주자들이 Regency Town으로 이사오기까지 22개월이 걸릴 것입니다. 비용의 70퍼센트는 SMP에 의해 지불되고, 나머지 비용은 시 정부에 의해 제공될 것입니다.

SMP는 우리 주에서 합리적인 가격으로 편안하고 편리한 주택들을 사람들에게 공급하는 것으로 잘 알려져 있습니다. 그들의 현재 매물인 Nixon Mansion과 Wayne Square는 6년 전에 지어졌는데 수요가 높아 대기 리스트가 깁니다.

SMP의 기획 부장인 Kevin Myer는 Regency Town이 도시의 상업 지역에서 차로 25분 떨어진 거리 이내에 개발될 것이라고 말했습니다. "Regency Town은 은퇴한 사람이나 중년 그리고 일상으로부터 벗어나 휴식을 취하려는 사람들에게 가장 적합하다"고 그는 말했습니다.

176 Spring Meadow Properties에 대하여 옳은 것은?
(A) 정부의 일부이다.
(B) 전국에 지점들이 있다.
(C) 온라인에만 이용 가능한 매물들의 목록이 있다.
(D) 사무실이 매일 문을 연다.

177 Wayne Square 유닛들의 특징으로 기술되지 않은 것은?
(A) 실내 주차 공간이 있다.
(B) 지역 학교에 접근하기 쉽다.
(C) 대중교통에 가까이 위치해 있다.
(D) 각 주택에 가구가 갖춰져 있다.

178 기사문이 Nixon Mansion과 Wayne Square의 주택들에 대하여 암시하는 것은?
(A) 많은 사람들이 그곳이 다른 곳보다 더 비싸다고 생각한다.
(B) 많은 사람들이 그곳에서 살고 싶어 한다.
(C) 22개월 전에 건설되었다.
(D) 도시의 도심 지역에서 너무 멀다.

179 Regency Town에 대하여 언급되는 것은 무엇인가?
(A) 지역 대학생들에게 가격이 알맞은 곳일 것이다.
(B) 건축 프로젝트가 Myer 씨에 의해 진행되고 있다.
(C) SMP는 그 단지에서 부동산 거래 사업에만 주력하고 있다.
(D) 건설 비용은 부분적으로 정부에 의해 지불될 것이다.

180 Regency Town은 다른 두 단지와 어떻게 다를 것인가?
(A) 은퇴한 사람들로 엄격히 제한될 것이다.
(B) 상업 지역에서 더 멀 것이다.
(C) 거주자들에게 임대료를 일 년에 한 번 내라고 요구할 것이다.
(D) 시 정부가 소유할 것이다.

Questions 181-185 refer to the following e-mails.

수신: Linda Park
발신: Jerry Gebhardt
날짜: 6월 11일, 목요일, 오전 11시
제목: 업데이트

마케팅과 유통 부서의 부장들이 여기 Neo-Altoona에 있는 그들 부서의 일자리를 위한 최종 후보자에 관한 보고서를 제출하였습니다. Stephen Portman은 Brad Triana와 David Harrelson에게 광고 직책에 대한 최종 면접을 위해 다시 오라고 요청하라고 했고, Jim Matthews는 제조 공정을 관리하는 직책에 대한 최종 면접에 Karen Simon을 초대해 달라고 요구하였습니다.

이 최종 면접자들에게 연락하면서 당신은 오찬 준비뿐만 아니라 면접 시간 및 날짜를 잡아야 할 필요가 있습니다. Portman 씨는 다가오는 목공 박람회 때문에 다음 주에 사무실을 비울 것이라는 점을 알아 두세요.

지원 절차를 도와주셔서 감사합니다. 저는 특히 촉박한 마감 일정에도 불구하고 초기 임무를 성공적으로 수행해 주셔서 감사를 표하는 바입니다.

안부를 전하며,

Jerry Gebhardt
인사부장

수신: Jerry Gebhardt
발신: Linda Park
날짜: 6월 12일, 금요일, 오후 3시
제목: 회신: 업데이트

Gebhardt 씨에게,

어제 언급하셨던 3명의 최종 후보자들에게 연락했습니다. 그들의 현재 상황을 확인했을 때 Karen Simon은 이미 경쟁사인 Oak Furnishing의 일자리 제안을 수락했다고 합니다. 이 내용을 Jim에게 알렸고, 그는 가능한 한 빨리 그녀를 대체할 만한 사람을 찾고 싶어 했습니다.

저는 6월 18일 목요일 본사에서 Brad Triana 씨와의 면접을 확정했고, 또한 Ruby Friday라는 식당에서 그와 함께 오찬을 가질 것입니다. 그러나 Harrelson 씨는 6월 20일까지 해외 출장중이어서, 이 문제를 당신과 논의할 필요가 있습니다.

Linda Park
업무 지원팀

181 첫 번째 이메일의 주된 목적은 무엇인가?
(A) 회사의 새로운 채용 공고를 게시하기 위해
(B) 취업 지원자들에게 연락하라고 부탁하기 위해
(C) 직무 연수 교육을 준비하기 위해
(D) 직원 부족에 관한 상황을 확인하기 위해

182 Neo-Altoona는 어떤 종류의 회사일 것 같은가?
(A) 가구 회사
(B) 회계 법인
(C) 마케팅 회사

(D) 식품 유통업체

183 Harrelson 씨에 대하여 암시되는 것은?
(A) 그는 본사에 입사하고 싶어 한다.
(B) 그는 이전에 Oak Furnishing에서 일했다.
(C) 그는 회계 분야에 경력이 있다.
(D) 그는 전에 Neo-Altoona에 방문한 적이 있다.

184 Matthews 씨는 무엇을 할 것 같은가?
(A) 식당 예약을 한다
(B) 가구 전시회에 참석한다
(C) 면접 볼 새로운 후보자를 선택한다
(D) Triana 씨에게 직접 연락한다

185 Park 씨는 무엇을 할 수 없었는가?
(A) Simon 씨에게 연락하기
(B) 그녀가 요청 받은 모든 약속의 일정을 잡기
(C) 부서장에게 변경 사항을 보고하기
(D) 이전의 절차들을 처리해서 Gebhardt 씨를 도와주기

Questions 186-190 refer to the following article, Web page, and online order form.

리버풀 (5월 20일) - 지난 몇 달 동안 새로운 지역 회사 하나가 리버풀의 식사 시간에 혁명을 가져오고 있습니다. 음식 배달 서비스업체인 Metro F&B 사는 18개월 전에 Susan Ariana에 의해 설립되었습니다. 이 회사는 웹 사이트를 통해 고객들에게 다양한 조리법을 제공하고 있습니다. 고객들이 식재료와 함께 가장 선호하는 조리법을 고르면 Metro F&B 사는 그들에게 매주 식사 패키지를 배송합니다.

Ariana 씨가 이 서비스를 시작한 이유는 그녀의 친구들이 너무 바빠서 규칙적으로 식사를 못했고, 건강 상태가 점점 안 좋아졌기 때문입니다. "저는 건강을 돌보지 못한 채 정신없는 삶을 이어가는 친구들을 위해 혁신적인 생각을 떠올려야만 했습니다."라고 그녀는 말했습니다. "그들은 직접 요리할 시간이 충분하지 않거나 요리 실력에 자신이 없기 때문에 주로 인스턴트 음식을 먹거나 포장 음식을 주문했습니다."

Ariana 씨는 지역 고객들에게 좋은 품질의 식단을 합리적인 가격에 제공하기 위해 배송 절차를 간단하게 하는 데 온 힘을 기울여 왔습니다. 그녀의 목표를 달성하기 위해 그녀는 지역의 작은 농장들과 공급업체들과 제휴를 맺기로 결정했습니다. 유통 경로를 간소화함으로써 Metro F&B 사는 식사의 신선도를 유지할 수 있고, 심지어 경쟁력 있는 가격까지 확보할 수 있습니다. 이러한 요인들 때문에 그녀의 사업은 리버풀 시민들에게 엄청나게 인기를 끌고 있습니다. 이러한 성공을 바탕으로 그녀는 내년에 사업을 맨체스터 지역까지 확장할 계획입니다.

---

http://www.evertonfarm.uk

홈	농산물	소식	연락

Everton 농장은 Metro F&B 사와 긴밀하게 협력하고 있습니다! 지난 20년 동안 저희는 품질 좋은 신선한 농산물을 계속 수확하고 있습니다. 우리는 그들에게 유기농 음식을 공급하면서 Metro F&B 사와 계속 협력해 나가기를 희망합니다.

여러분은 매일 오전 10시부터 오후 4시까지 저희 농장에 있는 부스에서 과일과 채소들을 구매하실 수 있습니다. 게다가 저희 식품들은 주말에는 Giant Eagle Market에서, 그리고 주중에는 Martin's Grocery에서 판매되고 있습니다.

---

http://www.metrofoodandbeverage.uk/order_form

Metro F&B 사
주문서
이름: Henry McGuire
이메일: h_mcguire@tofactory.com
전화: 746-4123-7413
선택된 조리법:
#08- 스리라차 랜치와 함께 제공되는 바삭한 후라이드 치킨 (5개)
#17- 또띠아 칩이 있는 매콤한 새우와 치즈 혼합 (3개)
#29- 케이준 샐러드와 함께 제공되는 소갈비살 (8온스) (2개)
총합: 60.00 달러 (신용 카드 끝자리 -6975로 지불)
배송일자 및 시간: 5월 20일 월요일 오후 5시

---

186 기사문의 목적은 무엇인가?
(A) 맛있고 가벼운 음식을 파는 장소를 설명하기 위해
(B) 지역 농장의 인기 이유를 설명하기 위해
(C) 한 인물이 새로운 사업을 시작한 의도를 보도하기 위해
(D) 유용한 요리 강습을 찾는 방법에 대해 말하기 위해

187 기사문에 따르면, 고객들이 Metro F&B 사를 좋아하는 이유는 무엇인가?
(A) 직원들이 친절하다.
(B) 편리한 위치에 있다.
(C) 가격이 저렴하다.
(D) 무료 배송을 제공한다.

188 Everton 농장의 웹 페이지에는 무엇이 알려져 있는가?
(A) 유통 과정
(B) 사업 제휴
(C) 재배 방법
(D) 취업 기회

189 Everton 농장에 관하여 가장 사실일 것 같은 것은?
(A) 유기농 식품을 기른다.
(B) 지역 매장에서만 농산물을 판매한다.
(C) 가족 소유의 사업이다.
(D) 다른 지역으로 확장할 것이다.

190 McGuire 씨에 대하여 추론할 수 있는 것은?
(A) 그는 오직 채소만 먹는다.
(B) 그는 Everton 농장과 제휴를 맺었다.
(C) 그는 5월 20일에 파티를 열 것이다.
(D) 그는 리버풀에 살고 있다.

Questions 191-195 refer to the following table of contents, article, and e-mail.

Worldwide News Magazine	3월 20일, 250호
목 차	
2 페이지	편집자 코멘트
> 전 세계 주간 뉴스 업데이트	
4 페이지	커버스토리
> 온라인에서 당신의 개인 정보는 안전합니까?	
7 페이지	온 더 테이블
> 국제 외교 분야의 두 게스트와 함께 논란이 많은 쟁점을 이야기하다.	
10 페이지	비즈니스 인사이트
> 호텔들의 예상치 못한 성장 - 오래된 건물들을 재건축하세요!	

15 페이지	음식과 건강
> 슈퍼 푸드: 채식주의자용 고기 - 채소로 만든 맛있는 음식들을 즐겨 보세요.	
21 페이지	스포츠
> 3월의 광란: 미국 대학 농구 연맹 토너먼트 결승전	

채소? 혹은 고기?
채소로 만든 맛있는 음식을 즐기실 수 있어요!

Joshua Nelson 작성

사람들은 소고기, 돼지고기, 그리고 닭고기 같은 다양한 육류를 즐깁니다. 그러나 지나친 육류 소비는 식단이 불균형한 사람들의 건강을 위협하고 있습니다. 요즘 많은 사람들이 건강을 걱정하고 있어서 채소가 많이 있는 영양가 높은 음식을 찾고 있습니다. 물론, 채소만 먹는 것은 식욕을 채울 수 없습니다. 이러한 문제를 해결하기 위해 콩으로 만들어진 "콩고기"라고 불리는 음식이 대중들에게 매우 인기가 있습니다. 애틀랜타 시에 있는 식당 Vegan Steak는 전례 없는 호황을 누리고 있는 중입니다. 주인이자 관리자인 Clara Kim 씨는 10년 전 당뇨병을 진단 받았다고 말했습니다. 그녀는 "저지방 채식 식단을 따르면서 저는 병으로부터 벗어날 기회를 가졌어요"라며 덧붙였습니다. 그녀는 식당에서 자신과 비슷한 문제를 겪고 있는 사람들에게 맛있는 야채 요리를 제공하는 일을 즐깁니다. 운이 좋게도, 애틀랜타의 많은 주민들은 그녀의 음식을 즐기고 그녀의 슈퍼 푸드로 건강을 유지하고 있습니다.

수신: Clara Kim
발신: Joshua Nelson
날짜: 3월 27일

Kim 씨에게,

지난주에 당신의 음식들을 맛볼 수 있도록 당신의 식당에 초대해 주셔서 감사합니다. 채식 버거가 매우 맛있었고 당신이 서빙한 차들 중에 제가 가장 좋아하는 모브 그린티와 정말 잘 어울렸습니다. 저는 진심으로 당신의 식당을 다시 한번 방문하기를 바라며, 당신이 <Worldwide News Magazine>에 실린 제 칼럼을 좋아하셨기를 바랍니다.

행운을 빕니다.

Nelson

191 잡지의 어떤 부분이 토론을 포함하고 있는가?
(A) 온 더 테이블
(B) 비즈니스 인사이트
(C) 음식과 건강
(D) 스포츠

192 Vegan Steak에 관한 글이 잡지 몇 페이지에 실려 있을 것 같은가?
(A) 7 페이지
(B) 10 페이지
(C) 15 페이지
(D) 21 페이지

193 기사문의 주된 주제는 무엇인가?
(A) 다가오는 요리 대회
(B) 농업의 최신 경향
(C) 지역 사업체의 성공
(D) 채소를 이용한 조리법

194 Nelson 씨에 대하여 추론할 수 있는 것은?
(A) 그는 요리 경연 대회를 열 것이다.
(B) 그는 조리법을 알고 싶어 한다.
(C) 그는 새로운 회사에 고용되었다.
(D) 그는 최근에 Vegan Steak에서 식사를 했다.

195 이메일에서 첫 번째 문단, 두 번째 줄의 단어 "paired"와 의미상 가장 가까운 것은?
(A) 지향하는
(B) 결합된
(C) 연장된
(D) 발생된

Questions 196-200 refer to the following Web site, online review, and booking confirmation.

http://www.guamzaza.net

Za Za 게스트 하우스
SUNRISE ST. VILLA I SABANA CIR 161, 96932 타무닝, 괌

괌에 있는 Za Za 게스트 하우스는 타무닝 지역에서 여러분께 아늑한 숙박 시설을 제공합니다. 이곳은 지역 식당들과 쇼핑 단지에서 걸어서 5분 거리, Tumon Beach에서 걸어서 10분 거리인 편리한 곳에 위치해 있습니다. 저희 건물 옆에 Sandcastle Guam이 있는데 그곳은 아름답고 불가사의한 외관으로 관광객들이 찾는 곳입니다.

세부 사항:

- 각 방에는 무료 세면도구와 개인 또는 공용 목욕탕이 있습니다.
- 공용 부엌은 거실과 함께 각 층의 중앙에 있습니다.
- 모든 손님들에게 지역 과일 주스와 함께 무료 괌 지역 조식이 제공됩니다.
- 비수기 (3월-6월/9월-11월)
  2인용 방 (60달러) / 3인용 방 (70달러_여분의 침대 포함) / 4인용 방 (80달러)
- 성수기 (7월-8월/12월-2월)
  2인용 방 (80달러) / 3인용 방 (90달러_여분의 침대 포함) / 4인용 방 (100달러)
- 체크인 시간: 오후 2시 / 체크아웃 시간 : 오전 11시
  (오후 6시 이후에 도착하시면, 늦은 체크인 요금으로 1인당 5달러가 부과될 것입니다.)
- 최소 2박 3일간의 숙박이 요구됩니다.

http://www.traveladvisor.com/zazaguesthouse_guam

타무닝, 괌: Za Za 게스트 하우스
8월 10일 Garry Hasselink에 의해 게시됨

저는 3월에 Za Za 게스트 하우스에서 4박 5일을 묵었습니다. 타무닝 지역에 많은 호텔들과 쉐어 하우스들이 있지만 저는 가성비 좋은 서비스들을 고려해 볼 때 Za Za가 최고의 장소라고 굳게 믿습니다. 이곳은 저에게 크고 개방된 거실과 시설이 완벽히 갖춰진 넓은 부엌을 제공했는데, 비록 서로 다른 나라와 문화권에서 온 사람들이지만 다른 손님들을 만나고 서로 이야기하기에 좋았습니다. 이것이 바로 제가 괌에서 기억에 남는 경험을 한 이유입니다. 만약 오후 6시 이후에 도착한다면 당신이 받은 비밀번호를 정문 옆의 키패드에 입력해야 한다는 것을 꼭 알아 두세요. 저는 이걸 잊어버려서 누군가 문을 열어줄 때까지 기다려야 했어요. 이 사소한 문제만 제외하면 저는 제 여행과 숙박을 진정으로 즐겼답니다.

http://www.guamzaza.net/confirmation_4810419

예약해 주셔서 감사합니다!
앞으로 있을 당신의 숙박을 위해 이 확인 세부 사항들의 사본을 출력해 두세요.

손님 이름: Victoria Brooks
손님 수: 1
예약 번호: 4810419
체크인: 5월 7일, 저녁 9시
체크아웃: 5월 8일, 오전 11시
지불 금액:
20달러 보증금
5달러 늦은 체크인 비용
60달러 방
총합: 85달러 (-2348로 끝나는 신용 카드로 지불)

*보안 비밀번호: 7340

언제든 문의가 있으시면 zazafront@guamzaza.com 또는 +01-471-3781로 저희에게 편하게 연락주세요.
곧 뵙기를 희망합니다!

Guam Za Za Guesthouse

196 Za Za 게스트 하우스는 어디에 위치해 있는가?
(A) 지역 명소에 인접하여
(B) 새로운 주거 지역 내에
(C) 대중교통 근처에
(D) 타무닝 언덕을 따라

197 Za Za 게스트 하우스에 관하여 무엇을 알 수 있는가?
(A) 공식적으로 조합을 만든다.
(B) 가이드 동행 투어를 손님들에게 제공한다.
(C) 무료 조식을 제공한다.
(D) 보증금으로 현금 결제를 요구한다.

198 Hasselink 씨는 Za Za 게스트 하우스에 관하여 무엇을 가장 좋아했는가?
(A) 관광 명소들에 근접함
(B) 편안한 공간
(C) 매력적인 외관
(D) 사교적인 분위기

199 Za Za 게스트 하우스는 Brooks 씨에게 어떻게 예외를 두었는가?
(A) 그녀의 숙박에 더 낮은 가격을 부과하여
(B) 그녀의 체크아웃 시간을 연장하여
(C) 그녀에게 하루만 숙박하는 것을 허락하여
(D) 그녀에게 늦은 체크인 비용을 면제하여

200 Brooks 씨에 대하여 추론할 수 있는 것은?
(A) 그녀는 게스트 하우스에 들어가기 위해 비밀번호를 기억해야 한다.
(B) 그녀는 게스트 하우스에 그녀의 저녁 식사를 준비하라고 요구했다.
(C) 그녀는 친구와 함께 Tumon Beach를 방문할 것이다.
(D) 그녀는 바다가 보이는 방을 요청했다.

4회

p.140

01	(A)	02	(C)	03	(C)	04	(B)	05	(B)
06	(D)	07	(A)	08	(C)	09	(C)	10	(C)
11	(A)	12	(B)	13	(A)	14	(B)	15	(C)
16	(B)	17	(A)	18	(A)	19	(A)	20	(A)
21	(B)	22	(C)	23	(B)	24	(C)	25	(B)
26	(A)	27	(B)	28	(B)	29	(A)	30	(A)
31	(A)	32	(B)	33	(D)	34	(C)	35	(B)
36	(B)	37	(A)	38	(C)	39	(D)	40	(C)
41	(C)	42	(A)	43	(C)	44	(D)	45	(A)
46	(A)	47	(A)	48	(B)	49	(B)	50	(C)
51	(D)	52	(B)	53	(C)	54	(C)	55	(C)
56	(C)	57	(D)	58	(C)	59	(C)	60	(B)
61	(B)	62	(A)	63	(D)	64	(B)	65	(A)
66	(D)	67	(C)	68	(B)	69	(B)	70	(C)
71	(A)	72	(C)	73	(D)	74	(C)	75	(C)
76	(A)	77	(C)	78	(C)	79	(C)	80	(D)
81	(A)	82	(D)	83	(A)	84	(B)	85	(D)
86	(C)	87	(C)	88	(B)	89	(D)	90	(B)
91	(D)	92	(A)	93	(C)	94	(D)	95	(C)
96	(D)	97	(B)	98	(A)	99	(C)	100	(B)
101	(A)	102	(D)	103	(A)	104	(C)	105	(C)
106	(D)	107	(B)	108	(B)	109	(A)	110	(B)
111	(D)	112	(A)	113	(C)	114	(D)	115	(A)
116	(C)	117	(B)	118	(C)	119	(C)	120	(C)
121	(D)	122	(A)	123	(C)	124	(B)	125	(B)
126	(B)	127	(C)	128	(C)	129	(C)	130	(C)
131	(C)	132	(A)	133	(C)	134	(C)	135	(A)
136	(A)	137	(D)	138	(C)	139	(C)	140	(A)
141	(B)	142	(A)	143	(C)	144	(B)	145	(A)
146	(C)	147	(C)	148	(C)	149	(C)	150	(B)
151	(C)	152	(B)	153	(C)	154	(C)	155	(B)
156	(C)	157	(A)	158	(C)	159	(B)	160	(D)
161	(D)	162	(B)	163	(A)	164	(C)	165	(D)
166	(D)	167	(D)	168	(C)	169	(C)	170	(B)
171	(A)	172	(C)	173	(A)	174	(B)	175	(C)
176	(C)	177	(B)	178	(C)	179	(C)	180	(D)
181	(D)	182	(C)	183	(C)	184	(C)	185	(C)
186	(A)	187	(B)	188	(C)	189	(C)	190	(C)
191	(C)	192	(D)	193	(C)	194	(C)	195	(C)
196	(C)	197	(A)	198	(B)	199	(B)	200	(C)

Part 1

1 (A) A man is holding some reading material.
(B) A man is sipping coffee.
(C) A man is leaning on the chair.
(D) A man is turning a page.

2 (A) They are looking in the same direction.
(B) They are standing in a circle.
(C) They have gathered in the square.
(D) They are holding hands.

3   (A) A woman is opening the car door.
    (B) Some vehicles are being parked on the street.
    (C) A woman is walking in the road.
    (D) There are some signs on both sides of the road.

4   (A) The bookcase is being assembled.
    (B) The chairs are unoccupied.
    (C) The computer monitor has been turned on.
    (D) Some papers have been placed in a file.

5   (A) Pedestrians are waiting for a traffic signal.
    (B) One of the women is pushing a stroller.
    (C) People are crossing the street with open umbrellas.
    (D) Some people are getting into the cars.

6   (A) Lampposts are illuminating the building.
    (B) A bus has stopped in a parking lot.
    (C) A structure is being built in the distance.
    (D) Some trees are casting shadows on the pavement.

Part 2

7   Where's the staff lounge room?
    (A) On the tenth floor.
    (B) Let's call the service center.
    (C) We need some rest.

8   When can we purchase jazz concert tickets?
    (A) The show starts at 7 P.M.
    (B) At the hall.
    (C) The day before the performance.

9   Have you found a competent dentist yet?
    (A) Brush your teeth.
    (B) No, around the corner.
    (C) Yes, I saw him last week.

10 Are you going to pay with cash?
    (A) It is recyclable.
    (B) They've already paid.
    (C) With a credit card.

11 Who's going to be present at Wednesday's meeting?
    (A) I'll be on vacation then.
    (B) Several slides.
    (C) I don't know who you are.

12 How can we promote our products to people in their twenties and thirties?
    (A) Jennifer is in her mid-thirties.
    (B) By using social media.
    (C) It's very impressive.

13 She has a copy of the sales report, doesn't she?
    (A) Yes, it's on her desk.
    (B) A broken copier.
    (C) Hader is a capable reporter.

14 Why don't you join us at the dinner party tonight?
    (A) Didn't you already register for it?
    (B) I'm too busy working on the project.
    (C) A membership card.

15 I hope Mr. Zhu likes the design of the café we came up with.
    (A) A new projector.
    (B) I'm satisfied with it.
    (C) He already approved it.

16 Why can't we replace the chairs in our office?
    (A) We have enough desks.
    (B) Due to the limited budget.
    (C) They should vote for a chairman.

17 Should we take the subway or a bus to the town hall?
    (A) Let's take my car.
    (B) The training session is down the hallway.
    (C) A traffic delay.

18 Who'll be promoted to department director?
    (A) That hasn't been announced.
    (B) George is in charge of the employee directory.
    (C) I think so.

19 I'm surprised we haven't received the updated company logo yet.
    (A) Didn't you get the e-mail?
    (B) Bring your receipt.
    (C) A graphic designer.

20 What do you think of the leadership seminar?
    (A) Actually, I attended a different session.
    (B) He was promoted to manager.
    (C) I'll lead the tour.

21 Where should I park the delivery van?
    (A) Yes, we can deliver on Saturdays.
    (B) Do you know where the loading dock is?
    (C) The park is on Main Street.

22 Aren't we supposed to take Highway 8 to the airport?
    (A) An accident on Highway 10.
    (B) The flight to Vietnam.
    (C) There's road construction going on.

23 Would you mind filling out a service request form?
    (A) I filled up my car with gas.
    (B) Do you have a pen?
    (C) The technician is coming tomorrow.

24 Didn't Dongmin leave the office at six yesterday?
    (A) Leave it on his desk.
    (B) Let me ask around six.
    (C) He stayed late to finish the project.

25 We still need to sign the contract with the travel agency, don't we?
    (A) My travel agent gave me the itinerary.
    (B) By next Friday.
    (C) I checked the earlier flight.

26 How were sales of our women's apparel last month?
    (A) They decreased by five percent.
    (B) She likes this brand very much.
    (C) By submitting a report.

27 Could you install the computer?
    (A) Set up a new shredder.
    (B) I'm about to take a break.
    (C) The office next door is noisy.

28 Should we use more funds to purchase printers or office furniture?

(A) Please move that chair.
(B) We've had the same printers for five years.
(C) They're affordable.

29. Ms. Smith can't go to the panel discussion today.
(A) Oh, then I'll take the notes.
(B) Actually, he is a good speaker.
(C) Conference room A.

30. When will that company introduce its healthy fruit drinks?
(A) Take a look at its Web site.
(B) I haven't tried healthy food yet.
(C) Apple, pineapple, and so on.

31. Do you want to start working on your speech?
(A) The banquet isn't until the tenth.
(B) He's changing topics.
(C) This microphone needs to be repaired.

Part 3

Questions 32-34 refer to the following conversation.

W Good morning. This is the facilities management office. How can I help you?

M Hi, I live in apartment 7B. I need someone to come here to check my water heater.

W All right. What seems to be the problem?

M Well, it was working well yesterday, but when I use it today, only cold water comes out. So I'm not able to take a shower.

W I'll send a technician as soon as possible. What's your phone number so that he can call you to make an appointment?

M It's 666-8920.

W Okay. One of our technicians will contact you soon.

32. Who most likely is the woman?
(A) A technician
(B) A property manager
(C) A tenant
(D) A security guard

33. What problem does the man have?
(A) There is a mistake in a contract.
(B) He cannot drink cold water.
(C) His apartment is too hot.
(D) A device is malfunctioning.

34. What information does the woman ask for?
(A) An address
(B) A code number
(C) A phone number
(D) An appointment time

Questions 35-37 refer to the following conversation.

M Hi, Emily. I want to tell you that I'm going to Canberra tomorrow to participate in a medical conference next Tuesday. I won't be back until Thursday.

W Yes, no problem. I already contacted Dr. Cooper from the Starfield Medical Center last week, and he will come in while you're away. Have you reserved a hotel room?

M Well, I'm planning to stay with my friend while I'm there. He's lived there for five years, and he's going to show me some famous landmarks in the city every day except Tuesday.

W That sounds interesting. I heard that there's so much to see and do there.

35. What is taking place next Tuesday?
(A) The opening of a medical center
(B) A professional convention
(C) A festival in Canberra
(D) A house party

36. What did the woman do last week?
(A) She participated in a conference.
(B) She talked with a doctor.
(C) She reserved a hotel room.
(D) She took a family vacation.

37. What is the man going to do most of his time in Canberra?
(A) Go sightseeing
(B) Stay at his hotel
(C) See patients
(D) Work on a new project

Questions 38-40 refer to the following conversation.

M Thanks for calling Hamilton Bookstore. What can I do for you?

W Do you have the book *How to Invest* by Eric Freeman?

M Hmm... Let me check. It looks like that item is currently out of stock. But a shipment containing that book is arriving here early next week.

W Oh, so I want you to do me a favor. Could you put a copy aside for me when it arrives?

M I'm sorry. Unfortunately, our policy does not permit us to hold copies for customers. However, I can call you as soon as the books are here at the shop. Please give me your phone number.

38. What most likely is the man's job?
(A) Clerk
(B) Patron
(C) Author
(D) Investor

39. What will happen next week?
(A) A book signing will end.
(B) A sale will begin.
(C) A store will move.
(D) A shipment will arrive.

40. What does the woman ask the man to do?
(A) Make a copy
(B) Exchange a book

(C) Hold an item
(D) Change a phone number

Questions 41-43 refer to the following conversation.

M	Hi, Ms. Taylor. There is going to be a big annual festival with thousands of visitors in this city next week. So I'm considering keeping the restaurant open later on those nights to get some extra business. I need more servers who can work late next week.
W	That sounds great. Can I work an extra shift because I need some money to fix my car? It's been making strange noises for the last few days.
M	Okay. When are you available next week?
W	Wednesday is my parents' wedding anniversary. So except for that day, I can work anytime.
M	I got it. I will schedule you for a couple of extra shifts.

41. Where do the speakers most likely work?
    (A) At a car dealer
    (B) At a convention hall
    (C) At a restaurant
    (D) At a city hall

42. What is the woman's problem?
    (A) Her vehicle needs to be repaired.
    (B) She wants to borrow money to buy a car.
    (C) She has never worked an extra shift.
    (D) She recently sold her car.

43. What does the woman mean when she says, "Wednesday is my parents' wedding anniversary"?
    (A) She wants to invite her parents to a restaurant.
    (B) She has to buy a gift before Wednesday.
    (C) She is not available on Wednesday.
    (D) She can work anytime next week.

Questions 44-46 refer to the following conversation with three speakers.

M	Ms. Sato, I'd like to introduce you to my coworker, Susan. She'll be joining the renovation project on your restaurant. Why we're here today is to see the site and to talk about some ideas.
W1	Oh, thank you for coming. It's nice to meet you, Susan. Today, I'd like to discuss what materials you should use for the flooring and walls.
W2	Of course. There are many great options that have various prices. Actually, if you choose something expensive, you'll get material that is durable and high in quality.
W1	Okay, but we have a limited budget. Before discussing any details, can I see the price list first?
M	Sure. Susan, why don't you show her the price section of the catalog?

44. Who most likely is Ms. Sato?
    (A) A real estate agent
    (B) An interior designer
    (C) A maintenance worker
    (D) A restaurant owner

45. What does Ms. Sato want to discuss first?
    (A) The costs of materials
    (B) A rental fee
    (C) Some flooring options
    (D) Some machinery upgrades

46. What will the speakers most likely do next?
    (A) Look at a catalog
    (B) Delay a meeting
    (C) Review some blueprints
    (D) Create an estimate

Questions 47-49 refer to the following conversation.

M	Good morning. I ordered a sofa and a table from your Web site last night, but I made a mistake when measuring my living room. I'm afraid the table may be too big to put in the middle of the room. Is it possible to change the size now?
W	Sure, I will change it to a smaller size. Actually, the table and the sofa will arrive unassembled. Don't worry. My delivery team will put them together tomorrow.
M	Oh, thank you. Unfortunately, I won't be at home tomorrow. Could you reschedule the delivery time for the following day?

47. What is the man concerned about?
    (A) The size of some furniture
    (B) The quality of a sofa
    (C) The place some items will be delivered to
    (D) The construction of a living room

48. What does the woman say her team will do at the man's house?
    (A) Remove some furniture
    (B) Clean a living room
    (C) Measure some items
    (D) Assemble some items

49. What does the man ask the woman to do?
    (A) Revise a contract
    (B) Change a delivery date
    (C) Deliver an item tomorrow
    (D) Bring some samples

Questions 50-52 refer to the following conversation.

W	Do you know Andrew, the new employee? Well, he handed in his first quarterly sales report yesterday. I just finished reviewing it, and it looks like our clothing items, especially men's clothing, are underperforming only at our branch here.
M	That's too bad.
W	In spite of the results, he insists that the company should still focus on selling men's clothing because the profit margin on these items is a lot higher than that of any other product.

M   That makes sense. I think Andrew should give a presentation for the employees in the Sales Department.

W   But this will be the first time he will give a presentation. Why don't you make the presentation instead?

M   I don't think so. It will be a good experience for the new employee. I'll arrange a meeting sometime next week. You should talk to Andrew about the presentation in advance.

50 What problem does the woman mention?
    (A) A proposal was rejected.
    (B) A sales position was already filled.
    (C) Products are not selling well.
    (D) A sales report has incorrect information.

51 Why does the woman say, "this will be the first time he will give a presentation"?
    (A) To praise a new employee
    (B) To criticize a coworker
    (C) To offer a position
    (D) To express her concern

52 What does the man ask the woman to do next?
    (A) Transfer to the Sales Department
    (B) Speak with a coworker
    (C) Schedule a meeting
    (D) Make a presentation

Questions 53-55 refer to the following conversation.

W   Alex, we should prepare for the upcoming safety inspection. Let's talk about what we're going to cover for it. I was thinking we should train the employees working on the assembly lines.

M   I agree. Workers often ask questions about safety rules. The training is mandatory, right? If not, it should be.

W   I don't think we should require all employees to come. Some people might already know the safety rules.

M   Well, why don't we ask our supervisor and hear what he thinks?

W   Okay, I'd also like to hand everyone a questionnaire asking them about their experience. It would help to find out what we need to do to prepare for the inspection.

53 What are the speakers talking about?
    (A) A security seminar
    (B) How to use some machines
    (C) A future inspection
    (D) Safety equipment

54 What aspect of the training does the woman disagree about?
    (A) Whether attendance should be compulsory
    (B) Whether refreshments should be served
    (C) How long it should last
    (D) When it should be announced

55 What does the woman want to distribute?
    (A) Employee directories
    (B) User manuals
    (C) Surveys
    (D) Some tools

Questions 56-58 refer to the following conversation.

W   I think we should update our brochures before summer. They don't include our discount coupons for the summer packages.

M   You're right. We should do that. Speaking of which, our Web site also needs to be upgraded because it has a lot of old information. It should have separate pages for each of our travel packages.

W   That's true, but it will take some time to design the Web site, and I think it would be a good idea if we hired a specialist to do that. We don't have enough time to focus on both the Web site and the brochure.

M   I agree. It might be a little tough, but I think it will be worth the effort if it means more bookings.

56 What type of business do the speakers work for?
    (A) A hotel
    (B) A printing company
    (C) A travel agency
    (D) An airline

57 What is the woman concerned about?
    (A) The cost of a design for a Web site
    (B) A deadline for updating brochures
    (C) The inaccurate travel itinerary
    (D) The time required to complete some work

58 What does the man agree with the woman about?
    (A) An itinerary should be changed.
    (B) The travel packages should be worth more.
    (C) They should hire an expert.
    (D) A supervisor has provided valuable feedback.

Questions 59-61 refer to the following conversation.

M   Clara, I looked over your winter jumper designs for the upcoming season. Do you have time to talk about them after your meeting?

W   Oh, my meeting was canceled a few minutes ago.

M   Okay, so let's discuss your drawings now.

W   Yes, what is your opinion?

M   I like the jumper designs overall, but I'm a little concerned about the collars and the number of inside pockets. I think there should be one more pocket inside.

W   I understand. It shouldn't be too hard to add another pocket or two to the designs. I'll go over my sketches right now and see what I can change in detail.

59 Which industry do the speakers most likely work in?
    (A) Architecture

(B) Furniture
(C) Apparel
(D) Tourism

60. What problem does the man mention?
(A) The color of a product is too bright.
(B) There aren't enough inside pockets.
(C) A design should be completely changed.
(D) A meeting should be delayed.

61. What will the woman most likely do next?
(A) Contact her manager
(B) Review some drawings
(C) Distribute design samples
(D) Change a color

Questions 62-64 refer to the following conversation and schedule.

M: The results of your physical checkup look good. You reduced your body fat to under 20%. Congratulations! You're in much better shape than you were when you visited our fitness center a month ago. What are you going to do to keep in good shape?

W: Well, I'd like to go jogging a lot more, but sometimes my knees hurt. I love aerobics and yoga, but I don't want to get injured. Is there something else I could do?

M: Sure, I suggest that you try swimming. It's a better exercise for your knees. You know we have a swimming class for adults at our center. Here is a brochure. You can sign up for a summer class.

W: I'm actually available on that day. I'll enroll in this. Thanks!

62. Who most likely is the man?
(A) A fitness trainer
(B) An athlete
(C) A medical doctor
(D) A receptionist

63. What does the woman ask the man about?
(A) A dietary regime
(B) The operating hours of a center
(C) Available class times
(D) Alternative types of exercise

64. Look at the graphic. When will the woman probably go to the fitness center in the summer?
(A) On Tuesdays
(B) On Wednesdays
(C) On Thursdays
(D) On Fridays

Questions 65-67 refer to the following conversation and departure board.

W: Hello, Mark. I have a problem. My flight for Budapest was supposed to leave at 11 o'clock, but it's been put off.

M: Really? I was expecting you to be here on time to meet with a potential client. You're supposed to be giving a presentation on the new wallpaper which our company is making this year.

W: Well, the delay is less than an hour, so I might get there in time.

M: I think it's not a good way because the schedule is too tight. I'm going to reschedule the meeting for tomorrow morning. The client is a famous interior designer, so if we sign a contract with her, we could make a lot of money. Remember that this is a very important meeting.

65. What kind of company do the speakers work for?
(A) A wallpaper manufacturer
(B) A hardware store
(C) An interior decorating company
(D) An airline

66. Look at the graphic. What is the status of the woman's flight?
(A) 20-minute delay
(B) On time
(C) 35-minute delay
(D) 50-minute delay

67. Why does the man change the meeting time?
(A) A potential client will be late.
(B) The woman's flight was canceled.
(C) The woman has a tight schedule.
(D) He wants to review a contract.

Questions 68-70 refer to the following conversation and table.

M: Joanne, can you tell me where I should put these books?

W: Yeah, that's our new shipment of translated foreign novels.

M: Well, that means they should go on the 1st floor, not the 2nd.

W: You're right. Foreign novels are located in our biggest section, so that's why we always display them at the front of the store. Oh, there's one more thing. You know that we are planning to hold a book signing. It'll be on the same floor but in the other section. So it would be helpful if you could clear off some of the tables by the door.

M: Sure. I'll do that after I organize these books on the shelves.

68. Where is the conversation most likely taking place?
(A) At a library
(B) At a bookstore
(C) At a publishing company
(D) At a real estate agency

69. Look at the graphic. Where will the book signing be held?
(A) 1F East
(B) 1F West
(C) 2F East

(D) 2F West

70. What will the man do next?
(A) Clean some tables
(B) Move some shelves
(C) Display some books
(D) Go to the second floor

Part 4

Questions 71-73 refer to the following excerpt from a meeting.

Thank you for coming on such short notice. But this meeting shouldn't last too long. I just want to review our company's plans for the bike competition that's happening next month. We'll be sponsoring all the food for the cyclists and spectators. It's going to be a long race. I think this is a good opportunity to promote some of our newest energy drinks such as Powerup and Monsteraid. Lucas, could you supervise the selection of the energy drinks for the athletes?

71. What kind of event is the speaker talking about?
(A) A race
(B) A luncheon
(C) A marathon
(D) An orientation

72. What does the company most likely sell?
(A) Beverages
(B) Footwear
(C) Clothing
(D) Bicycles

73. What does the speaker ask Lucas to do?
(A) Conduct a survey
(B) Distribute some drinks
(C) Visit a place
(D) Manage some items

Questions 74-76 refer to the following broadcast.

You're listening to the local evening news. And now for our top story. The Nagata Auto Company has announced plans to build a new production factory here in Charleston next year. This is very good news for our city, especially in terms of employment. The company is planning to hire approximately over 800 workers. In addition, there will be many construction jobs while the plant is being built. Nagata Yuto, the president of the Nagata Auto Company, stopped by the studio this evening to talk about the new assembly plant. We are looking forward to playing that interview now. But before we do that, let's take a short commercial break.

74. What is the broadcast about?
(A) A new facility
(B) A company acquisition
(C) A fundraising initiative
(D) A job fair

75. What advantage is expected for Charleston?
(A) A public library will be built.
(B) A hospital will provide more services.
(C) Employment will increase.
(D) Tourism will increase.

76. What will the listeners hear next?
(A) An advertisement
(B) An interview
(C) A traffic report
(D) A weather forecast

Questions 77-79 refer to the following excerpt from a meeting.

Hello, I'd like to discuss the pharmaceutical industry convention coming up in a month. As you know, the three of you have been chosen to attend. You'll be taking part in demonstrations and workshops promoting our new medicine. I know this will be your first time representing our company, but it is clearly a great opportunity to learn many things. I think you will probably have some questions while you're preparing for the event. I'd like to remind you that we have lots of the information about the convention available for you. I also went there last year. One more thing, you have to give a presentation to your colleagues on what you learn about our competitors and potential customers after returning from the trip.

77. What does the company sell?
(A) Home appliances
(B) Medical equipment
(C) Medicine
(D) Experiment equipment

78. What does the speaker mean when she says, "I also went there last year"?
(A) She does not want to go to the convention.
(B) She cannot share any information.
(C) She was disappointed by the convention.
(D) She is willing to help her coworkers.

79. What does the speaker ask the listeners to do when they return from the convention?
(A) Give a demonstration
(B) Identify potential customers
(C) Make a presentation
(D) Speak to their supervisor

Questions 80-82 refer to the following announcement.

Spring is approaching, so it is time for the annual music competition. We've already chosen ten local bands through a preliminary contest. Next Friday evening, come to Civil Park to listen to the best songs that selected local bands will play. This year's event will be better than ever. But the most important thing is that the audience is going to determine the winner. Just download our event application to your mobile phone. You can vote for your favorite performance on that app. We also need volunteers to help out with the food and beverage booths. Volunteers can watch the performance from seats that are right next to the stage. If you are interested in signing up, please get in touch with our event coordinator at 777-0909.

80. What type of event is the announcement about?
    (A) An art competition
    (B) A food festival
    (C) A local government election
    (D) A music event

81. Why does the speaker encourage the listeners to download an application?
    (A) To cast a vote
    (B) To look at a list of bands
    (C) To choose their favorite food
    (D) To check a schedule

82. What is a benefit for volunteers?
    (A) A complimentary ticket
    (B) A meal coupon
    (C) Free shuttle bus
    (D) Special seating

Questions 83-85 refer to the following telephone message.

Hi, Omar. It's David. I want to follow up with you about your upcoming travel to Eastwood for the motor show. Actually, I'm having trouble finding you a hotel. There is another big event in Eastwood during the exposition, so every hotel is already fully booked. But there are some places to stay in Chatswood. It will take about 30 minutes to get to the show by car from there. So you will have to drive a bit farther on the day of the event. However, I think we have no choice. Please get back to me as soon as possible. In addition, remember that you need to get your presentation approved by your manager before you leave. Thanks.

83. What problem does the speaker mention?
    (A) Finding accommodations
    (B) Reserving tickets for the auto show
    (C) Booking a flight
    (D) Preparing for a presentation

84. Why does the speaker say, "there are some places to stay in Chatswood"?
    (A) To offer a solution
    (B) To cancel a booking
    (C) To change the schedule
    (D) To reject a recommendation

85. What requires a manager's approval?
    (A) Travel reimbursements
    (B) Registration for an event
    (C) Equipment purchases
    (D) A conference presentation

Questions 86-88 refer to the following instructions.

Good morning! Thanks for coming to this training session. All employees will use this new tracking system for products from now on. It's not complicated, but some features are different from our old system. Let's look at the manual you received when coming to the meeting room. First, after checking the items you've got, scan and save them as item lists. Remember to hit "Save," not "Next." You have to save the product data before you can enter "Next." Look at the screen in front of the room. I'll show you how to use it. Oh, no. My computer seems to be frozen. Let me restart and try it again. I'm sorry for this interruption.

86. What is the purpose of the talk?
    (A) To assign a meeting room
    (B) To revise a manual
    (C) To provide some training
    (D) To introduce a new product

87. According to the speaker, what should the listeners remember to do?
    (A) Attend a demonstration
    (B) Fill out some paperwork
    (C) Save some data
    (D) Submit daily reports

88. Why does the speaker apologize?
    (A) Her computer didn't save some data.
    (B) Her device is malfunctioning.
    (C) The training is canceled.
    (D) A request has been denied.

Questions 89-91 refer to the following tour information.

Welcome to Sam's Farm. I've run this farm for over 20 years. Today, you'll have the opportunity to tour the fields and go inside our greenhouses to see a wide variety of produce. Our workers will also share some information about what we need to grow such high-quality crops. This is an outdoor tour, so please don't forget to take your hats, sunglasses, and anything else you need to protect yourself from the sun. I strongly suggest that you visit our farm store after the tour. All of our products are up to 30 percent off for visitors. Have a good time!

89. What field does the speaker work in?
    (A) Agriculture
    (B) Education
    (C) Distribution
    (D) Medicine

90. What does the speaker remind the listeners to do?
    (A) Purchase hats and sunglasses
    (B) Use sun protection
    (C) Get some discount coupons
    (D) Put their belongings in a locker

91. What does the speaker mean when he says, "All of our products are up to 30 percent off for visitors"?
    (A) He wants to emphasize that there are not many products left.
    (B) He is surprised by a discount.
    (C) He is disappointed that the merchandise is not selling well.
    (D) He wants the listeners to buy some produce.

Questions 92-94 refer to the following speech.

Hello, everyone. Today, I'm happy to introduce the new head of the Marketing Department, Ms. Rosa Jimenez. She comes to us from Mayforth Advertising with a wealth of experience. She has worked on many significant accounts, including the "For the Environment" campaign, which set a new standard for marketing strategy. She won the Innovative Marketer of the Year Award thanks to that campaign. Before we watch a short video about her outstanding work, I'm sure she'd like to say a few words. Let's give her a warm welcome.

92. What is the purpose of the speech?
    (A) To welcome a new employee
    (B) To present an award
    (C) To describe a new advertisement
    (D) To plan a marketing strategy

93. What does the speaker say about Rosa Jimenez?
    (A) She has appeared on TV commercials.
    (B) She doesn't have any experience in the field.
    (C) She has won an award.
    (D) She has been an accountant for years.

94. What will most likely happen next?
    (A) The meeting will end.
    (B) A short video will be shown.
    (C) Refreshments will be served.
    (D) A speech will be made.

Questions 95-97 refer to the following excerpt from a meeting and chart.

Let's look at the results of last quarter's fashion magazine sales. Now, I'd like to discuss how we can increase sales to the age group that made the least number of purchases. I think we could make a special issue geared toward the age group. Because people in this group spend the least amount of money and time on fashion, we should focus on fashion trends for them and sell the magazines at discounted prices. These could be arranged through our fashion coordinators. As the marketing director, I can give your opinions to them in person. So I'd like to hear your comments. Would anyone like to start?

95. Who most likely are the listeners?
    (A) Bookstore clerks
    (B) Magazine editors
    (C) Marketing employees
    (D) Fashion coordinators

96. Look at the graphic. Which group does the speaker suggest focusing on?
    (A) 25 and under
    (B) 26-35
    (C) 36-45
    (D) 46 and over

97. What does the speaker say he will do next?
    (A) Give his opinion
    (B) Listen to people's ideas
    (C) Contact a fashion coordinator
    (D) Receive funding for advertising

Questions 98-100 refer to the following excerpt from a meeting and menu.

I'd like to announce an important change before we open the restaurant. The shipment we were expecting from our seafood distributor won't arrive until next week, so we can't serve any seafood dishes for a few days. Instead, we'll make a double batch of Thursday's pasta and serve that on Friday as well. Please let our patrons know. Next, I'd like to introduce our new server, Peter Rauch. You will take turns training Mr. Rauch this week, and he will start serving customers next week. I attached his training schedule to the bulletin board. Please take a look at it during break time. If you have any questions about the training, ask me anytime. Thank you!

98. Look at the graphic. Which pasta does the speaker say will be served two days this week?
    (A) Bacon Cream
    (B) Seafood
    (C) Meatball
    (D) Tomato & Basil

99. Who is Peter Rauch?
    (A) A job applicant
    (B) A customer
    (C) A waiter
    (D) A chef

100. What did the speaker post on the bulletin board?
    (A) The restaurant's rules
    (B) A training timetable
    (C) A revised menu
    (D) The next meeting time

Part 5

101. 호텔 앞에서 분수대와 동상 사이에 있는 가판대를 찾으실 겁니다.

102. 이것은 귀하가 곧 Clear Eyesight Clinic에서 진료 예약이 있다는 알림입니다.

103. Jane 씨는 그녀가 졸업한 Bloomington 주립 대학교에서 학위를 받은 후 연구원으로 일을 시작했습니다.

104. 문화 지역은 해인사를 포함해서 나라에서 가장 오래되고 흥미로운 구조물들을 가지고 있습니다.

105. 이 건물에는 방이 부족하기 때문에 우리 사무실을 확장하려는 계획은 선택권이 제한되어 있습니다.

106. Tyler 씨는 고객 문제들을 처리하는 방법을 개선하는 데 있어서 그의 뛰어난 일 처리에 대해 인정을 받았습니다.

107. Del Posta Tribune의 소유주들은 2010년 이래로 웹상에서 그들의 기사문의 전자 버전을 이미 제공하고 있습니다.

108. 안내데스크에서 지불하시거나 여러분의 휴대 장비에서 저희의 무선 휴대 전화 지불 시스템을 사용해서 지불하실 수 있습니다.

109. 적절한 허가증 없이 수행되는 건설 작업이 우리 검사관에게 발견된다면 벌금이 부과될 것입니다.

110 교육 자료가 충분하지 않으니 당신이 대여한 어떤 것이든 빨리 반납해 주시기 바랍니다.

111 회사들이 우리에게 도움을 받으려는 이유는 경력직 직원의 대체자를 찾기 위해서입니다.

112 우리는 항상 가능한 한 가장 정확하게 예측하고자 애쓰지만 일부 배송물들은 수령하는 데 시간이 더 걸릴 수도 있습니다.

113 Mevius 항공사의 항공료는 뉴올리언스에서 출발하는 이코노미 항공편의 1인당 가격입니다.

114 최 씨가 고객 서비스 센터를 구조조정한 이래로 연간 수익이 상당히 증가했습니다.

115 인디애나 주 내에서 구매 가능한 매물들은 이미 새로운 쇼핑 단지용으로 확정되어 있습니다.

116 긴급 회의 때문에 Sue 씨는 컨퍼런스를 내일 오후로 재조정할 수 있는지 물었다.

117 일부 회사들은 학생들의 경력 개발을 위해 인턴십 프로그램을 만들었지만 다른 회사들은 이것을 채용하는 데 이용한다.

118 Charles Odell 씨는 은퇴 직전에 마케팅 분야에서 명성을 얻기 시작했습니다.

119 오래된 아파트가 안전상의 이유로 점검될 경우에만 모든 거주자들은 집 밖으로 나가도록 요구 받을 것입니다.

120 시 공무원들은 생태학적 오염도를 확인하고자 런던에 있는 템즈강의 상태를 면밀히 검사하고 있습니다.

121 우리의 편집장은 London Post 사가 다음 달부터 월간에서 격주로 발행 스케줄을 바꿀 것이라고 발표했습니다.

122 더 상세한 정보를 얻고 싶다면 저희 사무실에 언제든지 전화 주세요.

123 의류 회사들은 다가오는 특별 행사에서 이번 재고정리 판매에 관한 모든 적용 가능한 규정을 준수해야 합니다.

124 국가 의회는 외국 농산물 수입을 규제하는 새로운 법을 집행하기 시작했습니다.

125 우리 매장의 E-쿠폰으로 단골 고객들은 지정된 지역 내에서 식료품을 반값으로 구매할 수 있을 것입니다.

126 애틀랜타 시는 구직을 하려는 이주자들의 엄청난 유입을 겪어서 주택 부족 같은 문제들로 고통 받고 있습니다.

127 김해 국제 공항의 향후 개조 공사는 교통 혼잡을 완화하고 시설들을 개선할 것입니다.

128 그들의 주택 외관 개선을 요구하기 위해 Westgate 아파트의 세입자들은 의도적으로 임대료 납부를 지연시켰습니다.

129 펜실베이니아 주 내의 대학교 기숙사들은 주 정보 자금 조달을 통해 무료 재활용 쓰레기통을 받을 자격이 있다.

130 여러분이 이탈리아 요리 수업에 사전 등록하시면 신용 카드 수수료가 면제될 것입니다.

Part 6

Questions 131-134 refer to the following article.

Johnstown 위원회는 어제 도시 지역의 개울 복구 여부에 관한 결정을 미루었습니다. 위원인 Brandon Cohen 씨는 위원회가 승인하기 전에 추가적인 설문 조사와 연구가 고려되어야 한다고 발표하였습니다. 일부의 시 의회들만 이러한 종류의 건설 프로젝트를 실행하고 있습니다. 그러나 이런 사업은 향후 도시의 생태학적 환경을 고려하면 장기적인 관점에서 평가될 필요가 있습니다. 이러한 이유의 대응으로 주 정부는 물 재생 프로그램을 만들고자 노력하고 있습니다. 게다가 도시 환경과 관리를 위해 그 계획에 대한 대중들의 요구가 꾸준히 증가하고 있습니다.

133 (A) 자연 보호는 우리의 미래 세대를 위해 매우 중요합니다.
(B) 바이러스 때문에 개선 작업이 금요일에 진행될 것입니다.
(C) 일부의 시 의회들만 이러한 종류의 건설 프로젝트를 실행하고 있습니다.
(D) 설문 조사를 실시하기 위해서 우리는 개인 정보를 수집해야 합니다.

Questions 135-138 refer to the following e-mail.

수신: Aaron Whitman <aaron_w@ylang.net>
발신: Kazuki Burton <kazuki_burton@foxfirenet.com>
날짜: 8월 14일
제목: 설문 조사

Whitman 씨에게,

저는 Fox Fire Net Research의 직원이며, 미국에서 널리 알려진 리서치 기관입니다. 저희는 현재 서점과 온라인 소비자 행동에 관한 정보를 얻기 위해 온라인 설문을 진행하고 있습니다. 이 설문은 구매 습관에 영향을 미치는 요소들에 관한 올바른 정보를 모으기 위함입니다. 귀하는 <American Society Journal>의 정기 구독자이기 때문에 선정되었습니다. 설문지의 20개의 질문들에 응답하는 데 단 몇 분이면 됩니다. 귀하가 기꺼이 설문 조사를 작성해 주신다면 Public Journal Association Network를 통해 이용하실 수 있는 10퍼센트 할인을 받을 수 있습니다. 참여에 관심 있으시면 이 이메일에 답장해 주세요. 제가 설문 조사 웹 사이트 링크를 귀하에게 보내드릴 것입니다.

행운을 빌며,

Kazuki Burton
Fox Fire Net Research

138 (A) 귀하의 잡지와 논문 비용은 다음 달부터 오를 것입니다.
(B) 설문지의 20개의 질문들에 응답하는 데 단 몇 분이면 됩니다.
(C) 출판사는 고객들에게 책의 후기를 작성하라고 요구하는 경향이 있습니다.
(D) 우리의 엄선된 고객 리스트는 다양한 연령대를 포함합니다.

Questions 139-142 refer to the following letter.

독자님께,

귀하의 <Monthly Design> 잡지 구독이 곧 만료됩니다. 이번 달에 갱신하신다면 우리는 단 10권에 대한 가격으로 연간 구독을 제공할 것입니다. 게다가 당신은 우리의 최신 홈데코 잡지의 첫 호를 무료로 받을 것입니다.

구독을 갱신하지 않으시면 다음 달 말부터 잡지 제공을 중단할 것입니다. 그러나 당신은 추가 비용 없이 우리의 온라인 콘텐츠 대부분을 보실 수 있을 것입니다. 구독자분들은 구독이 끝나더라도 우리의 훌륭한 온라인 콘텐츠를 12개월 동안 계속 보실 수 있습니다. 그러므로 귀하의 사용자 이름과 비밀번호를 꼭 알아 두세요.

그럼 이만,

Eleanor Ricci
Monthly Design

142 (A) 그러므로 귀하의 사용자 이름과 비밀번호를 꼭 알아 두세요.
(B) 따라서 귀하는 한 달 이내에 우리에게 보낸 모든 기사에 대해 지불 받을 수 있습니다.
(C) 그러므로 귀하는 앞으로 허가 없이 우리 웹 사이트에 로그인할 수 없습니다.
(D) 그동안 귀하의 주소로 보내는 추가적인 인쇄 책자들은 더 이상 없을 것입니다.

Questions 143-146 refer to the following Web page.

국제 문학 기록 보관소에 오신 것을 환영합니다!

국제 문학 기록 보관소는 1920년대부터 오늘날까지 이르는 많은 문학 전집들이 있습니다. 1970년에 대중 문학 박물관 안에 하나의 섹션으로 설립된 이 기록 보관소는 디지털 형식의 문학과 함께 원본을 수집하고 보관합니다.

등록된 모든 사용자들은 일주일 대여 기간 동안 공개된 소설 대부분을 이용할 수 있습니다. 한 번에 대여할 수 있는 도서의 수에는 제한이 있다는 것을 알아 두세요. 게다가 사용자들은 박물관의 2층과 3층 선반에서 공개된 소설들을 볼 수 있습니다. 게시판에서 최근 변경된 이용약관을 검토해 보세요.

우리의 문학 작품의 원본들은 연구 또는 학술적 목적으로 승인된 사용자만 이용 가능합니다. 사용자로 등록하시려면 대출 데스크에서 가입하세요.

146 (A) 우리는 당신이 곧 자신만의 기록 보관소를 만들기를 희망합니다.
(B) 유감스럽게도 사용자들은 영화를 빌리실 수 없습니다.
(C) 사용자로 등록하시려면 대출 데스크에서 가입하세요
(D) 당신은 좋아하는 만큼 많은 책을 제출할 수 있습니다.

Part 7

Questions 147-148 refer to the following advertisement.

Butler Home Care Service

조경 서비스
- 나뭇가지 다듬기와 제거
- 잔디와 조경 유지보수

배수 서비스
- 물 고임 문제를 해결하기 위한 배수 시설 설치

관개 시스템 수리
- 손상된 잔디 스프링클러와 관개 장비 수리

여러분은 웹 사이트 www.butlerhomecare.com/3dvirtual에서 3D 가상 둘러보기 서비스를 통해 여러분의 새로운 조경의 낮과 밤의 모습을 보실 수 있습니다.

오늘 약속을 잡으시려면 저희에게 전화 주세요!
(790) 891-9247

147 이 회사는 어떤 유형의 사업을 하고 있는가?
(A) 주거 청소 서비스
(B) 잔디 깎는 기계 판매
(C) 정원 관리 서비스
(D) 컴퓨터 그래픽 디자인

148 고객들은 회사 웹 사이트에서 무엇을 할 수 있는가?
(A) 다른 지역 지점들을 확인한다
(B) 서비스 견적을 받는다
(C) 문의를 위해 라이브 채팅을 한다
(D) 작업 샘플들을 본다

Questions 149-150 refer to the following flyer.

Petersburg Gym
당신의 완벽한 몸을 만드세요

[5월 20일부터] 가입하는 첫 30명 무료!
오리엔테이션이 제공되는 무료 개인 훈련 및 가입비 무료

회원권 혜택
6개월 구매 시, 6개월 무료!
추가로! 한 달 무료 훈련!
20퍼센트 할인 - 5월 30일 종료
* 친구와 함께 등록하시면 두 분 다 5퍼센트 할인을 추가로 받으실 수 있습니다.

저희는 제공합니다
• 심장 강화 훈련
• 그룹 / 개인 훈련
• 웨이트 트레이닝
• 다이어트 프로그램 (영양)
• 시간 관리

149 전단지에 따르면, 센터에 가입하기 위한 이유는 무엇인가?
(A) 운동 장비에 익숙해지기 위해
(B) 야외 활동들을 경험하기 위해
(C) 건강 습관을 만들기 위해
(D) 운동 기구 구매 방법을 알기 위해

150 고객들은 어떻게 할인을 받을 수 있는가?
(A) 개인 강사와 훈련함으로써
(B) 다른 사람과 함께 등록함으로써
(C) 5월 이후 체육관에 가입함으로써
(D) 1년 회원권을 구매함으로써

Questions 151-152 refer to the following text-message chain.

Alex Scott [오전 10시 5분]	안녕하세요, Prepon 씨. 제가 월간 예산 보고서를 준비하고 있어서 데이터가 좀 필요해요. 좀 도와줄 수 있어요?
Robyn Prepon [오전 10시 5분]	어떤 일인데요?
Alex Scott [오전 10시 7분]	저는 내년의 잠재적 예산 책정 때문에 지난 3년 동안의 대차대조표와 우리 회사의 연간 순수익이 필요해요. 하지만 저는 이 데이터의 웹 저장장치에 접근할 수 없어요.
Robyn Prepon [오전 10시 8분]	오늘 오후에 제일 먼저 해 줄 수 있어요.
Alex Scott [오전 10시 9분]	제 생각엔 몇 분 안 걸릴 것 같은데요.
Robyn Prepon [오전 10시 10분]	알고 있지만 저는 마감 기한 때문에 엄청 바빠요. 그리고 저는 10분 후에 이사회 회의에 참석해서 안건을 기록해야 해요.
Alex Scott [오전 10시 12분]	이해했어요. 오늘 오후면 괜찮을 거예요.

151 Prepon 씨의 직업은 무엇일 것 같은가?
(A) 판매사원
(B) 법인 회계사
(C) 행정 조수
(D) 회사 웹 마스터

152 오전 10시 12분에, Scott 씨가 쓴 "오늘 오후면 괜찮을 거예요"는 무엇을 의미하는 것 같은가?
(A) 오후가 만나기 훨씬 좋다.
(B) 그는 오후에 퇴근할 것이다.
(C) 그는 오후 회의에 참석해야 한다.
(D) 그는 필요한 정보를 위해 기다릴 수 있다.

Questions 153-154 refer to the following Web advertisement.

http://www.daylightpainting.net/intro.html

저희는 일반 페인팅 회사와는 다른 선택권이라는 점에서 저희 스스로를 자랑스럽게 여깁니다. 저희는 페인팅 산업에서 거의 경험해 보지 못한 프로 정신으로 양질의 서비스를 제공하고 있습니다.

다년 간의 경험과 뛰어난 서비스를 지닌 Daylight Painting 사는 완전히 승인되고 보증된 페인팅 대행사입니다. 전문적인 도장공들을 찾고 계신다면 저희 회사는 여러분 집의 작업을 완수하기 위해 경험 많고 숙련된 노동자들을 제공해 드릴 수 있습니다. 저희는 집 내부, 전문적인 사무실, 상업 건물 외관 등의 도색을 해 왔습니다.

제한된 기간 동안 Greenville 지역의 집주인들은 Daylight Painting 사의 새로운 페인트칠 작업으로 많은 것을 얻으실 것입니다. 여러분은 6월 10일까지 정규 가격에 100달러 할인의 특별 프로모션 혜택을 받으실 수 있습니다. 아래의 웹 배너를 클릭하여 가능한 한 빨리 견적을 받아 보시고 무료 상담을 받아 보세요!

합리적인 가격으로 여러분의 집을 산뜻하게 만들 이 기회를 놓치지 마세요!

Daylight Painting
(981) 673-1289

무료 견적을 위해 저희에게 연락하세요

153 이 광고의 의도된 독자들은 누구인가?
(A) 지역 예술가들
(B) 집주인들
(C) Greenville의 세입자들
(D) 페인팅 상담가들

154 독자들은 어떻게 할인을 이용할 수 있는가?
(A) 회사 웹 사이트에 접속함으로써
(B) 전액 지불을 함으로써
(C) 6월 10일 전에 서비스를 이용함으로써
(D) 회사에 직접 방문함으로써

Questions 155-157 refer to the following schedule.

제 10회 연례 창작 글쓰기 국제 컨퍼런스
Edward 강당, Fordham 대학, 뉴욕시
4월 13일

*행사는 일정표에 명시된 모든 활동들을 포함합니다.

4월 12일 오후 6시 예비 소집	NY Publishing 사와 지역 협력체들에 관하여 공유하고 알아가기: Murray-Weige 홀, 515 E Fordham Rd, The Bronx, 뉴욕 10458
오전 10시 개회식	위치: 로비, Edward 강당, 415 E Fordham Rd
오전 11시 기조 연설	시연: ASPECT 사와의 협력 작업 관리하기 (Heather Bryant, Project Aspect의 설립자)
오후 12시 점심 식사	Aramak 식당, 캠퍼스 내 Leonard 홀 (다양한 식단이 준비됨)
오후 1시 강의	경쟁에서 협력으로: 미 동부의 여러 주에서 파트너십이 어떻게 지역 뉴스를 변화시키고 있는가 (Danny Rivera, 독립 제작자이자 Bronx 대학 언론학 겸임 교수)
오후 2시 5개의 회담	뉴욕 주위의 협력 프로젝트들에 관한 10분간의 열띤 발표들 • 동양 도시들의 이야기: Mike Piazza • 필라델피아 언론 협동 조합: Rebecca Beth • 어떻게 대학생들과 협력했는가: Andrew Tennent • 재진입 프로젝트 영향 보고: Maria Hill • 뉴햄프셔 뉴스 협동 조합: Nick Fury
오후 3시	휴식
오후 3시 30분 야외 활동	Blue Cap 여행사의 Nancy Gibbs와 함께 뉴욕 보도 현장 지점들을 걸어서 탐방하기

155 이 행사는 누구를 위해 의도된 것 같은가?
(A) 대학교 교직원들
(B) 언론인들
(C) 여행사 직원들
(D) 지역 사회 지도자들

156 누구의 발표가 대학생들과 연관되어 있을 것 같은가?
(A) Hill 씨
(B) Piazza 씨
(C) Tennent 씨
(D) Bryant 씨

157 행사에는 무슨 활동이 포함되어 있는가?
(A) 도시 견학
(B) 경력 상담
(C) 직업 체험 프로그램
(D) 고등학교 방문

Questions 158-160 refer to the following memo.

메모

여러분의 관리자들에게 공지 받았듯이 우리 주차 공간 공사가 4월 10일 금요일부터 시작될 것이고, 이번 달 말까지 지속될 것입니다. 전 직원들은 우리 건물 옆의 Tan Storage 창고에 주차가 허용될 것입니다. 여러분의 회사 사원증이 차량의 유리창에 보이게 두세요. 그렇지 않으면 예외 없이 차량들이 견인될 것입니다. 게다가 여러분의 차량을 지정된 구역인 Blue 주차장에 주차하시면 되는데 여긴 창고 건물 뒤에 위치해 있습니다. 걸어서 가면 주차장과 우리 사무실 간의 거리가 약간 멀어 보일 수 있지만 이러한 공간을 사용할 수 있어서 다행입니다.

이 프로젝트 동안 여러분의 인내에 감사를 전하기 위해 회사는 각 직원들에게 우리 사무실에 인접한 Donatello Dining 식당에서 사용할 수 있는 20달러짜리 선물 카드로 보상해 드릴 계획입니다. 게다가 여러분의 부서장이 로비에 있는 자판기에 쓸 수 있는 무료 커피 쿠폰을 배포할 것입니다.

여러분의 이해와 협조에 다시 한번 감사드립니다.

그럼 이만,

Kevin Caputo
총무과 부장, Terra System

158 Terra System에 대하여 언급된 것은?
(A) 주차 공간에 커피 자판기를 가지고 있다.
(B) 임시 주차 공간을 사용할 것이다.
(C) 회사 차량 사용자들을 위한 견인 서비스를 제공한다.
(D) Tan Storage 사의 소유주이다.

159 직원들은 인내한 것에 대해 어떻게 감사를 받을 것인가?
(A) 그들은 우대 주차 공간을 받을 것이다.
(B) 그들은 선물 카드를 받을 것이다.
(C) 그들은 추가 유급 휴가를 얻을 것이다.
(D) 그들은 조기 퇴근이 허용될 것이다.

160 [1], [2], [3] 그리고 [4]로 표시된 곳 중에 다음 문장이 들어가기에 가장 적합한 위치는 어디인가?
"게다가 여러분의 부서장이 로비에 있는 자판기에 쓸 수 있는 무료 커피 쿠폰을 배포할 것입니다."
(A) [1]
(B) [2]
(C) [3]
(D) [4]

Questions 161-163 refer to the following article.

Stout Global - 여러분의 꿈을 좇으세요!

로스앤젤레스 (9월 17일)—두 명의 형제 Eric Gardener와 Henry Gardener에 의해 설립된 매우 성공적인 인터넷 포털 기업 Stout Global 사는 Stout Global Innovation이라는 새로운 부서를 신설했다. 이 부서는 경영자들 사이에서는 비교적 잘 알려지지 않은 이름인 Heather Lopez가 이끌 것이다.

그녀는 그녀 스스로 관리직의 후보자가 되기를 원했다. 그녀는 지난 3년 동안 여러 혁신적이고 성공적인 제품을 만들면서 Stout 사의 연구 개발 부서를 이끌어 왔다. 그녀는 더 큰 창의적인 연구의 자유를 제공하는 Stout Global Innovation과 같은 환경에 합류하기를 진심으로 원했다.

그녀가 이끌어 갈 야심 찬 세 개의 프로젝트들과 그것들을 완수하기 위한 상당한 예산을 받았기 때문에 앞으로를 생각하면 잘 임명된 것 같다. Lopez 씨는 그 부서가 프로젝트들을 한 번에 수행할 것이라 설명했다. 세 개의 프로젝트들은 혁신적인 민간 교통수단, 다양한 식물들을 성장시킬 수 있는 건조 지역의 복구 체계 그리고 학생들이 모든 종류의 콘텐츠들을 전보다 더 효율적으로 학습할 수 있게 하는 이러닝 네트워크들을 포함한다.

161 Stout Global Innovation에 대해 언급되는 것은?
(A) 비밀 기관의 한 종류이다.
(B) 다른 건물을 사용한다.
(C) 임시 부서이다.
(D) 자금이 잘 지원된다.

162 Stout Global에 의해 채택되지 않은 계획은 무엇일 것 같은가?
(A) 전기를 이용한 개인 이동 수단
(B) 조력 발전기
(C) 반사막화 기술
(D) 진보된 학습 도구

163 Lopez 씨에 대하여 알 수 있는 것은?
(A) 그녀는 회사 내에서 선택되었다.
(B) 그녀는 곧 회사를 그만둘 계획이다.
(C) 그녀는 프로젝트들의 성공을 예상치 못했다.
(D) 그녀는 향후 대표 이사의 모든 업무를 떠맡을 것이다.

Questions 164-167 refer to the following e-mail.

수신: Ken Hyland <k.hyland@oxbridge.edu>
발신: Ian Raynold <i_raynold@bea.org>
제목: 연설 제안
날짜: 5월 1일

Hyland 교수님께,

저는 Bristol Enterprise Association(BEA)의 책임자입니다. 지난밤 저는 제 동료들과 Eberly 커뮤니티 센터에서 교수님의 포럼에 참석했습니다. 저희는 모두 교수님의 견해와 통찰력에 감명을 받았고, 저희 협회에서 유사한 포럼을 마련하기 위해 당신을 초대하고 싶습니다.

BEA는 브리스톨 시에 있는 지역 사회 단체들 중 하나입니다. 저희는 30개 이상의 기관들과 연합해 있고, 500여명의 회원들을 보유하고 있으며 이 수는 점점 증가하고 있습니다. 저희는 동료들에게 다양한 정보를 제공하기 위해 경력 상담과 취업 박람회 행사들을 개최하고 있고 인터넷 상에서 저희만의 취업 게시판을 운영하고 있습니다. 6월 2일에 경력 개발과 관련된 교수님의 논문을 발표해 주시겠습니까? 일반적으로 저희는 오후 1시에서 4시 사이에 모입니다. 저희 제안에 관심이 있으시다면 5월 10일 전에 연락 주십시오.

곧 교수님의 답을 듣기를 희망합니다.

그럼 이만,

Ian Raynold
Bristol Enterprise Association의 책임자

164 Raynold 씨는 Hyland 교수에게 왜 이메일을 보냈는가?
(A) 총회를 위한 약속을 잡기 위해
(B) 그에게 발표를 부탁하기 위해
(C) 그의 논문 출판을 제안하기 위해
(D) 종신 교수직 자리를 제안하기 위해

165 BEA가 회원들에게 제공하는 서비스로 언급되지 않은 것은?
(A) 취업 정보
(B) 경력 상담
(C) 모임 행사
(D) 주식 투자

166 BEA에 관하여 알 수 있는 것은?
(A) 20년 동안 운영되고 있다.
(B) 사업을 위한 정규 강좌들을 제공한다.
(C) 일 년에 한 번 모인다.
(D) 회원들을 위한 그들만의 회담을 개최한다.

167 첫 번째 문단, 두 번째 줄의 단어 "perspective"와 의미상 가장 가까운 것은?
(A) 검사
(B) 회계
(C) 처리, 가공
(D) 이해

Questions 168-171 refer to the following article.

당신의 나이가 얼마인지 간에 절대 늦지 않았습니다!
- 그의 모험은 아직 끝나지 않았다 -

(위스콘신, 2월 20일)—Chuck Franco 씨는 매디슨 시에서 25년 동안 피아노를 판매하고 수리하며 살았습니다. 4월부터 그는 유감스럽게도 일을 그만두고 밀워키에 있는 Wisconsin 예술 대학에서 새로운 경력을 시작하게 됩니다. Franco 씨는 피아노 조율과 관련된 고급 과정을 수강할 것이고 조교가 될 예정입니다. 그는 "저는 전에 했던 일을 사랑했고 지금은 제가 더 전문화된 기술들을 배우고 저의 현장 경험들을 공유할 시기입니다"라고 말했습니다.

비록 매디슨 시 내부와 주변의 거주자들은 그의 은퇴를 유감스러워했지만 대부분은 장인으로서 그의 새로운 도전을 진심으로 응원했습니다. 1994년 Franco 씨는 Madison Tune UP을 설립했고, 위스콘신 주 그리고 심지어 미국 밖에서도 좋은 명성을 얻어 왔습니다. 단골 고객들은 그와 곧 작별 인사를 나눌 시간이 왔다는 점에 아쉬워했습니다.

좋은 소식은 Franco 씨가 가게 문을 닫기 전에 재고들을 대중들에게 처분하고 싶어 한다는 것입니다. 이 기회에 사람들은 매우 할인된 가격으로 훌륭한 악기들을 구할 수 있습니다. 피아노의 추가적인 부속품들 또한 세일로 제공됩니다. 이 행사에 관심 있는 누구든 그의 매장을 방문하여 경쟁력 있는 가격으로 물건을 구입하실 수 있습니다. 그러니 그곳에서 그와 작별 인사를 나눌 이 기회를 놓치지 마십시오.

168 이 기사문의 목적은 무엇인가?
(A) 매디슨 시의 명문 대학을 홍보하기 위해
(B) 유명한 지역 음악가들을 소개하기 위해
(C) 악기 기술자를 소개하기 위해
(D) 고객들에게 온라인 혜택 세일을 알리기 위해

169 Franco 씨에 관하여 암시되는 것은?
(A) 4월부터 매디슨 시에서 일을 다시 시작할 것이다.
(B) 그는 25년 전에 밀워키에서 이사 왔다.
(C) 그는 음악 학사 학위를 받았다.
(D) 그는 이미 악기 관리에 명성이 있다.

170 Madison Tune UP에 대해 나타난 것은?
(A) 가게 임대료가 상당히 증가했다.
(B) 재고 정리 세일을 할 것이다.
(C) 가게 제품이 온라인에서 판매될 것이다.
(D) 전통 악기를 더 이상 판매하지 않는다.

171 [1], [2], [3] 그리고 [4]로 표시된 곳 중에 다음 문장이 들어가기에 가장 적합한 위치는 어디인가?

"Franco 씨는 피아노 조율과 관련된 고급 과정을 수강할 것이고 조교가 될 예정입니다."

(A) [1]
(B) [2]
(C) [3]
(D) [4]

Questions 172-175 refer to the following online chat discussion.

Bella Reynolds [오전 10시 15분]
여러분들도 아시다시피 제가 공지도 없이 편집장으로 승진했습니다. 급하게 진행되었기 때문에 여러분들이 저에게 많은 정보를 요청하시는 바입니다. 우리의 판매를 증진시키기 위하여 여러분들이 현재 하고 있는 것을 저에게 말해 주시겠어요?

Karl Murphy [오전 10시 16분]
음… 저는 개정된 사용자 인터페이스를 저희 일간지들을 위해 업데이트하고 있습니다. 저희는 3월 1일에 온라인으로 업그레이드 버전을 출판할 것입니다.

David Lennon [오전 10시 17분]
저희는 모두 이번 출판에 매우 흥분하고 있습니다. 구독자들이 저희의 향상된 온라인 시스템으로 인해 이전 기사들을 훨씬 더 쉽게 찾을 수 있을 것입니다. 이것은 다양한 모바일 장치들과 호환되고, 매우 사용하기 쉽습니다.

Bella Reynolds [오전 10시 18분]
우리에게 새로운 구독자를 모으는 일은 필수적인 일이죠. 그리고 그들을 끌어들이기 위해 더 혁신적인 방법을 고안해야 할 필요가 있어요.

Terra Mitchell [오전 10시 20분]
어디 봅시다… 저는 새로운 모바일 애플리케이션을 작업 중입니다. 그 앱은 고객의 필요에 맞게 맞춤 제작될 수 있습니다. 기능들 중 하나는 구독자들이 첫 페이지에 그들이 원하는 기사를 놓을 수 있다는 것입니다.

Karl Murphy [오전 10시 21분]
맞아요! Terra가 저에게 말하길 구독자들은 각 카테고리를 통해 이야기들을 선택할 수 있다고 했어요. 예를 들어 그들은 스포츠, 연예, 음식 등과 같은 특정 기사들을 그들의 첫 페이지에 놓을 수 있어요.

Bella Reynolds [오전 10시 22분]
그거 좋군요! 더 세부적인 사항들이 나오면 저에게 계속 알려 주세요.

Terra Mitchell [오전 10시 23분]
네, 저는 이번 금요일까지 이 애플리케이션의 개요와 모델을 준비하겠습니다.

Bella Reynolds [오전 10시 24분]
좋습니다. 저는 직접 이 절차들을 확인하고자 합니다. 내일 오전에 여러분 모두 제 사무실에서 봅시다.

172 글쓴이들은 어디에서 일하고 있을 것 같은가?
(A) 택배 회사에서
(B) 전자제품 회사에서
(C) 신문사에서
(D) 여행사에서

173 무엇이 개선되고 있는가?
(A) 신문의 전자 버전
(B) 인사 절차
(C) 건물 설계도
(D) 여행 패키지

174 오전 10시 22분에, Reynolds 씨가 "그거 좋군요"라고 쓴 의도는 무엇인가?
(A) 그녀는 Lennon 씨의 홍보 제안을 승인한다.
(B) 그녀는 Mitchell 씨가 개발 중인 기능을 좋아한다.
(C) 그녀는 사무 절차를 배워서 기쁘다.
(D) 그녀는 직원들의 현재 업무들에 만족한다.

175 내일은 어떤 일이 일어날 것 같은가?
(A) 휴대폰 출시
(B) 고객 설문 조사
(C) 시연
(D) 마케팅 홍보

Questions 176-180 refer to the following notice and e-mail.

반품 정책

우리 고객들에게 양질의 서비스를 제공하기 위해 Penta 사에서는 구매한 지 45일 이내에 모든 물품들을 교환이나 전액 환불해 드릴 것입니다. 환불 또는 교환 금액은 원래 가격에 상응할 것입니다. 저희는 고객분들이 아래의 규정들을 준수해 주시기를 권장하는 바입니다.

- 반품이나 교환을 요청하실 때 영수증 원본을 가져오셔서 제시해야 합니다.
- 영수증이 없으시면 구매 내역에 대한 신용 카드 청구서를 증빙하십시오.
- 결함이 있는 제품들은 구입일로부터 60일 안에 반품함으로써 전액 환불 받을 수 있습니다.
- 구매한 지 60일이 지난 후 결함이 있는 제품들을 반품하시면 원가의 절반 금액으로 환불 또는 교환 받을 수 있습니다.
- 매장 지점들이나 고객 서비스에 대한 문의가 있으시면 주저하지 마시고 cs_managing@pentaco.com으로 이메일을 보내 주시거나 수신자 부담인 +1-800-381-1923으로 전화주세요.

여러분의 협조에 감사드립니다.

수신: cs_managing@pentaco.com
발신: julia_sonya@nmail.com

관계자분들께,

제 이름은 Julia Sonya이고, 저는 귀사의 반품 정책에 대해 문의하고자 이 글을 씁니다. 저는 최근에 Eagleville Mall에 있는 귀사의 매장에서 운동화를 구매하였습니다. 그러나 구매한 지 일주일 만에 운동화 한쪽의 바닥이 떨어져 나갔고 이음새가 찢어졌습니다. 매장 직원이 저에게 그 운동화는 더 비싸기는 하지만 다른 브랜드들보다 훨씬 튼튼하고 더 편하다고 했습니다. 그의 추천 때문에 저는 주저 없이 구매를 결정했습니다. 하지만 저는 운동화의 내구성에 정말 놀랐고 실망했습니다. 물론, 왼쪽 신발은 괜찮은 상태이고 저는 오른쪽만 교환해서 그 신발을 계속 신고 싶습니다.

하지만 제가 영수증 원본을 잃어버렸고, 구매 당시에 현금으로 결제했습니다. 이 물품에 대한 구매 내역을 확인할 수 있는 방법이 있을까요? 제가 오른쪽 신발만 교환할 수 있나요?

가능한 한 빨리 귀사의 답을 듣고 싶습니다.

Julia Sonya

176 공지에 따르면, 결함 있는 제품들에 관하여 뭐라고 언급되는가?
(A) 비슷한 물품으로 교환될 수 있다.
(B) 마모에 대해 검사될 것이다.
(C) 전액 환불될 수 있다.
(D) 소매 지점에서 반품되어야 한다.

177 Sonya 씨는 왜 회사에 이메일을 썼는가?
(A) 그녀는 고객 서비스에 실망했다.
(B) 그녀는 반품 정책에 관한 질문이 있다.
(C) 그녀는 회사의 소매점들에 대해 알려고 한다.
(D) 그녀는 구매 절차를 확인하려고 한다.

178 Sonya 씨는 어떤 문제에 대해 말하고 있는가?
(A) 제품이 할인되지 않았다.
(B) 제품에 결함이 있다.
(C) 제품이 품절되었다.
(D) 제품의 색깔이 잘못되었다.

179 Sonya 씨는 그녀의 문제를 어떻게 해결하고 싶어 하는가?
(A) 교환함으로써
(B) 쿠폰을 받음으로써
(C) 구매 증명서를 받음으로써
(D) 매니저와 이야기함으로써

180 Sonya 씨가 규정을 지키지 못하는 이유는 무엇인가?
(A) 그녀는 포장 없이 물건만 반품했다.
(B) 그녀는 기한이 만료된 신용 카드로 지불했다.
(C) 그녀는 매장의 반품 기한을 지키지 않았다.
(D) 그녀는 지불 증명을 제시할 수 없다.

Questions 181-185 refer to the following article and e-mail.

영업을 멈추지 마세요!
Joe Klein, <Prime Magazine> 수석 작가 작성

3월 20일 — Isabella Jermain 씨는 2월 24일 매장을 떠나는 마지막 고객 몇 명을 보았습니다. 그녀는 Giant Eagle 마트의 매니저로 15년 이상 일했지만 그 마트는 문을 닫았습니다. Santa Barbara에 있는 이 매장은 가족 소유의 체인점 중 일부였는데, 이 기업은 Sheetz 사에 인수되었습니다.

샌프란시스코에 본사를 둔 Sheetz 기업은 미 서부 지역 곳곳의 매장들을 인수하고 있고, 그 매장들은 Sheetz 매장으로 빠르게 변화하고 있습니다. 이러한 빠른 전환은 기존의 고객들이 다른 마켓에서 쇼핑하는 것을 막을 것이라 생각됩니다. Jermain 씨와 대부분의 직원들은 여전히 매장에 남아 새로운 회사와 함께 일하고 있습니다. Jermain 씨는 정확히 그 인수가 얼마나 크고 복잡한지 알 수 없었습니다. "저는 처리 속도에 엄청 놀랐어요"라고 그녀가 말했습니다. "Sheetz 사의 직원들과 도급업자들이 3월 1일 저희 매장으로 몰려 들었습니다. 그들은 냉장고들을 치워 새로운 것들로 설치하고 벽을 도색하고 바닥재와 선반들을 교체하며 밤낮으로 일했습니다. 매장 앞의 거대한 'Sheetz'라는 간판은 이전 것과 교체되어 설치되었고, 그것은 순식간에 바뀌었습니다."

드디어 모든 제품들과 식료품들에 라벨을 붙여 새로운 가판대 위에 놓았습니다. 3월 12일 일요일에는 피곤하지만 웃고 있는 Jermain 씨가 새로운 Sheetz에서 리본을 자르고 고객들을 맞이하며 그곳에 있었습니다.

발신: Arnold Kane <a_kane@sheetz.com>
수신: Isabella Jermain <i_jermain@sheetz.com>
제목: 진전
날짜: 3월 15일

Jermain 씨에게,

저는 귀하가 매니저로서 남을 수 있었고 대부분의 기존 직원들도 함께 남았다는 점에 매우 감사합니다. 저는 여러분이 매우 헌신적인 팀이라는 것을 강하게 믿고 있으며, 그곳에서 당신들과 함께 일하게 되어 기쁩니다. 저는 Santa Barbara, Fresno, Palo Alto 그리고 Long Beach 같은 캘리포니아의 여러 매장들의 변화를 도왔는데, 여러분이 하신 것만큼 순조롭게 진행된 팀은 없었습니다.

여러분들의 뛰어난 협조에 감사드립니다. 저는 모든 것이 계속 잘 운영될 것이라 확신합니다. 다른 문의 사항이 있으시면 주저 말고 저에게 연락 주세요.

그럼 이만,

Arnold Kane
프랜차이즈 운영부 총괄 매니저
Sheetz 기업

181 Jermain 씨에 관하여 알 수 있는 것은?
(A) 그녀는 본사 부장으로 승진되었다.
(B) 그녀는 새로운 회사에서 퇴사하기로 결정했다.
(C) 그녀는 운영진에게 추가 직원 고용을 요청했다.
(D) 그녀는 동일한 직책으로 10년 이상 일하고 있다.

182 가장 최근의 Sheetz 가게는 언제 열었는가?
(A) 2월 24일에
(B) 3월 10일에
(C) 3월 12일에
(D) 3월 15일에

183 Kane 씨가 이메일을 보낸 이유는 무엇인가?
(A) 감사를 전하기 위해
(B) 새로운 매니저를 찾기 위해
(C) 매장의 판매 보고서를 요청하기 위해
(D) 개업 행사를 알리기 위해

184 Kane 씨는 Jermain 씨와 어디서 함께 일하였는가?
(A) 샌프란시스코
(B) 산타 바바라
(C) 롱비치
(D) 팔로알토

185 이메일에서, 두 번째 문단 첫 번째 줄의 단어 "run"과 의미상 가장 유사한 것은?
(A) 이해하다
(B) 경주하다
(C) 기능하다
(D) 열다

Questions 186-190 refer to the following Web pages and review.

| 홈 | 우리에 관하여 | 매물 | 연락 주세요 |

Delaney 부동산
Greensburg의 가장 새롭고 혁신적인 부동산 관리 그룹

우리의 목표는 매우 간단합니다!
고품질이고 편의시설이 많은 집들을 합리적인 임대료에 제공하기 위해 저희는 현재 다른 지역에 있는 오래된 네 개의 건물들을 리모델링하고 있습니다. 9월부터 새로운 매물들의 1년 임대가 가능할 것입니다.

이 페이지 상단의 매물 배너를 클릭해 보세요.
(건물 번호를 클릭하시면 사진들과 평면도를 보실 수 있습니다.)
 - 모든 Delaney 아파트 단지들은 주민들만을 위한 체육관과 추가 창고들을 가지고 있습니다.
 - 원룸은 한 달에 600달러에서 시작; 한 개의 침실이 있는 집은 한 달에 750달러에서 시작; 두 개의 침실이 있는 집은 한 달에 900달러에서 시작!

단기 임대가 필요하세요?
#606을 클릭하세요! - 이 단지의 1층은 도시에서 유일하게 단기 임대가 가능하며 모든 가구가 갖춰진 임대 공간입니다. (금액은 하루에 70달러부터 시작합니다. - 1주일 임대 시 10퍼센트 할인)

유의: 별표(*)가 되어 있는 매물들은 대학생들에게 적합하며, 시의 교육 재정 지원(EFA) 하에 임대료 할인 자격을 받을 수 있음 - 세부 사항을 보려면 www.greensburg.org/EFA에 접속하세요.

| 홈 | 우리에 관하여 | 매물 | 연락 주세요 |

자유롭게 아래의 매물들을 확인하세요.
건물 번호를 클릭해 보세요!

건물 번호	위치	인접 지역	입주 가능 날짜
#120 *	120 플레밍 가	존스 타운	9월 20일
#606	606 코트랜드 가	몬로빌	9월 10일
#990 *	990 워싱턴 드라이브	인디애나 밸리	9월 20일
#428	428 글렌데일 가	알투나	9월 1일

추가적인 정보를 알고 싶다면 이 페이지 상단의 "연락 주세요"를 클릭하여 저희에게 언제든지 연락해 주세요.

Greensburg 도시 생활
우리 지역의 집과 아파트에 관한 최신 업데이트

새로운 부동산 관리 그룹의 리모델링된 타운하우스들을 보세요.
10월 5일 Catherine James 게시

웹 사이트 상의 부동산 뉴스 기사와 후기들과 함께 저는 잠시 Delaney의 리모델링의 과정을 찾아 보았습니다. 저는 또한 그 부동산 그룹의 새로 소개된 거주자 포럼에 게시된 코멘트들을 읽어 보았고, 그것을 <GREEN REALTY NEWS>에 게시했습니다.

며칠 전에 저는 지인의 초대 덕분에 #990 건물에 방문할 기회가 있었습니다. 좀 작긴 했지만 최신 가전 제품을 포함하여 장비가 완전히 갖춰진 부엌이 인상 깊었습니다. 단지의 체육관은 훌륭한 운동 기구들로 잘 갖춰져 있었는데 추가 창고는 여전히 공사 중이었습니다. 제 친구가 말하길 다음 달에 마무리될 것이라 합니다. 게다가 단지의 동쪽은 여전히 수리와 개선 작업이 한창이었습니다. 그러나 그녀는 아직까지 소음은 신경 쓰이지 않는다고 했습니다.

전반적으로 그 건물의 아파트들과 타운하우스들은 매우 편해 보였지만 제공되는 공간에 비해 조금 비쌌습니다. 같은 지역에 있는 오크 그로브 가의 제 현재 아파트는 Delaney의 아파트와 가격은 같은데 더 넓습니다.

186 웹 페이지들에는 어떤 정보가 제공되지 않았는가?
(A) 도시 주변 지도 링크
(B) 부동산 중개업소의 강령
(C) 각 건물의 집들의 미리 보기 링크
(D) 단지 유닛들의 임대료

187 어떤 건물이 주간 임대를 제공할 것 같은가?
(A) #120
(B) #606
(C) #990
(D) #428

188 후기는 어디에 게시된 것 같은가?
(A) 관광객들을 위한 웹 사이트에
(B) 공공 게시판에
(C) 온라인 부동산 소식 사이트에
(D) 거주자들의 토론 포럼에

189 후기에 따르면, Delaney 부동산에 관하여 사실일 것 같은 것은?
(A) 입주일 전에 일부 개조 공사를 완수하지 못했다.
(B) 현재 공실인 매물이 없다.
(C) 피트니스 센터 사용을 위해 추가 비용을 부과한다.
(D) 도시의 EFA 프로그램과 무관하다.

190 James 씨가 살고 있는 동네는 어디인가?
(A) 존스 타운
(B) 몬로빌

(C) 인디애나 밸리
(D) 알투나

Questions 191-195 refer to the following article, form, and e-mail.

Seattle Daily

채용을 위한 대리사무소의 지원

Serra Jones 작성

시애틀 (5월 10일)—지역 회사들이 좋은 직원들을 찾는 것은 여러모로 힘든 일입니다. 그들의 채용 과정을 효율적으로 하기 위해서 일부 회사들은 채용 대리사무소를 고용합니다. 회사가 비정규직을 구하든, 아니면 경력직을 구하든 간에 이 과정을 외주에게 주는 것이 회사 스스로 진행하는 것에 비해 시간과 돈을 절약할 수 있습니다.

"비정규직에 유능한 직원들을 채용함으로써 회사들은 이익을 얻을 수 있습니다"라며 시애틀의 가장 오래된 채용 사무소 중 하나인 SA Headhunter 사의 본부장 Paul Kay 씨가 말했습니다. 게다가 그는 회사가 마주한 다급하고 예기치 못한 문제들을 해결할 수 있고, 심지어 정규직을 제안하기 전에 임시 직원들을 평가할 수 있다고 말했습니다.

우리 지역의 고용주들에게 도움을 주기 위해서 저희는 웹 사이트 www.seattledaily.com/job_bulletin에 엄선된 채용 대리사무소 목록을 게시했습니다.

SA Headhunter 사

[임시 직원 요청서]

고용주 정보

이 름	John Stockton
회 사	Three Rivers Accounting
산 업	회계 & 재정
전 화	702-183-1283
이메일	j_stockton@threerivers.net

업무 정보

필요한 인원 수	5-6
직책	사무 보조
근무 기간	약 한 달

설명
최근 저희는 주 정부와 몇몇 다른 회사들과 여러 중요한 회계 감사 계약을 맺었습니다. 이러한 업무들 때문에 다양한 종류의 문서들을 준비하고 분류해야 합니다. 주의 법에 따라 우리는 공적 및 사적 부문으로 그 문서들을 분류해야 합니다. 이상적인 지원자들은 법학이나 행정학을 전공하고 세심하게 문서를 검토할 수 있어야 합니다.

저희에 대해 어떻게 알게 되셨나요?
<Seattle Daily> 5월호의 2쇄 기사를 봤습니다

[제출해 주셔서 감사드립니다]

** 저희 직원이 24시간 이내에 당신에게 연락 드릴 것입니다.

발신: John Stockton <j_stockton@threerivers.net>
수신: Jane Fetterman <jane@saheadhunter.com>
제목: 회신: 귀하의 요청
날짜: 5월 23일

Fetterman 씨에게,

저는 귀하의 도움을 감사를 드리고자 합니다. 처음에 당신 회사와 같은 채용 사무소에 연락을 해서 이런 종류의 서비스를 통해 좋은 직원을 고용할 것이라는 확신이 없었습니다. 당신의 도움 덕분에 문제 없이 임시 직원을 채용할 수 있었습니다. 제가 온라인으로 제출하고 두 시간 만에 저에게 이메일을 주셨고, 단 8시간 만에 다음 서신에서 자격을 갖춘 직원들의 목록을 보내주셨습니다. 당신이 저희에게 추천해 주신 직원들은 성실하고 능숙하며 열정적입니다. 사실, 저희 인사과는 정규직을 위한 면접 기회를 그들 중 세 분에게 드리기로 결정했습니다.

그럼 이만,

John Stockton
인사과
Three Rivers Accounting

191 기사문에서 대행사의 서비스의 이점으로 언급되지 않은 것은?
(A) 회사 돈 절약하기
(B) 회사의 긴급 상황 해결에 도움 주기
(C) 전문적인 도움 받기
(D) 고용 절차를 수월하게 하기

192 Stockton 씨에 관해 암시된 것은?
(A) Jones 씨가 그를 면접했다.
(B) 그의 회사가 <Seattle Daily>의 웹 사이트에 목록으로 올라 있다.
(C) 그의 회사는 SA Headhunter 사보다 오래되었다.
(D) 그는 Jones 씨의 기사를 읽었다.

193 양식에서, 둘째 단락 셋째 줄의 단어 "duration"과 의미상 가장 가까운 것은?
(A) 총액
(B) 긴급
(C) 기간
(D) 추산

194 이메일의 목적은 무엇인가?
(A) 제공 받은 서비스에 감사를 표하려고
(B) 직원의 업무 습관에 관해 불평하려고
(C) 추가 직원 요청을 확인하려고
(D) 직원 알선업체에 일자리를 문의하려고

195 Fetterman 씨는 누구일 것 같은가?
(A) 임시 직원
(B) Stockton 씨의 조수
(C) SA Headhunter 사의 직원 알선 대리인
(D) 공무원

Questions 196-200 refer to the following text message, schedule, and e-mail.

수신: Joshua Storm
발신: Sophie Bell
전송: 8월 15일 오전 10시 30분

JD Wave Band가 예기치 못하게 다음 주에 있을 Georgia Festival 공연을 취소해야 한다고 해요. 오후 6시 30분 Madison Square 무대가 현재 이용 가능합니다. 귀하의 그룹이 여전히 공연에 관심이 있다면 가능한 한 빨리 저에게 알려 주세요. 저희는 다가오는 행사에 관한 소책자를 내일 출력해야 하거든요.

Georgia Festival
공연 일정
8월 25일 금요일

	오후 4시 30분	오후 5시 30분	오후 6시 30분	오후 7시 30분
Trevi Fountain 무대	Supersonic	Pirate Buccos	Cozy Comfy	
Penn Way 무대		Rising Sun		Lafayette Locals
Madison Square 무대	Bruno Brothers		Prism Band	

주의:
먼저 오신 50명은 주차에 20퍼센트 할인을 받을 것입니다. 외부 음식이나 음료가 허용되지 않지만 무료 다과들이 제공됨을 알아 두세요. 좌석이 따로 마련되어 있지 않기 때문에 참가자들은 자신의 야외용 의자나 담요를 가져오실 수 있습니다. 축제 날에는 비가 오지 않습니다. 웹 사이트인 www.georgiastate.org/stateweather을 통해 행사 날의 최신 날씨 정보를 확인해 보세요.

발신: r_lampard@waynestudios.com
수신: sophiebell@georgiastate.org
제목: 사진
날짜: 8월 30일
첨부: 분수를_넘어서.jpg

Bell 씨에게,

이번 축제는 정말 훌륭했어요! 당신이 저에게 보내 주신 티켓 덕분에 저는 우리 주의 자랑스러운 행사를 충분히 즐겼답니다. 비록 제가 행사 때 찍은 사진들을 아직 다 현상하지는 못했지만 제 생각에 정말 훌륭한 사진 한 장을 첨부했어요. Trevi Fountain 무대에 Cozy Comfy가 사진에 찍혔는데, 그 무대 뒤의 일몰 광경이 아주 아름다웠어요. 저는 확실히 이 사진이 웹 사이트의 축제 메인 페이지를 장식할 훌륭한 사진이라고 믿고 있어요. 남은 사진을 모두 본 후에 뛰어난 사진들의 목록을 만들어서 파일을 이메일로 보내 드리겠습니다. 이 사진들은 다음 축제 광고 자료로 활용될 수 있을 거예요.

행운을 빌며,

Ron Lampard
Wayne Studios

---

196 문자 메시지에 따르면, 8월 16일에 무엇이 일어나는가?
 (A) 무대들이 수리될 것이다.
 (B) Storm 씨가 축제에서 공연할 것이다.
 (C) 스케줄이 발행될 것이다.
 (D) JD Wave Band가 콘서트 투어를 시작할 것이다.

197 Storm 씨의 그룹 이름이 무엇인가?
 (A) Prism Band
 (B) Rising Sun
 (C) Supersonic
 (D) Bruno Brothers

198 행사에 대하여 암시되는 것은?
 (A) 주 내의 모든 거주자들은 주차가 무료이다.
 (B) 무료 음식이 이용 가능할 것이다.
 (C) 일부 좌석들은 추가 비용이 부과된다.
 (D) 활동 일정은 곧 재조정될 것이다.

199 Lampard 씨의 사진들에 대하여 암시되는 것은?
 (A) 주 공립 갤러리에 전시될 것이다.
 (B) 다음 행사의 광고에 사용될 수 있다.
 (C) 자선을 위한 기금 모금 이벤트에서 팔릴 수 있다.
 (D) 사진전을 위해 제출될 것이다.

200 Lampard 씨는 언제 이메일에 첨부된 사진을 찍었을 것 같은가?
 (A) 오후 4시 30분에
 (B) 오후 5시 30분에
 (C) 오후 6시 30분에
 (D) 오후 7시 30분에

5회

| p.182

01	(C)	02	(C)	03	(A)	04	(B)	05	(D)
06	(D)	07	(B)	08	(C)	09	(A)	10	(C)
11	(A)	12	(B)	13	(C)	14	(A)	15	(A)
16	(B)	17	(C)	18	(A)	19	(A)	20	(B)
21	(A)	22	(C)	23	(A)	24	(C)	25	(B)
26	(A)	27	(B)	28	(A)	29	(A)	30	(B)
31	(C)	32	(A)	33	(A)	34	(B)	35	(A)
36	(D)	37	(C)	38	(D)	39	(A)	40	(D)
41	(A)	42	(B)	43	(C)	44	(D)	45	(D)
46	(C)	47	(D)	48	(A)	49	(A)	50	(A)
51	(C)	52	(A)	53	(D)	54	(B)	55	(A)
56	(B)	57	(B)	58	(C)	59	(A)	60	(A)
61	(C)	62	(C)	63	(A)	64	(B)	65	(D)
66	(B)	67	(D)	68	(C)	69	(A)	70	(C)
71	(C)	72	(B)	73	(C)	74	(A)	75	(B)
76	(C)	77	(A)	78	(B)	79	(C)	80	(B)
81	(B)	82	(A)	83	(B)	84	(C)	85	(C)
86	(A)	87	(D)	88	(C)	89	(D)	90	(A)
91	(B)	92	(D)	93	(A)	94	(B)	95	(A)
96	(C)	97	(D)	98	(D)	99	(B)	100	(C)
101	(D)	102	(A)	103	(C)	104	(C)	105	(B)
106	(D)	107	(D)	108	(B)	109	(A)	110	(D)
111	(A)	112	(D)	113	(B)	114	(C)	115	(A)
116	(C)	117	(B)	118	(C)	119	(D)	120	(A)
121	(A)	122	(D)	123	(D)	124	(A)	125	(B)
126	(A)	127	(C)	128	(D)	129	(B)	130	(C)
131	(C)	132	(B)	133	(D)	134	(A)	135	(C)
136	(A)	137	(C)	138	(C)	139	(A)	140	(B)
141	(C)	142	(D)	143	(A)	144	(B)	145	(D)
146	(C)	147	(A)	148	(C)	149	(C)	150	(D)
151	(B)	152	(D)	153	(D)	154	(C)	155	(B)
156	(C)	157	(D)	158	(B)	159	(B)	160	(B)
161	(C)	162	(D)	163	(B)	164	(D)	165	(B)
166	(D)	167	(A)	168	(B)	169	(C)	170	(A)
171	(B)	172	(C)	173	(B)	174	(C)	175	(D)
176	(A)	177	(C)	178	(C)	179	(B)	180	(C)
181	(D)	182	(A)	183	(C)	184	(C)	185	(A)
186	(D)	187	(C)	188	(A)	189	(C)	190	(D)
191	(D)	192	(C)	193	(A)	194	(C)	195	(C)
196	(B)	197	(A)	198	(D)	199	(B)	200	(C)

Part 1

1. (A) They're playing guitars on the street.
   (B) They're checking the stage equipment.
   (C) One of the men is having his picture taken.
   (D) One of the men is repairing his instrument.

2. (A) He is putting on a mask.
   (B) He is putting away a microscope.
   (C) He is using medical equipment.
   (D) He is adjusting some protective gear.

3. (A) A woman is delivering a speech to the audience.
   (B) People are looking at a computer monitor.
   (C) People are watching a performance indoors.
   (D) A woman is raising her hand.

4. (A) She's taking some meat from the bowl.
   (B) She's standing behind the counter.
   (C) She's carrying a tray of food.
   (D) She's washing vegetables in the sink.

5. (A) Machines are being set up on a platform.
   (B) Windows are being washed.
   (C) One of the men is handing out tickets.
   (D) Some people are waiting in line.

6. (A) Tiles are being removed from the floor.
   (B) Some trees are being planted on a street.
   (C) Some cyclists are riding past a stone wall.
   (D) Some bicycles have been parked along a railing.

Part 2

7. Is there an awards ceremony at the restaurant tonight?
   (A) It was good.
   (B) Let me check the calendar.
   (C) He deserved it.

8. Could you pick Ms. Scott up from the hotel?
   (A) Pick it up for me.
   (B) We should make a reservation.
   (C) I already did that.

9. Who will get in touch with our contact at the public relations agency?
   (A) That assignment hasn't been given out.
   (B) Mr. Hampton apologized in public.
   (C) Three hours later.

10. What hotel did you stay at on your last business trip?
    (A) Two nights.
    (B) It's across the street.
    (C) I don't remember at all.

11. When are you leaving for Beijing?
    (A) At the beginning of next year.
    (B) From Seattle.
    (C) For a couple of months.

12. Where's the instruction manual for the air conditioner?
    (A) You need to read the instructions carefully.
    (B) I guess George has it.
    (C) It's behind schedule.

13. How many tickets should we issue for the train?
    (A) By Thursday at least.
    (B) I'm going on vacation next week.
    (C) Six in total.

14. Why is the Maintenance Department in a different building?
    (A) It temporarily moved due to the office renovations.
    (B) I go to the department store once a week.
    (C) It's far away from here.

15. How is the customer satisfaction survey going?
    (A) I've almost finished it.
    (B) I think it will be to your satisfaction.
    (C) Take bus number 52.

16. I'm not accustomed to that writer's novels.
    (A) For the book signing.
    (B) I'm sure you will like them soon.
    (C) That's a difficult request.

17. Mr. Hayward is the person who handled the transaction with the ABC Company, isn't he?
    (A) I prefer using public transportation for commuting.
    (B) He didn't give me a hand at all.
    (C) That's what I think.

18. Did you get the office supplies you ordered?
    (A) They're in the storeroom.
    (B) We are running out of some supplies.
    (C) The price was affordable.

19. Should this pamphlet be printed in color or in black and white?
    (A) Either is fine with me.
    (B) By express mail.
    (C) Sure, I will print them out.

20. Can you replace the ink cartridge?
    (A) The accounts manager.
    (B) No problem.
    (C) We'd better find a replacement for Erin.

21. Do you need to get a medical checkup?
    (A) Yes, I have an appointment this Friday.
    (B) I'm under pressure.
    (C) They issued a check.

22. I couldn't find any extra space for these files.
    (A) The data can be found in the file.
    (B) Could you please file these documents?
    (C) There is some in the downstairs office.

23. I will go to London on a business trip next week.
    (A) I've been there a couple of times.
    (B) Shall we arrange our itinerary for the trip?
    (C) The seller already sent the goods we purchased.

24. Didn't you go to the training session with me?
    (A) That was terrible.
    (B) Yes, I signed up for that.
    (C) When was that exactly?

25. Will the workshop be held at the Park View Hotel or the Riverside Hotel?
    (A) Perhaps at the end of the year.
    (B) That hasn't been decided yet.
    (C) The workshop will not delay.

26. Whose turn is it to take minutes?
    (A) William's, I think.
    (B) It will take a few minutes to finish.
    (C) Before you leave the office.

27. Would you like me to review the expense report this month?
    (A) I'm not sure I have time.
    (B) That'd be helpful.
    (C) Do you want an ocean view?

28. When is the application due?
    (A) 4 P.M. at the latest.
    (B) At the reception desk.
    (C) Yes, you can submit it.

29. Daniel reserved the convention hall yesterday, didn't he?
    (A) Actually, we changed the venue.
    (B) We've never used the dining hall.
    (C) It's on the right side of the hallway.

30. Where should I leave a sample of the redesigned catalog?
    (A) Every single day.
    (B) The front desk is that way.
    (C) Ms. Garcia resigned as manager yesterday.

31. Shouldn't our invoice have been sent by now?
    (A) It's not specified in this invoice.
    (B) Please keep your voice down.
    (C) Yes, it should be here now.

Part 3

Questions 32-34 refer to the following conversation.

> W: Good morning. I called yesterday to make a reservation for a table for tonight in the name of Amy Tanaka.
>
> M: Let me check the reservation, Ms. Tanaka. You have a party of six arriving at eight in the evening, right?
>
> W: Yes, but I just heard that three more people were invited to dinner. Could you change the reservation to nine people instead?
>
> M: We don't have a table large enough for that number of people. However, we have private rooms which can accommodate ten people. Would you like to change your reservation to the room?

32. Where does the man work?
    (A) At a restaurant
    (B) At a hotel
    (C) At a catering company
    (D) At a convention center

33. Why is the woman calling?
    (A) To alter a reservation
    (B) To rent a conference room
    (C) To purchase tickets
    (D) To order meals

34. What does the man suggest the woman do?
    (A) Change the booking time
    (B) Reserve a private room
    (C) Choose a different place
    (D) Cancel the reservation

Questions 35-37 refer to the following conversation.

W: Jonathan, we will have a meeting to discuss what to do during the workshop. Could you tell me when you are available at your earliest convenience?

M: Wasn't it canceled? Unfortunately, I have an appointment in Tokyo for the new product demonstration. So I can't make time for a meeting this week. Anyway, I want to make sure that the event will be held.

W: I heard the board of directors finally decided it will take place next week. Before you go to Tokyo, let's set up a meeting for today. Just check your schedule and let me know when is good for you.

35. What does the woman want to know?
    (A) The man's availability
    (B) The date of a workshop
    (C) The location of a function
    (D) The name of a product

36. What is the man most likely planning to do this week?
    (A) Drop by headquarters
    (B) Seek overseas markets
    (C) Open another branch
    (D) Prepare for an event

37. What is the man asked to do?
    (A) Provide a brief demonstration
    (B) Purchase additional equipment
    (C) Check his schedule
    (D) Explain his absence

Questions 38-40 refer to the following conversation.

M: Good morning. I'd like to watch a documentary film at this convention center today. I bought three tickets on the Web site last night, but I'm not sure the payment was authorized. Could you please check if my credit card has been accepted?

W: I'm sorry. A computer error occurred while we were uploading the new system yesterday, so all of our online services have been rejected. If you want, I can book tickets for you right away.

M: Okay, I'd like to book three tickets for *Back into the Wild*. Are tickets for the movie still available?

W: Of course. What time would you like to watch it? According to the schedule, there are two showings left.

38. What event does the man want to attend?
    (A) A celebration party
    (B) A press conference
    (C) The opening of a museum
    (D) A movie screening

39. According to the woman, what is the problem?
    (A) There was a problem with a Web site.
    (B) She cannot find her tickets.
    (C) The building is in need of renovations.
    (D) Free tickets are unavailable.

40. What information does the woman request?
    (A) Personal information
    (B) An address code
    (C) The method of payment
    (D) A preferred time

Questions 41-43 refer to the following conversation.

M: I've got some good news for you. Our manufacturing facility will be relocated to the business district just like you suggested a month ago. It's a perfect choice for our packaging firm.

W: I'm pleased to hear that! Has the date of the move been fixed?

M: That hasn't been decided yet, but I heard that our boss wants to relocate the facility by the first of December. However, we don't have much time this year to do that because of the company's plan to open a third branch in Chicago in November. I hope it would be better to move next year.

W: Well, we'll just wait and see what the board of directors decide at their meeting. They will definitely be eager to finalize the relocation as soon as possible.

41. Where do the speakers most likely work?
    (A) At a packaging company
    (B) At a glass factory
    (C) At a logistics firm
    (D) At a real estate agency

42. What will take place in November?
    (A) A board of director's meeting
    (B) A opening of a new branch
    (C) A relocation of a facility
    (D) A corporate merger

43. What does the woman imply when she says, "we'll just wait and see what the board of directors decide"?
    (A) She is unsatisfied about the rent.
    (B) She believes the space is too small.
    (C) She disagrees with a colleague.
    (D) She thinks the facility requires refurbishment.

Questions 44-46 refer to the following conversation.

W: We finally finished our new advertising project, Paul. Thank you for explaining how to use this new computer program.

M: We've gotten many inquiries about the program from other employees. It is likely that they are having difficulty making use of it, which has changed a lot compared to the previous version.

W: I hope I get familiar with this one as soon as possible since our team has a big project starting next week.

M: Once you're used to it, it will take less time to use this program than before. We are scheduled to hold a training session on the new software for the employees. I think that it will be very helpful to you.

44. What department does the woman work in?
    (A) Design
    (B) Sales
    (C) Quality Control
    (D) Advertising

45. How does the new program differ from the previous one?
    (A) It has a safer system.
    (B) It has more features.
    (C) It is more expensive.
    (D) It takes less time to use.

46. What does the man suggest the woman do?
    (A) Update some software
    (B) Speak to some of their co-workers
    (C) Take part in a training program
    (D) Demonstrate how to use some software

Questions 47-49 refer to the following conversation.

W   Linus, I heard that you are in charge of preparing gifts for visitors at our next exhibition. Is everything going to be all right?

M   The wholesaler sent the goods that I ordered for the gifts, but they are unpackaged. We need some small boxes to put the gifts in. Is there a store where I can purchase boxes near the office?

W   How about the stationery store on Lincoln Street? When I went there yesterday, the clerk said shoppers can get discounts on bulk purchases.

M   That sounds great. Do you know the phone number of the store? I should call before I go there and find out if it has the kind of boxes that I need.

47. Where do the speakers most likely work?
    (A) At a gift shop
    (B) At a radio station
    (C) At a stationery store
    (D) At a gallery

48. Why does the man want to purchase boxes?
    (A) To place some items in
    (B) To organize his office
    (C) To send some packages
    (D) To pack his personal belongings

49. What will the man probably do next?
    (A) Make a phone call
    (B) Visit the woman's office
    (C) Make a list of necessary items
    (D) Distribute complimentary gifts

Questions 50-52 refer to the following conversation with three speakers.

W   Adrian and Gregory, I just found some errors in the budget report that we made last week. I think we should get together to fix them and make a final version of it before we go to the next board meeting. Could you tell me when you are available?

M1 I'm going on leave next week, so we should have a meeting before this Friday.

M2 Actually, I have to work overtime all week long. If you don't mind, why don't we come to work and discuss it on the weekend?

W   Okay, then I'll arrange with the security guard to keep the main entrance open. Let's have a discussion about the matter then.

50. According to the woman, why do the speakers have to meet?
    (A) To modify some mistakes in a report
    (B) To make a budget for the current year
    (C) To give a product demonstration
    (D) To discuss a proposal

51. What problem do the men mention?
    (A) No room is available for a meeting.
    (B) A contract has expired.
    (C) Their availability is limited.
    (D) A request for leave was denied.

52. What will the woman arrange?
    (A) Free access to the office
    (B) More information on contractors
    (C) An orientation session for new employees
    (D) Precise budget allocations

Questions 53-55 refer to the following conversation.

W   Hi, Michael. I was about to call you to ask for help. Are you going to be in the office early on Sunday morning? I won't be able to come until lunchtime, so I wonder if you could open the store for me.

M   As it happens, I am working this weekend. As we are having a sale this week, it is expected that the store will be crowded with customers. By what time should I be here to open the store?

W   I think the store should be opened earlier than usual at around 8 o'clock. I'll let the head office know that you will open the store instead of me. Thank you.

53. What does the woman ask the man to do?
    (A) Go to the head office
    (B) Give her a ride to the office
    (C) Drop off the store key
    (D) Open a store

54. What does the man mean when he says, "As it happens, I am working this weekend"?
    (A) He cannot join the woman for lunch.
    (B) He accepts the woman's request.
    (C) He works every weekend.
    (D) He looks forward to working with the woman.

55. What does the woman say she will do?
    (A) Contact headquarters
    (B) Send a fax
    (C) Check her schedule
    (D) Put off an appointment

Questions 56-58 refer to the following conversation.

W Hello. I'm calling because I'd like to know the price to place an ad for a job opening in your magazine.

M I really appreciate that you contacted our magazine. Concerning the price, it depends on how long the advertisement will be posted. The normal price is 20 pounds per week. How many weeks do you want the recruitment notice advertised?

W I think it should be a 40-word advertisement and appear for two months. In that case, how much will it cost?

M If the ad is placed for more than four weeks, we offer a 30% discount on the whole price. In other words, you have to pay 112 pounds in total.

56 What are the speakers mainly discussing?
(A) A reimbursement process
(B) A cost of advertising
(C) Some budget cuts
(D) An advertising seminar

57 What information does the man ask the woman for?
(A) The purpose of the advertisement
(B) The period of the advertisement
(C) The type of advertisement
(D) The starting date of the advertisement

58 How can the woman get a discount?
(A) By paying more than 100 pounds
(B) By making a cash payment
(C) By placing an ad for a certain period of time
(D) By participating in a survey

Questions 59-61 refer to the following conversation.

W Charlie, I want to talk to you about our sales this month. Business has been really slow lately. It seems like we won't reach our sales goals for the month.

M Since the new DVD store opened across the street, we have lost a lot of customers. It's a really big problem. What do you suggest we do?

W We should come up with some ideas such as a buy-one-get-one-free offer in order to attract more customers.

M Okay, shall we have a lunch meeting? We have to try to get a competitive edge in the market.

59 What do the speakers sell?
(A) DVDs
(B) CD players
(C) Books
(D) Printers

60 What are the speakers concerned about?
(A) Their business has been underperforming.
(B) Their products are easily broken.
(C) Their company's stock price has declined.
(D) Other stores are selling the same products at cheaper prices.

61 What does the woman suggest?
(A) Using discount coupons
(B) Giving away new products
(C) Thinking about a sales strategy
(D) Asking for customers' feedback

Questions 62-64 refer to the following conversation and list.

W Did you see the notice about training programs? I registered for a class on how to use some computer graphic software.

M Yes, I was also thinking of signing up for the class, but the date is not good for me. I'm responsible for organizing a conference during the training time.

W That's too bad. Isn't there a chance that the class will be offered on other days?

M No, I already checked the schedule of the training programs, but there's only a single time slot on Monday for the graphic software class.

62 What is the man's problem?
(A) He isn't interested in any classes.
(B) He wasn't informed of the program.
(C) He has a schedule conflict.
(D) He forgot to organize a meeting.

63 What does the man say about the graphic software class?
(A) It will only be offered one time.
(B) It is offered every year.
(C) No textbook is required for it.
(D) He can take it online.

64 Look at the graphic. What class did the woman sign up for?
(A) Class A
(B) Class B
(C) Class C
(D) Class D

Questions 65-67 refer to the following conversation and schedule.

W Hello, Dan. I'm on my way to the head office for my scheduled meeting with our managing director, but I forgot to bring my laptop. Can you bring it to headquarters right now?

M Sure. But if you don't mind letting me know your laptop password, wouldn't it be much faster to send the files you need through e-mail?

W Well, I'd better have the laptop with me. All of the information about the company's finances is on that laptop's hard drive.

M No problem. It's 10:30. I'll go there now, and I guess it will take fewer than 30 minutes, but I'm afraid that you won't have enough time to review the materials.

65 What has the woman forgotten to bring?
(A) A key
(B) A phone
(C) A sample

302

(D) A computer

66. Look at the graphic. Which meeting will the woman attend?
(A) New products education
(B) Sales planning
(C) Quarterly financial review
(D) New employee orientation

67. What does the man say he will do?
(A) Send the woman an e-mail
(B) Stop by a computer repair shop
(C) Attend a meeting
(D) Head for headquarters

Questions 68-70 refer to the following conversation and survey.

M	Samantha, I heard that you did a market survey about the cosmetic IZ-2 that will be released next year. How did it go?
W	Well, we invited four retailers and demonstrated the product to them this afternoon. Most agreed that the quality of that cosmetic is excellent and that the price is affordable. However, some features didn't receive positive evaluations.
M	We need to discuss that data for the weekly meeting on Friday. Can you give the results to the Marketing Department as soon as possible?
W	Sure, I'll do that right away. There are four items that we need to talk about. First of all, we'd better deal with the one that received the least number of stars. We can handle the others next week.

68. Who did the woman meet this afternoon?
(A) Cosmetics manufacturers
(B) Marketing directors
(C) Retail representatives
(D) Customers

69. What does the man ask the woman to do?
(A) Send some information to another department
(B) Go to the Marketing Department
(C) Hold a press conference
(D) Test the company's new cosmetics

70. Look at the graphic. Which item will be discussed first?
(A) Quality
(B) Price
(C) Quantity
(D) Packaging

Part 4

Questions 71-73 refer to the following radio broadcast.

CBC News is glad to promote the yearly winter sports competition in December. We are recruiting amateur teams for curling from the local area. It is a great chance for people to compete against other competitors and to win a cash award. Other event categories include skiing, figure skating, and speed skating. Those who want to participate in this competition have to fill out an application form. It can be downloaded from our Web site at www.cbcnews.org, and should be submitted by the end of the week. Thank you.

71. Who is this announcement intended for?
(A) Journalists
(B) Ski instructors
(C) Winter sports athletes
(D) Newscasters

72. According to the speaker, what can listeners do on the Web site?
(A) Check out entry requirements
(B) Download an application form
(C) Install new apps
(D) Submit suggestions

73. What will happen at the end of the week?
(A) The winners will be announced.
(B) A competition will start.
(C) The deadline for applications will end.
(D) A sporting event will be officially held.

Questions 74-76 refer to the following telephone message.

Hello. This is Laura Walden. I'd like to file an insurance claim with People N Life. I have experience filing claims with other companies, but I am having trouble with the claim form on your Web site. Following the online instructions, I tried to submit my insurance details as requested. However, an error message popped up and indicated that my insurance was invalid although I entered the insurance reference number which was issued by someone on your staff. Please contact me at 204-5555-1324 in order to solve this matter. Thank you.

74. What kind of business is the speaker calling?
(A) An insurance firm
(B) A publishing company
(C) A community center
(D) A law firm

75. What is the speaker having trouble with?
(A) Connecting to the Internet
(B) Submitting a claim
(C) Canceling a contract
(D) Issuing a passport

76. What does the speaker ask the listener to do?
(A) Reschedule an appointment
(B) Send a reference letter
(C) Resolve the problem

(D) Transfer her some money

Questions 77-79 refer to the following talk.

> Thank you for joining us today on a tour at the Lower Mill Nature Reserve. We are proud that this is one of the finest reserves in the world for viewing wildlife. There are a wide range of animals here. During the tour, you are likely to come across wild animals. We're starting our tour from the lake, where a lot of different species of birds and water deer can be seen. This will be a great chance for you to see those kinds of animals in one place. <u>You're not aware of wild animals, aren't you?</u> So, if you want to learn more about the animals, you can sign up for an audio package, which includes a talk from one of our nature experts. Now let's begin the tour.

77 Who is the speaker?
    (A) A tour guide
    (B) A bus driver
    (C) A professor of zoology
    (D) A travel agent

78 What does the speaker imply when he says, "You're not aware of wild animals, aren't you"?
    (A) He wants the tour to be held more often.
    (B) He wants people to apply for an audio tour.
    (C) He wants to sign up for the tour for a cheap price.
    (D) He wants to meet a famous nature expert.

79 What will the listeners most likely do next?
    (A) Receive some audio players
    (B) Listen to an expert
    (C) Go around the area
    (D) Purchase tickets

Questions 80-82 refer to the following news broadcast.

> This is Gemma Walger with DYRN radio's weekly news report. The Department of Transportation just made a statement concerning the subway line extension at Wall Street Station. Owing to the heavy snow that hit the region last week, the extension work has been stopped for a while. The department indicated that construction will resume tomorrow, and the extended underground subway line is scheduled to be completed in January. After the completion, Wall Street Station will be connected to the city's main stations.

80 What construction project is the speaker discussing?
    (A) A parking lot
    (B) A subway line
    (C) A highway
    (D) A bus terminal

81 Why has construction been suspended?
    (A) There was a blackout in the city.
    (B) There were inclement weather conditions.
    (C) The city has insufficient funds.
    (D) There is a lack of workers.

82 According to the speaker, what will be available after the project is completed?
    (A) Access to the main stations
    (B) Lower fares
    (C) Extended service hours
    (D) More Wall Street Station exits

Questions 83-85 refer to the following telephone message.

> Good morning, Mr. Perlman. This is Michelle Gates. As you know, we're going to rent some vehicles for our annual workshop. It's very important that we carry some fragile instrument such as sound equipment and recording devices. So I'd like to contact the company that we borrowed cars from last year. <u>They're probably familiar with how to move those machines</u> because they've already done this kind of work. I'm expecting over 20 vehicles will be needed. In addition, outdoor furniture is required for an entertainment event. I'll send you a list of all the machines we need to relocate. Please read this information and call me back to discuss your decision. Thanks.

83 What is the speaker mainly discussing?
    (A) The types of projects assigned
    (B) Preparations for a company event
    (C) The status of some training materials
    (D) The location of a workshop

84 Why does the speaker say, "They're probably familiar with how to move those machines"?
    (A) To propose another option
    (B) To stress her dissatisfaction with a service
    (C) To give the reason for a choice
    (D) To agree with Mr. Perlman's opinion

85 What is the listener asked to do?
    (A) Book a flight
    (B) Rent some vehicles
    (C) Read some information
    (D) Invite some new employees

Questions 86-88 refer to the following announcement.

> Welcome to today's tour of our art exhibit. Our art gallery has a wonderful Impressionist exhibit these days. So this tour includes the work of Adams, who was both the last Impressionist and the precursor of modern art. Each painting of his was crafted from a wide range of colors and textures. As you'll notice, the subjects of his works are forests and lakes. The reason is that Mr. Adams derived his inspiration from nature scenery. Now, let's begin the tour. At the end of our tour, we'll go to the cafeteria, where you can enjoy dinner with the gallery director.

86 Who most likely is the speaker?
    (A) A tour conductor
    (B) A tourist
    (C) An artist
    (D) A product designer

87 According to the speaker, what kind of art did Mr. Adams create?
(A) Murals
(B) Abstract paintings
(C) Portraits
(D) Landscape paintings

88 What can the visitors do at the end of the tour?
(A) Go to the souvenir shop
(B) Take a picture with the tour guide
(C) Meet with the head of the gallery
(D) Listen to a lecture on art history

Questions 89-91 refer to the following telephone message.

Hi. This message is for Ryan at the Commercial Renting Agency. I'd like to inform you that my coworker and I decided to rent the office that you showed us last week. However, there is a big problem. The company that occupied the office left its office equipment and other items behind. We hope that all equipment can be removed from the office because we have some things to install there. So could you let me know how fast you can move those things? We need to know that before we rent the office. I'd appreciate your contacting me as soon as possible. Bye.

89 What happened last week?
(A) New employees were hired.
(B) An office was rented.
(C) A company was relocated.
(D) A property was shown.

90 What does the speaker inquire about?
(A) Removing some furniture
(B) Leasing a parking space
(C) Examining a contract
(D) Reconfirming a payment

91 What does the speaker ask the listener to do?
(A) Explain a renovation plan
(B) Give an estimated time for work
(C) Renew a rental contract
(D) Provide an accurate quotation

Questions 92-94 refer to the following news report.

In other news, the Littleton Construction Group announced that it's going to start construction on a new business park in Southhill right after the building permit is approved. Austin Wedge, the company's spokesperson, said that the company selected Southhill because of its closeness to the capital and the enormous potential for development. Southhill's mayor, Alan Houston, expressed support for the plan. On the other hand, he acknowledged that some local residents have expressed their concern about the creation of pollution in the area. However, the mayor stated that their anxiety will disappear once the construction plans have been released and that residents will be satisfied with the results. The plans are scheduled to be posted on the firm's Web site two weeks from now.

92 What is the news mainly about?
(A) A merger between two firms
(B) Projections of economic growth
(C) Public opinions regarding a construction project
(D) The construction of a business park

93 What are the residents worried about?
(A) Pollution levels may increase.
(B) There will be traffic problems.
(C) Business will be depressed.
(D) Property values will drop.

94 What will take place in two weeks?
(A) Construction work will start.
(B) Some information will be released.
(C) The renovation will be completed.
(D) A conflict between two companies will be resolved.

Questions 95-97 refer to the following recorded message and timetable.

You've reached Dr. Alice's office. We are located in the Alice Medical Center right next to the Hamilton Pharmacy. Our hours of operation are from Monday through Thursday from 8 A.M. to 6 P.M. On Tuesday, we conduct surgery until 10 P.M. Plus, we see patients on Friday from 8 A.M. to 7 P.M. every other week. Please make sure to make an appointment in advance to consult Dr. Alice. For a map of our location, just visit our Web site at www.alicehopital.com.

95 What kind of business is Alice's?
(A) A clinic
(B) An insurance agency
(C) A counseling center
(D) A pharmacy

96 Look at the graphic. Which day indicates the wrong business hours?
(A) Monday
(B) Tuesday
(C) Wednesday
(D) Friday

97 What does the speaker say is available on a Web site?
(A) A sign-up sheet
(B) A price list
(C) A contact number
(D) A map

Questions 98-100 refer to the following talk and map.

Attention, staff members. Please remember that the spring flower festival is supposed to take place tomorrow. Wellington Street's going to be closed because the parade will pass on it. There will be detour signs posted, but please be aware that nobody can use the road all afternoon tomorrow. Now, I need some people to help rearrange the office furniture due to the new employees. If you're willing to work a few extra hours, please raise your hand and let me write your name on a list.

98 Look at the graphic. Which building will be least affected by the festival?
(A) The post office
(B) The school
(C) The hospital
(D) The bookstore

99 According to the speaker, what will happen tomorrow?
(A) A subway station will be closed.
(B) There will be a restricted area.
(C) New employees will be hired.
(D) The furniture will be arranged.

100 What are the listeners asked to do to work extra hours?
(A) Confirm a list
(B) Write their names
(C) Raise their hands
(D) Attend an orientation session

Part 5

101 Meteora 프로젝트에서 경험한 문제점들을 고려하여 Evans 씨는 마감 기한 연장을 요구하였다.

102 완성된 양식들만 고려될 것이므로 지원 양식의 모든 부분을 작성하세요.

103 우리가 시간이 부족하기 때문에 Raymond 씨는 스스로 늦게까지 일할 수밖에 없었다.

104 공연의 일정들이 조정되어 현재 TD Broadband 케이블 구독자들이 매주 시청 가능하게 되었다.

105 Semi 씨는 Greensburg 사무소로부터 정보가 온 직후 그 자료들을 수정할 것이다.

106 전문가들의 도움 없이는 주식 거래가 힘들지만 우리의 새로운 온라인 시스템은 그 일을 쉽게 할 수 있다.

107 Berni 씨의 제안을 실행하는 것은 모두가 예상한 것보다 더 복잡했다.

108 주의 교육부는 다양한 현장 미술 워크숍들을 발표할 것이다.

109 우리는 8월 5일 금요일에 Apple Grand Ballroom의 시상식에서 당신의 업적을 축하하고 싶습니다.

110 James 씨가 마침내 최고경영자 자리에 오르게 된 본사에서 직원들을 기쁘게 하면서 판매 수치는 급성장했다.

111 이 쿠폰을 가지고 있으시면 몇몇의 특별한 장비를 할인된 가격으로 이용 가능할 것입니다.

112 회사 사장은 Jasmin 씨에게 O'Reilly 씨를 대신하여 계약 협상건들을 처리하라고 요구하였다.

113 자문위원은 우리 회사에서 신입 사원들을 위한 상세한 업무 편람을 만들어야 한다고 권유했다.

114 우리 환자들을 가능한 한 효율적이고 확실하게 모시기 위하여 저희는 예약 알림을 제공하고 있습니다.

115 인사과 직원 한 명이 취업 패키지에 관하여 신입 직원들이 무엇을 알아야 하는지 설명했다.

116 LEMI 그룹의 노력 덕분에 Kovalchick Center의 방문자 수가 두 배가 되었습니다.

117 모든 부서들은 새로운 시스템을 따르기 위해 매달 두 번째 월요일까지 Harbour 씨에게 자신들의 주문건을 제출해야 합니다.

118 TP Distribution의 부산 지점들의 폐점은 여러모로 생산과 효율성의 손실을 초래할 수 있다.

119 다음 주 금요일부터 시 정부는 건물 재건축의 규모를 제한하는 안전 규정을 집행할 것이다.

120 전 직원들은 정상 근무 시간 이후 건물 안에 있어야 할 때마다 그들의 직속 상관에게 허가를 받아야 한다.

121 Autobahn Motors에서 생산된 각 차량은 지역 판매점들에 보내지기 전에 여러 검사들을 거칩니다.

122 여러분은 내일 근무 시간이 끝날 때까지 일하거나 원래 예정된 대로 오후 5시에 일을 마치시면 됩니다.

123 물건 반품은 오직 구매 15일 이내에 승인된다는 것을 알아 두세요.

124 당신의 주문품을 포함한 소포가 일단 발송되면 귀하에게 도착하는 데 대략 2-3일 걸릴 것입니다.

125 우리의 봉급률은 관련 분야에서 직원들의 이전 경력에 따라 다르게 계산됩니다.

126 비록 거주자들은 도시의 경제를 활성화하는 계획에 일반적으로 동의하지만, 일부 사람들은 지역의 상업적인 개발을 반대하고 있다.

127 이 통행권으로 여러분은 반값으로 전시회들에 참석할 수 있을 뿐 아니라, 무료로 우리 워크숍에 참여할 수 있습니다.

128 우리의 아시아와 아프리카 시장은 회사의 지점들이 그 대륙들에 진출한 이래로 상당히 우세해지고 있다.

129 한 달이 지나도 수령 되지 않은 소포들은 저장 시설에 공간이 있는 곳은 어디든 보관되어야 한다.

130 당신에게 과다 청구된 200달러의 금액은 당신 계좌로 자동으로 입금되었습니다.

Part 6

Questions 131-134 refer to the following memo.

수신: 부서 관리자들
발신: 선임 디자이너, Kamil Graphic
제목: Tech Today Magazine 논평

최근 <Tech Today Magazine>의 논평은 우리 최신 노트북 컴퓨터들을 매우 칭찬했습니다. 특히 디자인과 성능이 대부분의 우리 경쟁사들과 구분되어 언급되었습니다.

그러나 그 논평이 완전히 긍정적인 것은 아니었습니다. 소비자 보고를 통해 제기된 내구성에 관한 문제는 여전히 남겨져 있습니다.

우리 연구는 내부 발열 시스템 때문에 플라스틱으로 만들어진 일부 부품들이 너무 취약하다고 밝혔습니다. 이것은 PC 본체 내부의 다른 구성요소들에 몇 가지 문제점들을 초래할 수 있습니다.

이 문제에 대하여 저는 두 가지 해결책을 권장하는 바입니다. 우선, 우리는 손상된 컴퓨터들을 무료로 수리해 줄 필요가 있습니다. 두 번째로, 다음 제품들에는 보다 내구성 있는 재료들을 사용해야 합니다.

저는 수요일까지 이것에 대한 당신의 평을 듣고 싶습니다.

134 (A) 저는 수요일까지 이것에 대한 당신의 평을 듣고 싶습니다.
(B) 출판사는 당신에게 곧 편집자의 연락처를 줄 것입니다.
(C) 모든 관리자들은 시스템을 업데이트할지 고려 중입니다.
(D) 새로운 정보를 얻으려면 우리에게 편하게 연락해 주세요.

Questions 135-138 refer to the following announcement.

우리 사무실들의 모든 컴퓨터들이 오늘 오후 필수 보안 소프트웨어 프로그램의 업데이트에 관한 알림 메시지를 받게 될 것입니다.

이 업데이트들은 오후 5시에 자동으로 시작될 것입니다. 컴퓨터의 속도가 평소보다 느리다는 것을 알게 되겠지만 설치 파일들이 설치되는 동안 여러분의 컴퓨터를 계속 사용하실 수 있습니다. 이 보안 업데이트가 준비된 이후 여러분은 컴퓨터를 재시작해야 합니다. 그러나 긴급한 업무가 있다면 업데이트를 할 시간이 있을 때까지 설치를 연기하실 수 있습니다. 저희는 이 일로 인해 방해와 불편을 드려 진심으로 사과를 드리는 바이고, 이해해 주셔서 감사 드립니다.

135 (A) 그러한 업데이트들은 다른 모바일 장치들과 연동됩니다.
(B) 그 질문들에 관해 저희에게 주저하지 말고 연락주세요.
(C) 이 업데이트들은 오후 5시에 자동으로 시작될 것입니다.
(D) 컴퓨터들의 최신 모델은 대중들에게 매우 인기가 있습니다.

Questions 139-142 refer to the following e-mail.

수신: <j_wick@gammamail.com>
발신: <customer@giantshopping.com>
제목: TFY 회원들을 위한 Coms 할인
날짜: 6월 20일

Wick 씨에게,

우리는 Coms에서 가장 인기 있는 여러 가지 컴퓨터와 액세서리의 가격을 인하하고 있음을 알려 드리려고 합니다. 게다가 Coms는 TFY 회원들이 한정 기간 내에 특별 프로모션 프로그램을 독점적으로 이용할 수 있게 해 드리고 있습니다. 귀하의 비회원들은 이용할 수 없는 특별 할인을 발견할 것입니다. Coms 데스크탑 컴퓨터, 노트북 컴퓨터, 태블릿과 같은 제품들을 최고 35%까지 할인 받으실 수 있습니다. 게다가 이 할인을 이용하는 고객분들은 연장된 보증 서비스와 기술 서비스를 받으실 수 있습니다. TFY 회원들이 구매하신 제품들이 다른 가게에서 더 낮은 가격에 판매되고 있다면 그 차액을 보상 받을 것입니다.

우리 회원들을 위한 특별 제안을 보시려면 여기를 클릭하세요.

140 (A) 물품들은 개인 용도로 구매하거나 선물로 보낼 수 있습니다.
(B) 귀하는 비회원들은 이용할 수 없는 특별 할인을 발견할 것입니다.
(C) 7월 25일 마감일 전에 조치가 취해져야 합니다.
(D) TFY 회원들이 최고의 고객 서비스를 받는다고 보고합니다.

Questions 143-146 refer to the following memo.

수신: Prudent Insurance 사 전 직원
발신: Kathy Stella, 최고 경영자, Prudent Insurance 사
제목: 인수합병 건
날짜: 8월 20일

저는 모든 직원분들께 Prudent Insurance와 Standard Bank 간의 합병이 8월 30일에 성사된다는 것을 알려 드리게 되어 기쁩니다. 그날 이후로, 회사의 이름은 Prudent Bancassurance Group이 될 것입니다. 이 합병은 우리가 유럽에서 상업 은행과 보험 회사 중에 가장 규모가 큰 제공 업체로 성장할 수 있게 할 것입니다.

근무 상황은 걱정하지 마세요! 현재 고용 계약에 기반하여, 여러분의 직책, 복지 혜택과 임금은 변화 없이 유지될 것입니다. 일부 개정이 필요할 경우에 대비하여 여러분의 문서를 철저히 살펴보세요.

합병으로 회사 규정 일부분이 변경될 것입니다. 이것들은 9월 2일 오후 2시 대강당에서 공식적인 회사 전체 회의 동안 공유될 것입니다. 합병에 관하여 문의가 있으시면 그곳으로 질문하러 편하게 오세요.

145 (A) 수정된 규정들은 Prudent 사와 Standard 사 사이에 협상 중일 것입니다.
(B) 우리 회사는 많은 부서에 더 많은 경력직 직원들이 필요합니다.
(C) 세 장의 추천서와 함께 공식 문서를 작성해 주세요.
(D) 일부 개정이 필요할 경우에 대비하여 여러분의 문서를 철저히 살펴보세요.

Part 7

Questions 147-148 refer to the following memo.

사무실 메시지

수신 : Chris Butterfield
발신 : Robert Dawson
시간 : 화요일, 오전 11시 25분

전화   직접 방문

메시지 :

Maria Hill 고객님이 와서, 인테리어 장식 프로젝트에 관하여 당신이 작업할 수 있는지 물었습니다. 듣자 하니, 그녀는 몇 가지 작업을 끝내야 하는 친구가 있습니다. 그녀는 저에게 그 공간의 사진을 보여 주었는데, 꽤나 큰 작업인 것처럼 보였습니다. 그녀는 가능한 한 빨리 연락을 달라고 요청했습니다.

서명 : *Robert Dawson*

147 Hill 씨가 왜 Butterfield 씨를 방문한 것 같은가?
(A) 잠재 고객의 일을 부탁하기 위해
(B) 프로젝트에 대해 그에게 감사를 전하기 위해
(C) 회의 일정을 확인하기 위해
(D) 일부 작업의 사진들을 요청하기 위해

148 Butterfield 씨는 메시지를 받은 후에 무엇을 할 것 같은가?
(A) 프로젝트를 시작한다
(B) 친구를 방문한다
(C) 전화를 한다
(D) 사진을 찍는다

Questions 149-150 refer to the following text-message chain.

Claire Barnes [오후 1시 27분]	안녕, 마이크! 나에게 이야기했던 금요일 포럼에 필요한 참고 도서를 아직도 찾고 있니? 지금 내가 도서관에 있어서 너를 도와주려고 하는데.
Mike Peterson [오후 1시 29분]	좋아! 그 책의 이름은 Dwinsky가 쓴 <영어의 기원과 역사>라는 책이야. 도서관 온라인 페이지에서 찾아봤을 때, 지금 대출 가능하다고 나왔어.
Claire Barnes [오후 1시 31분]	알겠어, 확인해 보고 찾아볼게.

Claire Barnes [오후 1시 38분]	찾았어! 내 이름으로 이 책을 대여할 수 있어. 하지만 3월 20일 전까지 반납해야 해. 그렇지 않으면 내가 연체료를 물어야 하거든.
Mike Peterson [오후 1시 40분]	그렇게 할게. 정말 고마워.

149 <영어의 기원과 역사>에 관하여 사실일 것 같은 것은 무엇인가?
(A) 도서관에서 찾기 어렵다.
(B) 교수에 의해 쓰여졌다.
(C) 포럼에서 언급될 것이다.
(D) 출판사에서 개정을 했다.

150 오후 1시 40분에, Peterson 씨가 "그렇게 할게"라고 쓴 의도는 무엇인가?
(A) 그는 혼자 책을 대여할 것이다.
(B) 그는 웹 사이트에서 그 책을 예약할 것이다.
(C) 그는 그 책을 도서관으로부터 직접 받을 것이다.
(D) 그는 제시간에 그 책을 반납할 것이다.

Questions 151-152 refer to the following receipt.

FACTORY's Supplies
Fleming Avenue 120번지
콜럼버스, 오하이오

품목 설명	금액
전기 드릴	40.00달러
	소계: 40.00달러
	쿠폰 할인: 15%
	세금: 2.15달러
	총합: 36.15달러

용도에 맞는 최상의 장비와 도구를 찾을 수 있는 FACTORY's에서 구매해 주셔서 감사합니다.
환불은 구매 후 2주 이내에만 승인됨을 알아 주세요. 당신이 구매하신 제품은 영수증 원본과 함께 포장되어야 함을 명심하세요.
저희는 조만간 다시 당신을 뵙기를 희망합니다!

수령일: 11월 20일

151 구매에 관하여 알 수 있는 것은?
(A) 구매된 물품은 절반 가격이다.
(B) 매장 쿠폰이 적용되었다.
(C) 구매자는 총 40달러를 지불하였다.
(D) 고객은 세금이 면제되었다.

152 FACTORY's Supplies에 대하여 추론할 수 있는 것은 무엇인가?
(A) 다양한 지역 지점들을 운영한다.
(B) 11월에 몇 개의 물품들만 할인했다.
(C) 구매자에게 청구 할인 프로그램을 제공한다.
(D) 구매 후 14일이 지나면 반품을 승인하지 않는다.

Questions 153-154 refer to the following advertisement.

Divine Memories Event Hall
6749 Winchester Rd, Memphis, TN 38115
전화: 901-244-6388   이메일: reservations@divinememories.net

9월 1일은 Memphis의 Winchester Road에 있는 Divine Memories Event Hall의 대규모 개점일이며, 우리는 일주일 내내 지역 회사들에게 방과 홀을 무료로 개방하여 기념할 것입니다. 무료 대여는 그 주 최대 4시간이며 선착순으로 진행됩니다.

우리의 모든 방들은 책상, 의자, 에어컨, 그리고 최신 시청각 장비를 구비하고 있습니다. 방의 크기나 경쟁력 있는 시간당 요금을 보시려면 저희 웹 사이트 www.divinememories.net을 확인해 보세요. 또한 저희만의 MV User Program을 소지하신 귀중한 고객분들이 이용할 수 있는 할인에 관한 정보도 찾아보실 수 있습니다.

개점까지 일주일 정도 남았지만 저희는 많은 관심을 기대하고 있습니다. 이 특별 제안을 이용하는 데 관심이 있으신 회사나 개인들은 미리 방을 예약하셔야 합니다. 예약은 온라인 또는 저희 유능한 직원들을 통해 하실 수 있고, 그들은 여러분이 가지고 있는 어떤 질문이든 도움을 드릴 수 있을 것입니다.

153 광고의 목적은 무엇인가?
(A) 새로운 회사를 위한 직원들을 구하기 위해
(B) 행사에 관한 정보를 확인하기 위해
(C) 사용자들에게 정책 변경을 알리기 위해
(D) 특별 혜택을 알리기 위해

154 Divine Memories Event Hall에 관하여 알 수 있는 것은?
(A) 이미 운영을 하고 있다.
(B) 이용 가능한 가장 큰 방들이 있다.
(C) 박식한 직원들을 보유하고 있다.
(D) 발표 장비 사용에 추가 비용을 부과한다.

Questions 155-157 refer to the following notice.

공지

수신: White Tower Square의 전 주민들

이것은 6월 20일 저녁 8시에 아파트 정문 옆 Ski-Hut Lodge에서 예정된 우리 세입자들을 위한 회의에 대한 알림입니다. 우리는 마당과 살수에 대한 지침과 관련된 문제를 논의하고자 합니다. 더 자세히 말하자면, 우리는 곧 있을 회의에서 현재 외주 업체인 TRES Cleaning & Landscaping 사와 계약을 갱신할지 말지 투표할 것입니다.

현재 안건에 생활 조건 개선에 대한 문제만 있으므로 6월 12일까지 www.whitetowersquare.net으로 Danny 씨에게 여러분의 의견이나 주제를 보내 주세요.

우리 단지에 살고 있는 어떤 사람이든 환영하고, 그곳에서 간단한 음식들을 제공할 것입니다.

관리 사무소
White Tower Square

155 이 공지문의 목적은 무엇인가?
(A) 새로운 규정을 설명하기 위해
(B) 세입자들에게 곧 있을 회의에 관하여 알리기 위해
(C) 새로운 아파트의 개관을 언급하기 위해
(D) 설문 조사의 결과를 발표하기 위해

156 6월 12일에 끝내야 하는 일은 무엇인가?
(A) 아파트로 이사하기
(B) 문제에 관해 투표하기
(C) 토론 주제들을 제안하기
(D) 회의에 참석하기

157 TRES Cleaning & Landscaping 사에 대하여 암시되는 것은?
(A) White Tower Square의 부동산을 소유했다.
(B) 그곳의 직원들은 회의에 참석할 것이다.
(C) 주택 청소 서비스만 제공한다.
(D) White Tower의 일부 주민들은 서비스에 만족하지 않을 수도 있다.

Questions 158-160 refer to the following invitation.

학문적 업적을 축하하여
Cam Union 대학은 표창합니다.
Canale Swain 박사

우리는 Swain 박사의 은퇴를 축하하기 위해 귀하를 초대하고자 합니다. 그는 지난 30여년 동안 제 2언어 작문의 교육 분야에 헌신해 왔습니다. 그의 마지막 강의 바로 후인 3월 17일 금요일 오후 6시 30분에 이 퇴임식에 참석해 주세요. 식사가 포함된 이 행사는 Rosewick 가의 인문 대학 건물 안에 있는 Léonard Hall에서 열릴 것입니다. 무료 주차는 현장에서 가능합니다.

여러분 재량껏 Swain 박사를 놀라게 할 선물을 가져오셔도 됩니다. 또한 모든 선물은 Swain 박사가 기여해 온 자선 단체인 State Literacy Foundation에 기부의 형태로 전달될 것을 알아 두세요.

---

158 Swain 씨는 누구일 것 같은가?
(A) 내과 의사
(B) 대학 교수
(C) 자선 단체 회장
(D) 정부 관리

159 초대 받은 사람들은 무엇을 하라고 요구 받는가?
(A) 그 행사를 비밀로 한다
(B) Swain 씨를 위해 선물을 가지고 온다
(C) 특별한 카드에 서명한다
(D) 각자의 음식을 가지고 온다

160 [1], [2], [3] 그리고 [4]로 표시된 곳 중에 다음 문장이 들어가기에 가장 적합한 위치는 어디인가?
"무료 주차는 현장에서 가능합니다."
(A) [1]
(B) [2]
(C) [3]
(D) [4]

Questions 161-163 refer to the following article.

Cal State 저널

캘리포니아, 4월 10일 — NMD Developments 사의 사장 Jerome Harts 씨는 회사가 주에서 가장 큰 쇼핑센터가 될 L.A. Giant Mall을 건설하는 일에 선정되었음을 발표했다. L.A. Giant Mall은 실내 운동 시설과 워터파크뿐만 아니라 600개 이상의 매장과 가게를 수용할 것이다.

NMD 사가 대형 쇼핑센터를 짓는 것은 처음이지만 그들은 이전에 샌프란시스코에서 NFL 축구 경기장과 다양한 고층 건물들과 같은 유사한 규모의 건물을 건설했다. 공사는 5월 20일에 시작할 예정이고, 쇼핑 단지와 테마파크는 이변이 없는 한 내년 가을에 대중에게 개관될 것이다.

NMD Developments 사는 매출이 10억 달러를 기록했고, 많은 회사와 정부 부처들과의 제휴를 통해 작년에 최고의 한 해를 보냈다. 빠른 성장 때문에 회사는 최근 그들의 업적과 캘리포니아 곳곳에 있는 신규 지점들의 개관을 축하하기 위해 많은 사람들을 초대했다. 새로운 샌디에고 지점에 있는 동안, Harts 씨는 무대에서 직원들에게 "운이 좋게도, 저희는 여러분들 덕에 승승장구하고 있습니다"라고 말했다. "이번 L.A. Giant Mall 입찰을 따내면서 우리는 국내 정상급 회사들 중 하나가 될 기회를 갖게 되었고, 건축 분야에서 우리의 입지를 견고히 할 수 있게 되었습니다."라고 덧붙였다.

L.A. Giant Mall을 건설한다는 NMD 사의 계약 소식은 회사의 주가 상승에 강력하면서도 긍정적인 영향을 미칠 것이다. 몇몇 전문가들은 다음 달까지 거의 35퍼센트가 증가할 수 있다고 예상했다. 이 프로젝트와 함께 회사는 국내 다른 주들로 사업을 확장하기 위한 초석을 마련할 수 있게 되었다.

---

161 기사문은 주로 무엇을 이야기하고 있는가?
(A) 두 건설사의 합병
(B) 사무실 이전
(C) 사업 계약 체결
(D) 쇼핑센터의 개관 행사

162 L.A. Giant Mall에 관해서 사실인 것은 무엇인가?
(A) 4월 30일에 공사가 끝날 것이다.
(B) 이번 여름에 영업할 것이다.
(C) 축구 경기장이 포함될 것이다.
(D) 캘리포니아에서 가장 큰 쇼핑센터가 될 것이다.

163 두 번째 문단, 여섯 번째 줄의 단어 "set"과 의미상 가장 가까운 것은?
(A) 설립된
(B) 설치된
(C) 예정된
(D) 조립된

Questions 164-167 refer to the following information.

Cox Net 사는 여러분이 필요한 모든 전산 장비로 소규모 회사를 도와드립니다. Cox Net 사는 지난 10여년 이상 운영되었고, 전산에 대한 도움이 필요할 때마다 Oregon 주의 많은 회사들이 선택했습니다. 저희는 양질의 서비스를 제공하고, 여러분의 회사가 고객들과 직원들을 위해 사업을 계속 원활하고 효율적으로 운영할 수 있도록 도움을 드립니다. 저희 회사는 다음을 포함하여 여러 방면으로 여러분의 회사를 도와 드릴 수 있습니다:

● 바이러스를 감지하는 최신 보안 소프트웨어 업데이트 또는 설치
● 최상의 인터넷 네트워킹 스테이션 설치
● 무료 기술 서비스에 대한 2년 보증서 제공
● 데스크톱과 노트북 컴퓨터 설치
● 장비가 완벽한 상태로 계속 작동되도록 관리

저희 회사의 세부적인 서비스들에 대하여 알고 싶으시면 망설이지 말고 461-1893-1782로 연락 주시고, 인증된 기술자들과 이야기 나눠 보세요. 저희는 전화나 웹상의 라이브 채팅을 통해 여러분의 문제를 해결하는 데 도움을 드릴 수 있어 기쁘며, 심지어 저희 전문가와 충분한 상담을 하도록 예약도 해 드리고 있습니다. 저희는 월요일부터 금요일까지는 오전 6시부터 저녁 8시, 토요일에는 오전 9시부터 오후 5시까지는 온라인과 오프라인 지원, 일요일에는 웹상에서만 오전 10시부터 오후 4시까지 이용하실 수 있습니다.

---

164 어떤 사업 분야가 광고되고 있는가?
(A) 전기 공학
(B) 에너지 보존

309

(C) 재무 컨설팅
(D) 정보 기술

165 Cox Net 사에 대해 암시되는 것은 무엇인가?
(A) 전국에 여러 상점을 가지고 있다.
(B) 설립된 지 10년이 넘었다.
(C) 현재 신입 직원들을 채용하고 있다.
(D) 신제품 라인을 막 출시했다.

166 정보에 따르면, 제공되지 않는 서비스는 무엇인가?
(A) 전자기기의 설치
(B) 업데이트된 보안 프로그램
(C) 전문가와의 상담
(D) 원격 지원 시스템

167 Cox Net 사가 전화 상담 서비스를 제공하지 않는 요일은?
(A) 일요일
(B) 월요일
(C) 금요일
(D) 토요일

Questions 168-171 refer to the following online chat discussion.

George McGuire [오후 5시 10분]
자, 여러분들 오늘은 어떤가요?

Jamie Chang [오후 5시 11분]
정말 좋아요. Tommy가 세 대의 세단을 판매했어요. Twain과 Matsuda는 각각 한 대씩이고요.

George McGuire [오후 5시 13분]
수요일 치고 나쁘지 않네요. 고객들 중에 차를 구매하려고 대출하실 분 있나요?

Jamie Chang [오후 5시 15분]
네, 모두요. 한 분은 연장된 보증도 구매하셨어요. Tommy가 오일 교환권 두 개를 포함했어요.

George McGuire [오후 5시 17분]
좋아요. 정비 부분은 어떤가요?

Kyrie Erving [오후 5시 20분]
저희는 오늘 6만 5천 달러 상당의 작업을 했어요. 대부분의 정비는 사전에 예약되었어요. 그런데 몇몇 다른 분들은 예약 없이 갑자기 오셨어요.

Jamie Chang [오후 5시 21분]
오! 기술자들이 처리하느라 엄청 바빴겠어요.

Kyrie Erving [오후 5시 24분]
제가 휴무인 직원에게 연락해서 좀 와서 도와달라고 해야 했어요.

George McGuire [오후 5시 26분]
저희는 내일 오후에 판매 구역으로 10대의 신형 세단과 20대의 신형 SUV를 입고시켜야 해요.

Kyrie Erving [오후 5시 30분]
제 직원 중 세 명에게 정비 구역에서 돌아오자마자 그것들을 검사하라고 요청할게요. 저희는 그날까지 주차장에서 차들을 빼놔야 해요. 어디에 그 차들을 둘까요?

George McGuire [오후 5시 32분]
사람들이 39번 Indi 고속도로를 운전하는 동안 그 차들을 잘 볼 수 있도록 우리 정문 바로 뒤의 첫 구역에 두었으면 해요. 지금은 이게 다예요. 퇴근합시다!

Jamie Chang [오후 5시 33분]
좋아요.

---

168 필자들은 어디에서 일하는 것 같은가?
(A) 택시 회사에서
(B) 자동차 대리점에서
(C) 주차장에서
(D) 은행에서

169 Erving 씨에 대해 암시되는 것은?
(A) 그는 새 차를 구매했다.
(B) 그는 오늘 일할 예정이 아니었다.
(C) 그는 정비공들을 감독한다.
(D) 그는 돈을 많이 썼다.

170 필자들이 일하는 곳에 관해 언급된 것은 무엇인가?
(A) 고속도로 근처에 있다.
(B) 월요일에는 보통 문을 닫는다.
(C) 수십 명의 직원이 있다.
(D) 내일 일찍 문을 열 것이다.

171 오후 5시 32분에 McGuire가 "퇴근합시다"라고 쓴 의도는 무엇인가?
(A) 그는 몇 가지 일을 더 마쳐야 한다.
(B) 그는 집에 갈 시간이라고 생각한다.
(C) 그는 자기 직원들이 한 일을 고마워한다.
(D) 그는 오늘 영업 실적에 매우 만족한다.

Questions 172-175 refer to the following e-mail.

수신: editor@albanytoday.com
발신: gloria_h@honorsociety.org
날짜: 12월 20일
제목: White Golden 상

편집자님께,

저는 12월 19일자 <Albany Today> 신문에서 Ronald Jackson 씨의 인터뷰 부분에 우려되는 점이 있어 이 이메일을 씁니다. 지난밤 시상식에 관한 그의 연설에서 몇 가지 실수들이 대중들을 혼란스럽게 할 수 있어서 저희는 그 실수들을 바로잡고 싶습니다. Jackson 씨는 그 행사를 "도시의 발전을 위한 프로젝트에 재정적으로 기여한 기관들을 축하하여"라고 설명하였습니다. 게다가 그는 우리의 비영리 기관인 Honor Society(HS)를 수상자로 언급했습니다. 그의 설명은 그 상이 주어진 이유에 대해 명확하게 드러내지 않았습니다. 기사문에 따르면, 우리가 원래 목표에 관련되지 않은 프로젝트들을 위해 기금을 모으는 것 같았습니다.

White Golden 상은 Honor Society에 주어지는 것이 아니라, 휴식 시간을 활용하여 도시 공동 구역을 청소했던 HS 직원들로 구성된 작은 지역 단체에게 주어진 것일 뿐입니다. 비록 Honor Society는 가끔 직원들에게 그런 일을 하도록 요구하지만 이번 사례는 우리 기관에 의해서 실행된 것이 아닙니다.

우리의 관대한 기부자들은 우리가 재정적으로 도움을 받거나 이러한 상들을 받으려는 의도가 없다는 사실을 아셔야 합니다. Jackson 씨의 인터뷰 대본에 명확한 정보를 추가해 주시겠어요? 그리고 저는 이 일을 가능한 한 빨리 처리해 주시길 요구합니다. 즉각적인 조치는 지역 라디오나 텔레비전 방송국에 소개되기 전에 행사에 관한 추가 혼란을 막을 수 있을 것입니다.

Gloria Han
미디어 홍보 관리자
Honor Society

172 이 이메일의 목적은 무엇인가?
(A) 상을 거절하기 위해
(B) 행사에 언론을 초대하기 위해
(C) 해명을 요구하기 위해
(D) 추가 근무를 한 직원들에게 감사하기 위해

173 일부 Honor Society 직원들은 무엇 때문에 인정 받았는가?
(A) 기금 조성의 결과물
(B) 자원 봉사
(C) 훌륭한 발표
(D) 향상된 성과

174 Jackson 씨에 대하여 암시되는 것은?
(A) 그는 이 이슈에 대해 Han 씨와 충분히 논의했다.
(B) 그는 실수로 누군가를 수상자로 지명했다.
(C) 그는 부정확한 정보를 가지고 연설을 했다.
(D) 그는 자선 단체에서 일을 해오고 있다.

175 [1], [2], [3] 그리고 [4]로 표시된 곳 중에 다음 문장이 들어가기에 가장 적합한 위치는 어디인가?

"그리고 저는 이 일을 가능한 한 빨리 처리해 주시길 요구합니다."

(A) [1]
(B) [2]
(C) [3]
(D) [4]

Questions 176-180 refer to the following schedule and article.

Davenport Novel Society 홈페이지 방문에 감사드립니다

저희와 Davenport Novel Society의 45주년 기념일을 축하해 주세요!
소설을 위한 학술자 포럼의 밤 (7월-8월)
Plazma 강당, 아이오와 대학교

6월 15일에 갱신됨

소설	날짜
<The Kite Runner>	7월 5일 금요일
<Cleaning Out the Closet>	7월 6일 토요일
<Faculty Room>	7월 10일 수요일
<The Shadow of America>	7월 12일 금요일
<Norwegian Forest>	7월 19일 금요일
<Beyond Atlantis>	8월 2일 금요일
<The Secret Life of Butterflies> (20석만 이용 가능)	8월 3일 토요일
<No Name Asian>	8월 7일 수요일
<For Banana Fish>	8월 9일 금요일
<The Others> (30석만 이용 가능)	8월 16일 금요일

다른 지시가 없다면 강당의 수용력 때문에 각 강의당 50석만 이용 가능합니다. 월간 회원권과 1회 참석권은 우리 웹 사이트 또는 강당 안내 데스크에서 구매할 수 있습니다. 월간 회원권 요금은 20달러이고, 1회 참석권은 5달러입니다. 월간 회원권은 늦어도 7월 2일까지 구매해야 합니다.

입장권을 구매하려면 **여기를 클릭**해 주세요.

<The Iowa Times>   *문화 부문*

Davenport Novel Society의 45주년 기념일 일정이 변경되었습니다

6월 20일—아이오와 주의 소설 애호가들은 Davenport Novel Society (DNS)의 45주년 기념 특별 포럼에 참석하길 기대하고 있습니다. 그러나 지난 20여년 동안 DNS의 학술자 포럼이 개최되었던 Plazma 강당이 7월과 8월 동안 재건축을 위해 일시적으로 문을 닫을 것입니다. 이것은 그 기관이 진행자를 변경해야 할 뿐만 아니라 대체 장소와 일정도 찾아야 한다는 것을 의미합니다. 소설 학회장은 변경 사항들이 다음과 같다고 이야기했습니다:

- <Cleaning Out the Closet>은 7월 20일 토요일에 논의될 것입니다.
- <Norwegian Forest>은 7월 17일 수요일에 논의될 것입니다.
- <No Name Asian>은 8월 8일 목요일에 논의될 것입니다.
- <For Banana Fish>와 이에 대한 포럼은 Charlotte Rivera에 의해 진행될 것입니다.

* 각 강의의 수용 인원은 변경되지 않을 것입니다.

포럼에서 여러분을 뵙겠습니다!

176 Davenport Novel Society에 대해서 알 수 있는 것은?
(A) 설립을 축하하고 있다.
(B) 최근에 회원 수를 감축하였다.
(C) 직책에 대한 지원서를 받고 있다.
(D) 전 세계에 널리 알려져 있다.

177 일정에 따르면, 월간 회원권에 관하여 사실인 것은?
(A) 1인당 5달러이다.
(B) 지역 자선 단체에 수익이 기부될 것이다.
(C) 웹 사이트를 통해 얻을 수 있다.
(D) 6월 15일까지 구매가 가능하다.

178 Plazma 강당에 대하여 암시되는 것은?
(A) 45년 전에 건설되었다.
(B) Davenport로 이전되었다.
(C) 건물 수리가 시작될 것이다.
(D) 최근 확장되었다.

179 원래 예정된 날짜보다 더 일찍 논의될 소설은 무엇인가?
(A) Cleaning Out the Closet
(B) Norwegian Forest
(C) No Name Asian
(D) For Banana Fish

180 Rivera 씨가 진행하는 포럼은 얼마나 많은 사람들이 참석하도록 허용될 것인가?
(A) 20명
(B) 30명
(C) 50명
(D) 80명

Questions 181-185 refer to the following e-mail and survey.

수신: Sam Bryant <s_bryant@gsu.edu>
발신: Anna Theron <a_theron@hallnet.com>
날짜: 3월 10일
제목: 겨울 인턴십 프로그램
첨부: Program_Survey_Form.pdf

Bryant 씨에게,

Niagara 지점의 Ontario Tourism Board에서 올해 우리 겨울 인턴십

프로그램에 참여해 주신 것에 감사 드립니다. 저희는 당신의 기여에 매우 감사 드리며 이것이 당신의 경력에 도움이 되었다고 생각하셨기를 바랍니다.

다가오는 시즌을 위한 우리 프로그램을 개선하기 위해 저희에게 당신의 피드백을 주셨으면 합니다. 이 이메일에 첨부된 파일을 다운로드 받으셔서 양식을 작성하고 이 이메일 주소로 보내주세요. 작성된 설문 조사들은 저희가 앞으로의 참가자들을 위해 이 첫 프로그램을 개선하는 데 도움을 줄 것이고, 당신과 함께 일한 부서 관리자에게 보내질 것입니다. 마케팅에서 일한 사람들은 Christian Paul에게 전달될 것입니다. 커뮤니케이션 서비스에서 일한 사람들은 Dixie Lynn에게 보내질 것입니다.

저희는 다음 여름 프로그램을 위한 기획 과정을 이미 시작했기 때문에 모든 설문 조사지를 3월 30일까지 수령했으면 합니다. 문의가 있으면 634-284-9123으로 편하게 연락 주시거나 planning@hallnet.com으로 이메일을 보내 주세요. 제가 근무 중이 아니라면 그 프로그램에 대하여 잘 알고 있는 제 부하 직원 Jerry Minnette와 이야기하셔도 됩니다.

당신의 헌신에 다시 한번 감사 드립니다.

진심으로,

Anna Theron
프로그램 담당자, Hallnet 사

인턴십 프로그램에 관한 설문 조사

이름: Sam Bryant
기간: 1월 5일 ~ 2월 20일
부서: 번역 서비스

오리엔테이션을 위한 모임이 유익하고 도움이 되었다.	예 [ ]	아니오 [X]	무응답 [ ]
내 업무가 흥미롭고 만족스러웠다.	예 [X]	아니오 [ ]	무응답 [ ]
나의 관리자로부터 즉각적인 피드백을 받았다.	예 [X]	아니오 [ ]	무응답 [ ]
나의 업무량에 만족했다.	예 [X]	아니오 [ ]	무응답 [ ]
다시 한번 그 프로그램에 참여하기를 고려한다.	예 [X]	아니오 [ ]	무응답 [ ]

개선을 위한 추가 코멘트

저는 Ontario 주립 대학에서 언어학을 전공하고 있고, 많은 외국인 관광객들과 만나고 이야기함으로써 저의 언어 능력도를 연습하는 것에 항상 흥미가 있습니다. 저는 이 경험이 매우 유익하고 제 경력을 발전시키게 했다고 확신합니다. 개선을 위해 제가 드리는 유일한 제안 하나는 오리엔테이션 모임 시간을 연장하는 것입니다. 그 강의는 시간의 압박 때문에 매우 정신없고 혼란스러웠습니다. 관리자들과 질의 응답 시간이 더 있었다면, 저희가 직무 설명과 귀사의 근무 환경을 이해하는 데 매우 도움이 되었을 것 같습니다.

181 이메일의 목적은 무엇인가?
(A) 신입 직원 채용 여부에 관해 묻기 위해
(B) 추천서를 받기 위해
(C) 프로그램에 지원하기 위해
(D) 정보를 요청하기 위해

182 인턴십 프로그램에 대하여 암시되는 것은?
(A) 새롭게 소개되었다.
(B) 학사 학위를 요구했다.
(C) 일회성 행사였다.
(D) 주 정부에 의해 운영되었다.

183 양식은 언제까지 돌려 보내져야 하는가?
(A) 1월 5일
(B) 2월 20일
(C) 3월 10일
(D) 3월 30일

184 Bryant 씨는 프로그램에 대해 누구에게 보고했을 것 같은가?
(A) Anna Theron
(B) Christian Paul
(C) Dixie Lynn
(D) Jerry Minnette

185 Bryant 씨에 대하여 알 수 있는 것은?
(A) 그는 현재 학생이다.
(B) 그는 일자리 제안을 수락할 수 있다.
(C) 그는 여행을 계획하고 있다.
(D) 그는 Niagara로 이동 중이다.

Questions 186-190 refer to the following notice, e-mail, and bill.

Kevin Lopez 박사의 사무실
6565 Fannin St, Houston, TX 77030, USA
+1 715-274-1284
kl_office@houstonmedic.com

Sharon Monica 씨에게,

저희의 우선 순위는 귀하의 건강을 유지하는 것입니다. 이것이 귀하에게 예약에 대해 다시 알려드리는 이유입니다.

6월 10일 목요일 오전 10시

저희 병원에 처음 방문하신다면 환자 정보 양식과 지불 관련 양식 작성을 위해 의사 선생님과의 진료 예약 20분 전에 도착해 주세요.

귀하의 예약을 변경하거나 취소하는 데 도움이 필요하시면 취소 수수료가 발생하지 않도록 최소 36시간 전에 저희에게 연락 주세요.

곧 뵙기를 희망합니다!

발신: s_monica@xmail.com
수신: kl_office@houstonmedic.com
날짜: 6월 5일 오후 4시 20분
제목: 진료 예약

알림을 보내 주셔서 감사합니다. 저는 지난 몇 주 동안 해야 할 일들이 많아 매우 바빴기 때문에 제 예약을 거의 잊어버릴 뻔했습니다. 저는 정기 검진을 받는 것이 중요하다는 것을 충분히 알고 있습니다. 하지만 저는 이번 주말까지 끝내야 하는 일들이 여전히 남아 있습니다. 6월 15일 화요일로 제 예약을 변경할 수 있을까요? 시간은 언제든 상관없습니다. 저는 문서 작성을 위해 20분 미리 도착하겠습니다.

게다가 다른 전문의가 제가 추가적인 내시경 검사를 받을 수도 있다고 했습니다. 저에게 그게 얼마나 효과가 있을지 모르겠습니다. 저는 Lopez 박사님과 그 검사를 등록해야 할지에 관한 문제를 논의하고 싶습니다.

감사합니다.
Sharon Monica

환자용 청구서

Sharon Monica 3891 Charlton Boulevard Houston, TX 77030	Kevin Lopez 박사 6565 Fannin St. Houston, TX 77030

서비스 요약	
신체 검사	220.00달러
내시경	130.00달러
계정 요약	
계정 번호	3754901-12854912
서비스 일자	6월 15일
총 비용	350.00달러
지불 방법	보험 [제공자 : Newlife Health]

비고

보험 회사에 청구되는 모든 비용은 제공자에 의해 승인되어야 합니다.
제공자가 그 비용을 승인하지 않는다면, 환자가 전액 지불의 의무를 집니다.
서비스를 승인하기 전 당신의 보험 회사에 확인해 보세요.

186 공지에서 제공된 정보가 아닌 것은?
(A) 약속 시간
(B) 약속 장소
(C) 취소 기한
(D) 예약 요금

187 Monica 씨에 대하여 암시되는 것은?
(A) 그녀는 Lopez 박사의 사무실 근처에서 일한다.
(B) 그녀는 최신 치료제를 받고자 한다.
(C) 그녀는 Lopez 박사의 신규 환자이다.
(D) 그녀는 늦은 취소 수수료를 지불해야 할 필요가 있다.

188 Monica 씨는 왜 이 이메일을 작성하였는가?
(A) 그녀의 예약을 변경하기 위해서
(B) 추가 정보를 요청하기 위해서
(C) 환자 설문지를 제출하기 위해서
(D) 새로운 약속을 잡기 위해서

189 Monica 씨의 방문에 관하여 사실일 것 같은 것은 무엇인가?
(A) 그녀는 예약한 것보다 늦게 도착했다.
(B) 오후에 방문했다.
(C) 그녀가 선호하는 날짜에 방문했다.
(D) 그녀는 추가적인 검사가 필요 없었다.

190 고지서에서, 비고 부분의 세 번째 줄 단어 "authorizing"과 의미상 가장 유사한 것은?
(A) 혼란스러운
(B) 공제하는
(C) 거절하는
(D) 허가하는

Questions 191-195 refer to the following advertisement, e-mail, and letter.

Banka Asset을 여러분의 친구들과 가족들에게 추천하고, 함께 혜택을 받으세요!

저희를 신뢰해 주셔서 감사를 드리고자 합니다. 플래티넘 회원으로서 귀하는 저희의 완벽한 재정 설계와 상품들을 이용하실 수 있고, 최상의 요금을 받으실 수 있습니다.

귀하가 새로운 계정을 개설하는 각각의 친구와 가족들에게 저희를 추천하였기 때문에 당신에게 30달러를 드리고자 합니다. 저희는 또한 Banka Asset의 온라인 계정 또는 Banka 주식 거래 계정으로 300달러 이상을 초기 예금하시면 그들에게 20달러를 드릴 겁니다. 그들이 해야 할 모든 것은 www.bankaco.com으로 로그인해서 프로모션 코드 BAP2981을 사용하시는 것입니다.

*이 제안은 완납하신 플래티넘 회원들에게만 적용됩니다. 추천 받으신 지인들은 전적으로 신규 회원이어야 합니다. 이미 저희 Banka Group의 계정을 가지고 계신 기존 회원분들은 참여하실 수 없습니다.

수신: Lora Houston <l_houston@speednet.com>
발신: Jason Kid <j_kid@speednet.com>
제목: Banka Asset 서비스
날짜: 1월 10일

안녕, Lora.

네가 어제 점심 식사 때 은퇴 후 너의 재정 설계를 어떻게 시작할지에 관하여 이야기했던 것이 기억 났어. 음, 여기에 너에게 재정적으로 도움을 줄 수 있는 것이 있어. Banka Asset은 새 계좌만 개설해도 너에게 20달러를 보상해 줄 거야.

나는 지난 3년 동안 그곳의 서비스를 이용해 왔고, 매우 만족하고 있어. 그것들은 안전하고, 사람들이 온라인 뱅킹과 관리 시스템을 사용하기 쉬워.

너의 우편함에 등록하는 방법을 설명해 놓은 전단지를 남겨 놓았어.

행운을 빌며,

Jason Kid

Lora Houston
Queens Avenue 720번지
인디애나, 펜실베이니아 15701

1월 17일

Houston 씨에게,

Banka Group의 계정을 개설해 주셔서 감사합니다. 저희는 방금 귀하의 이름으로 온라인 예금 계좌를 개설했습니다. 동봉된 이용약관과 지불 일정을 읽어 보세요.

귀하의 새 멤버십에 대해 감사를 전하기 위해 저희는 귀하의 Banka Asset 온라인 계정으로 20달러를 예치할 것입니다. 예치 금액은 계좌 개설일 2주 이내에 입금될 것입니다.

추가로, 귀하는 저희 웹 사이트 www.bankagroup.com을 통해 귀하의 계정으로 접속하실 수 있습니다. 우선, 저희가 아래에 제공한 임시 비밀번호와 식별 번호를 사용하실 수 있습니다. 사이트에 접속하자마자 귀하의 사용자 이름과 비밀번호를 재설정하세요.

계정 번호: 90342178023580
임시 비밀번호: tfc-ybm-1983-2019-zed

문의가 있으시면 1-729-1925-0183으로 언제든지 연락주세요.

진심으로,

Mark Tyler
신규 고객 계정 관리자

191 광고문은 누구를 대상으로 하는가?
(A) 잠재 고객들
(B) Banka Group의 직원들
(C) 주식 거래 대리인들
(D) 기존 계정 소지자들

192 Kid 씨는 왜 Houston 씨에게 이메일을 보냈는가?
(A) 투자 방법을 설명하기 위해서
(B) 보증 금액을 확인하기 위해서
(C) 그녀에게 좋은 금융 서비스를 추천하기 위해서
(D) 지역 금융 설계사를 소개하기 위해서

193 Kid 씨에 대하여 사실일 것 같은 것은?
 (A) 그는 Banka Asset의 플래티넘 회원이다.
 (B) 그는 항상 Houston 씨와 점심 식사를 하려고 만난다.
 (C) 그는 Banka Stock Trading에 채용되었다.
 (D) 그는 최근 새로운 주식 계좌를 개설하였다.

194 이메일에서 세 번째 문단, 첫 번째 줄의 단어 "flyer"와 의미상 가장 가까운 것은?
 (A) 신청서
 (B) 내역서
 (C) 유인물
 (D) 영수증

195 Houston 씨에 대하여 암시되는 것은?
 (A) 그녀는 Banka 사의 이전 고객이다.
 (B) 그녀는 Tyler 씨와 일한 적이 있다.
 (C) 그녀는 300달러 이상을 계좌에 예치했다.
 (D) 그녀는 언제 은퇴할지 고민 중이다.

Questions 196-200 refer to the following invoice and e-mails.

주문 확인
Edu Factory
피츠버그 Butler가 4312, 펜실베이니아 15201

전화: +1 412-687-2965
청구 정보: Latrobe Depót가 533, 펜실베이니아 15650, +1 724-537-5541
배송 주소: 청구 주소와 같음

| 주문 날짜: 4월 20일 (온라인 주문) | | 주문 번호: 218452185 | | |
| 배송 일자: 4월 25일 | | 예상 배송일: 5월 5일 | | |
제품 번호	설명	단가	수량	금액
BW 200	넓은 칠판 - 흰색	450.00달러	1	450.00달러
BW 220	매직펜 세트 - 검은색 보관함 - 짙은 회색	150.00달러	1	150.00달러
BP 178	태블릿 충전기 - 회색	120.00달러	1	120.00달러
BP 591	4개의 구역으로 나뉘어진 게시판 - 베이지색	200.00달러	1	200.00달러

지불: 4월 25일
신용 카드: XXXX XXXX XXXX 2418

소계 920.00달러
세금 80.00달러
배송 100.00달러
총합 1100.00달러

수신: customerservice@edufactory.com
발신: antoniomartial@comsmail.com
날짜: 5월 6일
제목: 주문 번호-218452185

관계자님께,

제 주문품은 어제 저희 집으로 배송되었습니다. 저는 BW 200 제품을 제외하고 모두 조립했습니다. 그러나 제가 포장을 열었을 때 사용설명서와 연결 부품 패키지가 물품과 함께 오지 않았다는 것을 알았습니다. 저는 그 부품을 조립할 수 없었습니다. 저에게 지시 사항과 장비를 바로 보내주실 수 있을까요? 저의 재택근무 사무실에서 다음 주부터 학생들을 받을 예정이라서 가능한 한 빨리 설치되어야 합니다.

감사합니다.

Antonio Martial

수신: antoniomartial@comsmail.com
발신: customerservice@edufactory.com
날짜: 5월 7일
제목: 회신: 주문 번호-218452185

Martial 씨에게,

저희는 조립 지시 사항과 연결 장비가 없다는 귀하의 이메일을 받았습니다. 저희는 오늘 빠른 우편으로 그것들을 발송했고, 내일 정오 전에 받아 보실 수 있습니다. 귀하에게 불편을 끼쳐 드려 진심으로 사과 드립니다. 훌륭한 고객 서비스를 제공하는 저희의 헌신을 보여드리기 위해 저희는 귀하의 주문에 대한 배송비를 환불해 드리고자 합니다. 이것은 다음 신용 카드 청구서에서 자동으로 차감될 것입니다.

최근에 저희 웹 사이트인 www.edufactory.com/cs_manual에 온라인 설명서를 추가했다는 것을 알아 두세요. 귀하의 모델 번호를 입력하시면 파일을 다운로드 받으실 수 있습니다. 파일 오른쪽 부분에 있는 검색창에 "조립"이라는 키워드를 입력하세요. 그렇게 하면 귀하는 설명 사진들을 보고 쉽게 제품을 조립하실 수 있습니다.

다시 한번 진심으로 사과 드리며,

Campbell Liu
고객 서비스 관리자

196 송장에 따르면, Martial 씨는 언제 그의 주문을 결제하였는가?
 (A) 그가 주문을 할 때
 (B) 주문이 배송되었을 때
 (C) 물건들을 수령했을 때
 (D) 그가 고객 서비스와 연락했을 때

197 Martial 씨는 어떤 제품을 조립할 수 없었는가?
 (A) 넓은 칠판
 (B) 보관함
 (C) 태블릿 충전기
 (D) 게시판

198 Martial 씨에 대해 사실인 것은?
 (A) 그는 배송 시 집에 없었다.
 (B) 그는 사무 가구를 훼손했다.
 (C) 그는 기본적인 가재 도구를 가지고 있지 않다.
 (D) 그는 자신의 재택 사무실을 가르치는 데 사용할 것이다.

199 Martial 씨는 얼마를 환불 받을 것인가?
 (A) 80달러
 (B) 100달러
 (C) 120달러
 (D) 155달러

200 두 번째 이메일에 따르면, 고객들이 현재 온라인에서 할 수 있는 것은?
 (A) 제품 환불을 요청하는 것
 (B) 청구서를 지불하는 것
 (C) 설명서를 이용하는 것
 (D) 제품 후기를 작성하는 것

ANSWER SHEET

ACTUAL TEST 1

No.

수험번호
성 명 / 한글 · 영자

LISTENING (PART I ~ IV)

NO	ANSWER	NO.	ANSWER	NO.	ANSWER	NO.	ANSWER
	A B C D		A B C D		A B C D		A B C D
1	Ⓐ Ⓑ Ⓒ Ⓓ	21	Ⓐ Ⓑ Ⓒ Ⓓ	41	Ⓐ Ⓑ Ⓒ Ⓓ	81	Ⓐ Ⓑ Ⓒ Ⓓ
2	Ⓐ Ⓑ Ⓒ Ⓓ	22	Ⓐ Ⓑ Ⓒ Ⓓ	42	Ⓐ Ⓑ Ⓒ Ⓓ	82	Ⓐ Ⓑ Ⓒ Ⓓ
3	Ⓐ Ⓑ Ⓒ Ⓓ	23	Ⓐ Ⓑ Ⓒ Ⓓ	43	Ⓐ Ⓑ Ⓒ Ⓓ	83	Ⓐ Ⓑ Ⓒ Ⓓ
4	Ⓐ Ⓑ Ⓒ Ⓓ	24	Ⓐ Ⓑ Ⓒ Ⓓ	44	Ⓐ Ⓑ Ⓒ Ⓓ	84	Ⓐ Ⓑ Ⓒ Ⓓ
5	Ⓐ Ⓑ Ⓒ Ⓓ	25	Ⓐ Ⓑ Ⓒ Ⓓ	45	Ⓐ Ⓑ Ⓒ Ⓓ	85	Ⓐ Ⓑ Ⓒ Ⓓ
6	Ⓐ Ⓑ Ⓒ Ⓓ	26	Ⓐ Ⓑ Ⓒ Ⓓ	46	Ⓐ Ⓑ Ⓒ Ⓓ	86	Ⓐ Ⓑ Ⓒ Ⓓ
7	Ⓐ Ⓑ Ⓒ Ⓓ	27	Ⓐ Ⓑ Ⓒ Ⓓ	47	Ⓐ Ⓑ Ⓒ Ⓓ	87	Ⓐ Ⓑ Ⓒ Ⓓ
8	Ⓐ Ⓑ Ⓒ Ⓓ	28	Ⓐ Ⓑ Ⓒ Ⓓ	48	Ⓐ Ⓑ Ⓒ Ⓓ	88	Ⓐ Ⓑ Ⓒ Ⓓ
9	Ⓐ Ⓑ Ⓒ Ⓓ	29	Ⓐ Ⓑ Ⓒ Ⓓ	49	Ⓐ Ⓑ Ⓒ Ⓓ	89	Ⓐ Ⓑ Ⓒ Ⓓ
10	Ⓐ Ⓑ Ⓒ Ⓓ	30	Ⓐ Ⓑ Ⓒ Ⓓ	50	Ⓐ Ⓑ Ⓒ Ⓓ	90	Ⓐ Ⓑ Ⓒ Ⓓ
11	Ⓐ Ⓑ Ⓒ Ⓓ	31	Ⓐ Ⓑ Ⓒ Ⓓ	51	Ⓐ Ⓑ Ⓒ Ⓓ	91	Ⓐ Ⓑ Ⓒ Ⓓ
12	Ⓐ Ⓑ Ⓒ Ⓓ	32	Ⓐ Ⓑ Ⓒ Ⓓ	52	Ⓐ Ⓑ Ⓒ Ⓓ	92	Ⓐ Ⓑ Ⓒ Ⓓ
13	Ⓐ Ⓑ Ⓒ Ⓓ	33	Ⓐ Ⓑ Ⓒ Ⓓ	53	Ⓐ Ⓑ Ⓒ Ⓓ	93	Ⓐ Ⓑ Ⓒ Ⓓ
14	Ⓐ Ⓑ Ⓒ Ⓓ	34	Ⓐ Ⓑ Ⓒ Ⓓ	54	Ⓐ Ⓑ Ⓒ Ⓓ	94	Ⓐ Ⓑ Ⓒ Ⓓ
15	Ⓐ Ⓑ Ⓒ Ⓓ	35	Ⓐ Ⓑ Ⓒ Ⓓ	55	Ⓐ Ⓑ Ⓒ Ⓓ	95	Ⓐ Ⓑ Ⓒ Ⓓ
16	Ⓐ Ⓑ Ⓒ Ⓓ	36	Ⓐ Ⓑ Ⓒ Ⓓ	56	Ⓐ Ⓑ Ⓒ Ⓓ	96	Ⓐ Ⓑ Ⓒ Ⓓ
17	Ⓐ Ⓑ Ⓒ Ⓓ	37	Ⓐ Ⓑ Ⓒ Ⓓ	57	Ⓐ Ⓑ Ⓒ Ⓓ	97	Ⓐ Ⓑ Ⓒ Ⓓ
18	Ⓐ Ⓑ Ⓒ Ⓓ	38	Ⓐ Ⓑ Ⓒ Ⓓ	58	Ⓐ Ⓑ Ⓒ Ⓓ	98	Ⓐ Ⓑ Ⓒ Ⓓ
19	Ⓐ Ⓑ Ⓒ Ⓓ	39	Ⓐ Ⓑ Ⓒ Ⓓ	59	Ⓐ Ⓑ Ⓒ Ⓓ	99	Ⓐ Ⓑ Ⓒ Ⓓ
20	Ⓐ Ⓑ Ⓒ Ⓓ	40	Ⓐ Ⓑ Ⓒ Ⓓ	60	Ⓐ Ⓑ Ⓒ Ⓓ	100	Ⓐ Ⓑ Ⓒ Ⓓ

READING (PART V ~ VII)

NO.	ANSWER	NO.	ANSWER	NO.	ANSWER	NO.	ANSWER
	A B C D		A B C D		A B C D		A B C D
101	Ⓐ Ⓑ Ⓒ Ⓓ	121	Ⓐ Ⓑ Ⓒ Ⓓ	141	Ⓐ Ⓑ Ⓒ Ⓓ	161	Ⓐ Ⓑ Ⓒ Ⓓ	181	Ⓐ Ⓑ Ⓒ Ⓓ
102	Ⓐ Ⓑ Ⓒ Ⓓ	122	Ⓐ Ⓑ Ⓒ Ⓓ	142	Ⓐ Ⓑ Ⓒ Ⓓ	162	Ⓐ Ⓑ Ⓒ Ⓓ	182	Ⓐ Ⓑ Ⓒ Ⓓ
103	Ⓐ Ⓑ Ⓒ Ⓓ	123	Ⓐ Ⓑ Ⓒ Ⓓ	143	Ⓐ Ⓑ Ⓒ Ⓓ	163	Ⓐ Ⓑ Ⓒ Ⓓ	183	Ⓐ Ⓑ Ⓒ Ⓓ
104	Ⓐ Ⓑ Ⓒ Ⓓ	124	Ⓐ Ⓑ Ⓒ Ⓓ	144	Ⓐ Ⓑ Ⓒ Ⓓ	164	Ⓐ Ⓑ Ⓒ Ⓓ	184	Ⓐ Ⓑ Ⓒ Ⓓ
105	Ⓐ Ⓑ Ⓒ Ⓓ	125	Ⓐ Ⓑ Ⓒ Ⓓ	145	Ⓐ Ⓑ Ⓒ Ⓓ	165	Ⓐ Ⓑ Ⓒ Ⓓ	185	Ⓐ Ⓑ Ⓒ Ⓓ
106	Ⓐ Ⓑ Ⓒ Ⓓ	126	Ⓐ Ⓑ Ⓒ Ⓓ	146	Ⓐ Ⓑ Ⓒ Ⓓ	166	Ⓐ Ⓑ Ⓒ Ⓓ	186	Ⓐ Ⓑ Ⓒ Ⓓ
107	Ⓐ Ⓑ Ⓒ Ⓓ	127	Ⓐ Ⓑ Ⓒ Ⓓ	147	Ⓐ Ⓑ Ⓒ Ⓓ	167	Ⓐ Ⓑ Ⓒ Ⓓ	187	Ⓐ Ⓑ Ⓒ Ⓓ
108	Ⓐ Ⓑ Ⓒ Ⓓ	128	Ⓐ Ⓑ Ⓒ Ⓓ	148	Ⓐ Ⓑ Ⓒ Ⓓ	168	Ⓐ Ⓑ Ⓒ Ⓓ	188	Ⓐ Ⓑ Ⓒ Ⓓ
109	Ⓐ Ⓑ Ⓒ Ⓓ	129	Ⓐ Ⓑ Ⓒ Ⓓ	149	Ⓐ Ⓑ Ⓒ Ⓓ	169	Ⓐ Ⓑ Ⓒ Ⓓ	189	Ⓐ Ⓑ Ⓒ Ⓓ
110	Ⓐ Ⓑ Ⓒ Ⓓ	130	Ⓐ Ⓑ Ⓒ Ⓓ	150	Ⓐ Ⓑ Ⓒ Ⓓ	170	Ⓐ Ⓑ Ⓒ Ⓓ	190	Ⓐ Ⓑ Ⓒ Ⓓ
111	Ⓐ Ⓑ Ⓒ Ⓓ	131	Ⓐ Ⓑ Ⓒ Ⓓ	151	Ⓐ Ⓑ Ⓒ Ⓓ	171	Ⓐ Ⓑ Ⓒ Ⓓ	191	Ⓐ Ⓑ Ⓒ Ⓓ
112	Ⓐ Ⓑ Ⓒ Ⓓ	132	Ⓐ Ⓑ Ⓒ Ⓓ	152	Ⓐ Ⓑ Ⓒ Ⓓ	172	Ⓐ Ⓑ Ⓒ Ⓓ	192	Ⓐ Ⓑ Ⓒ Ⓓ
113	Ⓐ Ⓑ Ⓒ Ⓓ	133	Ⓐ Ⓑ Ⓒ Ⓓ	153	Ⓐ Ⓑ Ⓒ Ⓓ	173	Ⓐ Ⓑ Ⓒ Ⓓ	193	Ⓐ Ⓑ Ⓒ Ⓓ
114	Ⓐ Ⓑ Ⓒ Ⓓ	134	Ⓐ Ⓑ Ⓒ Ⓓ	154	Ⓐ Ⓑ Ⓒ Ⓓ	174	Ⓐ Ⓑ Ⓒ Ⓓ	194	Ⓐ Ⓑ Ⓒ Ⓓ
115	Ⓐ Ⓑ Ⓒ Ⓓ	135	Ⓐ Ⓑ Ⓒ Ⓓ	155	Ⓐ Ⓑ Ⓒ Ⓓ	175	Ⓐ Ⓑ Ⓒ Ⓓ	195	Ⓐ Ⓑ Ⓒ Ⓓ
116	Ⓐ Ⓑ Ⓒ Ⓓ	136	Ⓐ Ⓑ Ⓒ Ⓓ	156	Ⓐ Ⓑ Ⓒ Ⓓ	176	Ⓐ Ⓑ Ⓒ Ⓓ	196	Ⓐ Ⓑ Ⓒ Ⓓ
117	Ⓐ Ⓑ Ⓒ Ⓓ	137	Ⓐ Ⓑ Ⓒ Ⓓ	157	Ⓐ Ⓑ Ⓒ Ⓓ	177	Ⓐ Ⓑ Ⓒ Ⓓ	197	Ⓐ Ⓑ Ⓒ Ⓓ
118	Ⓐ Ⓑ Ⓒ Ⓓ	138	Ⓐ Ⓑ Ⓒ Ⓓ	158	Ⓐ Ⓑ Ⓒ Ⓓ	178	Ⓐ Ⓑ Ⓒ Ⓓ	198	Ⓐ Ⓑ Ⓒ Ⓓ
119	Ⓐ Ⓑ Ⓒ Ⓓ	139	Ⓐ Ⓑ Ⓒ Ⓓ	159	Ⓐ Ⓑ Ⓒ Ⓓ	179	Ⓐ Ⓑ Ⓒ Ⓓ	199	Ⓐ Ⓑ Ⓒ Ⓓ
120	Ⓐ Ⓑ Ⓒ Ⓓ	140	Ⓐ Ⓑ Ⓒ Ⓓ	160	Ⓐ Ⓑ Ⓒ Ⓓ	180	Ⓐ Ⓑ Ⓒ Ⓓ	200	Ⓐ Ⓑ Ⓒ Ⓓ

ANSWER SHEET

ACTUAL TEST 2

LISTENING (PART I ~ IV)

READING (PART V ~ VII)

ANSWER SHEET

ACTUAL TEST 3

LISTENING (PART I ~ IV)

READING (PART V ~ VII)

ANSWER SHEET

ACTUAL TEST 4

LISTENING (PART I ~ IV)

READING (PART V ~ VII)

ANSWER SHEET

ACTUAL TEST 5

books.english.co.kr